Contents

Effective vocabulary learning

Word formation

Words and pronunciation

Connecting and linking words

Countables and uncountables

Topics

Feelings and actions

Basic concepts

Idiomatic expressions

Phrasal verbs and verb-based expressions

Varieties of English

Introduction

The first edition of *English Vocabulary in Use: upper-intermediate and advanced* was published in 1994. We felt it was time to revise the book for three main reasons. Firstly, technology and other social changes have brought a number of new words and expressions into everyday use. Secondly, we have collected feedback from users of the book all over the world who have made many helpful suggestions that we have been able to incorporate into our new edition. Thirdly, we have access to the Cambridge International Corpus to help inform the choice, presentation and practice of vocabulary items.

What is the same about the new edition?

It retains the features that have made it popular:

- The format of presentation on the left-hand page and practice on the right-hand page.
- It opens with a section on skills for vocabulary recording and memorising.
- It approaches English vocabulary from a range of different angles – looking not just at topics but also at word formation, at words and grammar, at functions like *Connecting and linking*, at concepts like *Time* or *Distance*, at varieties of English.
- It has a complete student-friendly answer key, containing not just the answers but also comments on them where appropriate.
- It contains language and usage notes that are ideal for the self-study learner.
- It contains four symbols to help identify useful common collocations, typical errors, notes about register and when to use a dictionary. (see p.1)
- There is a complete index at the back, listing all the key words and phrases covered.

What is different about the new edition?

In the new edition we have revised each unit to ensure that it is now at upper-intermediate level. We have done this by cutting words that were either too advanced or too easy, replacing them with words more relevant to the level. Frequency data from the Cambridge International Corpus helped inform our decisions here.

We have also clarified our presentation of vocabulary by adding artwork to make the vocabulary easier to understand. There is now more contextualisation of vocabulary and we have also provided more grammar and pronunciation information about the vocabulary we present.

In revising *English Vocabulary in Use: upper-intermediate* we have made considerable use of the Cambridge International Corpus of written and spoken English. This enabled us to check that the example contexts for the language presented were the most natural ones. Where necessary, we have suggested different, more frequent, collocations or contexts.

The process of updating the materials has also allowed us to introduce some new units as requested by teachers and students. You will, therefore, find that this edition contains units on: *Guessing and explaining meaning* (Unit 7), *Music* (Unit 47) and *Computers and the Internet* (Unit 58). Unit 17, *New words in English* has been totally revised to match changes in the language since our first edition.

In this second edition we have reorganised our units in a slightly more logical fashion and have introduced clearer headings for some of the sections. We have also created a new section, *Words and pronunciation*. In addition, we have made some other changes to the presentation materials and the exercises that we hope will make the book easier for students to use. The addition of colour in this edition will, we are sure, be a popular change.

We very much hope that students and teachers will continue to enjoy working with *English Vocabulary in Use: upper-intermediate* and will approve of the changes we have made.

Michael McCarthy and Felicity O'Dell (Cambridge, 2001)

Using this book

Why was this book written?

This book was written to help you to improve your English vocabulary. It will help you to learn not only the meanings of words but also how they are used. You can use this book either with a teacher or for self-study.

How is the book organised?

The book has 100 two-page units. In most units, the left-hand page explains the words and expressions to be studied in that unit. Where appropriate, it gives information about the meanings of words as well as how to use them. The right-hand page checks that you have understood the information on the left-hand page by giving you a series of exercises practising what you have just learnt. Occasionally the right-hand page will also teach you some more new words.

There is a key at the back of the book. It will help you learn more about the words and expressions studied in the unit. Some questions have only one correct answer. Other questions have more than one answer. You will find comments on the answers giving reasons why one answer may be more appropriate than another. You will also find suggested answers for more open-ended questions. These suggested answers are intended to be used as possible examples and are not the only correct answer.

There is an index at the back of the book. This lists all the words and phrases covered in the book and refers you to the units where these words or phrases are discussed. The index also tells you how difficult and unusual words are pronounced. It uses the International Phonetic Alphabet to do this and the symbols you need to know are listed on p.3.

How should I use this book?

The book is divided into a number of sections. Start by working through the first seven units. These units not only teach you some new vocabulary but they also help you with useful techniques for vocabulary learning in general. After completing those units, you might want to work straight through the book or you might prefer to do the units in any order that suits you. You may also like to visit the 'in Use' website at http://www.cambridge.org/elt/inuse/.

Key to symbols used in the margins

(!) indicates the type of error that students typically make with a word or expression.

(R) indicates a note about the language register, for example, whether a word or expression is formal or informal, slang or colloquial, or whether it is more commonly used in a written or spoken context.

 indicates a common collocation, where words frequently occur together.

 indicates where students are advised to refer to a dictionary.

What else do I need in order to work with this book?

You need some kind of vocabulary notebook or file where you can write down the new words you are learning. (See Unit 3 for advice on how to do this.)

You also need to have access to a couple of good dictionaries. This book selects the words that are most important for you to learn at your level and it gives you the most important information about those words but you will sometimes need to refer to a dictionary as well for extra information about meaning and usage. Some exercises tell you to use a dictionary; these help to train you in getting the best out of your dictionary. Firstly, you need an English–English dictionary for foreign learners. Good ones are The *Cambridge International Dictionary of English*, the *Longman Dictionary of Contemporary English*, the *Oxford Advanced Learner's Dictionary* and the *Collins Cobuild English Language Dictionary*, for example. Secondly, you will also find a good bilingual dictionary useful. Ask a teacher to recommend a good bilingual dictionary for you. (See Unit 5 for advice on using your dictionaries.) Don't forget that many dictionaries are available on CD-ROM. If you want more information about different types of dictionaries, visit Cambridge University Press's website at http://www.dictionary.cambridge.org/

Phonetic symbols

Vowel sounds

Symbol	*Examples*		
/iː/	sleep	me	
/i/	happy	recipe	
/ɪ/	pin	dinner	
/ʊ/	foot	could	pull
/uː/	do	shoe	through
/e/	red	head	said
/ə/	arrive	father	colour
/ɜː/	turn	bird	work
/ɔː/	sort	thought	walk
/æ/	cat	black	
/ʌ/	sun	enough	wonder
/ɒ/	got	watch	sock
/ɑː/	part	heart	laugh
/eɪ/	name	late	aim
/aɪ/	my	idea	time
/ɔɪ/	boy	noise	
/eə/	pair	where	bear
/ɪə/	hear	beer	
/əʊ/	go	home	show
/aʊ/	out	cow	
/ʊə/	pure	poor	

Consonant sounds

Symbol	*Examples*		
/p/	put		
/b/	book		
/t/	take		
/d/	dog		
/k/	car	kick	
/g/	go	guarantee	
/tʃ/	catch	church	
/dʒ/	age	lounge	
/f/	for	cough	
/v/	love	vehicle	
/θ/	thick	path	
/ð/	this	mother	
/s/	since	rice	
/z/	zoo	houses	
/ʃ/	shop	sugar	machine
/ʒ/	pleasure	usual	vision
/h/	hear	hotel	
/m/	make		
/n/	name	now	
/ŋ/	bring		
/l/	look	while	
/r/	road		
/j/	young		
/w/	wear		

1 Learning vocabulary – general advice

A What do you need to learn?

1 How many words are there in English? At least:
a) 10,000 b) 100,000 c) 250,000 d) 500,000

2 Winston Churchill was famous for his particularly large vocabulary. How many words did he use in his writing?
a) 10,000 b) 60,000 c) 100,000 d) 120,000

3 How many words does the average native English speaker use in his/her everyday speech?
a) 2,500 b) 5,000 c) 7,500 d) 10,000

4 How many words make up 45% of everything written in English?
a) 50 b) 250 c) 1,000 d) 2,500

5 What do you think are the most common 20 words in English?

To summarise some basic facts about English vocabulary:

- The most common words in English are the grammar words which you already know.
- There are many words in English you don't need at all.
- There are other words that you need simply to understand when you read or hear them.
- There are words which you need to be able to use yourself.

Clearly you need to spend most time learning this last group. In the text below underline the words you'd like to be able to use.

> English vocabulary has a remarkable range, flexibility and adaptability. Thanks to the periods of contact with foreign languages and its readiness to coin new words out of old elements English seems to have far more words in its core vocabulary than other languages. For example, alongside *kingly* (from Anglo-Saxon) we find *royal* (from French) and *regal* (from Latin). There are many such sets of words which add greatly to our opportunities to express subtle shades of meaning at various levels of style.

NOTE
You probably need only to **understand** the verb *coin* in the text, whereas most speakers of English probably need to **use and understand** words like *contact*, *add* and *opportunities*.

B What does knowing a new word mean?

It is not enough just to know the meaning (or meanings) of a word. You also need to know:
- which words it is usually associated with.
- its grammatical characteristics.
- how it is pronounced.
- whether it is formal, informal or neutral (See also Unit 4).

- Try to learn new words in phrases not in isolation.
- Write down words that commonly go together. These are called collocations:

  adjectives + nouns, e.g. rich vocabulary, classical music, common sense.
  verbs + nouns, e.g. to express an opinion, to take sides.
  nouns in phrases, e.g. in touch with, a train set, a sense of humour.
  words + prepositions, e.g. at a loss for words, thanks to you.
- Note special grammatical characteristics of new words. For example, note irregular verbs, e.g. take, took, taken; uncountable nouns, e.g. luggage; or nouns that are only used in the plural, e.g. clothes.
- Note any special pronunciation problems with new words.
- Make a note if the word is particularly formal or informal in character, in other words if it has a particular register.

1 How could you write these words in phrases to help you remember them?
  a) royal b) dissuade c) king d) up to my ears e) independent
  f) get married

2 What grammatical notes would you make beside the following words?
  a) scissors b) weather c) teach d) advice e) lose f) trousers

3 What might you note beside the following words?
  a) subtle b) catastrophe c) photograph/photographer d) answer

4 What might you note beside the following words about their register?
  a) guys b) persons c) people

5 What phrases could you pick out of the text about vocabulary in section A that could be useful to learn?

C Can you learn just by reading or listening to English?

You can help yourself to learn English vocabulary not only by studying with this book but also by reading and listening to English as much as you can. Rank each item below from 0 to 4 to describe how important this way of learning vocabulary is for you personally. (4 is the most important.) You can add other items to the list if you wish.

newspapers TV (cable/subtitled) magazines radio e.g. BBC World Service
video academic or professional literature cinema fiction comics
the Internet cassettes or CDs (music or spoken word) talking to native speakers

D How are you going to plan your vocabulary learning?

1 How many words and expressions do you intend to learn each week?
  a) 5 b) 10 c) 15 d) more than 15

2 Where and when are you going to learn them?
  a) on the way to school or work b) before dinner c) in bed d) other

3 How often are you going to revise your work?
  a) once a week b) once a month c) before a test d) once a year

2 Learning vocabulary – aids to learning

A Learning associated words together

- **Learn words with associated meanings together.**

Learning words together that are associated in meaning is a popular and useful way of organising your vocabulary study.

1 Complete the bubble network for the word CAT. Add as many other bubbles as you like.

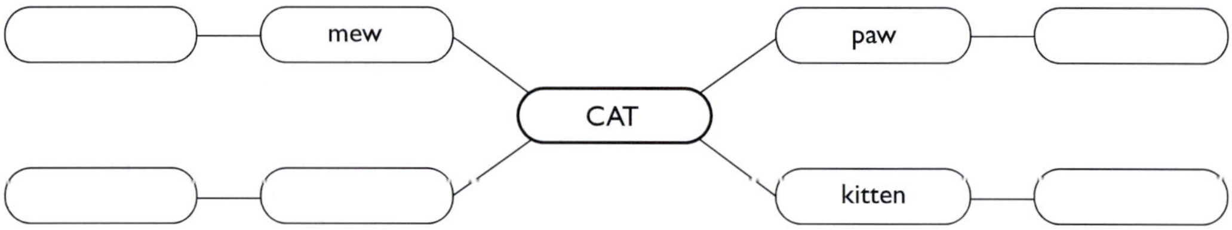

If possible, compare your network with those done by your classmates. Add any of their ideas that you like to your own network.

- **Learn words with a grammatical association together.**

2 Here are some groups of words, each of which has a grammatical connection. Can you see what the connection is? What other words could you add to these groups?

a) **child tooth mouse** b) **information furniture luggage**

- **Learn together words based on the same root.**

3 Can you add any words or expressions to these two groups?

a) **price priceless overpriced**
b) **handy single-handed give me a hand**

B Using pictures and diagrams

- **Pictures might help you to remember vocabulary.**

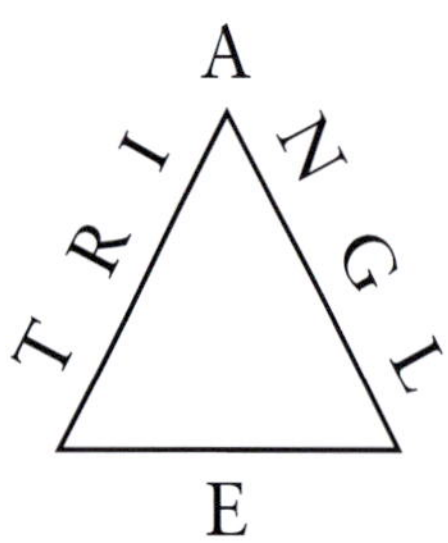

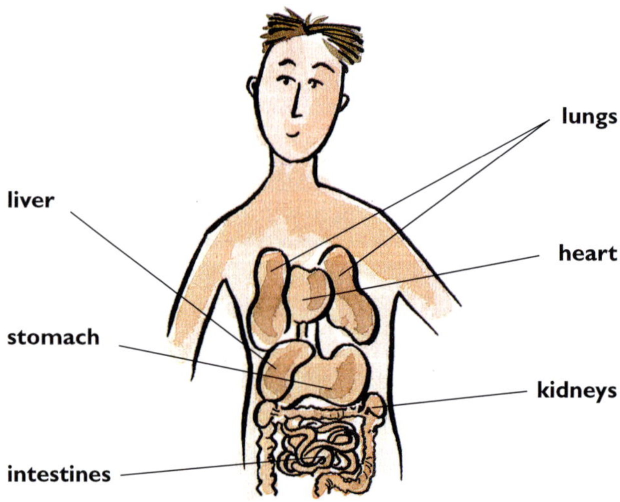

1 Can you draw any pictures that would help you remember the following vocabulary?

a circle to look a gift-horse in the mouth screwdriver

- **Word trees can be useful.**

2 Look at the word tree for **holiday**. Now complete a tree for **school**.

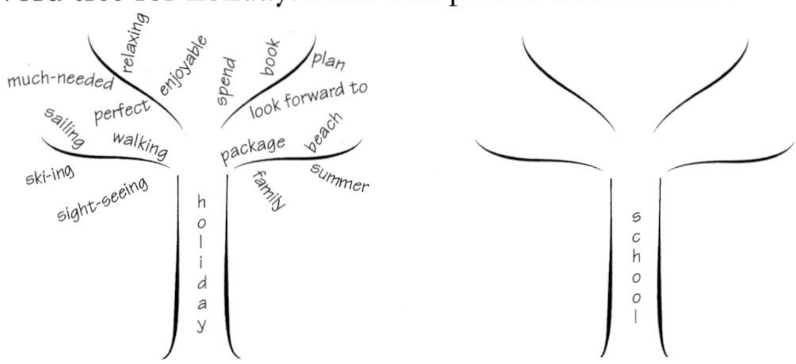

- **Word forks are good ways of learning adjectives and verbs.**

3 Look at complete word forks below. Finish the others.

original	
brilliant	
unusual	idea
great	
excellent	

shoot	
edit	
direct	a film
star in	
review	

magnificent	
breath-taking	
superb	view

kick	
hit	
bounce	a ball

- **Bubble networks can be a useful way of writing down phrasal verbs.**

4 Look at the example. The base verb goes at the centre of the network and is surrounded by the different prepositions which can be added to the base verb to make a phrasal verb. The final bubble contains an appropriate object or phrase to complete the relevant phrasal verb.

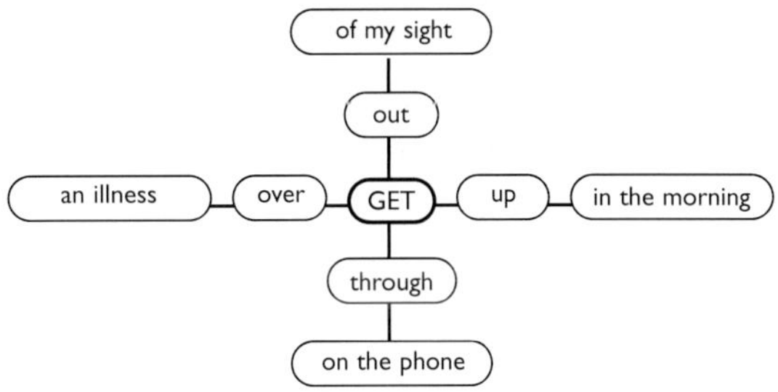

Write your own bubble network for *make*. Use a dictionary and look at Unit 89.

- **Tables can also help clarify collocations (words that are often associated).**

5 Look at the following example of a table:

	a car	*a motorbike*	*a train*	*a horse*	*a plane*
to fly					+
to drive	+		+		
to ride		+		+	

Now complete the following sentences.

a) She has always wanted to have the chance to .... a train.

b) Trainee pilots spend a long time learning how to .... different kinds of planes.

c) .... a motorbike can be very dangerous.

You will do more practice with these and other ways of writing down vocabulary in Unit 3.

3 Organising a vocabulary notebook

TIP All the time that you use this book, we advise you to keep a personal vocabulary notebook. There is no one correct way to organise a vocabulary notebook, but it is a good idea to think about possible ways of doing so. This unit gives some possibilities and examples.

A Organising words by meaning

Try dividing your notebook into different broad sections, with sections for **words for feelings, words to describe places, words for movement, words for thinking,** etc. In each section you can build families of words related in meaning, using some of the ways suggested in this unit.

B Using various types of diagrams

Words that can be grouped under a heading or a more general word can be drawn as a tree-diagram. (See also Unit 2.)

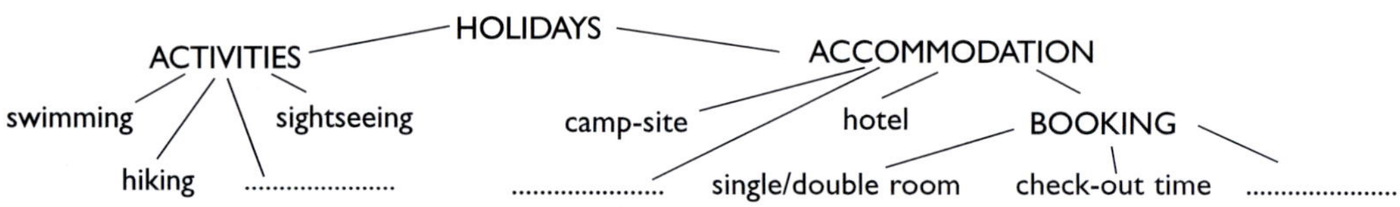

The dotted lines mean that you can add more words to the tree as you meet them.

A bubble network is also useful, since you can make it grow in whatever direction you want it to. (See Unit 2.)

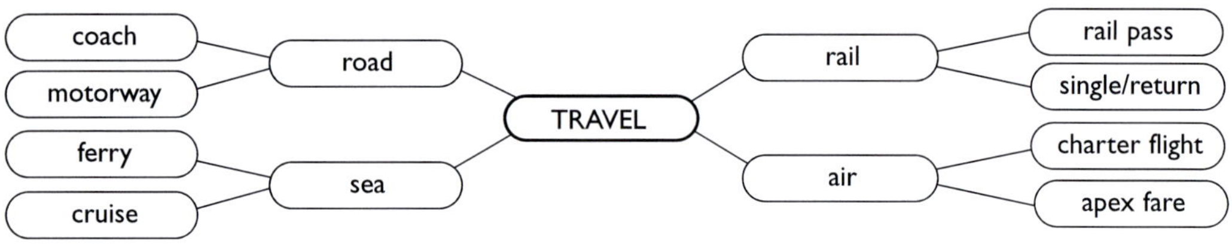

C Organising by word-class

A Spanish learner of English, Angeles, gave us an interview on how she marks word-class in her personal notebook. This is what she said:

> 'What I have just started doing is to write them depending on if they are verbs or nouns or adjectives or phrases. If they are phrases I write them in red and also the definition. If they are verbs, in black, and blue if they are nouns ... And if I write the Spanish translation I write it in another colour, so it's easy to see ... I draw some pictures too.'

D

When you find a synonym or an antonym of a word you already have in your book, enter it next to that word.

stop = cease ('cease' is more formal than 'stop')   urban ≠ rural

Exercises

3.1 **Here is a list of words a Spanish learner of English has made in her vocabulary notebook. How could she improve them and organise them better?**

clock – reloj
tell the time – decir la hora
rush – darse prisa
office – despacho
beneath
under
I must rush – tengo prisa/tengo que correr

drowsy – the room was hot and I got drowsy
wristwatch – reloj de pulsera
What time do you make it?
next to – junto a/al lado de
hands – the minute-hand (minutero)
wide-awake (fully awake)

3.2 **Here is a word-map, a variation on the bubble network. What word do you think should go in the middle?**

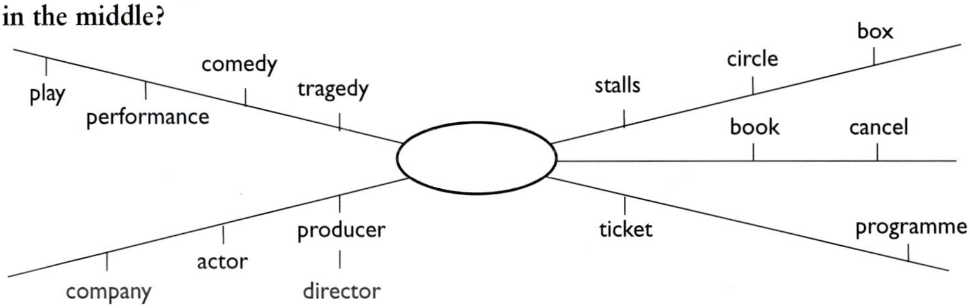

3.3 **One learner tested himself regularly with his notebook, covering up the word and trying to guess it from the translation he had written or from any other notes he had made. Here is his system.**

1 If the notes and/or translation were clear but he could not get the word, he made a small red mark in the margin. Three red marks meant that word needed extra attention and a special effort to learn it.
2 If the notes and/or translation could not help him guess the word, then the word got a blue mark. A blue mark meant 'Write more information about this word!'

What is your testing system? Try to invent one if you have not got one, or ask other people what they do. Try your system out and decide if it works.

3.4 **Making tables for word-classes is a good idea, since you can fill in the gaps over time. What would you put in the remaining gaps in the table?**

noun	*verb*	*adjective*	*person*
production	produce	....	producer
industry	....	industrial	....
export	....	....	....

Follow-up: Exchange tips on recording vocabulary in a notebook with at least two other people who are learning English or another language.

4 The names of English language words

A The names of basic parts of speech in English

article		noun		adverb				conjunction			gerund
↓		↓		↓				↓			↓
A	good	student	works	hard	at	her	books	and	she	enjoys	learning.
	↑		↑		↑				↑		
	adjective		verb		preposition				pronoun		

B Words relating to nouns

Look at the sentence *An artist loves beauty.* The word *artist* is **countable**, i.e. it has a plural form (artists), but *beauty* is **uncountable.** *Artist* is the **subject** of the verb as it describes who does the verb; *beauty* is the **object**, i.e. what is affected by the verb.

C Words relating to verbs

infinitive (go) **-ing form** (going) **past participle** (gone) **past tense** (went)

Go (go, gone, went) is an **irregular** verb whereas *live* (live, lived, lived) is **regular.** *Go* is also **intransitive** because it does not need an **object**, e.g. *Has Luis gone? Make* is **transitive** because it is followed by an **object** – you make something.

D Words relating to the construction of words

In the word, *irregularity*, *ir-* is a **prefix**, *regular* is a **root** and *-ity* is a **suffix.** *Thin* is the **opposite** or **antonym** of *fat* and *slim* is a **synonym** of *thin.* A **word family** is a set of words based on one root, e.g. *word, wordy, to reword.* A **phrase** does not include a **main verb** – 'in a word' is an example of a **phrase.** A **sentence** has a **main verb**; it begins with a **capital letter** and ends with a **full stop (or a question mark or an exclamation mark).**

E Words relating to pronunciation

A syllable /sɪləbəl/ is the minimum sound unit of a word consisting of one vowel and any consonants on either side. There are five **syllables** in the word 'monosyllabic' and the **stress** is on the fourth **syllable.**

F Words and their associations

There are different styles of speaking and writing appropriate to different situations. **Slang** is an extremely informal style; a **colloquial** style is suitable mainly for conversations, e.g. *He's a nice guy.* **Pejorative** words have a negative association. *Pig-headed* is **pejorative** whereas *determined*, which is very close in meaning, is not. **Collocation** refers to words which frequently occur together, e.g. *heavy rain, ginger hair.*

G Words describing punctuation

.	**full stop**	,	**comma**	;	**semi-colon**	’	**apostrophe**
-	**hyphen**	–	**dash**	!	**exclamation mark**	?	**question mark**
( )	**brackets**	“ ”	**inverted commas**	ANNE	**block capitals**		

Exercises

4.1 **Look at the paragraph about words and their associations in F opposite. Find at least three examples of each of the following:**

1 nouns ....
2 verbs ....
3 adjectives ....
4 adverbs ....
5 prepositions ....

Now mark the nouns you've written with a *C* (countable) or *UC* (uncountable). Mark the verbs *R* (regular) or *IR* (irregular) and *T* (transitive) or *IT* intransitive.

4.2 **Complete the following table.**

verb	*infinitive*	*-ing form*	*past participle*
define	....	....	....
mean	....	....	....
write	....	....	....

4.3 **Think about the word *informal*.**

1 What is its root, its prefix and its suffix?
2 What is its opposite or antonym?
3 Has it got any synonyms?
4 Name some words that are included in its word family.

4.4 **Look at all the words in bold (with more than one syllable) in sections E, F and G opposite. In each case mark which syllable is stressed.**

4.5 **Match the following colloquial words with their more formal equivalents in the box.**

1 chat (verb) 2 loo 3 chap 4 put up with 5 fiddle (noun)

man	violin	lavatory	converse	tolerate

4.6 **The following pairs of words are close in meaning but one word in each case is pejorative. Which?**

1 terrorist / freedom fighter
2 slim / skinny
3 fluent / wordy
4 mean / thrifty
5 cunning / shrewd
6 generous / extravagant

4.7 **The words in the box each collocate with one of the following words: *noun*, *verb* and *colloquial*. What are the collocations?**

EXAMPLE *abstract noun*

abstract	expression	intransitive	language	regular	uncountable

4.8 **Cover the left-hand page and write the names of the following punctuation marks.**

( ) .... ? .... ' .... , ...
; .... - .... – .... " " ....

5 Using your dictionary

A

Good dictionaries, especially learners' dictionaries, can tell you a lot more about a word than just its meaning, including (among other things):

- Word-class (usually abbreviations **n:** noun, **adj:** adjective, etc.), whether a noun is countable or uncountable, and whether a verb is normally transitive (needs an object) or intransitive (doesn't need an object).
- Synonyms and their differences, e.g. **mislay** and **misplace**
- Antonyms (opposites), e.g. **friend ≠ enemy/foe**
- Collocations (how words go together), e.g. **living** is often used in these collocations: **cost of living, make a living, standard of living, do something for a living**
- Pronunciation: this will mean learning some symbols which are different from the letters of the English alphabet.

θ	th in **th**ick	ð	th in **th**en	tʃ	ch in **ch**urch
ʃ	sh in **sh**e	dʒ	j in **j**am	ʒ	s in plea**s**ure
ŋ	ng in ri**ng**	æ	a in b**a**d	ɒ	o in t**o**p
ɔː	o in f**o**rm	ʊ	u in p**u**t	ə	a in **a**bout
ʌ	u in **u**p	ɜː	ir in b**ir**d		

  Most other symbols look just like ordinary letters of the English alphabet and their pronunciation is not too hard to guess. Check the table on p.3 if you're not sure.

- Word stress: often shown by a mark before the syllable to be stressed or by bold type, e.g. əd'ventʃə/, /**wes** tən/. Make sure you know how your dictionary marks stress.
- Usage: how a word is used and any special grammatical pattern that goes with it, e.g **suggest** + clause (not an infinitive) – I suggest **you ring her** right away.
- Whether a word is used for people and/or things. For example, look at this entry for **malignant:**

ma·lig·nant /mə'lɪgnənt/ *adj* **1** (of people or their actions) feeling or showing great desire to harm others; malevolent: *a malignant slander, attack, thrust.* **2 (a)** (of a tumour) growing uncontrollably, and likely to prove fatal: *The growth is not malignant.* **(b)** (of diseases) harmful to life.
▷ **ma·lig·nancy** /-nənsɪ/ *n* **1** [U] state of being malignant. **2** [C] malignant tumour.
ma·lig·nantly *adv.*

B

Don't forget that most words have more than one meaning. In this example, only the second meaning corresponds to the way **hairy** is used in this sentence:

It was a really **hairy** journey on the mountain road.

hairy /hɛəri¹/, **hairier, hairiest**. 1 Someone or something that is **hairy** is covered with hair. EG *...a plump child with hairy legs... ...a big, hairy man... The function of a mammal's hairy coat is to insulate the body.* — ADJ QUALIT

2 If you describe a situation as **hairy**, you mean that it is exciting, worrying, and rather frightening; a very informal use. EG *It got a little hairy when we drove him to the station with less than two minutes to spare.* — ADJ QUALIT = nerve-racking, scary

Exercises

5.1 With a *bilingual* dictionary, try a double search: look up a word in your language; the dictionary may give several possibilities in English. Look up each of those possibilities in the English section of the dictionary to see how they translate back into your language. This may help you to distinguish synonyms.

If you own a dictionary, make a little mark in the margin each time you look a word up. If a word gets three or more marks, it is worth an extra effort to learn it.
What other learning techniques are there for dictionaries?

5.2 Small bilingual dictionaries often just give three or four translations for a word you look up, without any explanation. Here are some pictures with translations you might find in such a dictionary. Which ones fit in the sentences? You may need to use a monolingual dictionary.

sofa divan
couch settee

boots bootees
wellingtons

sailing boat ketch
dinghy yacht

1 Come and sit on the .... and relax a while.
2 She bought a huge, luxury .... and went off round the world.
3 If you're going to stand in the water you should take your ....
4 It's not a proper yacht; it's just a tiny little ....

5.3 Which WORD for *casual* describes its use in these sentences?

cas·ual NOT INTERESTED /ˈkæʒ·ju·əl/ *adj* not taking or not seeming to take much interest; not caring • *The psychologist's* **attitude** *seemed far too casual, even brutal.* • *Security around the conference hotel seemed almost casual.* • *Although close to tears, she tried to make her voice sound casual.*
cas·ual·ly /ˈkæʒ·ju·ə·li/ *adv* • *"How would you kill someone, doctor?" the woman asked casually* (= as if it was not a serious matter).

cas·ual TEMPORARY /ˈkæʒ·ju·əl/ *adj* [before n] not regular or fixed; temporary • *The company is only taking on casual* **labour/labourers/workers**. • *Are you employed permanently or on a casual basis?* • *Casual* **sex/relationships** *can involve serious health risks.* • LP Work
cas·ual·ly /ˈkæʒ·ju·ə·li/ *adv* • *Eighty per cent of the workforce is employed casually, with no security.*

cas·ual CHANCE /ˈkæʒ·ju·əl/ *adj* [before n] not serious or considered; (done) by chance • *It was just a casual* **comment**, *I didn't mean it to be taken so seriously.* • *To a casual* **observer**, *everything might appear normal.* • *The new law is intended to deter the casual* **user** *of drugs.*
cas·ual·ly /ˈkæʒ·ju·ə·li/ *adv* • *He had information that he could not have acquired casually* (= by chance).

cas·ual INFORMAL /ˈkæʒ·ju·əl/ *adj* (of clothes) not formal or not suitable for special occasions • *For some people casual* **clothes** *means a shapeless T-shirt and old jeans, for others chinos and sweaters.* • LP **Shopping goods**

1 It was quite a casual outfit, just right for such an informal occasion.
2 I only said it casually, but it shocked her.
3 She has a very casual attitude to her work. She should take it more seriously.
4 I don't get a salary; I'm just a casual.

5.4 Pronunciation. What English words are these?

1 /edʒʊˈkeɪʃən/ ....
2 /ˈpæspɔːt/ ....
3 /ˈleŋθ/ ....
4 /ˈlɪbətɪ/ ....
5 /rəˈvɪʒən/ ....
6 /ˈbrʌðə/ ....

5.5 In the dictionary entry for *hairy* opposite how many synonyms can you find?

Follow-up: If you can access the Internet go to the web address for Cambridge University Press dictionaries at http://www.dictionary.cambridge.org/ and find out what different types of dictionaries are available for learners of English.

6 Revising vocabulary

A

Here is an extract from a book about language learning strategies on the importance of revising in an active way.

> Revising ... is especially useful for remembering new material in the target language. It involves looking back at what has been studied at different intervals, at first close together and then increasingly far apart. For example, Misha is learning a set of vocabulary words in English. He practises them immediately, waits 15 minutes before practising them again, and practises them an hour later, three hours later, the next day, two days later, four days later, the following week, two weeks later, and so on until the material becomes more or less automatic. In this way he keeps returning to these particular vocabulary words, even though he might be meeting more material in class. Each time he practises these vocabulary words, Misha does it in a meaningful way, like putting them into a context or recombining them to make new sentences. Naturally, the amount of time needed to make new material automatic depends on the kind of material involved.

B

Revising with this book

When you revise a unit, first read it through. Then look at anything you wrote in your vocabulary notebook, connected with the unit. Then, and most importantly, try to do something different with the new words and expressions in that unit in order to help fix them in your memory. Here are some suggestions:

- Highlight any words and expressions that you had forgotten or were not sure about.
- Look at the unit and choose six words and expressions that you particularly want or need to learn. Write them down.
- Look up any words that you selected in an English–English dictionary. Do these words have any other uses or associations that might help you learn them? Looking up the word, **heart**, for example, might lead you to **heart-broken** or **to have your heart in your mouth**. Write anything that appeals to you in an appropriate phrase or sentence.
- The dictionary can also help you find some other words based on the same root. Looking up the noun, **employment**, leads you to the verb, **employ**, to the nouns, **employer** and **employee**, and to the adjectives **employable, unemployed** and **self-employed.**
- Note the pronunciation of the words and expressions you wish to learn. Try to write them down in phonetic script. Use a dictionary to help you.
- In your notebook, write down the words and phrases from a unit in a different way – put them into a network or a table, perhaps.
- The next day, ask yourself: How much can I remember?
- Test yourself, cover part of a word or phrase. Can you complete the word or phrase?

When you have done all the steps above that you feel will be useful to you, close your book and notebook and remind yourself of what you have been studying. How much can you remember?

C Making the new words active

One of the great advantages of revising vocabulary is that it should help you to make the step from having something in your receptive vocabulary to having it in your active vocabulary. Encourage this process by:

- writing the words and expressions you are trying to learn in a sentence relating to your life and interests at the moment.
- making a point of using the new words and expressions in your next class or homework or in some other way.
- keeping a learning diary in which you note down things that particularly interest you about the words you have learnt.
- watching out for the words and expressions you are trying to learn in your general reading of English. If you come across any of them in use, write them down in their context in your diary or notebook.
- writing a paragraph or story linking the words and expressions you want to learn.

D What can you remember?

1 What do you remember now from the first five units in this book? Answer without looking back at the units.

2 Now read through the units again.

3 How much do you remember about the units now?

4 Choose at least one word and expression from each unit and work through all the suggestions made in B and C above. It may not always be appropriate in your future study to do all the steps in B but try them now for practice.

E Some plans for your work with this book

1 How often are you going to revise what you have done? (Every week? Every five units?)

2 Which techniques are you going to use for revising?

3 Now write yourself some notes to remind yourself of when you are going to revise. You might like, for instance, to write *revise vocabulary* in your diary for the next eight Fridays, if you decided to revise every week. Alternatively you could write **REVISE** in capital letters, after, say, every five units in the book.

7 Guessing and explaining meaning

A Inferring meaning from context

There are a number of clues which you may be able to use to help you work out the meaning of an unfamiliar word:

The context in which it is used

- Visual clues: a picture in a book or film footage in a TV news broadcast may help you.
- Your own background knowledge about a situation: for example, if you already know that there has just been an earthquake in Los Angeles, then you will find it easy to understand the word 'earthquake' when you hear a news broadcast about it.
- The immediate context (other words around the unfamiliar word): these may make the meaning absolutely clear: 'Suzanna picked one tall yellow gladiolus to put in her new crystal vase.' Even if you have never seen or heard the word 'gladiolus', it will probably be obvious to you from the context that it is a type of flower.
- Grammatical clues in the context: it is not difficult to understand that 'superstitious' must be an adjective in the sentence 'Marsha is very superstitious.' or that 'gingerly' is an adverb in 'Jackie tiptoed gingerly down the stairs.'

Similarity to other words you already know in English

A large number of words in English are made up of combinations of other words. You may never have seen the word 'headscarf', for example, but the meaning is easy to work out from its two components. Units 12–14 will help you improve your skills in understanding how English uses everyday words to build up new concepts.

Structure

A prefix or suffix may give you a clue, for example. Units 8–11 focus on different aspects of word formation in English and should help you exploit those clues in making sense of unfamiliar words.

Similarity to a word you know in your own (or some other) language

If your first language is of Latin or of Germanic origin, you will come across many words in English that resemble words in your own language. However, English has taken many words from many other languages too (see Unit 15). So make use of any other languages you know. But remember that some words are false friends – they sound as if they mean the same but in fact they have a different meaning. (A good dictionary will give lists of false friends for a lot of European languages.)

B Explaining unknown words

The following expressions can be useful when you are trying to explain what a word or expression means:

It's (a bit) like (a chair) ...

It's something you use for (painting pictures / cleaning the kitchen floor ...)

It's a kind of (bird / musical instrument / building ...)   It must / could be ...

TIP It will not be possible to work out the meanings of all the unfamiliar words that you come across but remember that you do not need to understand every word in a text in order to understand the whole text. When it is crucial to know a meaning, use the clues suggested in this unit and make a guess before checking the dictionary.

Exercises

7.1 **Look at the following text. Before you read it, see if you know what the underlined words mean.**

> A tortoise is a <u>shelled reptile famed</u> for its slowness and <u>longevity</u>. The Giant Tortoise of the Galapagos may attain over 1.5 metres in length and have a <u>lifespan</u> of more than 150 years. Smaller tortoises from Southern Europe and North Africa make popular pets. They need to be <u>tended</u> carefully in cool climates and must have a warm place in which they can <u>hibernate</u>.

Which of the underlined words can you guess from the context or using any other clues? First make a guess and then check your guesses in the key.

7.2 **Use the context to work out what the underlined words mean. Explain them using one or other of the expressions in B on the opposite page.**

1 Above the trees at the edge of the meadow, a <u>buzzard</u> hangs for a moment on the wind before soaring towards the hills.
2 According to some sources, the water <u>vole</u> is one of the most rapidly declining creatures in Britain and a new survey is now being carried out to determine how serious the threat of extinction really is.
3 Using a large <u>chisel</u> the police broke through the front door and surprised the robbers.
4 We ate a delicious chicken and noodle soup from a big <u>tureen</u> and enjoyed several bowls each.
5 When the soup is ready, <u>ladle</u> it into six warmed bowls.
6 We often used to walk up to the cliff top where we would <u>clamber</u> over the farmer's gate and go right to the edge where the view was better.
7 Some people get really <u>ratty</u> when they haven't had enough sleep.

7.3 **Use your knowledge of other basic English words to help you work out the meanings of the underlined words and expressions. Rewrite them using simpler words or explanations for the underlined words and phrases.**

1 It says on the can that this drink is <u>sugar-free</u>.
2 More and more shops now have their own special <u>store cards</u> and offer you a discount if you use one of them.
3 I find Mo a very <u>warm-hearted</u> person.
4 I've been <u>up to my eyes in work</u> ever since I got back from holiday.
5 We walked down a <u>tree-lined</u> street towards the station.
6 The little boys were fascinated by the <u>cement-mixer</u>.

7.4 **Use your knowledge of prefixes and suffixes to suggest what these phrases mean.**

1 to re-direct an envelope
2 uncontrollable anger
3 pre-dinner drinks
4 bi-monthly report
5 my ex-boss
6 anti-tourist feelings
7 to disconnect the telephone
8 undelivered letters

8 Suffixes

A Common noun suffixes

-er /ə/ is used for the *person* who does an activity, e.g. writ**er**, paint**er**, work**er**, shopp**er**, teach**er**.

You can use **-er** with a wide range of verbs to make them into nouns.
Sometimes the **-er** suffix is written as **-or** (it is still pronounced /ə/). It is worth making a special list of these as you meet them, e.g. act**or**, operat**or**, sail**or**, supervis**or**.

-er/-or are also used for *things* which do a particular job, e.g. pencil-sharpen**er**, bottle-open**er**, grat**er**, project**or**.

-er and **-ee** (pronounced /iː/) can contrast with each other meaning 'person who does something' (**-er**) and 'person who receives or experiences the action' (**-ee**) employ**er**/employ**ee** /emplɔɪj'iː/, send**er**/address**ee**, pay**ee** (e.g. of a cheque).

-(t)ion/-sion/-ion are used to form nouns from verbs, e.g.

complica**tion** pollu**tion** reduc**tion** altera**tion** dona**tion** promo**tion** admis**sion**

-ist [a person] and **-ism** [an activity or ideology]: used for people's politics, beliefs and ideologies, and sometimes their profession (compare with **-er/-or** professions above). e.g. Buddh**ism**, journal**ism**, Marx**ist**, typ**ist**, physic**ist**, terror**ist**.

-ist is also often used for people who play musical instruments, e.g. pian**ist**, violin**ist**, cell**ist**

-ness is used to make nouns from adjectives: good**ness**, readi**ness**, forgetful**ness**, happi**ness**, sad**ness**, weak**ness**. Note what happens to adjectives that end in **-y**.

B Adjective suffixes

-able/-ible /əbl/ with verbs, means 'can be done':
drink**able** wash**able** read**able** forgiv**able** ed**ible** [can be eaten] flex**ible** [can be bent]

C Verbs

-ise (or **-ize**) forms verbs from adjectives, e.g. modern**ise** [make modern], commercial**ise**, industrial**ise**.

D Other suffixes that can help you recognise the word-class

-ment: (nouns) excitement enjoyment replacement
-ity: (nouns) flexibility productivity scarcity
-hood: (abstract nouns especially family terms) childhood motherhood
-ship: (abstract nouns especially status) friendship partnership membership
-ive: (adjectives) passive productive active
-al: (adjectives) brutal legal (nouns) refusal arrival
-ous: (adjectives) delicious outrageous furious
-ful: (adjectives) forgetful hopeful useful
-less: (adjectives) useless harmless homeless
-ify: (verbs) beautify purify terrify

NOTE

The informal suffix **-ish** can be added to most common adjectives, ages and times to make them less precise, e.g. She's thirty**ish**. He has redd**ish** hair. Come about eight**ish**.

TIP When you are recording a new word in your vocabulary notebook, write any suffixes that go with it (e.g. *refuse – refusal*).

Exercises

8.1 **Use the *-er/-or*, *-ee* and *-ist* suffixes to make the names of the following. If you need to use a dictionary, try looking up the words in bold.**

Example: A person who plays jazz on the piano. a jazz pianist

1 The thing that **wipes** rain off your car windscreen.
2 A person who plays classical **violin.**
3 A person who takes professional **photographs.** (N.B. pronunciation)
4 A person who **acts** in amateur theatre.
5 The person to whom a cheque is **paid.**
6 A machine for **washing** dishes.
7 A person who **donates** their organs upon their death.
8 The person to whom a letter is **addressed.**

8.2 **Each picture is of an object ending in *-er*. Can you name them?**

1
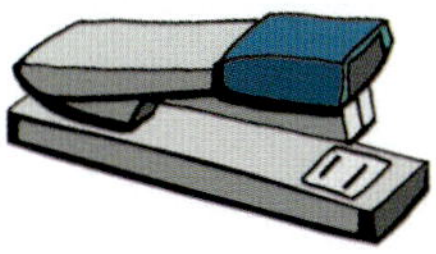
2
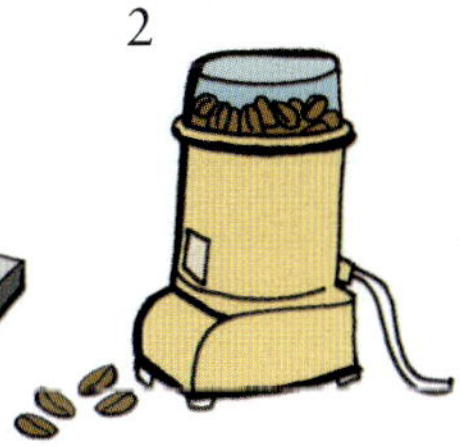
3

4

5
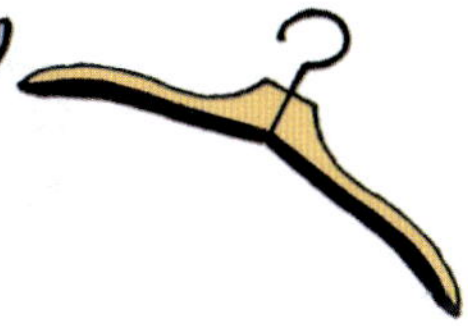

8.3 **List six jobs you would like to have in order of preference. How many different suffixes are there in your list? Do any of the job names not have a suffix? (e.g. pilot, film star)**

8.4 **Do these words mean a thing, a person, or both?**

1 a cooker	3 a ticket-holder	5 a cleaner	7 a drinker
2 a typewriter	4 a CD player	6 a smoker	8 a dresser

8.5 **Compete each of the second sentences by changing the words underlined in the first sentences. Use a suffix from the left-hand page and m ake any spelling changes needed.**

1 Most of his crimes can be <u>forgiven</u>. Most of his crimes are ....
2 The Club refuses to <u>admit</u> anyone not wearing shoes. The Club refuses .... to anyone not wearing shoes.
3 Her only fault is that she is <u>lazy</u>. Her only fault is ....
4 This firm has <u>produced</u> a lot in recent years. This firm has been very .... in recent years.
5 I found the book very <u>easy and pleasant to read</u>. I found the book very ....

8.6 **Can you think of anything in your country which should be *nationalised* (e.g. airlines), *privatised, standardised, modernised, computerised* or *centralised*?**

8.7 **Which word is the odd one out in each group and why?**

1 brotherhood neighbourhood manhood priesthood
2 tearful spiteful dreadful handful
3 appointment involvement compliment arrangement
4 worship kinship friendship partnership

9 Prefixes

A

Prefixes are often used to give adjectives a negative or an opposite meaning. For example, comfortable/**un**comfortable, convenient/**in**convenient and similar/**dis**similar are opposites. Other examples are '**un**just', '**in**edible', '**dis**loyal'. Unfortunately, there is no easy way of knowing which prefix any adjective will use to form its opposite.

TIP When you learn a new adjective note down whether it has an opposite formed with a prefix and, if so, what it is.

- **in**- becomes **im**- before a root beginning with 'm' or 'p', e.g. **im**mature, **im**patient, **im**partial, **im**probable. Similarly **in**- becomes **ir**- before a word beginning with 'r', and **il**- before a word beginning with 'l', e.g. **ir**replaceable, **ir**reversible, **il**legal, **il**legible, **il**literate.
- The prefix **in**- (and its variations) does not always have a negative meaning – often it gives the idea of inside or into, e.g. **in**ternal, **im**port, **in**sert, **in**come.

B

The prefixes **un**- and **dis**- can also form the opposites of verbs, e.g. tie/**un**tie, appear/**dis**appear. These prefixes are used to reverse the action of the verb. Here are some more examples: **dis**agree, **dis**approve, **dis**believe, **dis**connect, **dis**credit, **dis**like, **dis**mount, **dis**prove, **dis**qualify, **un**bend, **un**do, **un**dress, **un**fold, **un**load, **un**lock, **un**veil, **un**wrap, **un**zip.

C

Here are examples of other prefixes in English. Some of these words are used with a hyphen. Check in a dictionary if you're not sure.

prefix	*meaning*	*examples*
anti	against	anti-war antisocial antibiotic
auto	of or by oneself	autograph auto-pilot autobiography
bi	two, twice	bicycle bilateral biannual bilingual
ex	former	ex-wife ex-smoker ex-boss
ex	out of	extract exhale excommunicate
micro	small	micro-cassette microwave microscopic
mis	badly/wrongly	misunderstand mistranslate misinform
mono	one/single	monotonous monologue monogamous
multi	many	multi-national multi-purpose multi-media
over	too much	overdo overtired oversleep overeat
post	after	postwar postgraduate post-impressionist
pre	before	preconceived pre-war pre-judge
pro	in favour of	pro-government pro-revolutionary
pseudo	false	pseudo-scientific pseudo-intellectual
re	again or back	retype reread replace rewind
semi	half	semicircular semi-final semi-detached
sub	under	subway submarine subdivision
under	not enough	underworked underused undercooked

TIP Knowing about English prefixes can help you to understand the meaning of unfamiliar words.

Exercises

9.1 **Write the opposites of the words underlined. Not all the words you need are on the left-hand page.**

Example: He's a very honest man. ...dishonest...

1 I'm sure she's discreet.
2 I always find him very sensitive.
3 It's a convincing argument.
4 That's a very relevant point.
5 She's always obedient.
6 He's very efficient.
7 I always find her responsible.
8 He seems grateful for our help.
9 I'm sure she's loyal to the firm.
10 He's a tolerant person.

9.2 **Which negative adjective fits each of the following definitions?**

1 .... means not having a husband or wife.
2 .... means impossible to eat.
3 .... means unable to read or write.
4 .... means not having a job.
5 .... means fair in giving judgement, not favouring one side.
6 .... means unable to be replaced.

9.3 **Use the word in brackets to complete the sentences. Add the necessary prefix and put the word in the correct form.**

Example: The runner was ...disqualified... after a blood test. (QUALIFY)

1 Children (and adults) love .... parcels at Christmas time. (WRAP)
2 I almost always find that I .... with his opinion. (AGREE)
3 I'm sure he's lying but it's going to be hard to .... his story. (PROVE)
4 After a brief speech the Queen .... the new statue. (VEIL)
5 It took the removal men an hour .... our things from the van. (LOAD)
6 His phone was .... because he didn't pay his last bill. (CONNECT)

9.4 **Answer the following questions. The answers are all in the table opposite.**

1 What kind of oven cooks things particularly fast?
2 What kind of drug can help somebody with an infection?
3 What kind of company has branches in many countries?
4 How does a passenger aeroplane normally fly?
5 What is a student who is studying for a second degree?
6 What means 'underground railway' in the US and 'underground passage' in the UK?

9.5 **Using the table opposite construct words or phrases to replace the underlined words.**

Example: He's in favour of the American approach. ...He's pro-American...

1 The BBC tries to avoid pronouncing foreign words incorrectly.
2 Most people say they have to work too hard but are paid too little.
3 He dated his cheque with a date that was later than the real date.
4 She's still on good terms with the man who used to be her husband.
5 He made so many mistakes in the letter that he had to write it again.

Follow-up: Find two more examples for each prefix in C opposite. Use a dictionary if necessary.

10 Roots

A

Many words in English are formed from Latin roots. These words are often considered fairly formal in English. Here are some examples of the more common Latin roots, with some of the English words derived from them.

SPECT see, look

You should **respect** your parents / the laws of a country. [look up to]
The police **suspected** he was guilty but they had no proof. [had a feeling]
Many pioneers travelled west in America to **prospect** for gold. [search]

VERT turn

I tried the new make of coffee but I soon **reverted** to my old favourite brand. [went back]
Missionaries went to Africa to **convert** people to Christianity. [change beliefs]
The royal scandal **diverted** attention from the political crisis. [took attention away]

PORT carry, take

How are you going to **transport** your things to the States? [send across]
Britain **imports** cotton and **exports** wool. [buys in, sells out]
Our opinions are **supported** by a considerable amount of research. [held up]

DUC, DUCT lead

She was **educated** at a very small private school. [went to school]
He **conducted** the orchestra with great vigour. [led]
Japan **produces** a lot of electronic equipment. [makes]

PRESS press, push

She was **impressed** by his presentation. [full of admiration and respect]
This weather **depresses** me. [makes me feel miserable]
She always **expresses** herself very articulately. [puts her thoughts into words]

POSE, PONE place, put

The meeting has been **postponed** until next week. [changed to a later date]
The king was **deposed** by his own son. [put off the throne]
The government have **imposed** a sizeable tax increase. [put into force]

B

The examples above are of verbs only. Note that for all the verbs listed, there is usually at least one noun and at least one adjective as well. Here are some examples.

verb	*person noun*	*adjective*	*abstract noun*
inspect	inspector	inspecting	inspection
advertise	advertiser	advertising	advertisement
deport	deportee	deported	deportation
introduce	introducer	introductory	introduction
oppress	oppressor	oppressive	oppression
compose	composer	composite	composition

Exercises

10.1 **Complete as much as possible of the table with other forms of some of the words presented in B. Use a dictionary to help you if necessary.**

verb	*person noun*	*adjective*	*abstract noun*
convert	....	....	....
produce	....	....	....
conduct	....	....	....
impress	....	....	....
support	....	....	....
impose	....	....	....

10.2 **Fill in the gaps in the sentences below using words based on the root in brackets at the end of the sentence.**

1 The dictator's behaviour is typical of that of leaders of .... political regimes. (PRESS)
2 He was .... from the USA for having a forged passport. (PORT)
3 The magazine seems to have nothing in it but .... for cosmetics. (VERT)
4 May I .... you to the managing director? (DUC)
5 The tax .... decided I owed a lot of money. (SPECT)
6 The new take-away pizza place has a very good .... offer. (DUC)
7 Before you buy a new house be sure to .... it thoroughly. (SPECT)
8 Tchaikovsky .... some wonderful ballet music. (POSE)

10.3 **Can you work out the meanings of the underlined words in the sentences below? To help you, here are the meanings of the main Latin prefixes:**

intro: ***within, inward*** **o, ob:** ***against*** **in, im:** ***in, into*** **re:** ***again, back***
de: ***down, from*** **ex:** ***out*** **sub:** ***under*** **trans:** ***across***

1 She's a very <u>introspective</u> person and her husband's also very <u>introverted</u>.
2 He always seems to <u>oppose</u> everything I suggest.
3 I don't think it is healthy to <u>repress</u> one's emotions too much.
4 Perhaps you can <u>deduce</u> what the word means from the way it is formed.
5 The documentary <u>exposed</u> corruption in high places.
6 She tried hard to <u>suppress</u> a laugh.
7 She <u>transposed</u> the music for the flute.

10.4 **Below are some words based on Latin roots and their two part verb equivalents. Match each word with its synonym. Which in each pair is more formal?**

support put off oppose look at cut down deposit hold up
postpone turn away inspect go against divert reduce put down

Follow-up: Find three other words based on each of the roots listed in A opposite. Write an example phrase or sentence for each one.

11 Abstract nouns

A

An abstract noun represents an idea, experience or quality rather than an object that you can touch. For example, **happiness, intention** and **shock** are abstract nouns but pen, bed and trousers are not.

B

Suffixes are letters added to the end of words to make new words.
Certain suffixes are used frequently in abstract nouns. The most common are **-ment, -ion, -ness** and **ity**. The suffix **-ion** sometimes becomes **-tion, -sion, -ation** or **-ition.**
-ment, and **-ion**, are usually used to make verbs into abstract nouns.

The suffixes **-ness** and **-ity** are added to adjectives.

Here are some examples of abstract nouns using those suffixes.

achievement	action	aggressiveness	absurdity
adjustment	collection	attractiveness	anonymity
amazement	combination	bitterness	complexity
discouragement	illusion	carelessness	curiosity
improvement	imagination	consciousness	generosity
investment	production	friendliness	hostility
replacement	recognition	tenderness	prosperity
retirement	reduction	ugliness	sensitivity

C

Less common suffixes that form abstract nouns are **-ship**, **-dom**, **-th** and **-hood.**

The suffixes **-ship** and **-hood** are usually added to other nouns to form abstract nouns. The suffix **-th** is added to an adjective to form an abstract noun and **-dom** can combine with either a noun or an adjective.

Here are some examples of abstract nouns using those suffixes.

apprenticeship	boredom	breadth	adulthood
companionship	freedom	depth	brotherhood
membership	kingdom	length	childhood
ownership	martyrdom	strength	motherhood
partnership	stardom	warmth	neighbourhood
relationship	wisdom	width	(wo)manhood

D

Many abstract nouns do not use any suffix at all. Here are some examples.

anger	belief	calm	chance
faith	fear	humour	idea
luck	principle	rage	reason
sense	sight	speed	thought

TIP When you learn a new adjective, find out if it has an abstract noun based on the same root and note it down in your vocabulary book with the adjective, for example, warm, warmth (abstract noun).

You will find more examples of the use of suffixes in Units 8 and 10 and of abstract nouns in Units 64 and 65.

Exercises

11.1 **What is the abstract noun related to each of the following adjectives? All the nouns are formed in ways described on the opposite page although not all are listed opposite.**

EXAMPLE tender *tenderness*

1 affectionate	5 amused	9 attentive	13 equal
2 excited	6 graceful	10 happy	14 hopeful
3 kind	7 original	11 popular	15 resentful
4 secure	8 stupid	12 weak	16 wise

11.2 **Which verbs are related to these abstract nouns?**

EXAMPLE argument *argue*

1 collection	4 intensity	7 action	10 ownership
2 emptiness	5 strength	8 excitement	11 imagination
3 satisfaction	6 boredom	9 production	12 adjustment

11.3 **On the opposite page, find a synonym with the suffix in brackets, for each of the following nouns.**

EXAMPLE animosity (-ity) *hostility*

1 astonishment (-ment)	5 substitution (-ment)	9 vision (no suffix)
2 inquisitiveness (-ity)	6 fame (-dom)	10 liberty (-dom)
3 fraternity (-hood)	7 decrease (-tion)	11 fury (no suffix)
4 possibility (no suffix)	8 community (-hood)	12 wealth (-ity)

11.4 **Complete each of the quotations with one of the words in the box.**

imitation	advice	injustice	kingdom	darkness

1 'Better to light a candle than to curse the ....'
2 'Do not ask .... of the ignorant.'
3 'Better to suffer .... than to commit it.'
4 ' .... is the sincerest form of flattery.'
5 'It's easy to govern a .... but difficult to rule one's family.'

11.5 **Write your own quotations to describe the following abstract nouns. Perhaps you know a saying in your own language that you could translate into English?**

1 freedom 2 love 3 life 4 curiosity 5 imagination

Follow-up: Find at least one more noun using each of the suffixes in B and C.

12 Compound adjectives

A

A compound adjective is made up of two parts. It is usually written with a hyphen, e.g. **well-dressed, never-ending** and **shocking-pink**. Its meaning is usually clear from the words it combines. The second part of the adjective is frequently a present or past participle.

B

A large number of compound adjectives describe personal appearance.

Here is a rather **far-fetched** description of a person starting from the head down.

NOTE
Some compound adjectives use a hyphen before a noun but not after a noun (e.g. a well-known singer *but* That singer is well known.)

Tom was a curly-haired, sun-tanned, blue-eyed, rosy-cheeked, thin-lipped, broad-shouldered, left-handed, slim-hipped, long-legged, flat-footed young man, wearing an open-necked shirt, brand-new, tight-fitting jeans and open-toed sandals.

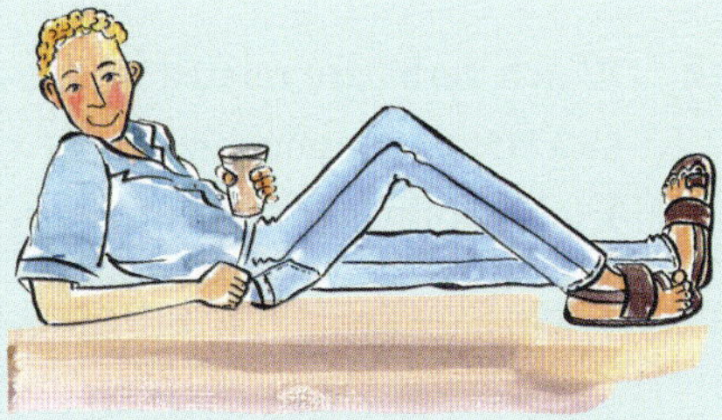

C

Other compound adjectives describe a person's character.

Melissa was **absent-minded** [forgetful], **easy-going** [relaxed], **good-tempered** [cheerful], **warm-hearted** [kind] and **quick-witted** [intelligent] if perhaps a little **big-headed** [proud of herself], **two-faced** [hypocritical], **self-centred** [egotistical] and **stuck-up** [snobbish (colloquial)] at times.

D

Another special group of compound adjectives has a preposition in its second part.

The workers' declaration of an **all-out** strike forced management to improve conditions.
Once there were fields here but now it's a totally **built-up** area.
That student's parents are very **well-off** but they don't give him much money and he is always complaining of being **hard-up**.
I love these shoes and, although they're **worn-out**, I can't throw them away.
This area was once prosperous but it now looks very **run-down**.

E

Here are some other compound adjectives with typical nouns.

air-conditioned rooms   bullet-proof windows on the president's car
cut-price goods in the sales   duty-free cigarettes   hand-made clothes
interest-free credit   last-minute revision for an exam   long-distance lorry driver
long-standing relationship   off-peak train travel   part-time job
remote-controlled toy car   second-class ticket   so-called expert   sugar-free diet
time-consuming writing of reports   top-secret information   world-famous film star

F

You can vary the compound adjectives listed by changing one part of the adjective. For example, **curly-haired, long-haired, red-haired** and **straight-haired; first-hand** (knowledge), **first-class** (ticket) and **first-born** (child).

TIP
When you come across a compound adjective that you want to learn, write it down in a phrase or sentence describing someone or something you know, for example, Maria is curly-haired, our second-hand car. Personalising the words in this way will help you to learn them.

Exercises

12.1 **Fill the blanks with the words from the box to form new compound adjectives. Use a dictionary if necessary.**

bald	bright	British	broad	brown	hands
dust	fire	fool	hard	round	home
hot	kind	high	narrow	pig	polo
problem	ready	single	soft	tax	wide

1 ....
.... -eyed
....

2 ....
.... -proof
....

3 ....
.... -minded
....

4 ....
.... -necked
....

5 ....
.... -made
....

6 ....
.... -free
....

7 ....
.... -headed
....

8 ....
.... -hearted
....

12.2 **Put the words in E opposite into any categories which will help you learn them.**

12.3 **List as many compound adjectives beginning with *self*, as you can. Mark them *P* or *N* for positive or negative characteristics, or write *neutral*.**

12.4 **Answer the questions by using a compound adjective which is opposite in meaning to the adjective in the question. Note that the answer may or may not have the same second element as the adjective in the question.**

EXAMPLE Is he working full-time? *No, part-time.*

1 Isn't she rather short-sighted?
2 Is your brother well-off?
3 Would you say the boy is well-behaved?
4 Are her shoes high-heeled?
5 Is this vase mass-produced?
6 Do they live in south-east England?

12.5 **Think of two more nouns that would frequently be associated with any ten of the compound adjectives listed in E opposite.**

12.6 **Add a preposition from the list below to complete appropriate compound adjectives.**

back	up	out	off	on	of

1 She's done the same low-paid job for so long that she's really fed-............ with it now.
2 The two cars were involved in a head-............ collision.
3 He has a very casual, laid-............ approach to life in general.
4 It'll never happen again. It's definitely a one-............ situation.
5 He's a smash hit here but he's unheard-............ in my country.
6 She bought a cut-............ paper pattern and made her own dress.

12.7 **Which of the adjectives from this unit could you use to describe yourself or your friends or members of your family?**

13 Compound nouns (1) noun + noun

A

A compound noun is a fixed expression which is made up of more than one word and functions as a noun. Such expressions are frequently combinations of two nouns, e.g. **address book, human being [person], science fiction** [fiction based on some kind of scientific fantasy]. A number of compound nouns are related to phrasal verbs and these are dealt with in Unit 14.

B

If you understand both parts of the compound noun, the meaning will usually be clear. Compound nouns are usually written as two words, e.g. **tin opener** [an opener for tins], **bank account** [an account in a bank], **pedestrian crossing** [a place for people to cross a road], but sometimes they are written with a hyphen instead of a space between the words, e.g. **pen-name** [a false name used by a writer, a pseudonym], **baby-sitter** [someone who sits with a baby/child while parents are out]. Sometimes they may be written as one word, e.g. **earring, trademark** [the symbol of a product].

C

Usually the main stress is on the first part of the compound but sometimes it is on the second part. In the common compound nouns below, the word which contains the main stress is underlined.

alarm clock	answering machine	blood donor	book token
burglar alarm	bus stop	contact lens	credit card
heart attack	package holiday	steering wheel	shoe horn
tea-bag	windscreen	windscreen wiper	youth hostel

D

Compound nouns may be countable, uncountable or only used in either the singular or the plural. The examples given in C are all countable compound nouns. Here are some examples of common uncountable compound nouns.

air-traffic control	birth control	blood pressure	computer technology
cotton wool	data-processing	food poisoning	hay fever [allergy to pollen]
income tax	junk food	mail order	pocket money

Here are some examples of common compound nouns used only in the singular.

arms race [countries wanting most powerful weapons]
brain drain [highly educated people leaving country to work abroad]
death penalty

generation gap	global warming	greenhouse effect
labour force	mother-tongue	
sound barrier	welfare state	

Here are some examples of common compound nouns used only in the plural.

grass roots	human rights	kitchen scissors	luxury goods
race relations	roadworks	sunglasses	traffic lights

TIP Compound nouns are particularly common when talking about new inventions or aspects of society in the modern world. Keep an eye open for more examples when you are reading a newspaper or magazine and note them down in a special section of your vocabulary notebook.

Exercises

13.1 **Complete these bubble networks with any appropriate expressions from the opposite page. Add extra bubbles if you need them.**

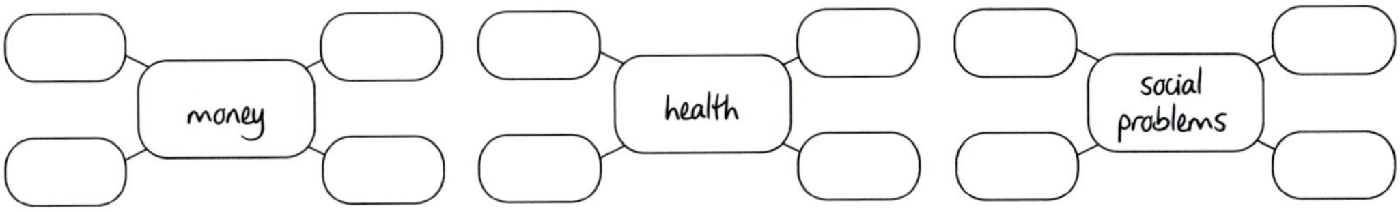

13.2 **In some cases more than one compound noun can be formed from one particular element. For example *blood pressure* and *blood donor*; *air-traffic control*, *birth control* and *self-control*. Complete the following compound nouns with a noun other than the one suggested opposite. Use your dictionary.**

1 .... token	4 blood	7 .... tax	10 .... lights
2 junk	5 tea	8 .... processing	11 .... food
3 sound	6 mother	9 .... crossing	12 .... race

13.3 **What are they talking about? In each case the answer is a compound noun opposite.**

EXAMPLE I had it taken at the doctor's this morning and he said it was a little high for my age. *blood pressure*

1 You really shouldn't cross the road at any other place.
2 It's partly caused by such things as hair sprays and old fridges.
3 She always has terrible sneezing fits in the early summer.
4 I can't understand why they spend so much on devising ways of killing people.
5 They say that working there is much more stressful than being a pilot.
6 The worst time was when I dropped one at the theatre and spent the interval searching around on the floor. I couldn't see a thing without them.
7 I don't think it should ever be used whatever the crime.
8 It's much easier not to have to make your own travel arrangements.
9 It took my mother ages to get used to leaving a message on mine!

13.4 **Now make up some sentences like those in exercise 13.3 relating to some of the new expressions you made in exercise 13.2.**

13.5 **Here are some compound expressions you have worked with in this unit. Explain what the significance of the nouns used in the compound are.**

EXAMPLE windscreen *a screen that protects a driver from the wind.*

1 book token	4 generation gap	7 luxury goods
2 burglar alarm	5 greenhouse effect	8 pocket money
3 food poisoning	6 kitchen scissors	9 welfare state

Follow-up: Find an article from a newspaper or magazine. (You can probably find one in an English-language textbook if you don't have easy access to English language newspapers or magazines.) Note down any examples of compound nouns that you find. Explain what the significance is of each of the parts of the compounds.

14 Compound nouns (2) verb + preposition

A

Some compound nouns are based on phrasal verbs, e.g. **takeover** / to take over. In sections B to E you will see these types of nouns in context. The meaning of the compound noun is given in brackets. To form the plural, 's' is added to the end, e.g. **pin-ups**.

B

Nouns based on phrasal verbs often have an informal feel to them and they are particularly common in newspaper reporting. Here are examples of such nouns in use.

In response to the pay offer, there was a **walk-out** at the factory. [strike]
There is going to be a **crack-down** on public spending. [action to prevent]
An inquiry into the recent **break-out** from the local prison has recommended measures to tighten security there. [escape]
Last month saw a tremendous **shake-up** in personnel. [change]
Last week we reported on the **break-up** of the mayor's marriage. [collapse]

C

A number of these nouns have economic associations.

The **takeover** of one of our leading hotel chains has just been announced. [purchase by another company]
We're trying to find some new **outlets** for our products. [places to sell]
Take your things to the **check-out** to pay for them. [cash-desk]
Cutbacks will be essential until the recession is over. [reductions]
Our profit was £1000 on a **turnover** of £10,000. [money passing through a company]

D

Some of these nouns are associated with technology and other aspects of modern life.

What the computer produces depends on the **input**. [information that is put in]
Output has increased thanks to new technology. [production]
We have a rather rapid staff **turnover**. [change]
Just after leaving school he went through the stage of being a **dropout**. [person who rejects society]
The consequences of **fallout** from Chernobyl are still being felt. [radio-active dust in the atmosphere]
I can easily get you a **printout** of the latest figures. [paper on which computer information has been printed]
A **breakthrough** has been made in AIDS research. [important discovery]

E

Some of the words can be used in more general circumstances.

Many of the problems were caused by a **breakdown** in communications. [failure]
The **outlook** for tomorrow is good – sunny in most places. [prospect]
There are **drawbacks** as well as advantages to every situation. [negative aspects]
The **outcome** of the situation was not very satisfactory. [conclusion]
TV companies always welcome **feedback** from viewers. [comments]
It was clear from the **outset** that the **set-up** would cause problems. [start; situation]
We parked in a **lay-by** on the **by-pass**. [parking space at the side of a road; road avoiding the centre of a town]
The **outbreak** of war took many people by surprise. [start of something unpleasant]

TIP Many, though not all, of these nouns are associated with phrasal verbs (the outbreak of war / war broke out). When you come across such a compound, check to see whether it is associated with a parallel phrasal verb and, if so, learn them together.

Exercises

14.1 **Here are some compound nouns based on phrasal verbs. Guess the meaning of the underlined word from its context.**

1 Because of the accident there was a three-mile tailback along the motorway.
2 Police are warning of an increased number of break-ins in this area.
3 The papers are claiming the Prime Minister organised a cover-up.
4 Unfortunately, our plans have suffered a setback.
5 I'm sorry I'm late. There was a terrible hold-up on the bridge.
6 The robbers made their getaway in a stolen car.

14.2 **Which of the words studied on the opposite page would be most likely to follow the adjectives given below?**

1 radioactive ....
2 nervous ....
3 computer ....
4 annual ....
5 final ....
6 sales ....
7 positive ....
8 drastic ....

14.3 **Fill in the blanks with an appropriate word from those on the left-hand page.**

1 A and C Ltd. have made a .... bid for S and M plc.
2 The Prime Minister yesterday announced a .... in the Cabinet.
3 The negotiations aim to end the 10-day-old ....
4 She provided some very valuable .... to the discussion.
5 CIRCUS LION IN HORROR ....
6 There's a terrible queue at this .... Let's find another one.
7 There has been a disturbing .... of violence in prisons recently.
8 The office wall was covered in ....

14.4 **Here are some more words made up of a noun + preposition. Choose a noun from the list to combine with the prepositions. Use your dictionary to help you.**

work hand hold clear write lie turn press write

1 Their car was a ....-off after the accident.
2 The lecturer distributed ....-outs before she started speaking.
3 Jack does a daily ....-out at the gym, starting with 20 ....-ups.
4 There is an interesting ....-up of the match in today's paper.
5 I'm giving my office a major ....-out this week.
6 Did you hear about the ....-up at our bank?
7 There was a surprisingly large ....-out at the concert.
8 I love having a ....-in on Sundays.

14.5 **These words are made up of the same parts but they have very different meanings. Explain the meaning of each of the words. Use your dictionary if necessary.**

1 outlook/look-out 2 set-up/upset 3 outlet/let-out 4 outlay/layout

14.6 **Choose eight of the words in this unit which you particularly want to learn and write your own sentences using them.**

15 Words from other languages

A

English has borrowed words from most of the other languages with which it has had contact. It has taken many expressions from the ancient languages, Latin and Greek, and these borrowings often have academic or literary associations. From French, English has taken lots of words to do with cooking, the arts, and a more sophisticated lifestyle in general. From Italian come words connected with music and the plastic arts. German expressions in English have been coined either by tourists bringing back words for new things they saw or by philosophers or historians describing German concepts or experiences. Words borrowed from other languages often relate to things which English speakers experienced from the first time abroad.

B

There are borrowings from a wide range of languages. For example, from Japanese, **tycoon, karate, origami, judo, futon** and **bonsai**. From Arabic, **mattress, cipher, alcove, carafe, algebra, harem** and **yashmak**. From Turkish, **yoghurt, jackal, kiosk, tulip** and **caftan**; from Farsi, **caravan, shawl, bazaar** and **sherbet**, and from Eskimo, **kayak, igloo** and **anorak**.

C

The map of Europe below shows the places of origin of some English words and expressions borrowed from some other European languages. Use a dictionary to check the meanings of any words you are not sure about.

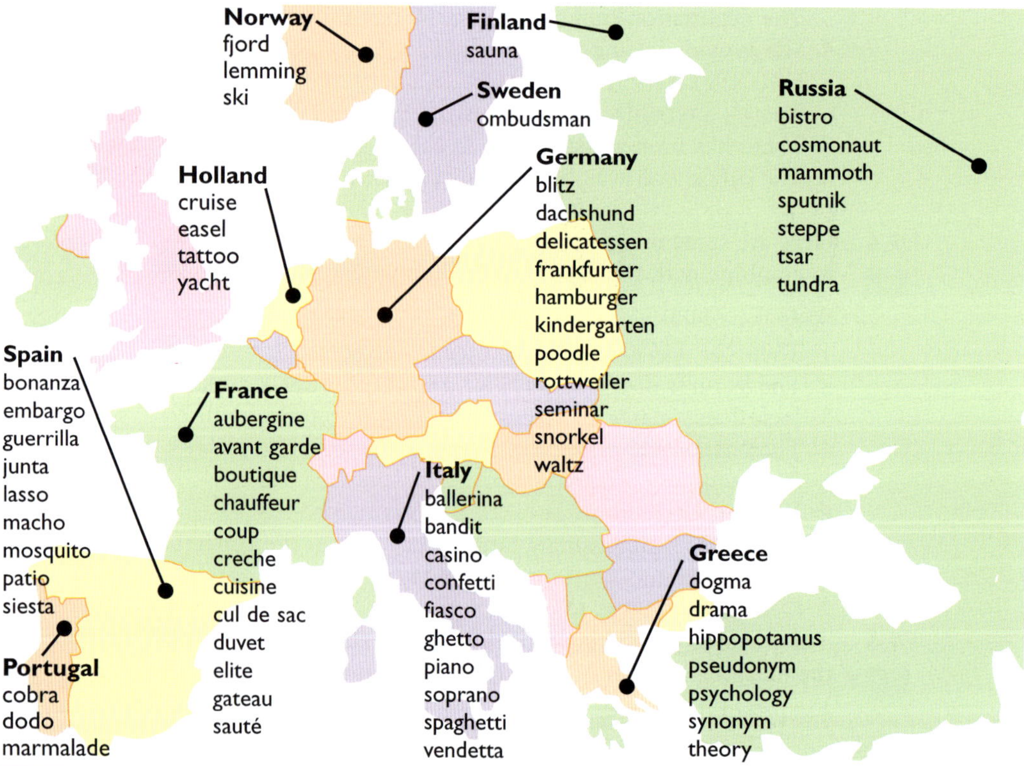

TIP English has borrowed very freely from other languages and you may well come across English words that you are familiar with from your own language. Note, however, that the pronunciation is often anglicised, so check in a dictionary.

Exercises

15.1 Which of the words listed opposite are also used in your language?

15.2 Is your own language represented on the opposite page? If so, can you add any words to the lists opposite? If not, do you know of any words English has borrowed from your language? (There are almost sure to be some.) Do the words mean exactly the same in English as in your language? Are they pronounced in the same way?

15.3 Look at all the words opposite and complete the following networks.

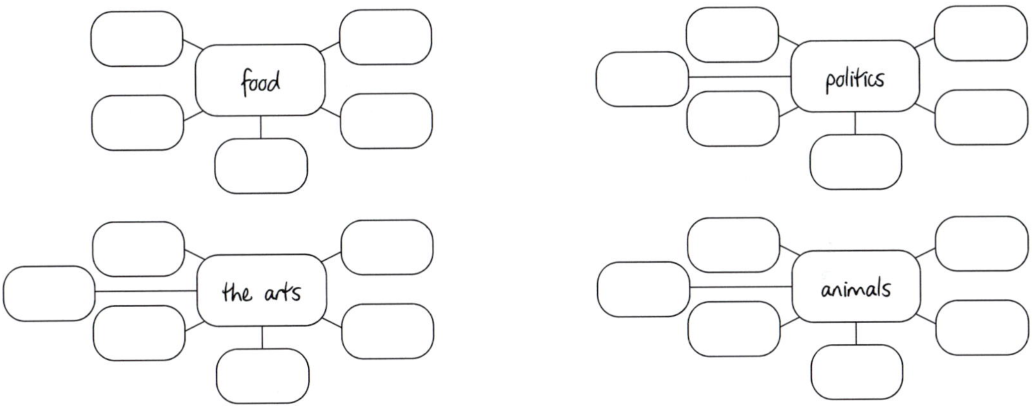

15.4 Make two or three other networks to help you to learn the words on the opposite page.

15.5 Match the adjectives on the left with the noun they are most likely to be associated with, on the right.

1 military	a kindergarten
2 strawberry	b casino
3 pop	c vendetta
4 Chinese	d embargo
5 ankle	e cuisine
6 total	f psychology
7 long-standing	g yoghurt
8 noisy	h coup
9 double	i tattoo
10 all-night	j duvet

15.6 What verbs collocate, in other words, are frequently used with the following nouns?

EXAMPLE *study* algebra

1 karate	3 futon	5 guerrilla	7 coup	9 siesta	11 sauna
2 kayak	4 embargo	6 cul de sac	8 confetti	10 cruise	12 seminar

15.7 Give three nouns likely to follow *macho* and *avant-garde*.

15.8 Have some words or expressions been borrowed from English into your own language? Give some examples. Have they kept exactly the same meaning as they have in English?

16 Abbreviations and acronyms

A

NOTE
When these abbreviations are stressed words in the sentence, the stress falls on the last letter, e.g. She works for the CIA. I heard it on the BBC.

Some abbreviations are read as individual letters.

WHO [W-H-O] World Health Organisation
ID Identity [an identity card or passport]
BBC British Broadcasting Corporation
GM(O) genetically modified (organism)
IRA Irish Republican Army
UN United Nations
PM Prime Minister
MP Member of Parliament

In the following three cases, the name of each country and the name of its secret police are pronounced as individual letters/numbers.

CIA (USA) **MI5** (UK) **KGB** (of the former USSR)

B

Some abbreviations are read as words; we call them acronyms.

NATO /neɪtəʊ/ North Atlantic Treaty Organisation
OPEC /'əʊ pek/ Organisation of Petroleum Exporting Countries
AIDS /eɪdz/ Acquired Immune Deficiency Syndrome
PIN /pɪn/ Personal Identity Number (e.g. for a bank or credit card)

Some acronyms have become so normal as words that people do not think of them as abbreviations any longer, and so they are not written all in capital letters.

laser **radar** **yuppy** **Esso**

C

Some abbreviations are only written forms; they are always pronounced as the full word.

Mr (Mister) Dr (Doctor) St (Saint or Street) Rd (Road)

D

Within a written text some abbreviations are used as notes to organise the language and give extra information to the reader.

etc. /et'setrə/ and so on [Latin *et cetera*]
i.e. (I-E): that is to say [Latin *id est*]
e.g. (E-G) for example [Latin: *exempli gratia*]
PTO (P-T-O) please turn over
NB (N-B) please note [Latin: *nota bene*]

E

Clippings: Some words are normally used in an abbreviated form in informal situations.

ad/advert (advertisement) **bike** (bicycle) **board** (blackboard) **case** (suitcase)
exam (examination) **fridge** (refrigerator) **lab** (laboratory) **phone** (telephone)
plane (aeroplane) **rep** (business representative) **TV** or **telly** (television)

F

Some abbreviations you might see on a letter/fax/envelope.

c/o care of [e.g. T. Smith, c/o J. Brown; the letter goes to J. Brown's address]
enc. enclosed [documents enclosed with a letter, e.g. enc. application form]
PS postscript [extra message after the letter has been ended]
asap as soon as possible [e.g. ring me asap]
RSVP (R-S-V-P) please reply [French; *répondez s'il vous plaît*]

Exercises

16.1 **What things in these addresses are normally abbreviated? How is *Ms* pronounced?**

1 Mister A. Carlton
Flat number 5
28, Hale Crescent
Borebridge

2 Ms P. Meldrum
care of T. Fox
6, Marl Avenue
Preston

3 N. Lowe and Company
7, Bridge Road
Freeminster
United Kingdom

16.2 **What do these abbreviations mean? Use a dictionary if necessary. Now group them according to groups A to D opposite.**

1 BSc 2 FBI 3 Fr 4 ext. 5 CD 6 asap 7 PIN 8 e.g. 9 Unesco

16.3 **'Translate' this note from the boss to a group of workers in an office, into full words.**

Memo from: Mr Richard Hedd (MD) **To:** All staff **Date:** 3/5/91 **Ref:** 04056/DC

May I remind you that all new lab equipment should be registered with Stores & Supplies, Room 354 (ext 2683). NB: new items must be notified before 1700 hrs on the last day of the month of purchase, i.e. within the current budgeting month. All a/c nos must be recorded.

Dick

16.4 **Explain 1–5 and match them with the contexts on the right.**

1 Students and OAPs: £1.50
2 WC Gents
3 US forces take 5,000 POWs
4 Ozone-friendly: CFC-free
5 Dep 1500 Arr 1742

on an aerosol can
in a newspaper headline
on a museum entrance
on an airline timetable
on a door in a pub or restaurant

16.5 **Complete the crossword.**

Across
3 Flying saucer
6 N, S, E or W?
8 Royal Navy
9 Rest in Peace
10 Short for biological(ly)
11 Music disc
12 &
13 Means 'especially'
15 British car-plate
17 America
19 Famous film alien from outer space
20 Short name for London Underground

Down
1 %
2 Same as 13 across
4 Refrigerators
5 Means 'or nearest offer'
7 Serious illness
10 'Please note' backwards
14 Place for a short drink?
16 British Telecom
18 South East

Follow-up: Check whether the dictionary you use has a special section on abbreviations and acronyms, or, if not, find out how the dictionary presents them.

17 New words in English

No language stands still. New words and expressions are always being created, sometimes just for fun or usually because something new is invented. Below are some relatively new words and expressions and new uses of old words. Note that all these new words had been in use for at least a few years before the publication of this book.

A Science, technology and medicine

cyberspace: the realm where electronic data are sorted or transmitted by computers
junk e-mail: unsolicited material, such as adverts, sent by e-mail
keypal: a kind of penfriend that you exchange e-mails with rather than letters
surfing the net: exploring the world-wide web
e-commerce: business based on the Internet
mouse potato: someone who spends a lot of time in front of a computer, especially on-line
information fatigue syndrome: a condition of psychological stress induced by trying to cope with too much information
eating disorder: a serious disturbance in eating habits often caused by emotional problems
GM foods: genetically-modified food, i.e. food adapted by use of biotechnology

B Entertainment

snowboarding: gliding on snow, upright on a large single ski
in-line skating: roller-skating or roller-blading with rubber wheels in a straight line
video jockey (VJ): a TV presenter of music videos
audio book: an audio recording of a book read aloud – sometimes in shortened form
drop-dead gorgeous: inspiring admiration for someone's attractiveness
bad hair day: a day when everything goes wrong and you feel unattractive

C Social trends

docusoap: a television genre showing people going about their ordinary lives
cybercafé: café where customers can eat and drink and also use the Internet
road rage: extreme anger experienced by drivers in stressful conditions, resulting in dangerous driving or attacks on other drivers
singleton: an unmarried man or woman
spin doctor: someone whose job it is to manipulate popular opinion in favour of politicians or other public figures
decluttering: the art of discarding unnecessary items
off-message: departing from the official party line
grey vote, grey pound: the voting or purchasing power of older people

D Employment

down-sizing: reducing the size of a company or organisation, usually by sacking people
outsourcing: employing outside workers to do work away from the company site
hot-desking: the practice of sharing desks or workstations between workers (rather than individuals having their own desks)
waitperson: waiter or waitress

Exercises

17.1 Here are some more new words and expressions. Match them with their definitions.

1 shopaholic	buying things by phone or computer
2 wannabe (informal)	a teenager highly skilled at using computers
3 snail mail	someone who is addicted to shopping
4 intermercial	disagreeably crude male behaviour
5 laddish	someone who aspires to be something or someone else
6 screenager	ordinary post rather than e-mail
7 to channel hop	a TV programme in which a hidden camera has filmed ordinary people going about their everyday lives
8 fly-on-the wall programme	to switch TV stations frequently, usually by using a remote control
9 tele-shopping	an advert distributed via the Internet

17.2 Choose a word from those defined opposite or in exercise 17.1 to fit into the following sentences.

1 Let's go to that .... You can send your e-mails while I have a coffee.
2 I've hardly ever used .... since I got my e-mail connection.
3 Most of my married friends think there's a lot to be said for being a ....
4 I like skiing but .... sounds too dangerous to me.
5 As people are tending to live longer these days, all political parties are trying to attract the ....
6 I hate the idea of .... as I want to keep my own photos and my personal stationery on my desk.
7 He's such a .... His only activity is surfing the net.
8 He lost the job he'd had for 20 years when the company began ....
9 The party was full of .... actors, all competing for the attention of the director.
10 I like to listen to an .... while I'm driving. It's as good as reading!

17.3 If you meet a new word it is often possible to work out its meaning from its context. Try and explain what the underlined words must mean.

1 I was driving too fast and, although there was no-one around, I was caught by a <u>speed camera</u> and had to pay a fine.
2 <u>Telebanking</u> is so much more convenient than having to find the time to go to the bank in their opening hours.
3 <u>Wet-biking</u>, increasingly popular with the braver water-sportsperson, is becoming a bit of a nuisance for swimmers.
4 Everyone posting to the list is requested to add a <u>sig</u> to the end of their e-mail.
5 He is writing an article on the horrific recent practice of <u>granny dumping</u>.
6 After the Princess's death in a car crash, the whole country was swept by <u>Dianamania</u>.
7 Many large shops now have their own <u>loyalty cards</u>.
8 There was so much sickness when the office moved that we began to wonder whether our new premises were affected by <u>sick building syndrome</u>.
9 She has <u>cyberphobia</u>; she refuses to go near a computer.
10 The area attracts quite a few <u>eco-tourists</u> who come to watch the wildlife.

18 Words commonly mispronounced

This page looks at some of the words which cause pronunciation difficulties for learners of English. The phonetic transcription is provided for some of the words below. If you are not sure of the pronunciation of any of the other words, check in the index at the back of the book or in a good learners' dictionary. Check that you understand the symbols and that you know how your dictionary indicates where the stress is.

A

To master English pronunciation it is helpful to learn the 20 phonetic symbols for English vowel sounds. It is not really necessary to learn the consonant symbols as it is usually not difficult to know how consonants should be pronounced. Vowels are important because the vowel letters can be pronounced in many different ways:

a	about /ə/ wander /ɑ/ last /aː/ late /eɪ/
i	alive /aɪ/ give /ɪ/
u	put /ʊ/ cut /ʌ/ cupid /juː/
ie	fiend /iː/ friend /e/ science /aɪə/
ei	rein /eɪ/ receive /ɪː/ reinforce /iːɪ/
e	met /e/ meter /iː/ /ə/
o	sorry /ɒ/ go /əʊ/ love /ʌ/ to /uː/
ea	head /e/ team /iː/ react /iːæ/
ou	our /aʊ/ route /uː/ would /ʊ/
oo	cool /uː/ cook /ʊ/ coopt /əʊɒ/

B

NOTE
/r/ is not silent in some varieties of English, for example American, Irish, Scottish.

The letters below in **bold** are silent in the examples:

p	**p**sychic /'saɪkɪk/ **p**sychiatry **p**neumatic recei**p**t **p**seudonym **p**sychology
b	com**b** /kəʊm/ dum**b** num**b** tom**b** clim**b** wom**b** lam**b**
b	dou**b**t /daut/ su**b**tle de**b**t de**b**tor
l	cou**l**d /kʊd/ shou**l**d ca**l**m ha**l**f ta**l**k pa**l**m wa**l**k sa**l**mon cha**l**k
h	**h**onour /ɑnə/ **h**onourable **h**onest **h**our **h**ourly **h**eir **h**eiress
t	whis**t**le /'wɪsəl/ cas**t**le lis**t**en fas**t**en sof**t**en Chris**t**mas
k	**k**nee /niː/ **k**nife **k**now **k**nob **k**nowledge **k**not **k**nit
r	ca**r**d /kaːd/ pa**r**k fa**r**m bu**r**n wo**r**k sto**r**m ta**r**t
r	(unless followed by a vowel) mothe**r** /'mʌðə/ siste**r** teache**r** wate**r**

C

Some two-syllable words in English have the same form for the noun and the verb. The stress is on the first syllable of the word when it is a noun and the second syllable when it is a verb, e.g. Wool is a major Scottish export. Scotland exports a lot of wool. Here are some other words like this.

conduct	conflict	contest	decrease	suspect
desert	import	increase	insult	transfer
permit	present	progress	protest	transport
record	reject	reprint	subject	upset

D

Here are a number of other words which are often mispronounced.

apostrophe /əpɒstrəfɪ/	catastrophe /kə'tæstrəfɪ/	cupboard /'kʌbəd/
recipe /'resɪpiː/	hiccough /'hɪkʌp/	sword /'sɔːd/
plough /plaʊ/	muscle /'mʌsəl/	interesting /'ɪntrəstɪŋ/

TIP
Multi-syllabic words in English tend to put their main stress on the third syllable from the end. Compare photograph, photography, photographically. Note that this rule does have exceptions!

Exercises

18.1 Mark all the silent letters in each of the following sentences.

1 They sang a psalm to honour the memory of the world-famous psychologist as she was laid to rest in the family tomb.
2 The psychiatrist was knifed in the knee as he was walking home.
3 He should have whistled as he fastened his sword to his belt.
4 You could have left me half the Christmas cake on Wednesday.

18.2 Which word is the odd one out in each of these groups?

1 worry sorry lorry
2 sword cord word
3 come some dome
4 head plead tread
5 doubt could shout
6 plough rough tough
7 land wand sand
8 soot root foot

18.3 What word could a poet use to rhyme with each of the words below? Use your dictionary to check the pronunciation.

1 hiccough ....pick up....
2 enough ....
3 plough ....
4 through ....
5 cough ....
6 though ....

18.4 Circle or highlight the stressed syllable in each of the underlined words.

1 They paid a £1 million <u>transfer</u> fee for <u>transferring</u> the player to their team.
2 Although they <u>suspected</u> several people were partly involved, the police decided to concentrate on Jo as the main <u>suspect</u>.
3 There are <u>conflicting</u> views as to the cause of the <u>conflict</u>.
4 All this <u>upset</u> over the wedding has really <u>upset</u> them.
5 The cost of living has <u>increased</u> while there has been a <u>decrease</u> in wages.
6 A work <u>permit</u> <u>permits</u> you to work for a period of six months.
7 I wish I could <u>record</u> a hit <u>record</u>!
8 Despite the disgraceful <u>conduct</u> of the audience, James went on <u>conducting</u> the orchestra.

18.5 Write out the words below using the normal English alphabet.

1 /mʌsəl/
2 /kə'tæstrəfi/
3 /'hæŋkətʃiːf/
4 /'kemɪkəl/
5 /'sʌtəl/
6 /rə'siːt/
7 /heɪt/
8 /'resɪpiː/

18.6 Underline the stressed syllable in each of the words below.

1 photograph photography photographer photographically
2 telephone telephonist
3 zoology zoologist zoological
4 arithmetic arithmetical arithmetician
5 psychology psychologist psychological
6 psychiatry psychiatric psychiatrist

Follow-up: Are there other words which you know you personally have particular problems pronouncing? You might like to ask a teacher to help you answer this question. Note any such words down with their phonetic transcription beside them.

19 Onomatopoeic words

Onomatopoeic words are those which seem to sound like their meaning. The most obvious examples are verbs relating to the noises which animals make, e.g. cows **moo** and horses **neigh**.

A

If the vowel sound in an onomatopoeic word is short, it usually signifies a short, sharp sound. If it is long (indicated in the International Phonetic Alphabet by :) then the word usually signifies a longer, slower sound. Compare **pip** /pɪp/ which is a short sound with **peep** /piːp/ which is a long sound.

B

Certain combinations of letters have particular sound associations in English.

gr- at the beginning of a word can suggest something unpleasant or miserable, e.g. **groan** [make a deep sound forced out by pain or despair], **grumble** [complain in a bad-tempered way], **grumpy** [bad-tempered], **grunt** [make a low, rough sound like pigs do, or people expressing disagreement or boredom], **growl** [make a deep, threatening sound].

cl- at the beginning of a word can suggest something sharp and/or metallic, e.g. **click** [make a short sharp sound], **clang** [make a loud ringing noise], **clank** [make a dull metallic noise, not as loud as a clang], **clash** [make a loud, broken, confused noise as when metal objects strike together], **clink** [make the sound of small bits of metal or glass knocking together]. Horses go **clip-clop** on the road.

sp- at the beginning of a word can have an association with water or other liquids or powders, e.g. **splash** [cause a liquid to fly about in drops], **spit** [send liquid out from the mouth], **splutter** [make a series of spitting sounds], **spray** [send liquid through the air in tiny drops either by the wind or some instrument], **sprinkle** [scatter small drops], **spurt** [come out in a sudden burst].

wh- at the beginning of a word often suggests the movement of air, e.g. **whistle** [a high-pitched noise made by forcing air or steam through a small opening], **whirr** [sound like a bird's wings moving rapidly], **whizz** [make the sound of something rushing through air], **wheeze** [breathe noisily especially with a whistling sound in the chest], **whip** [long piece of rope or leather or to hit with one of these].

-ash at the end of a word can suggest something fast and violent, e.g. **smash** [break violently into small pieces], **dash** [move or be moved violently], **crash** [suddenly strike violently and noisily], **bash** [strike heavily so as to break or injure], **mash** [make soft or pulpy by beating or crushing], **gash** [a long deep cut or wound].

-ckle, **-ggle**, or **-zzle** at the end of a word can suggest something light and repeated, e.g. **trickle** [to flow in a thin stream or drops], **crackle** [make a series of short cracking sounds], **tinkle** [make a succession of light ringing sounds], **giggle** [laugh lightly], **wriggle** [move with quick short twistings], **sizzle** [make a hissing sound like something cooking in fat], **drizzle** [small, fine rain].

Exercises

19.1 **Which of the consonant combinations listed in B opposite exist in your language? Do they ever have similar associations?**

19.2 **Which of the words from B fit best in the sentences below?**

1 She heard his key .... as it turned in the lock.
2 The blades of the propeller .... noisily.
3 I love to hear sausages .... in the pan!
4 They .... glasses and drank to each other's health.
5 There was a terrible car .... on the motorway today.
6 Everyone .... with disappointment at the news.
7 That baby loves .... in her bath.
8 It's not raining hard yet. It's just ....

19.3 **Almost all the words in B can be both nouns and regular verbs. There are, however, some exceptions. What are these words? Choose from the alternatives offered below.**

1 Which verb is irregular? whip, grunt, spurt, spit or wriggle?
2 Which word is only an adjective? gash, grumpy, wheeze, or whirr?
3 Which is both a verb and a noun but the noun has a different meaning? trickle, spray, growl, splutter, spit, splash or crash?

19.4 **Can you guess the meanings of the underlined words from their sounds?**

1 The child sploshed through the puddles.
2 If you have a sore throat, try gargling with some salt water.
3 I couldn't concentrate on the play because of the rustle of sweet papers behind me.
4 Speak up. Don't mumble.
5 Those stairs always creak.
6 He whacked the ball into the air.

19.5 **What words on the page opposite do these pictures represent?**

1

2

3

4

5

6

19.6 **Pair the words below so that in each case there is a noun and a matching verb.**

schoolchildren crackles tinkles a bad-tempered person or dog
the bell on a cat's collar a bored child clanks whistles a fire
giggle growls a church bell a steam train clangs wheezes
a bicycle chain wriggles someone with asthma

Follow-up: Look in your dictionary. Can you find any other examples of words beginning with *gr-*, *cl-*, *sp-* or *wh-* with the association described opposite?

20 Homonyms

A

Homonyms can be subdivided into **homographs** and **homophones. Homographs** are words which are written in the same way but have different meanings and may be pronounced differently. Compare **bow** in 'he took a **bow** /baʊ/ at the end of the concert' and 'he was wearing a **bow** /bəʊ/ tie'. **Homophones** are words with different meanings which are pronounced in the same way but are spelt differently, e.g. **bow** as in 'he took a **bow**' and **bough,** 'the **bough** of a tree'.

B

Here are some more examples of homographs with differing pronunciations.

I **live** in the north of England. /lɪv/
Your favourite rock group is singing **live** on TV tonight. /laɪv/
I **read** in bed each night. /riːd/
I **read** War and Peace last year. /red/
The **lead** singer in the group is great. /liːd/
Lead pipes are dangerous. /led/
The **wind** blew the tree down. /wɪnd/
Wind the rope round this tree. /waɪnd/
I **wound** my watch last night. /waʊnd/
He suffered a terrible **wound** in the war. /wuːnd/
Some students at Oxford spend more time learning to **row** well than studying. /rəʊ/
They shared a flat for ages until they had a **row** over money and split up. /raʊ/
They stood in a **row** and had their photo taken. /rəʊ/
This book is called *English Vocabulary in* **Use**. /juːs/
You must know how to **use** words as well as their meaning. /juːz/
They lived in a large old **house**. /haʊs/
The buildings **house** a library and two concert halls as well as a theatre. /haʊz/
The **sow** has five piglets. /saʊ/
The farmers **sow** the seeds in the spring. /səʊ/
Bathing the baby at night may help it to fall asleep. /baːθɪŋ/
(*On a sign at a beach*) No **bathing** /beɪðɪŋ/

TIP A very large number of words in English are homographs or homophones. If a word that you read or hear in English seems strange in its context, it may well be because it is not being used in the sense that you are familiar with. Use your dictionary carefully to check for extra meanings.

C

Here are some of the many examples of homophones in English.

air/heir	aloud/allowed	break/brake	fare/fair
faze/phase	flu/flew	grate/great	groan/grown
hoarse/horse	its/it's	lays/laze	mail/male
meat/meet	mown/moan	our/hour	pale/pail
pane/pain	pair/pear/pare	peal/peel	place/plaice
practise/practice	pray/prey	raise/rays	read/reed
rein/rain	right/rite/write	sale/sail	scene/seen
sight/site	so/sew	sole/soul	some/sum
steak/stake	tea/tee	there/their/they're	through/threw
tire/tyre	toe/tow	waist/waste	wait/weight
weak/week	weather/whether	whine/wine	would/wood

Exercises

20.1 **Each underlined word rhymes with, or sounds similar to, one of the words in brackets; choose the matching word.**

1 The girl I live with knows a good pub with live music. (five/give)
2 The main house houses a collection of rare stamps. (mouse/browse)
3 It's no use. I can't use this gadget. (snooze/juice)
4 You sow the seeds while I feed the sow. (cow/go)
5 The violinist in the bow tie took a bow. (now/so)
6 He's the lead singer in the group 'Lead piping'. (head/deed)
7 What a row from the last house in the row! (plough/though)
8 Does he still suffer from his war wound? (found/tuned)
9 I wound the rope around the tree to strengthen it against the gale. (round/spooned)
10 It's quite hard to wind in the sails in this wind. (find/tinned)

20.2 **Write the word in phonetic script in the correct spelling for the context.**

EXAMPLE I really must do some more exercise or I'll never lose /weɪt/ *weight*

1 Watching TV game shows is such a /weɪst/ of time.
2 There is a hole in the /səʊl/ of my shoe.
3 He broke a /peɪn/ of glass in the kitchen window.
4 The eldest son of the monarch is the /eə/ to the throne.
5 You are not /ə'laʊd/ to talk during the test.
6 Let's /'præktɪs/ our swimming together this evening.
7 He's going /θruː/ a rather difficult /feɪz/ at the moment.
8 Don't throw away that orange /piːl/. I need it for a recipe.

20.3 **Write one sentence using both of the words corresponding to the phonetic script.**

EXAMPLE /peɪl/ *She was quite pale after the exertion of carrying such a heavy pail of water.*

1 /ðeə/	3 /'præktɪs/	5 /waɪn/	7 /saɪt/	9 /hɔːs/
2 /ɪts/	4 /greɪt/	6 /breɪk/	8 /preɪ/	10 /reɪz/

20.4 **Homophones and homographs are at the root of many jokes in English. Match the first part of each of these children's jokes with the second part and then explain the play on words involved in each.**

1 What do you get if you cross a sheep and a kangaroo?	Let's play draughts.
2 What did the south wind say to the north wind?	A drum takes a lot of beating.
3 Why did the man take his pencil to bed?	A woolly jumper.
4 Why is history the sweetest lesson?	He wanted to draw the curtains.
5 What's the best birthday present?	Because it's full of dates.

20.5 **Choose pairs of words from C opposite to describe the pictures below.**

1a 
2a 
3a 
4a 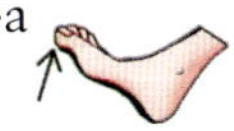

1b 
2b 
3b 
4b 

21 Time

A One thing before another

Before I went to work I fed the cat. [+ clause: most typical]
Before going to work I wrote some letters. [+ -ing form: formal/written style]
I had written to her **prior to** meeting the committee. [formal/written style]
It was nice to be in Venice. **Previously** I'd only been to Rome. [fairly formal, more informal would be **Before that, I** ...]
I was in the office from 2.30. I was out **earlier on**. [before then, fairly informal]
The city is now called Thatcherville. **Formerly** it was Grabtown. [fairly formal, typically written; used when something has changed its name, state, etc.]

B Things happening at the same time

While I waited, I read the newspaper. [or, more formal: While waiting, I read ...; the waiting and reading happen together.]
As I was driving to work, I saw an accident. [**As** describes the background when something *happens* in the foreground. **As** cannot be immediately followed by *-ing*.]
I saw her **just as** she was turning the corner. [precise moment]
She was entering **at the very time / the very moment** I was leaving. [these two are stronger and more precise than **as** or **just as**]
Whenever I watch a sad film, I cry. [every time]

During and **throughout** are different:
During the war, I lived in Dublin. **Throughout** the war, food was rationed.
During does not specify *how long* within a period of time. **Throughout** means *from the beginning to the end* of a period of time.

C One thing after another

After I'd locked up, I went to bed. [or, more formal: **After** lock**ing** up; we do not usually say 'After **having** locked up ...', which is very formal style.]
First we went to theatre. Then / **After that**, we had a meal.
He fell ill and was admitted to hospital. He died soon **afterwards**. [In these two examples, **after that** and **afterwards** are interchangeable.]
Following my visit to Beijing, I bought several books about China. [fairly formal]

D Time when

When I'm rich and famous. I'll buy a yacht. [*Don't say*: 'When I will be rich ...']
As soon as we've packed we can leave. [immediately after]
Once we've finished we can go and have a coffee. [less specific]
The moment/the minute I saw his face I knew I'd met him before.
I stayed in that hospital **the time (that)** I broke my leg.
I met Polly at Ken's wedding. **On that occasion** she was with a different man. [more formal]

E Connecting two periods or events

Dinner will be ready in about an hour. **In the meantime**, relax and have a drink. [between now and the meal]
The new computers are arriving soon. **Till then**, we'll have to use the old ones.
I last met him in 1985. **Since then** I haven't seen him.
By the time I retire, I will have worked here 26 years. [*Don't say*: 'By the time I will retire ...']

Exercises

21.1 **Look at these pages from the personal diary of Laura, a businesswoman who travels a lot, then do the exercise.**

Mon 12	Paris - day 5 Pompidou Centre then theatre	Up early. Said goodbye to Nick and left. Saw bad accident on motorway.	Fri 16
Tue 13	Been away 6 days! Paris OK, but miss home.	Answered all the mail, then felt I could watch TV!	Sat 17
Wed 14	Left Paris 10 am. Huge pile of mail waiting!	Lots of phone calls! Sandra, Joyce and Dougy all in a row! Lazy day!	Sun 18
Thu 15	Manchester, then Glasgow. Met Maura at Nick's.	book tickets for Dublin 24th!	Notes

Fill in the blanks with connectors. An example is given.

1 Prior... to going to Manchester, Laura was in Paris.
2 Her next trip after Glasgow is on 24th. .... she can have a quiet time at home.
3 She was in Paris for over a week. .... she got home there was a big pile of mail waiting for her.
4 .... she was at Nick's place on the 16th, she met Maura.
5 She went to the theatre in Paris on Monday. ...., she had been to the Pompidou Centre.
6 .... she had said goodbye to Nick, she left.
7 .... she answered all her letters, she felt she could watch TV for a while.
8 .... she put the phone down it rang again. This time it was Dougy.

21.2 **Make more sentences with connectors you haven't used, based on the diary information.**

21.3 **Think of things that are true for you in these situations and complete the sentences. Add more sentences if you can. An example is given.**

1 While I'm asleep, ...I usually dream a lot...
2 After I've eaten too much, ...
3 The moment I wake up, I ....
4 Throughout my childhood I ....
5 I'm doing vocabulary right now. Earlier on, I was ....
6 Once I've finished my language course, I'll ....
7 Before I go on holiday, I always ....
8 Following an argument with someone, I always feel ....

Follow-up: Try and get hold of a news report in English. Underline all the time connectors and see if there are any which you can add to those on the left-hand page.
If you find any, write a whole sentence in your notebook showing how the connector is used.

22 Condition

A

NOTE
Don't confuse **in case of** with **in case.** 'Take your umbrella **in case** it rains' means 'it isn't raining but it might rain'.

In addition to *if*, there are several other words and phrases for expressing condition.

1 You can't come in **unless** you have a ticket. [... if you do not have a ticket]

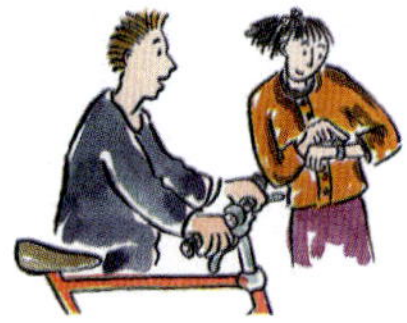

2 You can borrow the bike **on condition that** you return it by five o'clock.

3 **In case of** fire, dial 112. [When there is ...; usually seen on notices; you can also say **in the event of**.]

4 You can stay, **as long as** you don't mind sleeping on the sofa. [less formal than **so long as** and less formal and not so strong as **on condition that**]

Providing (that) or **provided (that)** can also be used in examples 2 and 4. They are less formal and not so strong as **on condition that** but stronger and more restricting than **as long as**, e.g. **Provided/Providing** you don't mind cats, you can stay with us.

B

Note the use of **supposing** and **what if** (usually in spoken language) for possible situations in the future. **What if** is more direct.

MICK: Paul's coming tomorrow. He'll help us.
ALICE: **Supposing / What if** he doesn't turn up; what shall we do then?

C

NOTE
In the examples in A, B and C the present tense is used in the conditional clause. *Don't say:* Take your umbrella in case it will rain.

Conditions with -ever

The **-ever** suffix means 'it does not matter which ...'. The stress is normally on *ever*.

However you do it, it will cost a lot of money.
You'll get to the railway station, **whichever** bus you take.
Whoever wins the General Election, nothing will really change.
That box is so big it will be in the way **wherever** you leave it.

These four sentences can also be expressed using **no matter**. Note the *stress*.
No matter *how* you do it, it will cost a lot of money.
You'll get to the railway station, **no matter** *which* bus you take.

D

Some nouns which express condition

Certain **conditions** must be met before the Peace Talks can begin. [rather formal]
A good standard of English is a **prerequisite** /prɪˈrekwɪzɪt/ for studying at a British university. [absolutely necessary; very formal word]
What are the entry **requirements** /rəˈkwaɪəmənts/ for doing a diploma in Management at your college? [official conditions, rather formal]
I would not move to London **under any circumstances**. [fairly formal]

Exercises

22.1 **Fill the gaps with a suitable word from A and B opposite.**

1 You can come to the party .... you don't bring that ghastly friend of yours.
2 .... emergency in the machine-room, sound the alarm and notify the supervisor at once.
3 .... I hear from you, I'll assume you are coming.
4 A person may take the driving test again .... they have not already taken a test within the previous fourteen days.
5 .... I lent you my car, would that help?

22.2 **The pictures show conditions that must be met to do certain things. Make different sentences using words and phrases from the opposite page.**

EXAMPLE *You can have a passenger on a motorbike provided they wear a helmet* or *Unless you wear a helmet, you can't ride on a motorbike.*

1

2

3

4

22.3 **Change the sentences with *-ever* to *no matter*, and vice versa.**

1 Wherever she goes, she always takes that dog of hers.
2 If anyone rings, I don't want to speak to them, no matter who it is.
3 No matter what I do, I always seem to do the wrong thing.
4 It'll probably have meat in it, whichever dish you choose. They don't cater for vegetarians here.
5 No matter how I do it, that recipe never seems to work.

22.4 **What would your answers be to these questions?**

1 Are there any prerequisites for the job you do or would like to do in the future?
2 Under what circumstances would you move from where you're living at the moment?
3 What are the normal entry requirements for university in your country?
4 On what condition would you lend a friend your house/flat?

23 Cause, reason, purpose and result

A Cause and reason

NOTE
Note the use of 'the fact that' when 'owing to' is followed by a full clause. We cannot say 'Owing to (that) the meeting was cancelled ....

You probably know how to use words like **because, since** and **as** to refer to the **cause** of or **reason** for something. Here are some other ways to express cause and reason.

Owing to the icy conditions, the two lorries collided. [rather informal]
Owing to the fact that the conditions were icy ...
The collision was **due to** the icy conditions.
The collision **was caused by** ice on the road.
The cause of the collision was ice on the road.

Here are some other 'cause' words and typical contexts. They are all rather formal, and more suitable for written use.

The rise in prices **sparked (off)** a lot of political protest. [often used for very strong, perhaps violent, reactions to events]
The President's statement **gave rise to / provoked / generated** a lot of criticism. [slightly less strong than **spark (off)**]
The new law has **brought about / led to** great changes in education. [often used for political/social change]
This problem **stems from** the inflation of recent years. [explaining the direct origins of events and states]
The court-case **arose from / out of** allegations made in a newspaper. [the allegations started the process that led to the court-case]

B Reasons for and purposes of doing things

Her **reason for** not going with us was that she had no money. *or* **The reason (why)** she didn't go with us was that ... [less formal]

The following sentences are all fairly formal, and more frequent in written English:

I wonder what his **motives** were **in** sending that letter? [purpose]
I wonder what **prompted** him to send that letter? [reason/cause]
She wrote to the press **with the aim of** exposing the scandal. [purpose]
I've invited you here **with a view to** resolving our differences. [sounds a bit more indirect than **with the aim of**]
He refused to answer **on the grounds that** his lawyer wasn't there. [reason]
The purpose of her visit was to inspect the equipment.

C Results

Most of these expressions are fairly formal, and more frequent in written English:

He did no work. **As a result / As a consequence / Consequently**, he failed his exams.
The **result/consequence** of all these changes is that no-one is happy any more.
[The examples with **consequence/consequently** sound more formal than **result**]
His remarks **resulted in** everyone getting angry. [verb + **in**]
The events had an **outcome** that no-one could have predicted. [result of a process or events, or of meetings, discussions, etc.]
The **upshot** of all these problems was that we had to start again. [less formal than outcome]
When the election results were announced, chaos **ensued**. [very formal]

TIP When recording these expressions in your notebook, don't forget to write the prepositions that go with them (e.g. result *in*, consequence *of*).

Exercises

23.1 **Make full sentences using 'cause and reason' words from A opposite.**

EXAMPLE closure of 20 mines → strikes in coal industry The closure of 20 mines sparked (off) a lot of strikes in the coal industry.

1 announcement → strong attack from opposition
2 new Act of Parliament → great changes in industry
3 signal failure ← train crash
4 violent storm → wall collapsed
5 food shortages → serious riots in several cities
6 food shortages ← bad economic policies

23.2 **Make two sentences into one, using the 'reason and purpose' words in brackets. Look at B opposite if you aren't sure.**

EXAMPLE There was a controversial decision. She wrote to the local newspaper to protest. (prompt) The controversial decision prompted her to write to the local newspaper to protest.

1 I didn't contact you. I'd lost your phone number. (reason)
2 I will not sign. This contract is illegal. (grounds)
3 The government passed a new law. It was in order to control prices. (aim)
4 She sent everyone flowers. I wonder why? (motives)
5 The salary was high. She applied for the job. (prompt)

23.3 **Use the pictures to describe the *causes* and *results* of events in different ways.**

1 The road was blocked.

2 Everyone got a refund.

3 The customers got angry.

4 We had to walk home.

23.4 **Fill in the missing words.**

1 My reasons .... not joining the club are personal.
2 The purpose .... this pedal is to control the speed.
3 I came here .... the aim .... resolving our dispute.
4 His stupidity has resulted .... us having to do more work.
5 All this arose .... one small mistake we made.
6 It was done .... a view .... lowering inflation.
7 That press article has given rise .... a lot of criticism.

24 Concession and contrast

Concession means accepting one part of an idea or fact, but putting another, more important argument or fact against it.

Although they were poor, they were independent.
He is a bit stupid. He's very kind, **nevertheless**.

A Verbs of concession

example		*paraphrase and comments*
I **acknowledge/accept** that he has worked hard but it isn't enough.	→	I agree but ... [**accept** is less formal than **acknowledge**]
I **admit** I was wrong, but I still think we were right to doubt her.	→	I accept I'm guilty of what I'm accused of.
I **concede** that you are right about the goal, but not the method.	→	You have won this point in our argument. [rather formal, used in debates/arguments]

B Adverbs and other phrases showing contrast

The first four are fairly informal:
OK, you're sorry. **That's all well and good**, but how are you going to pay us back?
You shouldn't seem so surprised. **After all**, I did warn you.
It's all very well saying you love dogs, but who'll take it for walks if we *do* get one?
He *is* boring, and he *is* rather cold and unfriendly, but, **for all that**, he *is* your uncle and we should invite him.
These are more formal:
Admittedly, she put a lot of effort in, but it was all wasted.

I expected Mr Widebody to be fat. **The reverse was true.**

We're not almost there at all. **Quite the opposite**; we've got five miles to go yet.

In Europe they use metric measurements. **In contrast**, the USA still uses many non-metric measurements.
It's not actually raining now. **On the other hand**, it may rain later, so take the umbrella.

NOTE
On the other hand means 'that is true *and* this is also true if we look at it from a different viewpoint'. **On the contrary** is a rather formal expression which means 'that is *not* true, the opposite is true', e.g. The medicine did little to help her. On the contrary it made her feel even more sick.

C Collocating phrases for contrast

When it comes to politics, Jim and Ann are **poles apart**.
There's a **world of difference** between being a friend and a lover.
There's a **great divide** between left and right wing in general.
A **yawning gap** divides the rich and poor in many countries.
There's a **huge discrepancy** between his ideals and his actions.

Exercises

24.1 **Rewrite these sentences using the most likely verb from A opposite (there is usually more than one possibility).**

1 I know that you weren't solely to blame, but you must take *some* responsibility.
2 OK, OK, I was wrong, you were right; he *is* a nice guy.
3 The company is prepared to accept that you have suffered some delay, but we do not accept responsibility.
4 She didn't deny that we had done all we could, but she was still not content.

24.2 **Write a *beginning* for these sentences, as in the example.**

1 I expected Mary to be tall and dark. The reverse was true; she was short, with fair hair.
2 .... On the other hand, it does have a big garden, so I think we should rent it.
3 .... On the contrary, the number of cars on the road is increasing yearly.
4 .... In contrast, the traffic in Britain drives on the left.
5 .... Quite the opposite; I feel quite full. I had a huge breakfast.

24.3 **Try to do this word puzzle from memory. If you can't, look at C opposite.**

Across
1 a .... gap
3 a .... of difference
5 a .... discrepancy
7 .... apart

Down
2 poles ....
4 a great ....
6 a yawning ....

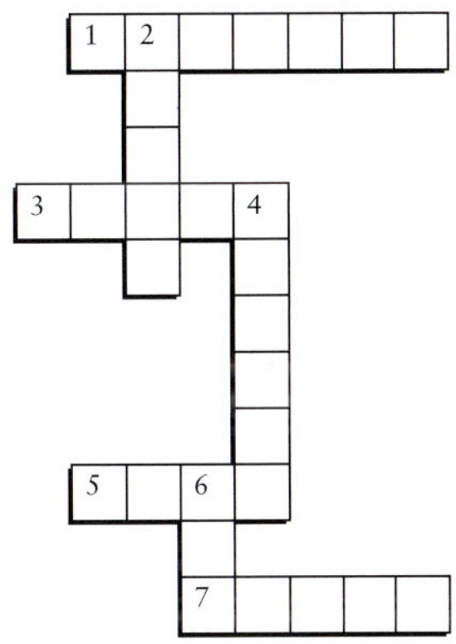

24.4 **Now use the phrases from the word puzzle in 24.3 to make comments on these statements.**

1 Some people believe in nuclear weapons, some in world disarmament.
2 She says one thing. She does quite the opposite.
3 Jim believes in God. Sandra's a total atheist.
4 Being a student's one thing; being a teacher's quite another.

24.5 **Complete the sentences with phrases from B opposite.**

1 OK, you've cleaned the kitchen, ..., but what about the dining-room?
2 No need to panic. ...., it doesn't start till six.
3 She's bossy and sly, but ...., she *is* a friend.
4 .... saying you'll pay me back soon; *when* is what *I* want to know!

24.6 **Choose between *on the other hand* and *on the contrary*.**

1 I'm not worried; ...., I feel quite calm.
2 It's expensive, but ...., we do need it.

25 Addition

You already know words like **and, also** and **too**. Here are some more.

A Words for linking sentences/clauses

®

sentence/clause 1	*and*	*sentence/clause 2*
For this job you need a degree.	**In addition***	you need some experience.
Video cameras are becoming easier to use.	**Furthermore** **Moreover** /mɔːˈrəʊvə/ **What's more****	they're becoming cheaper.
It'll take ages to get there and it'll cost a fortune.	**Besides*****	we'll have to change trains three times at least.
Children should respect their parents.	**Equally** **Likewise**	they should respect their teachers.
We'll have all the stress of going to court and giving evidence.	**On top of (all) that******	we'll have to pay the lawyers' bills.

* **in addition** is more formal than **and** or **also/too**.

** **furthermore** and **moreover** are normally interchangeable, and are both rather formal; **what's more** is informal; **what is more** is rather formal.

*** a more emphatic way of adding information; similar in meaning to **anyway**.

**** even more emphatic: used mostly in informal spoken English.

You can also use **plus**: To keep fit you need a good diet **plus** regular exercise. [normally used to connect noun phrases, but can connect clauses in informal speech]

B Words at the end of clauses/sentences

They sell chairs, tables, beds, **and so on / etc.** /etˈsetrə/. [**and so on** is more informal than **etc.**]
It'll go to the committee, then to the board, then to another committee, **and so on and so forth.** [informal; suggests a long continuation]
He was a good sportsman and an excellent musician **into the bargain / to boot**. [informal; emphasises the combination of items]

C Words that begin, or come in the middle of, clauses/sentences

NOTE
The words and expressions in C are followed by nouns, noun phrases, or -ing. *Do not say:* As well as she speaks French, she also speaks Japanese. You say: As well as **speaking** French, she ....

Further to my letter of 18/9/01, I am writing to ... [formal opening for a letter]
In addition to winning the gold medal, she also broke the world record.
In addition to his BA in History, he has a PhD in Sociology. [fairly formal]
He's on the school board, **as well as** being a local councillor.
Besides / Apart from having a salary, he also has a private income.
Apart from her many other hobbies, she restores old racing cars.
Jo Evans was there, **along with** a few other people who I didn't know.

TIP When learning connecting words such as those in this unit, make a note about the formality of the word where appropriate. It is possible to sound too formal in conversation if you use connectors only normally found in writing or formal speech.

Exercises

25.1 **Fill in the gaps in this letter with suitable adding words and phrases. Try to do it without looking at the opposite page.**

Dear Mr Coldheart,

.... (1) my letter of 16.3.94, I should like to give you more information concerning my qualifications and experience. .... (2) holding a Diploma in Catering, I also have an Advanced Certificate in Hotel Management. The course covered the usual areas: finance, front services, publicity, space allocation .... (3).

I also wish to point out that .... (4) holding these qualifications, I have now been working in the hotel trade for five years. .... (5), my experience prior to that was also connected with tourism and hospitality.

I hope you will give my application due consideration.

Yours sincerely,

Nora Hope

25.2 **Rewrite the sentences using the word or phrase in brackets at the end.**

1 Physical labour can exhaust the body very quickly. Excessive study can rapidly reduce mental powers too. (equally)
2 My cousin turned up and some schoolmates of his came with him. (along with)
3 He owns a big chemical factory and he runs a massive oil business in the USA. (as well as)
4 She was my teacher and she was a good friend. (into the bargain)
5 I'm their scientific adviser and act as a consultant to the Managing Director. (in addition to)

25.3 **Correct the mistakes in the use of addition words and phrases in these sentences.**

1 I work part-time as well as I am a student, so I have a busy life.
2 Besides to have a good job, my ambition is to meet someone nice to share my life with.
3 Alongside I have many other responsibilities, I now have to be in charge of staff training.
4 In addition has a degree, she also has a diploma.
5 Likewise my father won't agree, my mother's sure to find something to object to.
6 To boot she is a good footballer, she's a good athlete.
7 He said he'd have to first consider the organisation, then the system, then the finance and so forth so on.

25.4 **What adding words/phrases can you associate with these pictures?**

1

2

3

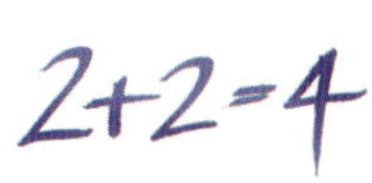

4

26 Text-referring words

A

Text-referring words take their meaning from the surrounding text. For example, this sentence in isolation does not mean much:

We decided to look at the problem again and try to find a solution.

What problem? The words **problem** and **solution** help organise the argument of the text, but they do not tell us the topic of the text. They refer to something somewhere else.

Here are some examples. The word in bold refers to the underlined words.

Pollution is increasing. The **problem** is getting worse each day.
Should taxes be raised or lowered? This was the biggest **issue** in the election. [topic causing great argument and controversy]
Whether the war could have been avoided is a **question** that interests historians.
Let's discuss crime. That's always an interesting **topic.** [subject to argue about or discuss, e.g. in a debate or in an essay]
Punishment is only one **aspect** of crime. [part of the topic]

B Problem-solution words

Text-referring words are often used with 'problem-solution' types of text, where a problem is presented and ways of solving it are discussed. In the following example, the words in bold concern a problem or a solution. Try to learn these words as a family.

> The **situation** in our cities with regard to traffic is going from bad to worse. Congestion is a daily feature of urban life. The **problem** is now beginning to **affect** our national economies. Unless a new **approach** is found to control traffic, we will never find a **solution** to the **dilemma**.

In the dialogue below, two politicians are arguing. Note how the words in bold refer to parts of the argument.

> A: **Your claim** that we're doing nothing to invest in industry is false. We invested £10 billion last year. You've ignored **this fact**.
> B: But the investment has all gone to service industries. **The real point** is that we need to invest in our manufacturing industries.
> A: **That argument** is out-of-date in a modern technological society. **Our position** has always been that we should encourage technology.
> B: But **that view** won't help to reduce unemployment.

The following problem-solution words are grouped in families associated with the key-words in bold. The prepositions normally used with them are given in brackets.

situation: state of affairs, position (with regard to)
problem: difficulty [more formal], crisis, matter
response: reaction (to), attitude (to)
solution: answer (to), resolution (to), key (to), way out (of)
evaluation [of the solution]: assessment, judgement

Exercises

26.1 **Draw lines from the left-hand column to the right-hand column joining each sentence with a suitable label, as in the example.**

1 The earth is in orbit around the sun.	problem
2 World poverty and overpopulation.	evaluation
3 God exists and loves everybody.	fact
4 I've run out of cash.	belief
5 It has proved to be most efficient.	view
6 They should get married, to my mind.	issue

26.2 **Fill the gaps with an appropriate word to refer to the underlined parts of the sentences.**

1 So you were talking about animal rights? That's quite a big .... nowadays.
2 We are running out of funds. How do you propose we should deal with the ....?
3 Is there life on other planets? This is a .... nobody has yet been able to answer.
4 (*Teacher to the class*) You can write your essay on 'My best holiday ever'. If you don't like that ...., I'll give you another one.
5 She thinks we should all fly around in tiny little helicopters. This .... to the traffic problem in cities is rather new and unusual. I wonder if it is viable?

26.3 **These newspaper headlines have got separated from their texts. Put each one with a suitable text.**

NEW APPROACH TO CANCER TREATMENT

NEW ARGUMENT OVER ECONOMIC RECESSION

SCIENTIST REJECTS CLAIMS OVER FAST FOOD

PRIME MINISTER SETS OUT VIEWS ON EUROPEAN UNION

SOLUTION TO AGE-OLD MYSTERY IN KENYA

SITUATION IN SAHEL WORSENING DAILY

1 ... she said if the world community failed to respond, thousands of children could die and ...

2 ... tests were being carried out to see if the new drug really did ...

3 ... there was no proof at all that such things were harmful, and in ...

4 ... the bones proved beyond doubt that human beings had inhabited the region during ...

5 ... also said that he believed that most people had a similar vision of ...

6 ... The Minister denied that this was true and said instead that the evidence pointed to ...

26.4 **Answer these questions with regard to yourself.**

1 What's your approach to learning vocabulary?
2 What aspect of your work/studies do you find most interesting?
3 Which topics in this book are most useful?

27 Discourse markers in speech

A

Discourse markers are words and phrases which organise, comment on or in some way frame what we are saying or writing. An example from spoken language is **well**:

A: So you live in Boston? B: **Well**, near Boston.

Well here shows that the speaker is aware he/she is changing the direction of the conversation in some way (not giving the expected 'yes' answer). In other words, **well** is a comment on what is being said. Another example is how teachers use words like **right** and **OK** to organise what is happening in a classroom:

Right/OK, let's have a look at exercise 3.

B

Here are some common markers which organise the different stages of a conversation.

Now, what shall we do next? **So**, would you like to come to the table now, please?
Good, I'll ring you on Thursday, then. **Well then**, what was it you want to talk about?
Now then, I want you to look at this picture. [said by someone in control of the conversation, e.g. a teacher]
Fine/Great, let's leave it at that, then, shall we?

C

In these mini-dialogues, the markers in bold *modify* or *comment* on what is being said:

A: It's cold isn't it?
B: Yeah.
A: **Mind you**, it is November, so it's not surprising.
[an afterthought, used like however]

A: It's quite a problem ...
B: **Listen/Look**, why don't you let me sort it out?
A: Would you? Thanks a lot.
[introducing a suggestion/point]

A: What's her number?
B: **Let me see**, I have it here somewhere ...
[a hesitation – gaining time]

A: And he said he was go –
B: Well, that's typical!
A: **Hang on / Hold on!** Let me tell you what he said!
[preventing an interruption]

Here are some other similar markers.

I can't do that. **You see**, I'm not the boss here. [explaining]
He was, **you know, sort of ...** just standing there. [hesitation]
So that's what we have to do. **Anyway**, I'll ring you tomorrow. [signalling that the speaker thinks the topic or the conversation can now close]
It rained all day yesterday. **Still**, we can't complain, it was fine all last week. [contrasts two ideas with one another]
We shouldn't be too hard on him. **At the end of the day**, he's only a child. [the most important point or argument is ...]

In informal spoken language, people often use the letters of the alphabet (usually no more than a, b and c, to list points they want to make.

FRED: Why aren't you going this evening?
BOB: Well, **a** I haven't got any money, and **b** it's too far anyway.

TIP It's sometimes difficult to catch markers when they are used in rapid speech, but when you are in a position to listen in a relaxed way to someone speaking English (for example, if you are not the person being spoken to, or you are listening to informal speech on radio or TV), concentrate on listening for markers.

Exercises

27.1 **Underline all the discourse markers in this monologue. Not all of them are on the left-hand page.**

'Well, where shall I start? It was last summer and we were just sitting in the garden, sort of doing nothing much. Anyway, I looked up and ... see, we have this kind of long wall at the end of the garden, and it's ... like ... a motorway for cats, for instance, that big fat black one you saw, well, that one considers it has a right of way over our vegetable patch, so ... where was I? Yes, I was looking at that wall, you know, day-dreaming as usual, and all of a sudden there was this new cat I'd never seen before, or rather, it wasn't an ordinary cat at all ... I mean, you'll never believe what it was ...'

27.2 **Here are some small dialogues where there are no markers used at all, which would be unusual in real informal conversation. Add markers from the opposite page and from exercise 1 above, where you think the speakers might use them.**

1 A: Are you a football fan?
B: I like it; I wouldn't say I was a fan.

2 A: I'll take care of these.
B: That's everything.
A: See you next week.
B: That was a very useful meeting.

3 A: It was last Monday. I was coming home from work. I saw this ragged old man approaching me. I stopped him ...
B: Jim Dibble!
A: Let me tell you what happened first.

4 A: Which number is yours?
B: *(pause)* ... it's that one there, yes, this one.

5 A: He's looking exhausted.
B: Yes, he is.
A: He has an awful lot of responsibility, so it's hardly surprising.

6 A: What do you mean, 'cold'?
B: She's not friendly, very distant. Last week I gave her a jolly smile and she ... scowled at me.
A: What do you expect? I've seen the way you smile at people, it puts them off.

27.3 **Which marker fits best into the sentences? Rewrite the sentences with the markers included.**

at the end of the day still a, b, c, etc. anyway

1 Yes, there is a lot of work to do. I must rush now, I'll call you tomorrow.
2 There's two reasons I think he's wrong. People don't act like that, and Paul would certainly never act like that.
3 Money is not the most important thing in life. I really do believe that.
4 I never got a chance to tell him. I'm seeing him next week. I'll tell him then.

Follow-up: If you can, make a recording of a natural conversation between English speakers (get their permission, but don't say why you need it). What markers do they use?

28 Discourse markers in writing

In this unit we look at how certain common words and phrases are used to organise written texts.

A Organising a formal text

First / Firstly / First of all, we must consider ...
Next, it is important to remember that ...
Secondly and **thirdly** are also used with first/firstly for lists.
Finally/Lastly, we should recall that ... [*not* 'at last']
Turning to the question of foreign policy, ... [changing to a new topic]
Leaving aside the question of pollution, there are also other reasons ... [the writer will not deal with that question here]
In parenthesis, let us not forget that ... [making a point that is a side issue, not part of the main argument]
In summary, to sum up, we may state that ... [listing / summing up the main points]
In sum, the economic issues are at the centre of this debate. [listing / summing up the main points: much more formal]
In conclusion / to conclude, I should like to point out that ... [finishing the text]

B Markers for explaining, exemplifying, rephrasing, etc.

To learn new words properly a lot of recycling is needed; **in other words / that is to say**, you have to study the same words over and over again. [**That is to say** is much more formal]
Some English words are hard to pronounce, **for example / for instance**, 'eighth'.
It might be possible, **say**, to include the parents in the discussion. [similar to **for example**; note the commas before and after; **say** is also common in spoken language]
The Parliament has different committees. **Briefly**, these consist of two main types. [the explanation will be short and not comprehensive]
She is, **so to speak / as it were**, living in a world of her own. [makes what you are saying sound less definite/precise; **As it were** is more formal.]

C Signposts around the text

These are words and phrases that point the reader to different parts of a text.

The following points will be covered in this essay: ... [used to introduce a list]
It was stated **above/earlier** that the history of the USA is ... [earlier in the text]
See page 238 for more information. [go to page 238]
Many writers have claimed this (see **below**). [examples will be given later in the text]
A full list is given **overleaf.** [turn the page and you will find the list]
For **further** details/discussion, see Chapter 4. [more discussion/details]
May I **refer you to** page 3 of my last letter to you? [formal; May I ask you to look at / read]
Ⓡ **With reference to** your fax of 28th May 2000, ... [formal; often used at the beginning of a letter to link it with an earlier text]

TIP Make a separate list of markers for spoken and written English. You may end up sounding too formal or too informal if you do not distinguish between those found in writing and those common in speech.

Exercises

28.1 **Fill the gaps with typical written-text markers. The first letter of each phrase/word is given.**

Points for discussion – crime and punishment:

F............ (1), it is important to understand why people commit crimes, i............ (2), what are the motives which make people do things they would never normally do? F............ (3), a young man steals clothes from a shop; is it because he is unemployed? a drug addict? mentally disturbed? N............ (4), it is essential to consider whether punishment makes any difference, or is it just, a............ (5), a kind of revenge? L............ (6), how can we help victims of crime? I............ (7), how can we get to the roots of the problem, rather than just attacking the symptoms?

28.2 **Match the markers on the left with the appropriate function on the right.**

1 Leaving aside ...	change the topic
2 In parenthesis, ...	read something earlier in the text
3 Turning to ...	this will not be discussed
4 In conclusion ...	this document is about another one
5 With reference to ...	to finish off
6 See above ...	as an aside / secondary issue

28.3 **Which marker(s) ...**

1 is based on the verb 'to say'?
2 is based on the verb 'to follow'?
3 is a form of the word 'far'?
4 contains something you find on trees?
5 contain the word/syllable 'sum'? There are three of them.

28.4 **Write a short letter to the Editor of a newspaper about a report in that paper the previous week that a local hospital is going to close. You think the hospital should not close because:**

The nearest other hospital is 50 kilometres away.
It is being closed for political reasons, not genuine economic ones.
200 people work at the hospital; they will lose their jobs.
The hospital makes an important contribution to the local economy.
It is the only hospital in the region with a special cancer unit.

Try to include as many as possible of these markers:

with reference to   firstly, secondly, thirdly, etc.   leaving aside
the following   to sum up   briefly   that is to say   finally

29 Uncountable nouns

Countable nouns can be used with **a/an** and made plural (e.g. **a hat, two hats**). Uncountable nouns are not normally used with a(n) or the plural, e.g. **information,** *not* 'an information', or 'some informations'. You can learn uncountable nouns in groups associated with the same subject or area. Here are some possible headings.

A Travel

NOTE
Travel is also an uncountable noun, e.g. Travel broadens the mind.

luggage
baggage (*Am. Eng.*)

accommodation

money
currency

equipment
(e.g. *for skiing*)

information

B Day-to-day household items

soap

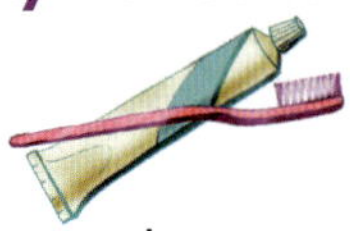
toothpaste

paper

washing-up liquid

shoe polish

washing powder

C Food

The word **food** is uncountable, and so are many food names. Try adding more uncountable words to this list.

sugar **rice** **spaghetti** **butter** **flour** **soup**

D Abstract uncountable nouns

She gave me some **advice** on how to study for the exam.
I picked up some interesting **knowledge** on that course.
She's made a lot of **progress** in a very short time.
She has done some **research** on marine life.
They've done a lot of **work** on the project.

E Material and resources

For making clothes, furniture, etc.: **cloth** (e.g. cotton, silk) **leather** **wool**
For buildings: **stone** **brick** **plastic** **wood/timber** **concrete** **glass**
For energy: **coal** **oil** **petrol** **gas** **electricity**

F Typical mistakes

Don't say: What a terrible weather! She has long hairs. I have a news for you. We bought some new furnitures. *Say*: What terrible weather! She has long hair. I have some news for you. We bought some new furniture.

TIP Always mark an uncountable noun with (U) in your vocabulary notebook, or write 'some ...' or 'a lot of ...' before it.

(See Unit 33 for ways of making uncountable nouns countable.)

Exercises

29.1 **Decide whether these sentences need the indefinite article *a(n)*. Not all of the nouns are on the left-hand page. Use a dictionary that tells you whether the nouns are countable.**

1 He gave us all .... advice on what to take with us.
2 I'm sorry. I can't come. I have .... homework to do.
3 She's doing .... investigation of teenage slang in English for her university project.
4 You'll need .... rice if you want to make a Chinese meal.
5 Paul's getting divorced? That's .... interesting news!
6 I have to buy .... film for the holiday. I think I'll get about five rolls.
7 We saw .... beautiful silk and .... cotton in Thailand.

29.2 **List these words in two columns side by side, one for *uncountables* and one for *countables*. Then join the words which have similar meaning.**

tip clothing case information job advice
travel garment trip work baggage fact

29.3 **Imagine you are going away for a week's holiday and you pack a suitcase with a number of things. Make a list of what you would pack and tick (✓) all the items on your list that are *uncountable* nouns in English.**

29.4 **Correct the mistakes in these sentences.**

1 We had such a terrible weather that we left the camp-site and got an accommodation in town instead.
2 In the North of England, most houses are made of stones, but in the South, bricks are more common.
3 I love antique furnitures, but I would need an advice from a specialist before I bought any. My knowledges in that area are very poor.
4 Her researches are definitely making great progresses these days. She has done a lot of original works recently.

29.5 **Personal qualities and skills use a lot of uncountable nouns. For example, we might say that a secretary should have *intelligence*, *reliability*, *charm* and *enthusiasm*. These are all uncountable nouns. Choose from the list and say what qualities these people should have. Say whether they need *some*, *a lot* or *a bit* of the quality. Use a dictionary for any difficult words.**

jobs: soldier nurse teacher explorer actor athlete writer surgeon receptionist
qualities: patience courage determination goodwill charm stamina reliability loyalty energy experience commitment talent creativity intelligence training imagination

29.6 **Could I have ...? Practise asking for these everyday items and decide whether you must say *a* or *some*.**

vinegar duster needle thread sellotape tea-bag shoe polish

30 Words that only occur in the plural

A Tools, instruments, pieces of equipment

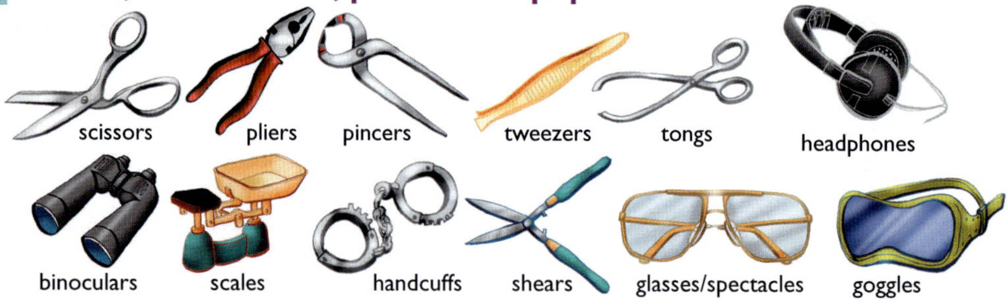

B Things we wear

C More useful words

When I move to London, I'll have to find **lodgings**. [e.g. a room in a flat]
When will the **goods** be delivered? [articles/items]
The architect inspected the **foundations** before declaring that the **premises** were safe. [under the building / the building itself]
The military **authorities** have established their **headquarters** in the old Town Hall.
The **acoustics** in the new opera-house are near-perfect. [quality of the sound]
The **contents** /ˈkɒntents/ of the house were sold after her death.
Looks are less important than personality in a partner.
As you come to the **outskirts** of the village, there are **traffic-lights**. Turn left there. [the beginning or end of the village]
The **stairs** are a bit dangerous; be careful.
The **proceeds** of the concert are going to the children's fund. [money from selling tickets]
A terrorist has escaped from prison. Her **whereabouts** are unknown. [where she is]

D Words with plural form but used mostly with singular verbs

Names of some games: **billiards** **dominoes** **draughts** **darts** **bowls** **cards**
Names of subjects/activities: **physics** **economics** **classics** **gymnastics** **aerobics** **athletics** **maths**

Some words look plural, or may be thought of as plural, but are not, e.g. **means, news, spaghetti** (an Italian plural form), **series.**
There was a **series** of programmes on TV about Japan.
Is there a cheap **means** of transport I could use to get there?

Exercises

30.1 **Make a list of (a) subjects you studied at school or elsewhere, and (b) your leisure interests. How many of the words are plural? Use a dictionary if necessary.**

30.2 **Which things listed on the left-hand page can be used to:**

1 cut a hedge? shears
2 help you to read small print?
3 cut paper?
4 hold your trousers up?
5 get a splinter out of your skin?
6 look at distant objects?
7 get a nail out of a piece of wood?
8 keep a prisoner's hands together?

30.3 **How many articles on the clothes line are plural nouns?**

30.4 **Fill the gaps with an appropriate plural-form noun.**

1 (*To a child*) Come on! Get your .... on! It's time to go to bed.
2 The .... of the rock concert are going to the international 'Save the Children fund'.
3 The .... in the new concert hall are superb. I've never heard such clear sound.
4 The escaped prisoner is tall, dark and has a beard. His .... are unknown.
5 You don't have to wear .... to ride a horse, but it's much more comfortable.
6 The .... have forbidden the import of all foreign ....

30.5 **Odd one out. In each group, one of the nouns is always used in the plural. Which one?**

1 sock trouser slipper
2 billiard squash tennis
3 knife scissor razor
4 tracksuit costume dungaree

30.6 **In this silly story, change the singular nouns to plural where appropriate. Change the verbs where necessary.**

I decided that if I wanted to be a pop star I'd have to leave home and get lodging in London. I finally got a room, but it was on the outskirt of the city. The owner didn't live on the premise, so I could make as much noise as I liked. The acoustic in the bathroom was fantastic, so I practised there. I made so much noise I almost shook the foundation! I went to the headquarter of the Musicians' Union, but a guy there said I just didn't have a good enough look to be famous. Oh well, never mind!

31 Countable and uncountable nouns with different meanings

A

When we use a countable noun we are thinking of specific **things** that can be counted (e.g. two glasses). When we use it as an uncountable noun we are thinking of **stuff** or **material** or the **idea of a thing in general** (e.g. this door is made of glass).

stuff/materials		*things*	
glass		a glass / glasses	
cloth		a cloth	
fish		a fish	
work		a work	

Be careful! there's broken **glass** on the road. I need **a cloth** to wipe the table.
We had **fish** for dinner. Hamlet is one of Shakespeare's most famous **works**.

Here are some more nouns used in both ways. Make sure you know the difference between the uncountable and the countable meanings.

drink / a drink **hair / a hair** **paper / a paper** **land / a land**
people / a people **home / a home** **policy / a policy** **trade / a trade**

Drink was the cause of all his problems. [alcohol]
There's **a hair** in my sandwich, a dark one; it must be yours.
Did you buy **a paper** this morning? [a newspaper]
I love meeting **people** from different countries. [individuals]
The different **peoples** of Asia. [races / national groups]
Her grandmother lives in a **home**. [an institution]
I've lost an important insurance **policy**. [a document]
Trade with China has increased. [imports and exports]

B

The names of food items often have a different meaning depending on whether they are used as countable or uncountable nouns (see **fish** above).

coffee/tea 

→ a **coffee** and two **teas** 

potato  → just two **potatoes**, please! 

would you like some **chocolate**?  → would you like **a chocolate**? 

salt and **pepper**  → **a pepper** 

a hot dog with **onion**  → **an onion** 

Exercises

31.1 **Would you normally expect to find these things in most people's houses/flats/garages/gardens? In which room or place? Answer for both meanings (countable and uncountable).**

EXAMPLE an iron Yes, most people have an iron to iron their clothes; they might keep it in the kitchen somewhere. Most people don't normally keep iron (the metal) at home, but they might have things made of iron (e.g. a frying pan) in the kitchen.

1 a cloth
2 a wood
3 a fish
4 pepper
5 glass
6 paper
7 drink
8 a tape
9 a rubber

31.2 **Which question would you ask?** ***Could I have/borrow a ...?*** **or** ***Could I have/borrow some ...?***

EXAMPLE cake Could I have some cake?

1 iron

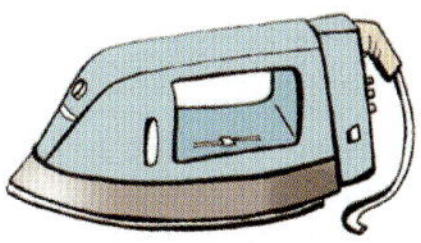

4 paper

2 pepper

5 rubber

3 chocolate

6 glass

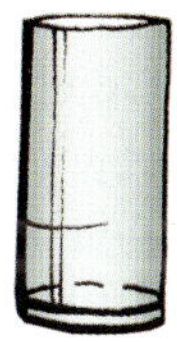

31.3 **Answer these remarks using the word in brackets, as in the example. Use** ***a(n)*** **or** ***the*** **if the meaning is countable.**

EXAMPLE Oh dear! I've spilt water on the floor! (cloth) Never mind. Here's a cloth; just wipe it up.

1 How did you get that puncture in your car tyre? (glass)
2 I was surprised to hear that old Mrs Jones doesn't live with her family any more. (home)
3 What do you think my son should do? He's just left school and he's not really academic. He needs a job. (trade)
4 Why did you choose this house in the end? (land)
5 Mum, what's the *Mona Lisa*? (work)
6 How can I find out what the restrictions are on this car insurance? (policy)

31.4 **What is the difference between (a) and (b) in each pair?**

1 a) Have some sauce with your hot dog.
  b) Shall I make a sauce with the fish?
2 a) PLANT AND HEAVY MACHINERY CROSSING (road sign)
  b) I've bought you a house plant.
3 a) Can I have some light?
  b) Can I have a light?

32 Collective nouns

Collective nouns are used to describe a **group** of the same things.

A People

a **group** of people (smaller number)

a **crowd** of people (large number)

a **gang** of thieves (rather negative)

B Words associated with certain animals

A **flock** of sheep or birds, e.g. geese/pigeons; a **herd** of cows, deer, goats; a **shoal** /ʃəʊl/ of fish (or any particular fish, e.g. a **shoal** of herring/mackerel – note the use of singular here); a **swarm** /swɔːm/ of insects (typically flying ones, e.g. a **swarm** of bees/gnats). A **pack** of … can be used for dogs, hyenas, wolves, etc. as well as for (playing) cards.

C People involved in the same job/activity

A **team** of surgeons/doctors/experts/reporters/scientists/rescue-workers/detectives arrived at the scene of the disaster.

These nouns are used with singular or plural verbs, depending on your point of view.

The **crew** was/were saved when the ship sank. [workers on a ship/ambulance/plane]
The **company** is/are rehearsing a new production. [group of actors]
The **cast** is/are all amateurs. [actors in a film or theatre production]
The **public** has/have a right to know the truth. [the people as a whole]
The **staff** are on strike. [normally used with a plural verb; general word for groups who share a place of work, e.g. teachers in a school, people in an office]

D Physical features of landscapes

In the picture we can see a **row** of cottages near a **clump** of trees with a **range** of hills in the background. Out on the lake there is a small **group** of islands.

E Things in general

a **pair** of birds sitting on a branch [two of anything that are the same]
a **couple** of strawberries [vague way of saying two, not necessarily exactly the same]
a **pile/heap** of papers [or clothes, dishes, toys, etc.]
a **bunch** of flowers [or grapes, bananas etc.]
a **stack** of chairs [or tables, boxes, logs, etc.]
a **set** of tools [or pots and pans, dishes, etc]

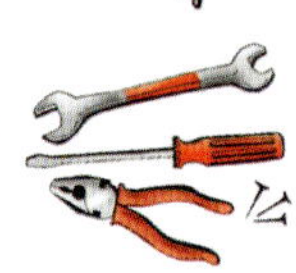

Exercises

32.1 Fill each gap with a suitable collective noun.

1 There are .... of mosquitoes in the forests in Scandinavia in the summer.
2 As we looked over the side of the boat, we saw a .... of brightly coloured fish.
3 There was a .... of youths standing on the corner; they didn't look very friendly.
4 You'll see a .... of cards on the bookshelf. Will you fetch them for me, please?
5 A .... of biologists is studying marine life in this area.
6 Look at that .... of birds on that tree. Both of them have beautiful markings. I wonder what they are?
7 Could you put a .... of spoons of sugar in this coffee for me, please? It's very bitter. Yes, just two, that's fine. Thanks.

32.2 In each case, one of the examples is wrong. Which one?

1 Company is often used for actors / opera singers / swimmers
2 Cast is often used for people in a play / a book / a film
3 Crew is often used for the staff of an ambulance / a plane / a hospital
4 Pack is often used for cats / dogs / wolves
5 Flock is often used for sheep / pigeons / pigs

32.3 Draw a line from the left-hand column to the right-hand column.

1 a clump of	houses
2 a range of	flies
3 a gang of	fir-trees
4 a swarm of	elephants
5 a row of	bed-linen
6 a heap of	mountains
7 a herd of	schoolkids

32.4 Rewrite these sentences using collective words. Don't forget to change the verb to singular or plural where necessary.

1 There are some tables on top of one another in the next room.
2 There are a large number of people waiting outside.
3 The people who work there are very well-paid.
4 A large number of sheep had escaped from a field.
5 She gave me six identical sherry glasses.
6 She gave me five or six beautiful roses.

32.5 Some collective nouns are associated with words about using language. Underline any you can see in this next text and make a note of them in your vocabulary notebook.

THE JOURNALISTS raised a whole host of questions about the actions of the police during the demonstration. There had been a barrage of complaints about police violence. The Chief of Police replied that he was not prepared to listen to a string of wild allegations without any evidence. In the end, he just gave a series of short answers that left everyone dissatisfied.

Follow-up: How would you translate the expressions you underlined in Exercise 32.5 into your own language?

33 Making uncountable nouns countable

A

You can make many uncountable nouns singular and countable by adding a **piece of** or **a (little) bit of**. Similarly you can make such nouns plural with **pieces of** or **bits of**. (**Bit** is less formal than **piece** and they are not always interchangeable. **Bit** can be used with all types of nouns. **Piece** tends to be used more with uncountable nouns. **Bit** suggests a smaller amount than **piece**.

She bought an attractive old **piece of** furniture at the auction sale.
How many **pieces of** luggage have you got with you?
The police collected **bits of** information from different sources.
Chopin wrote some wonderful **pieces of** music.
Before you go to England I should give you two **bits of** advice ...
He spends all his money buying new **bits of** computer equipment.

B

A number of other words go with specific uncountable nouns.

Weather

Today's weather has been variable. In the north there were heavy **showers** (**of rain**). The sunny **spell** (**of weather**) that we have had this last week has continued in much of the south although there were occasional **rumbles of thunder** and **flashes of lightning** in some areas with some quite loud **claps of thunder** in one or two areas. These were followed by a few **spots of rain** but **gusts of wind** soon blew them away and the sunshine returned. (See also Unit 36 for more weather words.)

Groceries

'I need a **loaf of** bread, a couple of **slices of** ham, two **bars of** chocolate, a **tube of** toothpaste, two **cartons of** milk and three **bars of** soap.'
[**slice** can also be used with toast, bread, meat and cheese.]

Nature

Look at the ladybird on that **blade of** grass!
What's happened? Look at that **cloud of** smoke hanging over the town!
She blew little **puffs of** smoke out of her cigarette straight into my face.
Let's go out and get a **breath of** fresh air.
Put another **lump of** coal on the fire, please. [**lump** can also be used with 'sugar']

Other

I had an amazing **stroke of** luck this morning.
I've never seen him do a **stroke of** work. [only in negative sentences]
I've never seen him in such a **fit of** temper before.
The donkey is the basic **means** of transport on the island.
Tights must be the most useful **article/item of** clothing ever invented.
There was an interesting **item of** news about France on TV last night.

NOTE
A stroke of used with luck or work give them greater emphasis than **a bit of**.

C

The phrase **a state of** can serve to make an uncountable noun singular. The nouns used with **state** are usually abstract and include chaos, emergency, tension, confusion, health, disorder, uncertainty, poverty, agitation, disrepair and flux [continuous change], e.g. **a state of** emergency.

Exercises

33.1 **Match the words in the list on the left with the words they collocate with on the right.**

1 a stroke		lightning
2 a shower		coal
3 an article		grass
4 a lump	of	news
5 a flash		rain
6 a blade		clothing
7 an item		thunder
8 a rumble		luck

33.2 **Change the uncountable nouns to countable nouns in the following sentences by using either *a piece of* or *a bit of* or one of the more specific words listed in B opposite.**

EXAMPLE Could you buy me some bread, please? Could you buy me a loaf of bread, please?

1 My mother gave me some advice that I have always remembered.
2 Suddenly the wind almost blew him off his feet.
3 We had some terribly windy weather last winter.
4 Would you like some more toast?
5 He never does any work at all in the house.
6 Let's go to the park – I need some fresh air.
7 I can give you some important information about that.
8 We could see smoke hovering over the city from a long way away.
9 There is some interesting new equipment in that catalogue.
10 I need to get some furniture for my flat.

33.3 **Use words from C opposite to fit the clues for the puzzle below.**

1 My granny wouldn't be in such a bad state of .... now if she hadn't smoked all her life.
2 The government announced a state of .... after the earthquake.
3 We fell in love with the house although it was in a dreadful state of ....
4 We are still in a state of .... as to who has won the election.
5 Although this is supposed to be an affluent society, many people are still living in a state of ....

33.4 **Make up a puzzle of your own like the one above using the language practised in this unit. If possible, test a friend.**

33.5 **Now decide who or what might be in the following states and write your own sentences using these expressions.**

1 chaos 2 flux 3 confusion 4 tension

34 Containers and contents

A

There are a number of special words in English which are used to describe different kinds of containers. Look at the following pictures.

B

Here is some additional information about each of these types of containers.

container	*usually made of*	*typical contents*
bag	cloth, paper, plastic	sweets, shopping, letters
barrel	wood and metal	wine, beer
basket	wicker, metal	shopping, clothes, waste paper
bottle	glass, plastic	milk, lemonade, wine
bowl	china, glass, wood	fruit, soup, sugar
box	cardboard, wood	matches, tools, toys, chocolates
bucket	metal, plastic	sand, water
can	tin	cola, beer
carton	card	milk, yoghurt, 20 packets of cigarettes
case	leather, wood, cardboard*	jewellery, spectacles, wine
crate	wood, plastic	bottles
glass	glass	milk, lemonade, wine
jar	glass, pottery	jam, honey, olives, instant coffee
jug	pottery	milk, cream, water
mug	pottery	tea, coffee, cocoa
pack	card	cards, six cans of cola/beer
packet	card, paper	cigarettes, tea, biscuits, cereal
pan	metal	food that is being cooked
pot	metal, pottery	food, plant
sack	cloth, plastic	coal, letters, rubbish
tin	tin	peas, baked beans, fruit
tub	wood, zinc, card	flowers, rainwater, ice-cream
tube	soft metal, plastic	toothpaste, paint, ointment

*A case of wine is usually a cardboard box of wine, containing 12 bottles. Half a case is six bottles.

Exercises

34.1 Complete the blanks in the shopping list without looking at the opposite page.

2 .... of milk
4 .... of cola
a .... of condensed milk
a .... of chocolate biscuits
a .... of cigarettes
a large .... of matches
a .... of honey
6 .... of crisps

34.2 Try the following quiz about the words on the opposite page.

1 Which two of the containers listed would you be most likely to find holding flowers in a garden?
2 Which three are you most likely to find in a cellar?
3 Which six would you be likely to find in an off-licence (a shop which sells alcoholic drink)?
4 Which five would you be most likely to see on the breakfast table?
5 Which ones does a postman carry with him?
6 Which two are often used for carrying shopping?
7 How many cigarettes would you expect to find in (a) a carton (b) a packet?

34.3 Name the containers and their contents.

1

2

3

4

5

6

7

8

9

10

11

12

34.4 Think of other words which are often used with the following containers.

EXAMPLE *shopping, wastepaper, linen* basket

1 .... box
2 .... bottle
3 .... bag
4 .... jug
5 .... glass
6 .... pot

Follow-up: Look in a kitchen cupboard or a supermarket. How many of the things that you see can you name? You will find more useful vocabulary for this exercise in Units 33 and 48.

35 Countries, nationalities and languages

A Using 'the'

Most names of countries are used without 'the', but some countries and other names have 'the' before them, e.g. **The United States / US(A), The United Kingdom / UK, The Netherlands, The Philippines, The Commonwealth.**

Some countries may be referred to with or without 'the', (the) **Lebanon,** (the) **Gambia,** (the) **Ukraine,** (the) **Sudan.** The forms without 'the' are more common.

B Adjectives referring to countries and languages

With **-ish**: British Danish Flemish Irish Polish Spanish Turkish
With **-(i)an**: American Australian Brazilian Canadian Korean Russian
With **-ese**: Chinese Japanese Maltese Portuguese Taiwanese Vietnamese
With **-i**: Bangladeshi Iraqi Israeli Kuwaiti Pakistani Yemeni
With **-ic**: Arabic Icelandic Slavonic

Some adjectives are worth learning separately, e.g. **Cypriot, Dutch, Greek, Swiss, Thai.**

C Nationalities

Some nationalities and cultural identities have nouns for referring to people, e.g. **a Finn, a Swede, a Turk, a Spaniard, a Dane, a Briton, an Arab.** In most cases we can use the adjective as a noun, e.g. **a German, an Italian, a Belgian, a Catalan, a Greek, an African, a European.** Some need woman/man/person added to them (you can't say 'a Dutch'), so if in doubt, use them, e.g. **a Dutch man, a French woman, an Irish person, an Icelandic man.**

D World regions

E People and races

People belong to **ethnic groups** and **regional groups** such as **Afro-Caribbeans, Asians** and **Latin Americans.** What are you? (e.g. **North African, Southern African, European, Melanesian**)

They speak **dialects** as well as languages. Everyone has a **native language** or **first language;** many have **second** and **third languages.** Some people are expert in more than one language and are **bilingual** or **multilingual.**

Exercises

35.1 **Ways of learning nationality and language adjectives: some adjectives can form regional groups, e.g. Latin American countries are always described by *-(i)an* adjectives.**

1. Complete the list of Latin American adjectives. Look at a world map if you have to. Brazilian, Chilean, ...
2. Adjectives of former European socialist bloc countries and parts of the former Soviet Union also end in *-ian*. Complete the list. Hungarian, Armenian ...
3. What other regional groupings can you see on the left-hand page? (e.g. many *-ish* adjectives are European)

35.2 **Famous names. Can you name a famous ...**

EXAMPLE Argentinian sportsman or woman? Diego Maradonna

1. Chinese politician?
2. South African political leader?
3. Pole who became a world religious leader?
4. Italian opera singer?
5. Irish rock-music group?

35.3 **All these nationality adjectives have a change in stress and/or pronunciation from the name of the country. How do we pronounce the adjectives? Use a dictionary for any you don't know. Use phonetic script if possible (see Unit 5).**

EXAMPLE Canada → Canadian → /kə'neɪdɪən/

1 Panama → Panamanian
2 Cyprus → Cypriot
3 Ghana → Ghanaian
4 Jordan → Jordanian
5 Egypt → Egyptian
6 Fiji → Fijian

35.4 **Correct the mistakes in these newspaper headlines.**

1 Princess to marry a French? Royal sensation!

2 Britains have highest tax rate in EU

3 Rwandese refugees leave UN camps

4 POLICE ARREST DANISH ON SMUGGLING CHARGE

5 Iraqian delegation meets Pakistanian President

35.5 **World quiz**

1. What are the main ethnic groups in Malaysia?
2. Which countries, strictly speaking, are in Scandinavia?
3. What are the five countries with the highest population?
4. How many languages are there in the world?
5. Where is Kiribati?
6. Where do people speak Inuit?
7. What are the five most widely spoken languages?

Follow-up: Make sure you can name your own nationality, country, region, ethnic group, language(s), etc. in English.

36 The weather

A Cold weather

In Scandinavia, the **chilly**(1) days of autumn soon change to the cold days of winter. The first **frosts**(2) arrive and the roads become icy. Rain becomes **sleet**(3) and then snow, at first turning to **slush**(4) in the streets, but soon **settling**(5), with severe **blizzards**(6) and **snowdrifts**(7) in the far north. **Freezing**(8) weather often continues in the far north until May or even June, when the ground starts to **thaw** /θɔː/(9) and the ice **melts**(10) again.

(1)cold, but not very (2)thin white coat of ice on everything (3)rain and snow mixed (4)dirty, brownish, half-snow, half-water (5)staying as a white covering (6)snow blown by high winds (7)deep banks of snow against walls, etc. (8)when temperatures are below 0° centigrade (9)change from hard, frozen state to softer state (10)change from solid to liquid under heat

B Warm/hot weather

close /kləʊs/ [warm and uncomfortable] **stifling** [hot, uncomfortable, you can hardly breathe] **muggy** [very warm and a little damp] **humid** [hot and damp, makes you sweat a lot] **scorching** [very hot, often used in positive contexts] **boiling** [very hot, often used in negative contexts] **mild** [warm at a time when it is normally cold]
Note also: We had a **heatwave** last month. [very hot, dry period]

C Wet weather

This wet weather scale gets stronger from left to right.

damp → **drizzle** → **pour down** (verb) / **downpour** (noun) /ˈdaʊnpɔː/ → **torrential rain** /təˈrenʃəl/ → **flood** /flʌd/

Autumn in London is usually **chilly** and **damp** with **rain** and **drizzle**.
It was absolutely **pouring down**. *or* There was a real **downpour**.
In the Tropics there is usually **torrential rain** most days, and the roads often get **flooded**. *or* There are **floods** on the roads.
This rain won't last long; it's only a **shower**. [short duration]
The **storm** damaged several houses. [high winds and rain together]
We got very wet in the **thunderstorm**. [thunder and heavy rain]
Hailstones were battering the roof of our car. [small balls of ice falling from the sky].
Note also **hail** (uncountable): There was **hail** yesterday.
The sky's a bit **overcast**; I think it's going to rain. [very cloudy]
We had a **drought** /draʊt/ last summer. It didn't rain for six weeks.

D Mist and fog

Nouns and adjectives: **haze/hazy** [light mist, usually caused by heat] **mist/misty** [light fog, often on the sea, or caused by drizzle] **fog/foggy** [quite thick, associated with cold weather] **smog** [mixture of fog and pollution (**smoke** + **fog**)]

E Wind

There was a gentle **breeze** on the beach, just enough to cool us.
There's a good **wind** today; fancy going sailing?
It's a very **blustery** /ˈblʌstrɪ/ day; the umbrella will just blow away.
There's been a **gale** warning; it would be crazy to go sailing.
People boarded up their windows when they heard there was a **hurricane** on the way.

Exercises

36.1 Match each word with a word from the box.

1 thunder 2 torrential 3 down
4 heat 5 hail 6 snow 7 gale

stones	drift	storm	warning
rain	wave	pour	

36.2 Fill the gaps with words from the left-hand page.

My first experience of real winter weather was when I went to Northern Canada. I was used to the sort of snow that falls in London, which quickly turns into brown ....(1) with all the people walking on it. In fact, most of the time I was in London, it didn't really snow properly, it was mostly ....(2). Apart from that, British winters meant a bit of white ....(3) on my garden and occasionally having to drive very carefully on icy roads early in the morning. I had never experienced the ....(4) and ....(5) that can paralyse a whole city in less than an hour and close roads completely. However, when the earth finally ....(6) and all the snow ....(7) away in spring, everything comes to life again and looks more beautiful than ever.

36.3 What kinds of weather do you think caused the following to happen? Write a sentence which could go *before* each of these.

1 We had to sit in the shade every afternoon.
2 The sweat was pouring out of us.
3 I could hardly breathe; I wished it would rain to cool us down.
4 Cars were skidding out of control.
5 The postman had to use a boat to get around.
6 They had to close the airport; the snow was a metre deep.
7 We were able to sit in the garden in the middle of winter.
8 The earth became rock-hard and a lot of plants died.
9 It blew the newspaper right out of my hands.
10 A row of very big trees had been blown over.
11 I could hardly see my hand in front of my face.

36.4 What types of weather are bad and good for doing these things?

EXAMPLE skiing *bad: mild weather which makes the snow melt; good: cold, clear days*

1 Planting flowers in a garden
2 Having an evening barbecue
3 Going out in a small sailing boat
4 A day of sightseeing in a big city
5 Camping out in a tent
6 Looking at ships through binoculars

36.5 This chart shows anyone who wants to visit the West of Ireland what weather to expect at different times of the year. Make a similar chart for your country or home region.

Dec–Mar	*April–June*	*July–Aug*	*Sep–Nov*
coldest months; usually quite wet; snow on hills	generally cool, often wet and windy but improving	warmest months; bright with showers; cool sea breezes	often mild becoming cold; mist and fog

Follow-up: watch the weather forecast on an English-language TV channel (e.g. The BBC World Service or CNN), or listen to one on the radio, or look at one on the Internet, e.g. at http://www.cnn.com Note how many words from this unit are used.

37 Describing people: appearance

A Hair, face, skin and complexion /kəm'plekʃən/

She's got **straight hair** and she's **thin-faced** (*or* she's got **a thin face**).

She's got **long, wavy** hair and she's **round-faced** (*or* she's got a **round face**).

She's got **curly hair** and is **dark-skinned** (*or* she's got **dark skin**).

He's got a **crew-cut.**

He's **bald** /bɒld/ and has freckles.

He's got a **beard** and **moustache** /məs'tæʃ/ and has a **chubby** face.

He's got **receding** hair and a few **wrinkles** /'rɪŋkəlz/.

He used to have **black** hair but now it's gone **grey**, almost **white**.

What sort of person would you find attractive? **Blonde, fair, dark** or **ginger-haired / red-haired.**
She has such beautiful **auburn** hair. /'ɔːbən/ [red-brown]
Fair and **dark** can be used for hair, complexion or skin.

B Height and build

a rather **plump** or **stout** man

a **slim** woman [positive]

a **skinny** person [rather negative]

an **obese** couple /əʊ'biːs/ [negative, very fat]

Fat may sound impolite. Instead we often say **a bit overweight.** If someone is broad and solid, we can say they are **stocky.** A person with good muscles can be **well-built** or **muscular.** If someone is terribly thin and refuses to eat, they may be **anorexic** /ænə'reksɪk/.

C General appearance

She's a very **smart** and **elegant** woman, always **well-dressed;** her husband is quite the opposite, very **scruffy** and **untidy-looking / messy-looking.**
He's very **good-looking**, but his friend's rather **unattractive.**
Do you think **beautiful** women are always attracted to **handsome** men? I don't. I think **personality** matters most.
First impressions are always important. [your first reaction to someone]

TIP The suffix **-ish** is useful for describing people (see Unit 8). She's **tallish.** He has **brownish** hair. He must be **thirtyish.**

Exercises

37.1 Answer these remarks with the opposite description.

EXAMPLE A: I thought you said he was the short, chubby one.
B: No, no, no, not at all, he's the tall, thin-faced one.

1 A: Was that his brother, the dark-skinned, wavy-haired one?
B: No, completely the opposite, his brother's …
2 A: She's always quite well-dressed, so I've heard.
B: What! Who told you that? Every time I see her, she's …
3 A: So Charlene's that rather plump, fair-haired woman, is she?
B: No, you're looking at the wrong one. Charlene's …
4 A: So, tell us about the new boss; good looking?
B: No, I'm afraid not; rather …
5 A: I don't know why, but I expected the tour-guide to be middle-aged or elderly.
B: No, apparently she's only …

37.2 Write one sentence to describe each of these people, giving information about their hair and face, their height and build and general appearance.

1 you yourself
2 your best friend
3 a neighbour
4 your ideal of a handsome man / a beautiful woman

Now, in the same way, describe somebody very famous, give some extra clues about them, e.g. He's/She's a *pop star/politician*. Can someone else guess who you are describing?

37.3 From these jumbled words, find combinations for describing people, as in the example. Not all of the words are on the left-hand page. Some of the combinations are hyphenated. Use a dictionary if necessary. You can use the words more than once.

EXAMPLE good-looking

looking round mixed over well dressed legged
haired complexion good long race weight
middle stocky faced red aged build tanned

37.4 WANTED! MISSING! Complete the gaps in these police posters.

WANTED FOR MURDER

Ian Prowse
White, height 6ft,
..........................-faced,
.... hair,
.... skin

Wanted for Armed Robbery

Sandra King
White, height 5ft 4,
.... hair,
.... build,
..........................-faced

Missing

Louise Fox
age 7,
Asian appearance
..................................,
....
hair.

Wanted
dead or alive

Jack 'Dagger'
Flagstone 6ft
.... , with
.... and ....;
.... build.

Follow-up: Make a collection of descriptions of people from newspapers and magazines. Court/crime reports, celebrity and gossip pages of magazines, and the personal columns where people are seeking partners are good places to start.

38 Describing people: character

A Intellectual ability

Ability: intelligent bright clever sharp shrewd able gifted talented brainy (colloquial)

Lacking ability: stupid foolish half-witted simple silly brainless daft dumb dim (the last four are predominantly colloquial words)

Clever, in a negative way, using brains to trick or deceive: cunning crafty sly

B Attitudes towards life

Amal is **pessimistic** while Nita is **optimistic** – he always expects the worst to happen while she looks on the bright side.

It is strange that one of the twins is so **extroverted** while the other is so **introverted** – Ben loves being the focus of attention while Bill would far rather be alone with his thoughts.

I feel very **tense** (*or* **wound-up / stressed-out****) after a very busy day at work but, after a hot bath and a nice cup of tea, I'll soon feel **relaxed.**

Jane is very **sensible** – she'd never do anything stupid. In other words, she's very practical and **down-to-earth.**

Rupert is very **sensitive** – he gets very **upset** (or **worked-up**, more colloquial), if he feels people are criticising him.

C Attitude towards other people

Enjoying others' company: sociable gregarious*
Disagreeing with others: quarrelsome argumentative
Taking pleasure in others' pain: cruel sadistic
Relaxed in attitude to self and others: easy-going even-tempered laid-back**
Not polite to others: impolite rude ill-mannered discourteous*
Telling the truth to others: honest trustworthy reliable sincere
Unhappy if others have what one does not have oneself: jealous envious

D One person's meat is another person's poison

Ⓡ

Some characteristics can be either positive or negative depending on your point of view. The words in the right-hand column mean roughly the same as the words in the left-hand column except that they have negative rather than positive connotations.

determined	→	obstinate stubborn pig-headed
thrifty/economical	→	stingy mean tight-fisted miserly*
self-assured/confident	→	self-important arrogant full of oneself**
unconventional/original	→	eccentric odd peculiar weird**
frank/direct/open	→	blunt abrupt brusque curt
broad-minded	→	unprincipled permissive
inquiring*	→	inquisitive nosy**
generous	→	extravagant
innocent	→	naive
ambitious	→	pushy**
assertive	→	aggressive bossy**

* These words are much more common in written than in spoken English.
** These words are much more common in spoken than in written English.
(See also Units 11, 12, and 82).

Exercises

38.1 **Match these words with their opposites.**

1 clever	introverted
2 extroverted	tight-fisted
3 rude	courteous
4 cruel	gregarious
5 generous	kind-hearted
6 unsociable	half-witted

38.2 **Do you think that the speaker likes or dislikes the people in these sentences?**

1 Di's very thrifty.
2 Molly's usually frank.
3 Liz is quite broad-minded.
4 Sam can be aggressive.
5 Dick's quite bossy.
6 I find Dave self-important.
7 Don't you think Jim's nosy?
8 Jill is very original.

38.3 **Reword the sentences in 38.2 to give the opposite impression (negative rather than positive or vice versa).**

EXAMPLE *Di's very stingy.*

38.4 **Magazines often publish questionnaires which are supposed to analyse aspects of your character. Look at the words below and then match them to the corresponding question.**

EXAMPLE If you arrange to meet at 7 p.m., do you arrive at 7 p.m.?
reliable

pessimistic argumentative sensitive sociable
extravagant assertive inquisitive

1 Do you prefer to be in the company of other people?
2 Look at the picture. Do you think 'my glass is half empty'?
3 Do you find it easy to tell your boss if you feel he or she has treated you badly?
4 Do you always look out of the window if you hear a car draw up?
5 Do you often buy your friends presents for no particular reason?
6 Do you frequently disagree with what other people say?
7 Do you lie awake at night if someone has said something unkind to you?

38.5 **What questions like those in 38.4 could you ask to find out if a person is the following:**

1 thrifty 3 sensible 5 even-tempered 7 obstinate
2 blunt 4 intelligent 6 original 8 stressed-out

38.6 **Can you complete each of these word forks?**

1 self-............ (............ / .... / ....)
2 ....-tempered (............ / .... / ....)
3 ....-minded (............ / .... / ....)

Write a sentence to illustrate the meanings of each of your words.

38.7 **Choose five or six adjectives from the opposite page which you think best describe either your own or a friend's character. How do you or your friend demonstrate these characteristics?**

EXAMPLE *Sociable – I am sociable because I love being with other people.*

39 Relationships

A Types of relationships

Here is a scale showing **closeness** and **distance** in relationships in different contexts.

	CLOSER ⟵⟶	MORE DISTANT
friendship:	best friend good friend	friend (casual) acquaintance
work:	close colleague /ˈkɒliːg/	colleague/workmate
love/romance:	lover steady boy/girlfriend	ex-*
marriage:	wife/husband/partner	ex-*

*ex- can be used with or without (informally) another word: She's my **ex**. (girlfriend, etc.)

Mate is a colloquial word for a good friend. It can also be used in compound nouns to describe a person you share something with, e.g. **classmate, shipmate, workmate, flatmate.** The stress is on the first word in each case: /ˈklɑːsmeɪt/

Workmate is usual in non-professional contexts or in informal contexts; **colleague** is more common among professional people, and sounds more formal.

Fiancé/ée /fiːˈɒnseɪ/ can still be used for someone you are engaged to, but a lot of people feel it is dated nowadays. You will sometimes see **husband-/wife-to-be** in journalistic style.

English has no universally accepted words for 'person I live with but am not married to', but **partner** is probably the commonest.

B Liking and not liking someone

core verb	*positive*	*negative*
like	love adore	dislike hate
worship	idolise /ˈaɪdəleɪz/	can't stand loathe /ləʊð/
respect	look up to admire	look down on despise
attract	be attracted to fancy	repel leave someone cold

She doesn't just like Bob she **idolises** him. I **can't stand** him.

I really **fancy** Lisa, but her friend just **leaves me cold / doesn't do anything for me.** [more colloquial]

Fancy is informal. **Repel** is very strong and rather formal.

C Phrases and idioms for relationships

Jo and I **get on well (with each other).** [have a good relationship]

Adrian and Liz **don't see eye to eye.** [often argue/disagree]

I've **fallen out with** my parents again. [had arguments]

Tony and Jane have **broken up / split up.** [ended their relationship]

George is **having an affair** with his boss. [a sexual relationship, usually secret]

Children should respect **their elders.** [adults/parents, etc.]

Let's try and **make it up.** [be friends again after a row]

She's **my junior** / I'm **her senior** / I'm **senior to her**, so she does what she's told. [refers to position / length of service at work]

(See Unit 65 for more words relating to likes and dislikes.)

Exercises

39.1 **Use words with the suffix *-mate* to rewrite these sentences.**

1 This is Jack. He and I share a flat.
2 My grandad still writes to his old friends he was at sea with.
3 We were in the same class together in 1988, weren't we?
4 She's not really a friend, she's just someone I work with.

39.2 **How many relationships can you find between the people in column A and column B, using words from the left-hand page?**

EXAMPLE *John Silver and Lorna Fitt were once colleagues.*

A

John Silver: owns a language school for business people in Bath. Worked at the Sun School, Oxford, 1994–5.

Josh Yates: politician, was married to Eve Cobb 1983–1990. Met Bill Nash a couple of times.

Ada Brigg: was married to Bill Nash 1991–4. Swam for Britain in 1992 Olympics.

Ana Wood: has lived as a couple (unmarried) with Bill Nash for the last five years.

B:

Nora Costa: was in GB Olympic swimming team in 1992. Was in same class at school as Ada Brigg.

Bill Nash: works every day with John Silver. Shared a flat years ago with Eve Cobb.

Fred Parks: politician. Knew Ada Brigg years ago, but not very well.

Lorna Fitt: taught at Sun School, Oxford, 1990–7. Lives with Josh Yates.

39.3 **What do you think the relationships between the people below would be like? Use the verbs, phrases and idioms opposite.**

1 teenage music fan
(a) parents (b) pop star (c) strict teacher (d) mate
2 secretary
(a) another secretary (b) boss (c) very attractive workmate
3 45-year-old
(a) teenagers (b) ex-husband/wife

39.4 **The person who typed this book has got some of the phrases and idioms opposite mixed up with one another. Correct them.**

1 Jo and Phil don't get on eye to eye.
2 I fell up with my parents last night. It wasn't my fault.
3 We had a quarrel but now we've made it well.
4 Do you think Jim and Nora are making an affair? I do.
5 I see very well with all my colleagues at work.
6 She should learn to respect her olders.
7 Jo's attractive, but her mate just makes me cold completely.

40 At home

A Places in the home

TIP

If you visit an English-speaking country, go to a department store or a supermarket and look at the names of everyday things for the home. This is a good way of getting vocabulary that is not in dictionaries.

You probably already know the names of most rooms and locations in a typical home. Here are some less common ones and what they are for.

master/main bedroom: the largest, most important bedroom
spare bedroom/guest (bed)room: not used every day; visitors can stay there
utility room: usually just for washing machine, freezer, etc.
shed: small building separated from the house usually for storing garden tools
attic/loft: space in the roof of a house used for storing things; it can also be converted into an extra living space with stairs leading up to it (**loft/attic conversion**)
cellar: room below ground level, no windows, used for storing things
basement: room below ground level, windows, for living/working
study: a room for reading/writing/studying in
landing: flat area at the top of a staircase
hall/hallway: open area as you come into a house
porch: covered area before an entrance-door
pantry or **larder:** large cupboard (usually big enough to walk into) for storing food
terrace or **patio:** paved area between house and garden for sitting and eating, etc.
drive: short road leading from the street to the house or garage; you can drive/park on it

B Small objects in the home

Some everyday objects are often difficult to name and are often not listed in dictionaries.

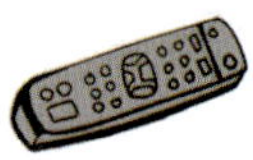
remote control

power point and plug

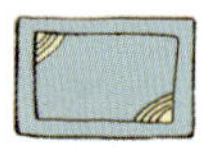
table-mat

coaster

corkscrew

tea-towel

washing-up liquid

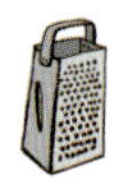
grater

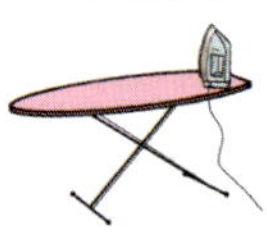
ironing-board /ˈaɪənɪŋ bɔːd/

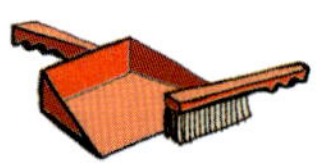
dust-pan and brush

bin-liners

chopping board

C Types of houses/places people live

detached house: not joined to any other house
semi-detached house (informal: **semi-**): joined to one other house
self-contained flat: does not share facilities with any other
terraced house: joined to several houses to form a row
cottage: small house in the country or in a village
bungalow: house with only one storey (no upstairs)
bedsit: bedroom and living room all in one
villa: large house with big gardens or a rented house in a holiday resort/tourist area
time-share: holiday flat or house where you have the right to live one or two weeks a year

Exercises

40.1 **Where in a typical house would you look for the following things?**

1 a rake
2 cutlery
3 dental floss
4 a coat-hanger
5 suitcases
6 a tumble-dryer
7 a power point
8 a porch
9 a grater
10 old empty boxes

40.2 **Fill in the room and place labels on the plan of the house.**

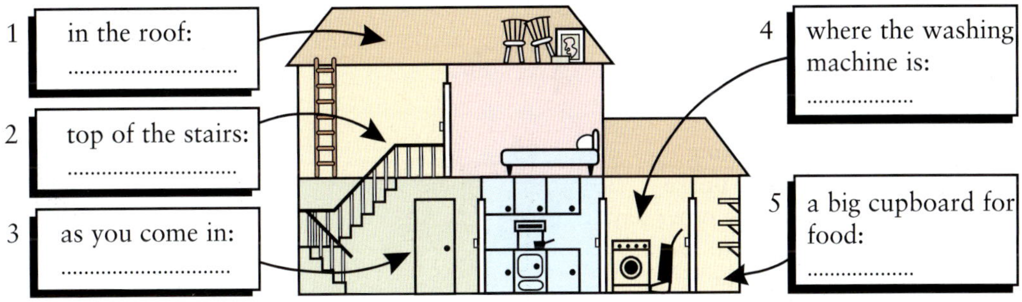

40.3 **Fill the gaps with a suitable word.**

1 I've got a darkroom in the .... where I develop films. It's perfect because there are no windows down there.
2 Is there a .... where I can plug in this radio?
3 Put a .... under your drink in case you mark that side-table. It's an antique.
4 I've emptied the waste-bin. Are there any more ....? Where are they?
5 We keep our skis up in the .... They're out of the way up there.
6 You'll find the garden-chairs in the .... at the bottom of the garden. Bring them up and we'll have a drink on the .... and watch the sunset.
7 The light-switch for the stairs is on the .... just by your bedroom door.
8 I've moved to a .... now I can't manage the stairs any more at my age.
9 This is the .... bedroom; we sleep in here. You'll be in the .... bedroom; that's this one here.
10 Leave your car in the ...., just in front of the garage. It'll be safe there.

40.4 **Answer these questions about yourself and if possible, ask someone else too.**

1 Is your house detached? What sort is it if not?
2 Are time-shares common in any part of your country?
3 Do houses still have pantries in your country?
4 Is it common to rent bedsits in your country? If so, what sorts of people do so?

40.5 **Everyday objects. Answer these questions.**

1 How can you make very small pieces of cheese to sprinkle on a dish?
2 What might you fetch if someone dropped a saucer and it broke into small pieces on the floor?
3 What could you put under a dinner plate to prevent it marking the table?
4 How can you switch off the TV without leaving your chair?
5 How can you cut vegetables without marking the kitchen work-surface?

41 Everyday problems

A Things that go wrong in houses and flats

The lights are not **working**; there must be a **power cut**.

Oh no! The bathroom's **flooded**! Get a mop, quick! /ˈflʌdɪd/

The door-handle's **come off**.

The batteries **have run out / are dead**. I'll have to get some more.

The washing machine **broke down** the other day. I'll have to do the laundry by hand.

Oh dear! This chair's **broken**. I wonder how that happened.

This pipe's **leaking**.

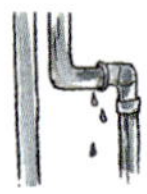

I'm sorry, your cup's **chipped**.

B Everyday minor injuries

She **twisted her ankle** coming down the stairs.

I **cut** my finger while I was slicing potatoes. [broken skin with blood coming out]

I **bumped/banged** my head on the cupboard door and got a bruise. /bru:z/

Sharon **fell down** and **grazed** her knee this morning. [red with broken skin, but no blood]
Graze, cut and **bruise** can be used as verbs or as countable nouns.

C Other everyday problems

I've **mislaid** Bob's letter. Have you seen it anywhere? [put it somewhere and can't find it]
She **spilt** some coffee on the carpet. I hope it doesn't **stain**. [leave a permanent mark]
The sink is **blocked**. Have you been throwing the tea-leaves in there again? [the water will not drain away]
I'm afraid I've **dented** your car. I'm really sorry. I'll pay for the repairs. [bent the metal a little bit by hitting something]
I've **locked myself out**. Can I use your phone to ring my wife?
The car **won't start**. I hope it's nothing serious. Perhaps the battery's **flat**.
The kitchen clock's **slow/fast/stopped**. What time d'you make it?

Exercises

41.1 **What do you think happened to make these people do/say what they did?**

EXAMPLE We had to send for a plumber. *Maybe a pipe was leaking/the bathroom was flooded.*

1 I had to call out our local mechanic.
2 Our neighbours let us use their washing machine.
3 Don't worry, it often does that; I'll screw it back on.
4 Come here and I'll put a plaster on it.
5 Luckily, that was all it was; the skin was broken a bit, but there was no blood.
6 How many batteries does it take? I'll get some for you.
7 I don't know where you've put them. Try the bedside table.

41.2 **Odd one out. Which of the three words is the odd one out in each case?**

EXAMPLE spill flood chip *chip the other two involve liquids*

1 break down smash break
2 run out stain stop
3 leak come off chip
4 cut bruise flood

41.3 **What would you do if ...**

1 you mislaid your credit card?
2 you noticed your guest's glass was chipped?
3 one of your coat-buttons came off?
4 your dishwasher broke down?
5 you bruised your forehead?
6 your watch was slow?

41.4 **Here is a matrix. There are the names of things and things that can go wrong with them. Not all of the words are on the left-hand page. Use a dictionary for any you are not sure of. Put a tick (✓) for things that *most typically* go together, as in the example.**

	cake-tin	vase	elbow	clock	moped	sink
banged						
cracked						
broken down						
dented						
stopped				✓		
blocked						

41.5 **Complete these sentences using words and phrases from the opposite page.**

EXAMPLE We had to use candles because ... *there was a power cut.*

1 I didn't look where I was going as I walked through the low doorway and ...
2 The wind blew the door shut and I realised I'd ...
3 I would ring her but I'm afraid I've ...
4 I can't take a photo, my camera's ...
5 I tried to run over the rocks but I ...

42 Global problems

A Disasters/tragedies

NOTE
injure /'ɪndʒə/ [people], damage /'dæmɪdʒ/ [things]: 200 people were injured. Buildings were damaged.

earthquakes [the earth moves/trembles]

drought /draʊt/ [no rain]

explosions [e.g. a bomb]

hurricanes/tornadoes /tɔː'neɪdəʊz/ **typhoons** [violent winds / storms]

volcanoes /vɒl'keɪnəʊz/ [hot liquid rock and gases pour from a mountain]

famine /'fæmɪn/ [no food]

floods [too much rain]

major accidents [e.g. a plane crash]

epidemics [diseases affecting large numbers of people]

war / civil war [civil war is war between people of the same country]

Disasters not caused by human beings can be called **natural disasters.**

Verbs connected with these words

A volcano has **erupted** in Indonesia. Hundreds are feared dead. The flu epidemic **spread** rapidly throughout the country. Millions are **starving** as a result of the famine. A big earthquake **shook** the city at noon today. The area is **suffering** its worst drought for many years. Civil war has **broken out** in the north of the country. A tornado **swept** through the islands yesterday.

B Words for people involved in disasters/tragedies

The explosion resulted in 300 **casualties.** /'kæʒəltiːz/ [dead and injured people]
The real **victims** of civil war are children left without parents. [those who suffer the results]
There were only three **survivors** /sə'vaɪvəz/. All the other passengers were reported dead. [people who live through a disaster]
Thousands of **refugees** /refju'dʒiːz/ have crossed the border looking for food and shelter.
During the battle, the **dead** and **wounded** /'wuːndɪd/ were flown out in helicopters. [**wounded**: injured in a battle / by a weapon]

C Headlines

Here are some headlines from newspapers all connected with diseases and epidemics. Explanations are given.

/'reɪbiːz/ disease can be caused by bite from a dog, fox, etc: very serious

> **Rabies** out of control in many parts of Asia

> **Cholera** and **typhoid** injections not needed says Tourism Minister

/'kɒlərə/ /'taɪfɔɪd/ diseases causing sickness, diarrhoea etc.; caused often by infected food and water

/mə'leərɪə/ usually caught because of mosquito bites

> New **malaria** drug tested

tropical disease; skin goes yellow

> **yellow fever** figures drop

acquired immune deficiency syndrome; often caused by sexual contact or contact with contaminated blood

> New **AIDS** unit to be opened this month

/'leprəsɪ/ terrible skin disease; leaves the skin deformed

> Minister says fight against **leprosy** goes on

Exercises

42.1 **What type of disaster from the list in A opposite are these sentences about? Why?**

EXAMPLE The lava flow destroyed three villages. volcano; lava is the hot rocks and metal

1 The earth is cracked and vegetation has withered.
2 The tremor struck at 3.35 p.m. local time.
3 People had boarded up shops and houses during the day before, and stayed indoors.
4 Shelling and mortar fire could be heard all over the town.
5 Witnesses said they saw a fire-ball fall out of the sky.
6 People had to stay in the upper floors and sometimes on the roofs of their homes.

42.2 **Complete the missing items in this word-class table, using a dictionary if necessary. Where there is a dash (–), you do not need to write anything.**

verb	*noun: thing or idea*	*noun: person*
....	explosion	–
....	....	survivor
injure	....	....
starve	....	....
erupt	....	–

42.3 **In these headlines, say whether the situation seems to be getting *worse* or *better*, or whether a disaster has *happened* or has been *avoided/prevented*.**

1 Poison gas cloud spreads
2 POLICE DEFUSE TERRORIST BOMB
3 OIL SLICK RECEDES
4 AIDS time-bomb ticking away
5 All survive jumbo emergency landing
6 Flood warnings not heeded in time

42.4 **Fill the gaps with a suitable word from B opposite. Try to work from memory.**

1 Another 50 people died today, all .... of the famine.
2 The government agreed to allow 3,000 war .... to enter the country.
3 It was the worst road accident the country has ever seen, with over 120 ....
4 A: Were there any .... when the ship sank? B: I'm afraid not.
5 The .... and .... were left lying on the battlefield; it was a disgrace.

42.5 **Which diseases are we talking about? Try to do this from memory.**

1 One that can be caused by a mosquito bite.
2 One that leaves the skin badly deformed.
3 One you can get by drinking infected water.
4 One you can get from an animal bite.
5 One that makes the skin go yellow.

Do people get any of these diseases in your country?

Follow-up: Look at an English-language newspaper and see how many of the global problems mentioned in this unit are reported. Cut out any articles you find, and make a list of the vocabulary for each topic in your notebook.

43 Education

A Stages in a person's education

Here are some names that are used to describe the different types of education in Britain.

play school/group nursery school /'nɜːsrɪ/	pre-school (2–5 years old)	mostly play with some early learning
infant school junior school	primary (5/6–12/13)	basic reading, writing, arithmetic, art, etc.
comprehensive school or grammar school sixth form college (16–18)	secondary (12/13–16/18)	wide range of subjects in arts and sciences and technical areas
college or university	further/higher (18+)	degrees/diplomas in specialised academic areas

Comprehensive schools in the UK are open to all and are for all abilities. You can only get into a **grammar school** by competitive entry (an exam). **Public schools** in the UK are very famous **private schools. Colleges** include **teacher-training colleges, technical colleges** and **general colleges of further education.**

B Exams and qualifications

take/do/sit an exam **resit** an exam (take it again because you did badly first time)
pass (get the minimum grade or more) / **do well in** (get a high grade) an exam **fail** (you do not get the minimum grade) / **do badly in** (you fail, or don't do as well as expected / as well as you wanted) an exam

Before an exam it's a good idea to **revise** for it. If you **skip classes/lectures**, you'll probably do badly in the exam. [informal; miss deliberately]

Some schools give pupils **tests** regularly to check their progress. The **school-leaving exams** are held in May/June. In England, these are called **GCSEs** (age 16) and **A-levels** (age 18). In some schools, colleges and universities, instead of tests and exams there is **continuous assessment** with **marks**, e.g. 65%, or **grades**, e.g. A, B+, for essays and projects during the term. If you pass your university exams, you **graduate** /'grædʒʊeɪt/ (get a degree), then you're a graduate /'grædʒʊət/ and you may want to go on to a **post-graduate** course.

C Talking about education

In colleges and universities, there are usually **lectures** (large classes listening to the teacher and taking notes), **seminars** (10–20 students actively taking part in discussion etc.) and **tutorials** (one student or a small group, working closely with a teacher).

A **professor** is a senior university academic who is a well-known specialist in his/her subject. University and college teachers are usually called **lecturers** or **tutors.**

Asking somebody about their country's education system.

What age do children start school at?
What's the **school-leaving age**?
Are there **evening classes** for adults?
Do you have **state** and **private universities**?
Do students get **grants** for **further education**?

Exercises

43.1 Fill the gaps in this life story of a British woman.

At 5, Nelly Dawes went straight to ....(1) school because there were very few ....(2) schools for younger children in those days. When she was ready to go on to secondary school, she passed an exam and so got into her local ....(3) school. Nowadays her own children don't do that exam, since most children go to a ....(4) school. She left school at 16 and did not go on to ....(5) education, but she works during the day, then goes to ....(6) at the local school once a week to learn French. She would like to take up her education again more seriously, if she could get a ....(7) or scholarship from the government. Her ambition is to go to a ....(8) and become a school-teacher.

43.2 Correct the mis-collocations in these sentences.

1 I can't come out. I'm studying. I'm passing an examination tomorrow.
2 Congratulations! I hear you succeeded your examination!
3 You can study a lot of different careers at this university.
4 I got some good notes in my continuous assessment this term.
5 She's a professor in a primary school.
6 He gave an interesting 45-minute conference on Goethe.
7 She got a degree in personnel management from a private college.
8 When I was 12, we started having French seminars at school, and I fell in love with the language.

43.3 What questions could you ask to get these answers?

1 No, they have to finance their own studies.
2 There isn't much difference; it's just that one gets money from the government and the courses are free, the other depends on fee-paying students.
3 Well, they learn one or two things, like recognising a few numbers, but most of the time they just play.
4 Because I wanted to be a teacher, no other reason.
5 It's sixteen, but a lot of kids stay on until eighteen.
6 I've been revising/studying for an exam.
7 No, ours are given in grades, you know, B1, C, A, that sort of thing.
8 No, I was ill. I didn't miss it deliberately.
9 They are exams taken in England at 18 years old, which you need in order to get into university.

43.4 Make a table for the various stages and types of education in your country, like the table in A opposite. How does it compare with the UK system and with the system in other countries represented in your class or that you know of? Is it possible to find satisfactory English translations for all the different aspects of education in your country?

Follow-up: The education system in the USA is a bit different from in the UK. Find out what the following terms mean in the US education system.

high-school college sophomore graduate school

44 Work

A

Some job-titles are found in a wide range of different workplaces. The broad meanings are given here. The right-hand page exercises will help you work out more precise meanings.

director (member of the board of a company) **executive** /ɪɡ'zekjətɪv/ (important person who makes big decisions) **administrator** (person who runs the office day-to-day) **clerk** /klaːk/ (ordinary office worker) **skilled worker** (trained to do specific tasks, e.g. building a computer) **unskilled worker** (doing a job that needs no training) **labourer** (does hard, physical work) **receptionist** (visitors must check in with them) **public relations officer** (gives information to the press, TV, etc. about the company) **safety officer** (makes sure machines, etc. are not dangerous to use) **security officer** (makes sure thieves/criminals cannot enter) **union representative** (looks after the staff's interests) **economist** (expert in financial matters) **personnel officer** (takes care of administration for new and existing employees) **sales assistant** (sells goods to the public) **education officer** (organises training, classes, etc. for employees) **research-worker** (investigates and develops new products) **supervisor** (makes sure workers are doing their job properly)

B

Here are some **professions** (jobs that require considerable training and/or qualifications) and trades (skilled manual jobs requiring on-the-job and other training).

lawyer **dentist** **hairdresser** **mechanic** **architect** /'aːkɪtekt/ **priest**
farmer **vet** **librarian** **physiotherapist** /fɪzɪəʊ'θerəpɪst/ **child-minder**
police officer **accountant** **engineer** **scientist** **chef** /ʃef/ **firefighter**
civil servant **tailor/dressmaker** **designer** **builder** **carpenter** **plumber**

C

Collocations of words connected with work

It's not easy to **get/find work** round these parts. I've been **offered work / a job** in Paris.
What d'you **do for a living**? I'm **in publishing/banking**, etc.
It's hard to **make a living** as a freelance writer. [earn enough money to live comfortably]
She's not prepared to **take on that** job. [suggests 'having personal responsibility']

hours of work

to do shift-work or to work shifts [nights one week, days the next week]
to be on flexi-time [flexible working hours]
to work nine-to-five [regular day work]

***not* working**

to go/be on strike [industrial dispute]
to get the sack [thrown out of your job]
to be fired [more formal than 'get the sack'; often used as a direct address: 'You're fired!']
to be made redundant [thrown out, no longer needed]
to be laid off [more informal than 'made redundant']
to give up work [e.g. in order to study]
to be on / take maternity (woman) or paternity (man) leave [before/after the birth of a baby]
to be on / take sick leave [illness]
to take early retirement [retire at 55]

other useful expressions

to be a workaholic [love work too much]
to be promoted [get a higher position]
to apply for a job [fill in forms, etc.]

Exercises

44.1 **Which of the job-titles in A opposite would best describe the following?**

1 The person who represents the workers' interests in disputes with the management in a factory.
2 A person who has a high (but not the highest) position in a company and whose job it is to make important decisions.
3 An important person in a company who sits on the board.
4 A worker whose job requires no special training, for example, an office cleaner.
5 A person generally in charge of the day-to-day organisation of a company/department.
6 The person who makes sure there are no risks of accidents from machinery, etc.
7 A person whose job it is to keep an eye on the day-to-day work of other workers.
8 A person who does hard physical work.
9 The person who handles applications for vacant posts.
10 The person who gives out information to the press for a company.
11 The person who makes sure all the doors and windows have good locks on them.
12 The person you first speak to when you arrive at a company as a visitor.

44.2 **Using the expressions in C opposite, say what you think has happened / is happening.**

EXAMPLE I'm not working now; the baby's due in 3 weeks. *She's on maternity leave.*

1 I lost my job. They had to make cutbacks.
2 He's enjoying life on a pension, although he's only 58.
3 One week it's six-to-two, the next it's nights.
4 They've made her General Manager as from next month!
5 I was late so often, I lost my job.
6 I get in at nine o'clock and go home at five.
7 Your trouble is you are obsessed with work!

44.3 **Whose job do these things belong to?**

EXAMPLE bucket ladder leather *window cleaner*

1 board overhead projector chalk
2 scalpel mask forceps /ˈfɔːseps/
3 fax machine filing cabinet stapler
4 make-up script microphone
5 tractor plough barn
6 sewing machine scissors needle

44.4 **Would you call the following a *trade*, a *profession* or an *unskilled job*?**

1 vet
2 chef
3 plumber
4 architect
5 electrician
6 dressmaker
7 cleaner
8 tailor
9 refuse collector /ˈrefjuːz/
10 lawyer

44.5 **Fill in the collocations.**

I'd love to ....(1) a job in journalism, but it's not easy without qualifications. Since I have to earn a ....(2) somehow, I'll have to get ....(3) wherever I can find it. I've been ....(4) some part-time work editing a typescript for a book, but I'm not sure I want to .... it ....(5) .

44.6 **Think of five people you know who work for a living. Can you name their jobs in English? If you cannot, look them up in a good bilingual dictionary, or in a thesaurus.**

45 Sport

A Some sports whose names you may not know

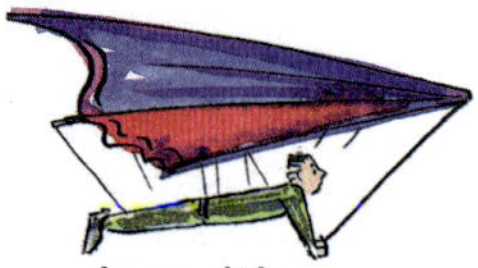
hang-gliding

windsurfing

(ten-pin) bowling

scuba-diving

cross-country skiing

show-jumping

fencing

snooker/pool/billiards /ˈbɪljədz/

motor-racing

archery

B Equipment – what you hold in your hand

golf – **club** squash/tennis/badminton – **racket** darts – **dart** archery – **bow**
cricket/table-tennis/baseball – **bat** (ice) hockey – **stick** snooker/pool/billiards – **cue**
canoeing – **paddle** rowing – **oar** fishing – **rod/line**

C Athletics – some field events

discus

javelin /ˈdʒævlɪn/

high-jump

long-jump

pole-vault /ˈpəʊl vɒlt/

She's a great **sprinter** [fast over short distances]. She's running the **final leg** in the **relay**. I hope no-one drops the **baton**.
He's a great **long-distance** runner. [e.g. 5000 metres, marathon]
Jogging round the park every Saturday's enough for me. It keeps me fairly fit.

D Verbs and their collocations in the context of sport

Our team **won/lost** *by* three **goals/points**.
She **broke** the Olympic **record** last year.
He **holds the record** for the 100 metres breast-stroke.
Liverpool **beat** Hamburg 4–2 yesterday.
The team have never been **defeated**. [more formal than **beat**]
How many **goals/points** have you **scored** this season?
I think I'll **take up** bowling next spring and **give up** golf.

E People who do particular sports

-er can be used for many sports, e.g. footballer, swimmer, windsurfer, high-jumper, cricketer, golfer, etc. **Player** is often necessary, e.g. tennis-player, snooker-player, darts-player, and we can also say football-player, cricket-player. Some names must be learnt separately, e.g. canoeist, mountaineer, jockey, archer (**not** archerer), gymnast.

Exercises

45.1 Which of the sports opposite are these people probably talking about?

1 The ball has a natural curve on it so it doesn't go in a straight line on the ground. You have to aim away from the centre of the pins.
2 Provided it's not too windy at the top, there's no problem.
3 It is incredibly noisy, fast and dangerous, but it's really exciting to watch.
4 You have to jump over a series of different jumps without knocking the posts off.
5 It's all a matter of balance really. But sometimes you can't help falling in the water.
6 You need a good eye and a lot of concentration, especially to hit the centre of the board.

45.2 Name one *other* piece of equipment necessary to play these sports apart from the item given, as in the example. What special *clothing*, if any, is worn for each sport?

EXAMPLE golf: clubs, ...balls...

1 archery: bow, ...
2 badminton: racket, ...
3 hockey: stick, ...
4 baseball: bat, ...
5 darts: darts, ...

45.3 Fill the gaps with suitable verbs.

1 Were many records .... at the Olympics?
2 We've been .... so many times we deserve to be bottom of the league!
3 Congratulations! How many points did you .... by?
4 You should .... jogging. That would help you lose weight.
5 Who .... the world record for the 1000 metres? Is it a Russian?
6 I only ever once .... a goal, and that was sheer luck.

45.4 What do you call a person who ...?

1 does the long-jump? a long-jumper
2 rides horses in races?
3 drives cars in races?
4 throws the discus/javelin?
5 does gymnastics?
6 plays hockey?
7 plays football?
8 does the pole-vault?

45.5 Make sure you know which sports these places are associated with, as in the example. Use a dictionary if necessary.

1 court tennis, squash, etc.
2 course
3 ring
4 pitch
5 rink
6 alley
7 piste

Follow-up: Look at the sports page of one or two newspapers (either in English or in your own language). Are there any sports mentioned not listed in A opposite? If so, what are their English names? Use a bilingual dictionary if necessary. Make sure you know the English names for any sport you do, any equipment and clothing you use to do it, and the place where you do it. Use a dictionary if necessary.

46 The arts

A Things which generally come under the heading of 'the arts'

- LITERATURE: novels, biographies, short stories, drama, poetry
- PERFORMING ARTS: theatre, dance, cinema, ballet, opera, concerts: classical/rock/country and western
- FINE ART(s): sculpture, painting, architecture, ceramics (making pots, bowls, etc.) /sə'ræmɪks/

The arts (plural) covers everything in the network. **Art** [singular, uncountable] usually means **fine art**, but can also refer to technique and creativity.

Have you read the **arts page** in the paper today? [that part of the newspaper that deals with all the things in the network]
She's a great **art lover**. [loves painting and sculpture]
Shakespeare was skilled in **the art of poetry**. [creative ability]

Dance usually refers to modern artistic dance forms: **ballet** /'bæleɪ/ usually has a more traditional feel, unless we say **modern ballet**. *Remember*: a **novel** is a long story, e.g. 200–300 pages; a piece of short prose fiction, e.g. 10 pages, is a **short story**.

(!) *Use of the definite article*

When we refer to a performing art in general, we can leave out the definite article.

Are you interested in (the) **cinema/ballet/opera/theatre**?
But: Would you like to come to the **cinema/ballet/opera/theatre** with us next week? [particular performance]

B Describing a performance

We went to see a new production of Hamlet last night. The **sets**[1] were incredibly realistic and the **costumes**[2] were wonderful. It was a good **cast**[3] and I thought the **direction**[4] was excellent. Anthony O'Donnell **gave** a marvellous **performance**[5]. It **got rave reviews**[6] in the papers today.

[1]scenery, buildings, furniture on the stage or in a studio; [2]clothes the actors wear on stage; [3] all the actors in it; [4]the way the director had organised the performance; [5]and [6] note these typical collocations; [6] means 'got very enthusiastic comments'

C Words connected with events in the arts

There's an **exhibition** of paintings by Manet **on** in London.
They're going to **publish** a new **edition** of the **works** of Cervantes next year.
The Opera Society are doing a **performance** of *Don Giovanni*.
Our local cinema's **showing** *Titanic* next week.

Note: **What's on at** the cinema/theatre, etc. next week? (note the two prepositions)

Exercises

46.1 Which branch of the arts do you think these people are talking about?

EXAMPLE It was a strong cast but the play itself is weak. Theatre

1 It's called *Peace*. It stands in the main square.
2 Animation doesn't have to be just *Disney*, you know.
3 It was just pure movement, with very exciting rhythms.
4 It doesn't have to rhyme to be good.
5 Oils to me don't have the delicacy of water-colours.
6 Her design for the new city hall won an award.
7 I like to read them and imagine what they'd be like on stage.
8 The first chapter was boring but it got better later.
9 I was falling asleep by the second act.
10 Overall, the performance was good, though the tenor wasn't at his best.

46.2 Definite article or not? Fill the gap with *the* if necessary.

1 The government doesn't give enough money to .... arts.
2 She's got a diploma in .... dance from the Performing Arts Academy.
3 I've got some tickets for .... ballet. Interested?
4 .... art of writing a short story is to interest the reader from the very first line.
5 I can't stand .... modern poetry; it's so pretentious.
6 I was no good at .... art at school. What about you?

46.3 Each one of these sentences contains a mistake of usage of words connected with the arts. Find the mistake and correct it. You may need a dictionary.

EXAMPLE The scene at this theatre projects right out into the audience.
not 'scene' but 'stage' (the place where the actors perform)

1 What's the name of the editorial of that book you recommended? Was it Cambridge University Press?
2 'I wandered lonely as a cloud' is my favourite verse of English poetry.
3 He's a very famous sculpture; he did that statue in the park, you know, the one with the soldiers.
4 Most of the novels in this collection are only five or six pages long. They're great for reading on short journeys.
5 There's an exposition of ceramic at the museum next week.
6 The sceneries are excellent in that new production of *Macbeth*, so dark and mysterious.
7 What's in the Opera House next week? Anything interesting?

46.4 Ask *questions* for which these remarks would be suitable answers.

EXAMPLE It's an oil on canvas. What sort of painting is it?

1 Yes, it got rave reviews.
2 No, I'm not really a concert-goer, but thanks anyway.
3 Oh, there are some beautiful old buildings and some ugly new ones.
4 The cast were fine, but the direction was weak.
5 A new Hungarian film; fancy going to see it?

Follow-up: Make sure you can name all the parts of a typical theatre in English. A picture-dictionary might help you.

47 Music

A Buying music

Many people now buy music on CD though some people prefer tapes (audio cassettes).

album [a recording of a selection of songs/tracks/pieces of music on a CD or cassette]
hit singles [best selling songs issued individually]
lead singer [main singer in a band]
backing [the group providing the background music/vocals for the song]

B Types of music

TIP

You can learn vocabulary by listening to songs in English. Note that pop singers sometimes break the 'rules' of standard grammar. Check with a teacher if something seems strange to you.

Music can be described in terms of the instrument(s) playing it: piano music, guitar music, big band music, instrumental music [instruments only with no vocals (voices, singing)], electronic music [played by a synthesiser], orchestral music.

STYLE

- **chamber music** [written for a small group of orchestral instruments]
- **blues**
- **heavy metal**
- **folk** [traditional]
- **jazz**
- **soul**
- **pop**
- **classical**
- **country and western** [a style of US music based on western and southern folk music]

The dinner was lovely, but the **background music** was just too loud. We couldn't talk.
It's difficult to concentrate on work when there's **dance music** playing.
The **soundtrack** of that film is fantastic. I think it won an Oscar. [music for a film]
I don't really like restaurants where they play **muzak**. [recorded, light music played continuously in public places; you can also say **canned music** or **piped music**]
Music can be described in terms of its period or place of origin:
contemporary / modern / 20th century / sixties / Irish / Indian music

C Other adjectives used to describe music

live /laɪv/ recorded deafening loud rousing soft sweet innovative
tuneless discordant tuneful soothing relaxing peaceful modern

D Things you do with music

She **plays the piano** very well, but she doesn't **read music**. She's got **a good ear**. [informal]
She can **pick out** any tune on the piano. [informal] She doesn't have to **practise** much at all. She's a **natural**. [informal]. She can **play by ear**.
He's very **musical**. He **wrote an arrangement of / arranged** a Bach symphony for the band.
You can **play a tune** on an instrument or you can **whistle** [make a sound by pushing air through your lips] or **hum** [sing with lips closed]. You can **make music** in lots of ways.
I've some new **chords** on the guitar [several harmonising notes played at the same time]
I have to **practise** my **scales**, but it's boring. [sets of notes moving up and down in steps]

Exercises

47.1 **Explain the difference between:**

1 a track and an album
2 a CD and a cassette
3 a lead singer and a backing group
4 a hit and a single
5 orchestral music and chamber music
6 country music and folk music
7 muzak and disco music
8 soothing music and discordant music

47.2 **What styles of music do you think the people below might be playing?**

1

2

3

4

47.3 **Look at the adjectives in C opposite. Divide them into those that have positive associations and those that have negative associations.**

47.4 **Find the words in Section D on the opposite page that fit in these sentences.**

1 I started to learn the piano when I was a kid but I always made a fuss when I was told to .... every day and eventually gave up.
2 If you don't know the words of the song just .... along as the others sing.
3 My brother is learning the guitar and he can already play a few basic ....
4 A student opera singer lives in the flat next to mine and she spends hours practising every day – not songs, just .... I think I'll have to move.
5 This music was originally written for the violin but it has been .... quite successfully for the guitar.
6 Paul can play anything. He's got a good ....
7 I always know when the postman is there as I can hear him .... very tunefully.
8 In primary school young children practise .... music with all sorts of different things – even, say, with tins containing buttons.

47.5 **Answer these questions about music.**

1 Can you remember the name of the first single you ever bought? Who was it by?
2 Which songs are currently big hits in your country?
3 Which of the kinds of music listed in B on the opposite page do you particularly enjoy?
4 Are there any other kinds of music that are not listed that you like?
5 Are there any kinds of music listed that you dislike? Why do you dislike them?
6 Do you like to have background music while you are working? If so, what kind of background music do you like?
7 Can you read music? Can you explain the basic system used for writing music?
8 Can you play any musical instruments and how well do you play them?
9 What musical instrument and what kind of music would you like to be able to play well and why?

Follow-up: If possible, find a cassette or CD sleeve which has English on it. Note down any useful vocabulary that it contains.

48 Food

A

Here are some types of meat. The animals they come from are given in brackets:
red meat: **beef** (cow), **lamb** (lamb), **mutton** (sheep), **venison** (deer)
white meat: **veal** (calf), **pork, ham, bacon** (pig), **chicken** (chicken), **turkey** (turkey)
Chicken, turkey and **duck** are sometimes referred to as **poultry** /'pəʊltrɪ/.
Fish: **cod, hake, plaice, mackerel, herring, sardine, trout, salmon**
Seafood: **prawns, shrimps, crab, lobster, crayfish, squid, cockles, mussels, oysters**
Vegetables: **cabbage, cauliflower, broccoli, spinach, cucumber, leeks, mushrooms, courgettes** /kɔː'ʒetz/ (*Am. Eng*: zucchini), **aubergines** /'əʊbəʒiːnz/ (*Am. Eng*: egg plants)
Spices: **curry** [a mixture of spices such as **cumin, cardamom, coriander, paprika, turmeric, ginger**], **cinnamon, nutmeg**

Herbs:

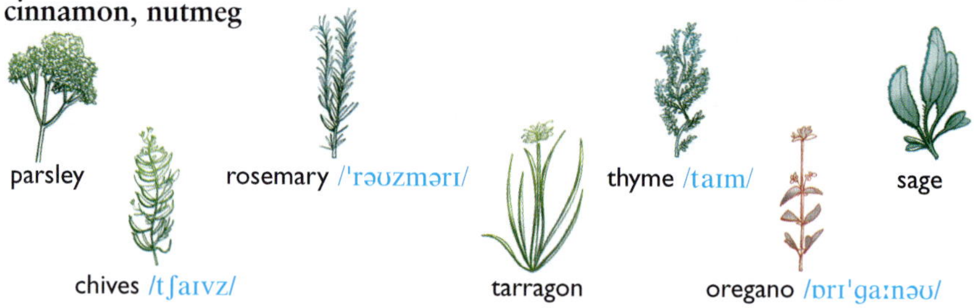

B Flavours and tastes – adjectives and some opposites (≠)

sweet ≠ **bitter** [sharp/unpleasant] **sour** [e.g. unripe fruit]
hot, spicy [e.g. curry] ≠ **mild** **bland** [rather negative]
salty [a lot of salt] **sugary** [a lot of sugar] **sickly** [too much sugar]
savoury /'seɪvərɪ/ [pleasant, slightly salty or with herbs]
tasty [has a good taste/flavour] ≠ **tasteless** [no flavour at all] **delicious**

C General appearance, presentation and quality

These chips are terribly **greasy** /'griːsɪ/ / **oily**. [too much oil/fat]
This meat is **over-cooked/overdone / under-cooked/underdone.**
British cooking can be very **stodgy.** /'stɒdʒɪ/ [heavy, hard to digest]
Mm, this chicken's **done to a turn.** [just perfect, not overdone]
These pistachio nuts are terribly **more-ish.** [informal; you want to eat more]

D Ways of cooking food – verbs

Lamb chops are nice **barbecued.** /'baːbəkjuːd/ [over hot coals, usually outdoors]
Have you **seasoned** the stew? /'siːzənd/ [added herbs/spices/salt/pepper]

E Courses and dishes

In the UK a meal in a restaurant would typically be three courses: a **starter** [light snack/appetiser], a **main course** [the most important/substantial part of the meal], followed by a **dessert** [sometimes called a **sweet/pudding/afters**, especially at home].

Exercises

48.1 **To learn long lists of words, it is sometimes helpful to divide them up into groups. Try dividing the vegetable names into groups, in any way you like, e.g. 'vegetables which grow underground' (potatoes, carrots etc.). If possible, compare your answers with someone else's. There are some words which are not given opposite. Use a dictionary if necessary.**

aubergine leek cucumber spinach carrot potato cauliflower
green/red pepper courgette sweetcorn lettuce onion rice pea cabbage
garlic radish bean shallot turnip asparagus beetroot celery

48.2 **Use the taste and flavour words opposite to describe the following.**

1 Indian curry
2 pizza
3 sea water
4 an unripe apple
5 a cup of tea with five spoonfuls of sugar
6 strong black coffee with no sugar
7 factory-made white bread

48.3 **Sort these dishes out under the headings *starters*, *main courses* or *desserts*.**

chicken casserole coffee gateau fresh fruit salad sorbet Irish stew
pâté and toast prawn cocktail rump steak chocolate fudge cake
grilled trout shrimps in garlic

48.4 **What might you say to the person/people with you in a restaurant if …**

1 your chips had too much oil/fat on them?
2 your dish had obviously been cooked too much / too long?
3 your piece of meat was absolutely perfectly cooked?
4 your dish seemed to have no flavours at all?

48.5 **How do you like the following foods prepared? Use words from D opposite and look up others if necessary. What do you like to put on the foods from the list in the box?**

a leg of chicken eggs potatoes cheese sausages
a fillet of cod prawns mushrooms

salt pepper vinegar mustard brown sauce ketchup
salad dressing oil mayonnaise lemon juice

48.6 **Food quiz.**

1 Which are *fish* and which are usually called *seafood*?
prawns sardines squid oysters mackerel mussels hake
crab plaice trout lobster cod sole whiting

2 What do we call the *meat* of these animals?
calf deer sheep (two names) pig (three names)

3 Which of these fruit grow in your country/region? Are there others not listed here?
peach plum grapefruit grape nectarine star-fruit blackcurrant
raspberry strawberry melon lime kiwi-fruit mango pear pineapple

Follow-up: Make sure you can name or at least describe the most important foods of your country or culture in English. Use a bilingual dictionary if necessary.

49 The environment

A You have to be careful about the use of 'the' with features of the environment.

	use with the?	*example*
countries	no	France
countries which are in a plural form	yes	The USA
countries when limited by time	yes	The Japan of today
individual mountains	no	Mount Everest
mountains in the Bernese Oberland	yes	The Jungfrau /ˈjʊŋfraʊ/
mountain chains	yes	The Himalayas /hɪməˈleɪjəz/
islands	no	Sicily
groups of islands	yes	The West Indies
rivers	yes	The Volga
oceans	yes	The Pacific
seas	yes	The Mediterranean /medɪtəˈreɪnɪən/
gulfs, bays and straits	yes	The Gulf of Mexico / The Bay of Biscay
lakes	no	Lake Erie
currents	yes	The Gulf Stream

B Look at this encyclopedia entry about Iceland. Note the words in bold.

Iceland An island republic in the North Atlantic. The **landscape** consists largely of **barren plains** [flat land where little grows] and **mountains**, with large **ice fields** particularly in the south west. The island has **active volcanoes** [they still erupt] and is known for its **thermal** [hot] springs and **geysers** [warm water that fountains out of the ground]. With less than 1% of the land suitable for growing **crops** [food that is grown], the nation's **economy** is based on fishing, and fish products account for 80% of the exports. Area: 103,000 km^2. **Population**: 227,000. **Capital**: Reykjavik.

C Here are some other nouns which are useful when talking about the environment. Check their meanings in a dictionary if necessary.

Where land meets sea: coast, shore, beach, cliff, cape, peninsula, cove, bay, gulf

Words connected with rivers: source, tributary, waterfall, mouth, valley, gorge, delta, brook, stream, estuary

Words connected with mountains: foot, ridge, peak, summit, glacier

D There are many environmental problems in the world today.

The air, rivers and seas are all **polluted**, especially in **over-populated** and heavily industrialised regions. Poor **waste disposal** is the cause of much of this **pollution.**

Overfishing has depleted the numbers of fish in the oceans.

The **destruction of the ozone layer** is leading to climatic changes and what is known as **the greenhouse effect.**

The **destruction of the rainforests** is causing widespread ecological problems.

Battery farming provides large amounts of food but it involves keeping animals in crowded and unnatural conditions.

TIP Write down the English names for the main geographical features in your country. Check how these names are pronounced as English may have taken the names of the features from your language but may have anglicised their pronunciation.

Exercises

49.1 **Label the pictures below.**

49.2 **In the paragraph below all the instances of *the* have been omitted. Insert them wherever they are necessary.**

Brazil is fifth largest country in world. In north, densely forested basin of River Amazon covers half country. In east, country is washed by Atlantic. Highest mountain chain in South America, Andes, does not lie in Brazil. Brazil's most famous city is Rio de Janeiro, former capital. Capital of Brazil today is Brasilia.

49.3 **Can you answer the following general knowledge questions about the environment?**

1 What is the highest mountain in Africa?
2 What is the longest river in Europe?
3 Where is the highest waterfall in the world?
4 Name another country, apart from Iceland, which has geysers and hot springs.
5 What is a delta and which famous river has one?
6 Where are the Straits of Gibraltar and the Cape of Good Hope?

49.4 **Complete the paragraph below about your own country, or any other country that interests you. Remember to use 'the' whenever it is necessary.**

............(1) is a ....(2) in ....(3). The countryside is ....(4) in the north and ....(5) in the south. The country's economy is based on ....(6). The best-known river in ....(7) is ....(8). The most famous chain of mountains is ....(9) and the highest mountain in that chain is ....(10). ....(11) is a major environmental problem in ....(12) today.

49.5 **Give two nouns from the opposite page to go with the adjectives below. Try not to repeat any of the nouns you choose.**

1 sandy 2 steep 3 shallow 4 rocky 5 turbulent 6 dangerous

49.6 **Answer these questions about being environmentally friendly.**

1 Why do environmentalists say we should avoid spray cans?
2 Why are environmentalists in favour of practising organic farming and using unleaded petrol?
3 Why do environmentalists encourage us to use recycled paper and bottle banks?
4 What else are environmentalists in favour of?

50 Towns

A

The words, **city** and **town**, are sometimes used interchangeably but a city is generally large with a wider range of facilities. This is a description of Cork, one of Ireland's main cities. Which words or phrases might be useful for describing your own or another town?

Cork city is the major metropolis of the south; indeed with a population of about 135,000 it is the second largest city in the Republic. The main business and shopping centre of the town lies on the island created by two channels of the River Lee, with most places within walking distance of the centre. (The buses tend to be overcrowded and the one-way traffic system is fiendishly complicated.) In the hilly area of the city is the famous Shandon Steeple, the bell-tower of St Anne's Church, built on the site of a church destroyed when the city was besieged by the Duke of Marlborough. Back across the River Lee lies the city's cathedral, an imposing 19th century building in the French Gothic style. Cork has two markets. Neither caters specifically for tourists but those who enjoy the atmosphere of a real working market will appreciate their charm. The Crawford Art Gallery is well worth a visit. It regularly mounts adventurous exhibitions by contemporary artists. The fashionable residential districts of Cork city overlook the harbour. There are other residential areas on the outskirts.

B

Here are some of the facilities that you might find in a town.

Sports: swimming pool   sports centre   golf course   tennis courts   football pitch   skating rink
Cultural: theatre   opera house   concert hall   radio station   art gallery
Educational: school   college   university   library   adult education centre   museum
Catering, accommodation and night-life: restaurant   nightclub   take-away   hotel   B & B (bed and breakfast)   youth hostel   disco   estate agency   housing estate
Transport: bus service   taxi rank   car hire   car park   parking meters
Other: health centre   law courts   registry office   citizens' advice bureau   job centre   bottle bank   department store   chemist's   garden centre   police station   Town or City Hall   suburbs   industrial estate

C

Here is a grid showing the typical problems of large cities now.

problem	*effect*	*cause*
traffic jams	traffic very slow commuters get very stressed	too much traffic especially in the rush-hour
slums	housing in a bad condition	poverty – people don't have money to spend on housing
vandalism	pointless destruction of property	poverty, lack of hope
overcrowding	difficult living conditions	too many people living in one place
pollution	deterioration in health	traffic and industrial
crime	See Unit 61	poverty, inequality

D

Here are some useful adjectives for describing towns: picturesque, historic, spacious, elegant, magnificent, atmospheric, quaint, lively, hectic, deserted (e.g. at night), bustling, crowded, packed, filthy, run-down, shabby

TIP Find some information about your own town or area written for English speaking visitors. Make a note of any useful vocabulary that you find in it.

Exercises

50.1 **Check that you understand the text about Cork by answering the following questions.**

1 Where is Cork?
2 Where is the shopping and business centre of Cork?
3 What is Cork's traffic system like?
4 What is special about the site of St Anne's Church?
5 In what style is the architecture of Cork Cathedral?
6 Can you buy souvenirs at the markets?
7 Why is the Crawford Gallery worth visiting?
8 Where do Cork people live?

50.2 **The description of Cork comes from a guidebook for tourists. Write sentences about a town of your choice, using the following expressions from the text.**

the second/third/fourth ...est   in the Victorian/Georgian/Classical
the main ... area of the town lies within walking distance of   built on the site
Baroque/French Gothic style   cater   tend to be   to overlook
whether or not it merits   well worth a visit / visiting   to mount an exhibition
those who enjoy   a working market/museum/steam railway/model
on the outskirts   to appreciate the charm

50.3 **Look at the list of facilities listed in B opposite. Think of a town and tick all those facilities which the town has.**

50.4 **Suggest three words which would collocate well with each other of the nouns below, as in the examples. The words do not have to be on the left-hand page.**

1 .... museum	3 .... college	5 ...night........... .... club ....
2 ...leisure......... .... centre	4 .... court	6 .... agency ....

50.5 **What facilities would your ideal town have? Name the three most important facilities for you in each of the categories listed in B opposite. You may choose facilities other than those listed opposite if you wish.**

50.6 **Are any of the problems mentioned in C opposite to be found in your town or a town you know well? Could you suggest a solution for these problems?**

50.7 **Write sentences about any towns you know, using each of the adjectives in D.**

EXAMPLE *The most picturesque part of my town is the old market-place.*

Follow-up: Design a brochure about your own town or another town you know well.

51 The natural world

A Animals

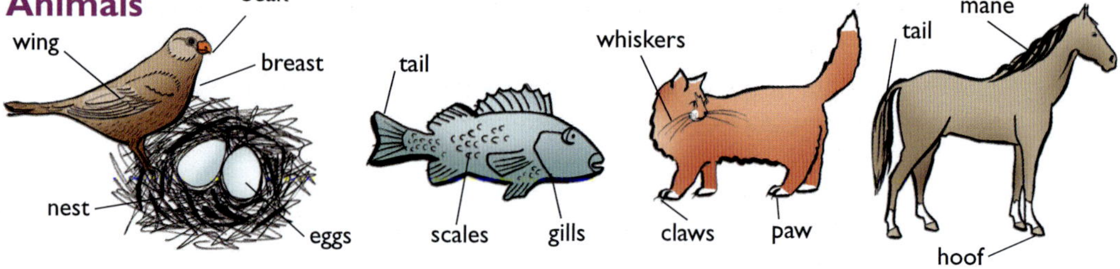

B Flowers and trees

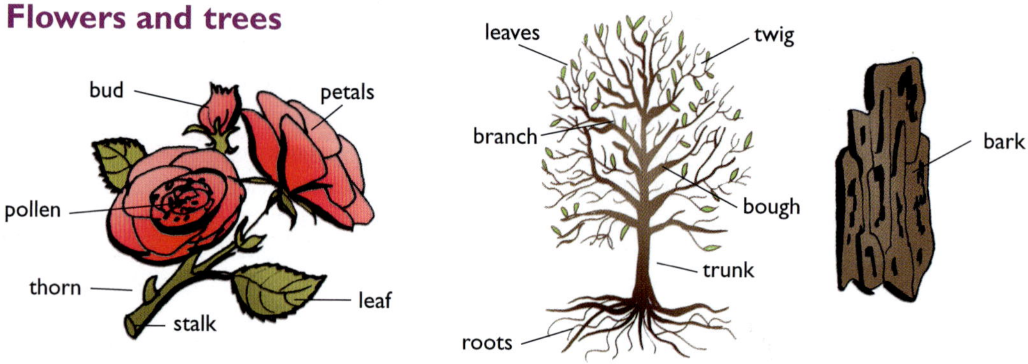

C Specific animals

Here are the English names of some more unusual creatures.

D Names of trees

Here are the names of some of the commonest British trees. You are likely to meet these words if you read fiction or poetry in English.

E Some verbs for talking about the natural world

Our apple tree **flowers/blossoms** in April. / Let's **pick** some flowers (not pick up). / Farmers **plant, fertilise** and **harvest** their crops.

> **TIP** A good bilingual dictionary will help you to find the words for the most frequent flowers, animals and trees in your area, if they are not included on this page.

Exercises

51.1 Can you answer the following general knowledge questions about the natural world?

1 Is the shark a fish or a mammal?
2 Are the following trees deciduous [lose their leaves in winter] or evergreen [green all year round] – oak, willow, pine, chestnut?
3 What does the bee take from flowers to make honey?
4 Name three animals that hibernate [go to sleep] in winter.
5 What might a British boy or girl say while pulling the petals off a daisy?
6 Name three flowers and three birds in English.
7 Which is the fastest of all land animals?
8 What plants or animals are the symbols of (a) England and (b) New Zealand?
9 What plant or animal is the symbol of your country?
10 What do fish use their gills for?
11 Which of these creatures is extinct [not alive any more] – emu, dinosaur, phoenix?
12 Can you name an endangered species [species at risk of becoming extinct]?

51.2 Divide these words into two or three groups in any way that seems appropriate to you:

hedgehog mane petals eagle oak willow worm bark

51.3 Fill in the blanks in the sentences below using words from the opposite page.

1 A tree's .... go a long way under ground.
2 A cat sharpens its .... against the .... of a tree.
3 Most fruit trees .... in spring.
4 Flowers will not .... unless they get enough water and light.
5 The horse is limping. It must have hurt its ....
6 Flowers last longer in a vase if you crush the end of their ....
7 A flower that is just about to open is called a ....
8 Take care not to prick yourself. That plant has sharp ....
9 If we pick up those ...., we can use them to start the fire.
10 .... use a kind of radar to find their way around.
11 .... move very, very slowly.
12 Most crops in thc UK arc .... in the autumn.

51.4 Look at this description of a chimpanzee from a children's book. Underline four or five collocations used in the text.

Chimpanzees are many people's favourite great apes, but they are not the cuddly creatures often portrayed in the media. Wild chimps are intelligent, powerful animals that live in complex communities. They often work together to hunt other animals and they have even been known to wage war on their own kind. They have developed a marvellous range of tool-using skills, and have been able to adapt to both forest and savannah regions in central and western Africa. But what makes chimpanzees so fascinating is their close relationship to humans. Not only do they look like us, but they often seem to behave like us as well.

51.5 Use the collocations you underlined in exercise 51.4 to write sentences of your own about any of the animals you have worked on in this unit.

52 Clothes

A

At this level you probably already know most of the everyday words for clothes. Here are some items of clothing or parts of them which are perhaps less familiar.

NOTE
Most items of clothing covering the legs are plural words only. If you wish to count them, you need to say, e.g. 'six pairs of trousers'. (See Unit 33.)

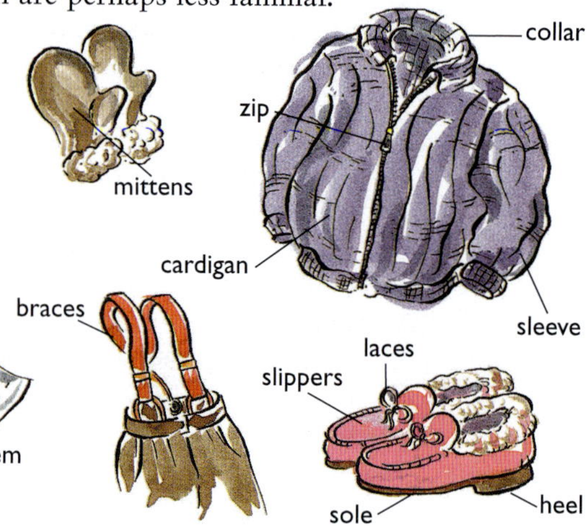

B Verbs associated with clothing

Can I **try on** these grey shoes in the window?
I love **dressing up** for parties as I normally wear jeans.
The skirt is too tight and too short – it needs **letting out** and **letting down**.
The dress is too loose and too long – it needs **taking in** and **taking up**.
He **changed out of** his weekend clothes **into** his uniform.
Red usually doesn't **suit** people with ginger hair.
Her black bag **matches** her shoes.
Those shoes don't **fit** the boy any more. He's **grown out** of them.

C Adjectives for describing people's clothing

How things fit: **baggy** **loose** **tight** **close-fitting**
Style: **long-sleeved** **sleeveless** **V-neck** **round-neck** **pleated**
How people look: **elegant** **smart** **scruffy** **chic** **trendy** **messy** **old-fashioned** **fashionable** **well-dressed** **badly-dressed**

D Materials which clothes are often made of

A **silk** shirt feels soft and light but also warm. **Cotton** shirts are cool but they need ironing. **Velvet** skirts are rich and warm for winter parties. Jeans are usually made of **denim**. **Suede** is a kind of **leather** but it isn't shiny. **Nylon**, **polyester** and **lycra** are artificial fibres.

We get **wool** from sheep; **woollen** clothes keep you warm when it's cold. All the above words for materials except **wool** and **woollen** can be nouns or adjectives.

E Adjectives used to describe the patterns on materials

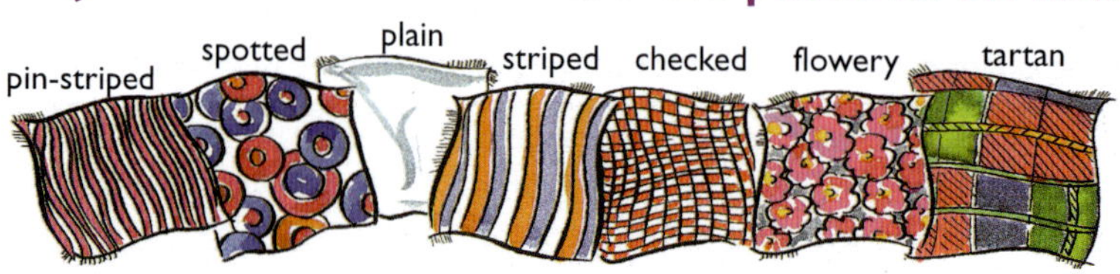

See Unit 37 for more useful vocabulary for describing someone's appearance.

Exercises

52.1 **Which of the words illustrated in A fit best in the following sentences?**

1 I must get my black shoes repaired. One .... is broken and both the .... have holes in them.
2 Do up your .... or you'll fall over.
3 There's someone at the door. You'd better put your .... on before you open it.
4 Put your .... on – this floor is very cold.
5 I've eaten too much – I'll have to loosen my ....
6 I've almost finished making my dress for the party but I've still got to take up the .... and sew on some ....

52.2 **Complete these sentences with any appropriate word. Use *pair* where it is necessary.**

1 Many women wear nighties in bed whereas most men and children wear ....
2 Blue .... are a kind of international uniform for young people.
3 It's too cold for .... Put your trousers on.
4 I need some new underwear. I'm going to buy three new .... today.
5 I've got a hole in my tights. I'll have to get a new ....
6 I've got a hole in my tights. I'll have to get some new ....

52.3 **Write three items of clothing that collocate with these materials.**

EXAMPLE velvet *ribbon, skirt, jacket*

1 silk 2 cotton 3 leather 4 woollen 5 suede 6 denim

52.4 **Describe in as much detail as possible what the people in the pictures are wearing.**

52.5 **Put the right verb, *match*, *suit* or *fit*, into each of these sentences.**

1 The blue dress .... her properly now she's lost some weight.
2 The blue of her dress .... the blue of her eyes.
3 That blue dress .... the girl with the blonde hair.

52.6 **Describe in as much detail as you can how (a) you and (b) someone else you can see are dressed.**

53 Health and medicine

A What are your symptoms?

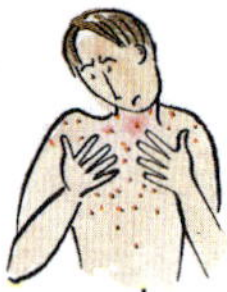
rash

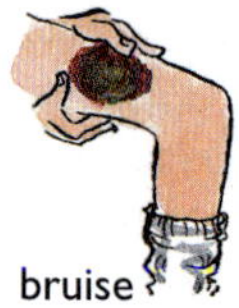
bruise

lump

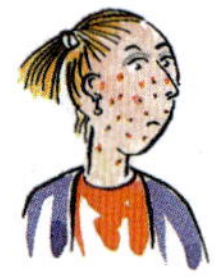
spots

a black eye

I've got a **cold** / a **cough** / a **sore throat** / a **temperature** [a higher temperature than normal] / a **stomach ache** / **chest pains** / **earache** / a **pain** in my side / a **rash** on my chest / **spots** / a **bruise** on my leg [e.g. after playing football] / a **black eye** [e.g. after being hit in the eye] / a **lump** on my arm / **indigestion** [after eating too fast] / **sickness and diarrhoea** /daɪə'rɪə/ [an upset stomach which makes you vomit and need to go to the toilet frequently] / **sunburn** / **painful joints** [e.g. ankles, knees, wrists, shoulders] / **blisters** [after wearing new, tight shoes].

I **feel sick** / **dizzy** [my head is spinning] / **breathless** / **shivery** [cold and hot] / **faint** [light-headed].

I am **depressed** / **constipated** [not able to go to the toilet] / **tired all the time.**

I've **lost my appetite** / **voice**; I can't sleep, my nose **itches** [I want to scratch it], my leg **hurts.**

B What do doctors do?

They take your temperature, listen to your chest, look in your ears, examine you, take your blood pressure, ask you some questions and weigh and measure you before sending you to the hospital for further tests.

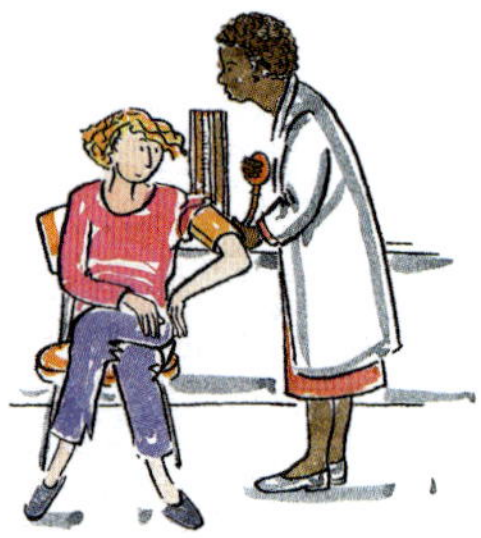

C What's the diagnosis?

You've got **flu** / **chickenpox** / **mumps** [singular noun] / **pneumonia** /njə'məʊnɪə/ / **rheumatism** /'ruːmətizəm/ an **ulcer** / a **virus** / a **bug** / **something that's going round.**

You've **broken your wrist** and **sprained/dislocated your ankle.**

You're **pregnant** / a **hypochondriac** /haɪpə'kɒndrɪæk/.

He **died of lung cancer** / a **heart attack** / a **brain haemorrhage** /'hemərɪdʒ/ **AIDS.**

D What does the doctor prescribe?

a) Take one tablet three times a day after meals.
b) Take a teaspoonful of medicine last thing at night.
c) Rub this ointment on you and don't spend too long in the sun without suncream.
d) We'll get the nurse to put a bandage on your wrist.
e) You'll need to have some injections before you go to the Amazon.
f) I'll ask the surgeon when he can fit you in for an operation.
g) You'll have to have your leg put in plaster until the break mends.
h) I think you should have total bed rest for a week.

E What might the doctor ask you?

What would you say if the doctor asked you the following questions?

Do you have health insurance?
Are you taking any medication?
Have you ever had any operations?
Are you allergic to anything?

Exercises

53.1 **Match the diseases with their symptoms.**

1 flu	swollen glands in front of ear, earache or pain on eating
2 pneumonia	burning pain in abdomen, pain or nausea after eating
3 rheumatism	rash starting on body, slightly raised temperature
4 chickenpox	dry cough, high fever, chest pain, rapid breathing
5 mumps	headache, aching muscles, fever, cough, sneezing
6 an ulcer	swollen, painful joints, stiffness, limited movement

53.2 **What does the doctor or nurse use the following things for?**

EXAMPLE stethoscope *For listening to a patient's chest.*

1 thermometer 2 scales 3 syringe 4 scalpel

53.3 **Look at the statements (a) to (h) in D opposite. Which do you think the doctor said to each of the following patients?**

1 Anne with bad sunburn.
2 Jo who's broken her leg.
3 John who's off to the Tropics.
4 Paul with flu.
5 Liz with a bad cough.
6 Sam who needs his appendix out.
7 Rose suffering from exhaustion.
8 Alf who's sprained his wrist.

53.4 **Complete the following table.**

noun	*adjective*	*verb*
....	breathless	....
....	faint	....
....	shivery	....
....	dislocated	....
ache	....	....
treatment	....	....
....	swollen	....

53.5 **What medical problems might you have if ...**

1 you wear shoes that rub?
2 you eat too fast?
3 you smoke a lot?
4 you play football?
5 you go skiing?
6 you stay out in the sun too long?
7 you eat food you're allergic to?
8 you run unusually fast for a bus?
9 you eat food that is bad?
10 a mosquito bites you?
11 you get wet on a cold day?
12 you think you're ill all the time?

53.6 **Think of illnesses you (or members of your family or friends) have had. What were the symptoms and what did the doctor prescribe?**

Follow-up: Look at the health page of a magazine or newspaper. Make a note of any new vocabulary on the theme that you find there. Look in your medicine cabinet at home, at school or work. Can you name everything that you find there?

54 Travel

A Here is some basic travel vocabulary.

transport type	*different kinds of vehicle*	*parts of vehicle*	*people working with it*	*associated facilities*
road	sports car, estate car, bus, coach, tram, van, lorry	boot, engine, gears, steering-wheel, brakes, tyres	driver, mechanic, chauffeur, bus-conductor	petrol station, garage, service station
rail	passenger train, freight train, local train, express	sleeping-car, buffet, restaurant-car, compartment	engine-driver, ticket collector, guard, porter	waiting-room, ticket office, signal-box
sea	fishing-/rowing-boat, liner, ferry, yacht	engine-room, deck, bridge, gangplank	captain, purser, docker, steward(ess)	port, buoy, customs, light-house, docks
air	aeroplane, jet, helicopter, supersonic aircraft	cockpit, nose, tail, wings, aisle /aɪjəl/, joystick	pilot, ground staff, steward, cabin crew, air traffic controller	duty-free shop, departure lounge, runway

B Words at sea

At sea – a bedroom is a **cabin**, a bed is a **bunk**, the kitchen on a ship is a **galley**, right is **starboard** and left is **port** and the group of people who work on the ship is called the **crew**. These terms are also used for an aircraft. Sailors also refer to their vessels as 'she' rather than 'it'.

C Journey, trip, travel, voyage

A **trip** is shorter than a **journey**: What **was the journey like**? We **had a long journey** by coach from the north to the south of the country. We **took a trip / went on a trip** to the beach last weekend. [**go on a trip** suggests an organised short excursion, whereas **take a trip** or **have a trip** could be something you do yourselves in your own car.

(!) **Travel** is a general word. It is a noun and a verb: **Travel** broadens the mind. How did you **travel** round Australia? We hitch-hiked. *Note*: We never say 'a travel'. It is an uncountable noun.

Voyage means a long journey usually by sea, though this use is quite formal. It is often used in other contexts with discovery. Learning English is a voyage of discovery!

D Some words connected with travel

Last week he **flew** to New York. It was an early-morning **flight**. The **plane** was to take off at 6 a.m. and **land** at 7 a.m. He was **stranded** at the **airport**. The **plane** was **delayed** by fog. Air **passengers** often suffer such delays.

Trains always **run on time** here. You have to **change** trains at Crewe.

We are **sailing** on the QE2. It **sets sail** at noon. It will **dock** in New York at 6 p.m. I hope the sea won't be **rough** – I might be **seasick**.

The **ship** was **wrecked**. The passengers were **marooned** on a desert island.

Our **car does 10 km to the litre**. It **goes** quite **fast**. We can usually **overtake** other cars.

The car **swerved** into the middle of the **road** to avoid the **cyclist**.

He **backed/reversed** the car into the **drive** and **parked** in front of the house.

Exercises

54.1 **Label the diagram below. Use a dictionary to help you if necessary.**

54.2 **Here are some more words which could have been included in the table in A opposite. Where would they fit into the table?**

bonnet balloon deck-chair guard's van mast petrol pump
bus driver anchor glider oar rudder left luggage lockers
check-in desk control tower canoe dual carriageway

54.3 **Choose the best word *flight, journey, trip, travel* or *voyage* to fit these gaps.**

1 I would love to .... round the world in a balloon.
2 The *Titanic* sank on its maiden ....
3 How long does the .... from New York to Rio take?
4 She says her hobbies are reading, golf and ....
5 When they were in Cairo they took a .... to see the Pyramids.
6 Getting from London to the north of Scotland involves an overnight train ....

54.4 **Fill in the blanks. Most of the words you need can be found opposite.**

Yesterday John was supposed to take a ....(1) from London to Amsterdam. He got up very early, put his luggage in the ....(2) of his car and tried to start the engine. It wouldn't start. John lifted the ....(3) but he couldn't see what the matter could be. He immediately called his local ....(4) to ask them to send a ....(5) at once. Fortunately, the garage had a man free and he was with John within ten minutes. He quickly saw what the matter was. 'You've ....(6) of petrol,' he said. John felt very foolish. 'Why didn't I ....(7) everything last night?' he wondered. Despite all this, he got to the airport, checked in quite early and then went straight through to the ....(8) to read a newspaper while he waited. Soon he heard an announcement. 'Passengers on flight BA 282 to Amsterdam are informed that all flights to and from Amsterdam are ....(9) because of a heavy snowfall last night.' 'If only I had decided to go by ....(10),' John thought. 'It would probably have been quicker in the end and even if I sometimes feel sick on the ....(11), it can be quite pleasant sitting in a ....(12) on the deck, watching the seagulls and the other ....(13). The ....(14) on a ship seem to produce much better food than those on an aircraft too.'

54.5 **Write two advantages and two disadvantages for each of the four forms of travel opposite.**

55 Holidays

A Places to stay and types of holiday

camp-site: a place where you can pitch a **tent** or park a **caravan**
self-catering flat: a flat which you rent; you cook for yourself
guesthouse: accommodation like a hotel but cheaper and with fewer services
youth hostel: cheap accommodation, mainly for young people, with, perhaps, ten or more people sleeping in bunk beds in one room
holiday camp: a place providing holiday accommodation in little chalets or flats, with restaurants, bars, swimming pools and lots of other facilities and entertainment for when visitors want a break from sun-bathing
time-share apartment: accommodation of which you share ownership with a number of people, for example you own a twelfth of the apartment so you have the right to stay there for one month every year.

package holiday: a holiday in which you pay for travel, accommodation and food (even occasionally excursions) in advance
cruise: a holiday spent touring on a boat, stopping off to go sight-seeing at different ports

B

The language of holiday brochures is often quite exaggerated. Here are some typical adjectives with nouns that they collocate with.

breath-taking views/scenery/pistes (ski slopes) [breath-taking (like **stunning**) suggests that something is so magnificent that it takes your breath away]
exclusive access/club/shops [only the most special people can use the facilities]
exhilarating feeling/ride/moment [makes you feel excited and full of energy]
exotic beauty/charm/location [unusual and much more exciting than one's everyday reality]
glamorous surroundings/film star/hotel [especially exciting and attractive]
intoxicating views/air/fragrance [makes you feel excited and emotional]
legendary hospitality/figure/status [so special that it has been famous for some time]
luxurious cruise ship/accommodation/lifestyle [provides great comfort]
mighty river/cathedral/oak [large and powerful]
picturesque streets/villages/cottage [as pretty as a picture]
sublime pleasure/simplicity/skill [heavenly or divine]
unsurpassed opportunity/beauty/quality [nothing better exists]
unspoilt charm/village/woodland [still in a beautiful and natural state]

TIP To find more useful language relating to holidays, get some holiday brochures or other tourist information written in English. You could either try the embassies of those countries or a travel agency. Ask for the information in English. Note down any useful new words and expressions that you learn from it. Think about what the writer was trying to suggest through his or her choice of words.

Exercises

55.1 Which of the holiday places and types of holiday in A have you or any of your friends had experience of? What are the advantages and disadvantages of each? Try and find at least one advantage and one disadvantage for each, even if you have no experience of them.

55.2 Complete this table. Use a dictionary to help you, if necessary.

adjective	*noun*	*verb*
exhilarating	....	....
glamorous	....	....
intoxicating	....	....
legendary	....	–
luxurious	....	....

55.3 Fill in the gaps in this postcard with appropriate adjectives from Section B on the opposite page.

Hi,
Am having a wonderful holiday here. The town here is very old and .... (1) The guidebook says it is remarkable for its .... (2) charm and it is right! It is surrounded by magnificent mountains and yesterday I went for an .... (3) climb. Even though it isn't too expensive, the hotel is quite .... (4) and the view from my balcony is .... (5).
Wish you were here!
Love P

Mr J. P. Jenkins
47 Bernard Street
Cambridge
CY4 5PT

55.4 Complete these sentences with a word from the opposite page.

1 As soon as we got to the camp site we .... our tent.
2 At the youth hostel Jimmy insisted on sleeping in the top ....
3 They stayed in a nice little .... at a holiday camp with two bedrooms and its own living area.
4 Our hotel offers you unsurpassed .... for unbeatable prices.
5 Take a memorable cruise along the .... Mississippi.
6 Visitors to our hotel have .... access to our own private beach.
7 Experienced skiers can try the most breath-taking of ....
8 Be thrilled by visiting the castle of the .... Count Dracula!

55.5 There are six typical language mistakes in the paragraph below. Underline and correct them.

The Smiths stayed at a camping last summer because all other kinds of holiday accommodations are too expensive for them. Every day Mrs Smith had a sunbath, Mr Smith made a sightseeing and the children made a travel around the island. One day they made an excursion to a local castle.

55.6 Write a holiday advertisement for a place you know well. Use as many of the words from Section B opposite as possible.

56 Numbers and shapes

A

Notice how the following are said in English.

28% twenty-eight per cent 10 m × 12 m ten metres by twelve metres
10.3 ten point three

Note that decimal fractions are separated by a dot and not a comma in English and this is pronounced *point*.

$1\frac{2}{3}$ one and two thirds
$\frac{4}{5}$ four fifths $\frac{9}{13}$ nine thirteenths *or* nine over thirteen
4^2 four squared 7^3 seven cubed 8^4 eight to the power of four
32°C *or* F thirty-two degrees centigrade/Celsius *or* Fahrenheit
1,623,457 one million, six hundred and twenty-three thousand, four hundred and fifty-seven

(!) Note how commas separate each set of three numbers in long numbers.
When saying a long number, you pronounce each set of up to three digits separately with rising intonation, until the last set – where the intonation falls at the end to make it clear that the number is complete.

B Two-dimensional shapes

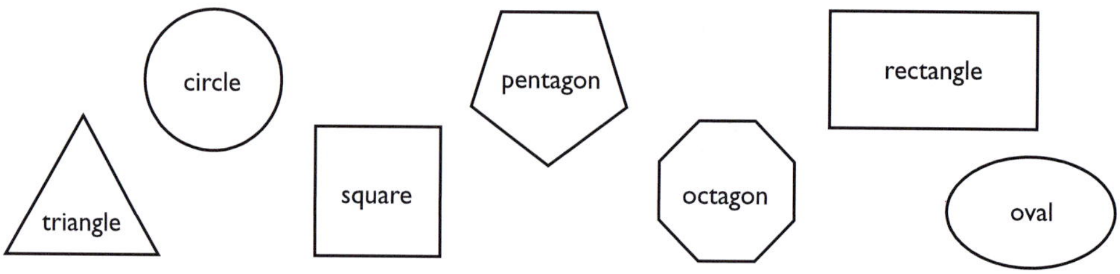

A **rectangle** has four **right angles**.
A **circle** is cut in half by its **diameter**. Its two halves can be called **semi-circles**.
The **radius** of a circle is the distance from its centre to the **circumference**.

C Three-dimensional shapes

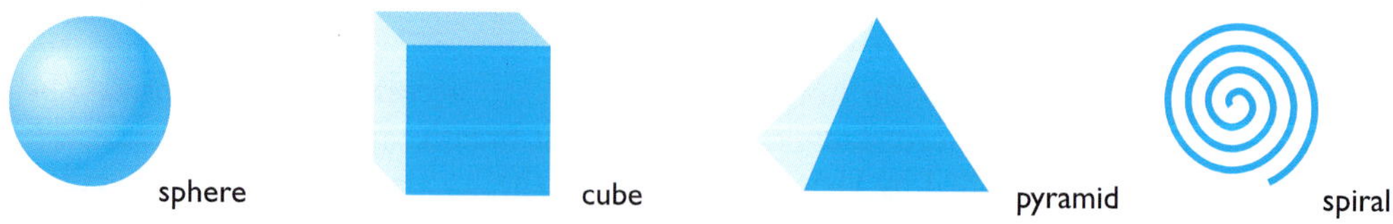

The two halves of a sphere can be called **hemispheres**.

D

Here are the four basic processes of arithmetic.

+ **addition** - **subtraction** × **multiplication** ÷ **division**

$2x + 3y - z = 3z/4x$ Two *x* plus three *y* minus *z* equals three *z* divided by four *x*. *or* Three *z* over four *x*.

6 × 7 = 42 Six **times** / **multiplied by** seven is forty two. *or* Six sevens are forty two.

Exercises

56.1 How numerate are you? Try this numbers quiz.

1 Name the first four odd numbers.
2 Name the first four even numbers.
3 Name the first four prime numbers.
4 Give an example of a decimal fraction.
5 Give an example of a vulgar fraction.
6 How do you read this formula and what does it represent: $e = mc^2$?
7 How do you read this and what does it represent: 2 p*r*

56.2 Write the following in words rather than in figures or symbols.

1 2% of the British population owned 90% of the country's wealth in 1992.
2 0°C = 32°F
3 62.3% of adults have false teeth.
4 $\frac{2}{3} + \frac{1}{4} \times 4^2 = 14\frac{2}{3}$.
5 2,769,425 people live here.

56.3 Look at the shapes in B and C opposite. What is the adjective relating to each of the shapes illustrated? Use a dictionary if necessary.

56.4 Read the underlined words aloud.

1 Oxygen accounts for <u>46.6%</u> of the earth's crust.
2 The highest waterfall in the world is Angel Falls in Venezuela with a drop of <u>979 m</u>.
3 The top coffee-drinking country in the world is Finland where <u>1,892</u> cups per annum are consumed per head of the population.
4 The tallest church is the Chicago Methodist Temple which is <u>173 m</u> or <u>568 ft</u> high.
5 The commonest item of lost property on London transport is the umbrella. <u>23,250 umbrellas</u> were handed in to London transport lost property offices in <u>1987/8</u>.
6 The country with the most telephones in the world is Monaco. It has <u>733 telephones per 1,000 population</u>.
7 The smallest country in the world is the Vatican City with an area of <u>0.4 sq km</u>.
8 The nearest star to earth is Proxima Centauri. It is <u>33,923,310,000 km</u> from earth.

56.5 Draw the following shapes.

1 A right-angled triangle with two equal sides of about two centimetres in length. Draw a small circle at the centre of the triangle and then draw lines from the centre of the circle to each of the angles of the triangle.
2 A rectangle with diagonal lines joining opposite angles.
3 An octagon with equal sides. Draw an oval in the middle of the octagon.
4 A cube of roughly 3 cm by 3 cm by 3 cm.

Follow-up: Write down some numbers that are important for you – your age, any numbers in your address, your telephone number and similar numbers for any of your friends, any other numbers that are significant for you at work or in your study. Practise saying these numbers in English.

57 Science and technology

A

You are probably familiar with the traditional branches of science e.g. chemistry, physics, botany and zoology. But what about these newer fields?

genetic engineering: the manipulation of genetic material (DNA) of living things to alter hereditary traits
ergonomics: the study of the design of physical working spaces and how people interact with them
molecular biology: the study of the structure and function of the organic molecules associated with living organisms
cybernetics: the study of the way information is moved and controlled by the brain or by machinery
information technology: the study of technology related to the transfer of information (computers, digital electronics, telecommunications)
bioclimatology: the study of how climate affects living things
geopolitics: the study of the way geographical factors help to explain the basis of the power of nation states
nuclear engineering: the study of the way nuclear power can be made useful
cryogenics: the study of physical systems at temperatures less than 183°C
astrophysics: the application of physical laws and theories to stars and galaxies
voice technology: technology which enables machines to interpret speech

B

Here are some of the modern inventions which we are now becoming quite used to.

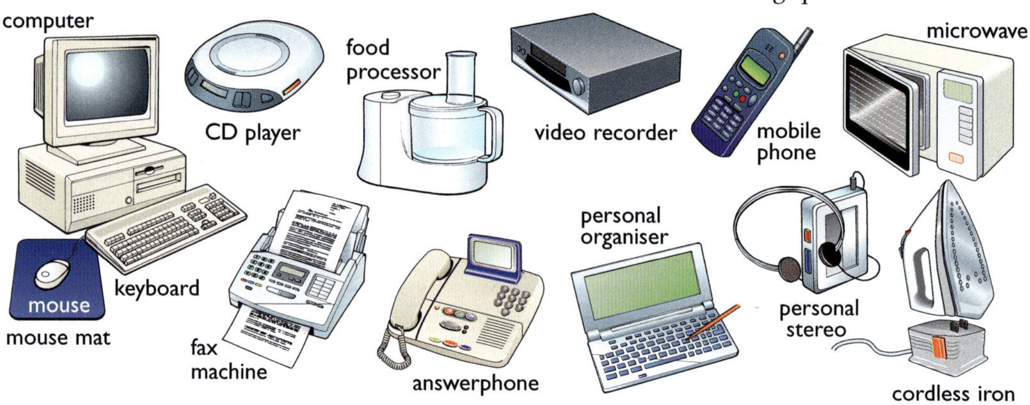

C

The verbs in the sentences below are all useful in scientific contexts.

He **experimented** with a number of different materials before **finding** the right one.
The technician **pressed** a button and lights started **flashing**.
When she **pulled** a lever, the wheel began to **rotate**.
The zoologist **dissected** the animal.
When they were **combined**, the two chemicals **reacted** violently with each other.
After **analysing** the problem, the physicist **concluded** that there was a flaw in his initial hypothesis.
James Watt **invented** the steam engine and Alexander Fleming, another Scot, **discovered** penicillin.
After **switching on** the computer, **insert** a floppy disk into the disk drive.
You must **patent** your invention as quickly as possible.

See Unit 58 for words relating to Computers and the Internet.

Exercises

57.1 Complete the following list with the name of the specialists in the particular fields.

science	scientist	science	scientist
chemistry	....	information technology	....
physics	....	cybernetics	....
zoology	....	civil engineering	....
genetics	....	astrophysics	....

57.2 Below you have some of the amazing achievements of modern technology. Match the names on the left with the definitions on the right.

1 video recorder	a kind of sophisticated typewriter using a computer
2 photocopier	a machine which records and plays back sound
3 fax machine	a machine which records and plays back sound and pictures
4 tape recorder	a camera which records moving pictures and sound
5 modem	a machine for chopping up, slicing, mashing, blending, etc.
6 camcorder	a machine which makes copies of documents
7 word processor	a machine which makes copies of documents and sends them down telephone lines to another place
8 food processor	a piece of equipment allowing you to send information from one computer down telephone lines to another computer

57.3 Write descriptions like those in exercise 57.2, for the following objects.

1

2

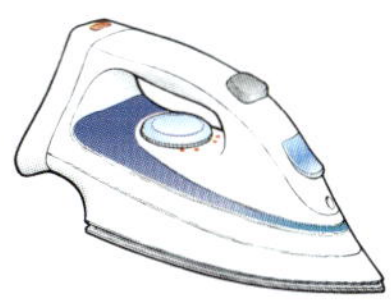

3

4

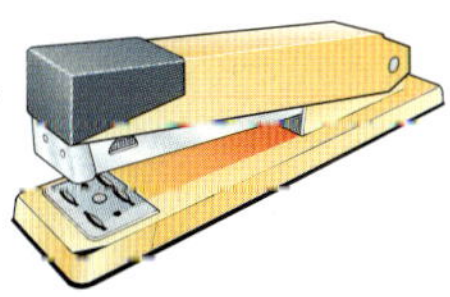

5

57.4 What are the nouns connected with the following verbs?

1 discover	3 rotate	5 patent	7 dissect	9 combine
2 invent	4 conclude	6 analyse	8 experiment	

57.5 Give each of the sciences in A opposite a number from 0 to 5 depending on whether it doesn't interest you at all (0) or interests you enormously (5). Similarly mark each of the inventions in B, 0 to 5, depending on how important they are to you in your life.

Follow-up: Increase your knowledge of scientific vocabulary by reading articles of general scientific interest in English language newspapers or magazines. If possible, get a textbook in English for schoolchildren studying a branch of science that you have studied. Choose a book where the science is relatively easy for you so that you can concentrate on the English used.

58 Computers and the Internet

Nowadays computers are everywhere. Even people who don't own or operate computers are exposed to computer terminology. This unit explores some of the most common words and expressions associated with computers and the Internet.

A Personal computers

Here are some words associated with personal computers.

personal computer / PC / desktop computer: a computer that fits on a desk, used by individuals at work or at home
laptop (computer): a lightweight portable computer that usually fits in a briefcase
palmtop (computer): one small enough to fit in your hand
hardware: computer equipment or machinery
software: programs that you put into a computer to make it run
floppy (disk) / diskette: a small plastic disk that stores (a limited amount of) information. A floppy can be inserted into a computer and taken out.
hard disk: a device inside a computer that stores large amounts of information
disk drive: an apparatus that allows information to be read from a disk or stored
modem: a piece of equipment that sends information from one computer along telephone lines to another computer
scanner: machine for transferring pictures and texts into a computer
to **download:** to transfer data or software from a large computer to a smaller one
RAM (random access memory / memory: the memory available on a computer to store and use information temporarily, usually measured in **megabytes**)
spreadsheet (program): a program or the grid you create with it to perform mathematical operations
computer graphics: pictures, images, and symbols that you can form on a computer
word processing: writing and storing printed text on a computer
virus: hidden instructions in a program designed to destroy information

B The Internet

The Internet / 'the net': a network connecting millions of computer users worldwide. You can access information on the Internet or send and receive **e-mail** (electronic mail) from a computer, through a modem.

Here is a small sampling of other words and expressions associated with the Internet.

World Wide Web / 'the Web': a huge portion of the Internet containing linked documents, called pages
to surf the net / the Web: to navigate around the Internet, sometimes aimlessly
website / home page: a document on the Web giving information about a person or institution
newsgroup: a meeting place on the Internet for discussion of a particular topic
chat room / chat forum: a group of people who have the same interests who e-mail one another live as a group
FAQ: 'frequently asked questions', a list of common questions and helpful answers

(See Unit 57 on technology, and Unit 16 on abbreviations.)

Exercises

58.1 **Match the words to the pictures below.**

laptop	desktop computer	mouse	floppy disk drive
floppy disk	printer	spreadsheet	

1 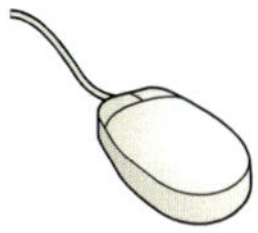

2 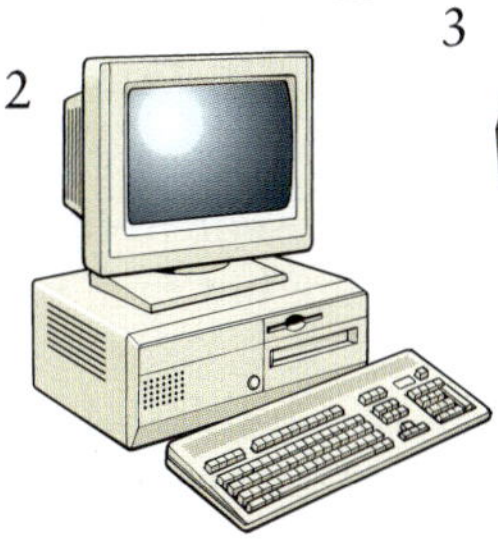

3 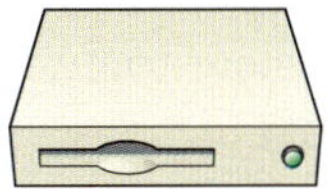

4 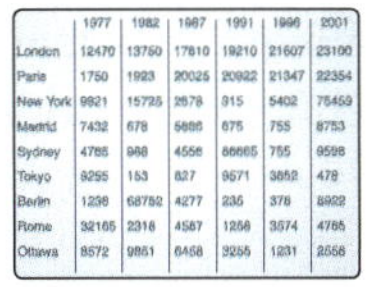

	1977	1982	1987	1991	1996	2001
London	12470	13750	17810	19210	21607	23100
Paris	1750	1923	20025	20922	21347	22354
New York	9921	15725	2578	915	5402	75459
Madrid	7432	678	5886	675	755	8753
Sydney	4785	988	4556	86665	755	9598
Tokyo	8255	153	827	9571	3852	478
Berlin	1236	68752	4277	235	378	8922
Rome	32165	2318	4587	1256	3574	4785
Ottawa	8572	9851	6458	9255	1231	2558

5 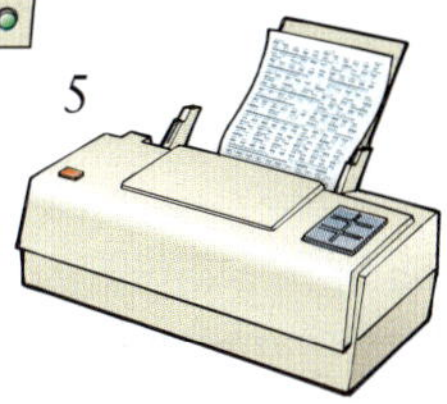

6 

7 

58.2 **Fill in the blanks with appropriate words from the opposite page.**

1 It's so easy to use a .... when you want to send photographs to friends by e-mail. It's just like using a photocopier.
2 I've lost a lot of data. I wonder if my computer has a ....
3 I'm always impressed by people who carry their .... on aeroplanes and work on them during the flight.
4 Those .... disks don't store nearly enough information. You really need to use your .... disk for all the data you want to store.
5 If you want some photos of the USA, you could just try .... the Web. You'll be amazed how many you can find.
6 I belong to a great .... There are about ten people who are all interested in 1960s music. We e-mail one another almost every day, and can talk live to one another.
7 I .... a good program from the Internet the other day. Would you like a copy?
8 Do you ever visit any .... for pop stars or film stars? Some of them have photos and music too.

58.3 **Here are some other words associated with computers and the Internet. Use them to complete the text. Use your dictionary if you need to. Remember to use the appropriate form of the verbs.**

down	scan	click	attachment	crash

The other day I ....(1) some photos I'd taken, so that I could send them to a friend in Australia. However, as I was doing the last one, I just ....(2) the mouse and the program ....(3). It was very annoying! Then, when I got it started again, I tried to send the photos by e-mail, as an ....(4) but the server was ....(5), and so I just gave up, I was so frustrated!

58.4 **Do you use a computer regularly? If so, what do you use it for? Do you have access to the Internet? If so, what do you use it for?**

59 The press and the media

A

The term the **mass media** in English refers basically to TV, radio and newspapers: means of communication which reach very large numbers of people. This page looks at some useful words for talking about the mass media and about **publishing** in general.

B Radio and television

Types of programmes: documentaries news broadcasts current affairs programmes soap operas [continuing stories about the lives of a set of characters] quizzes sitcoms [comedies centring around a set of characters in a particular situation] drama chat shows detective stories sports programmes weather forecasts music programmes game shows [where contestants compete for prizes] variety shows commercials [adverts]

A **serial** is a story that continues from one **programme** or **episode** to the next. A **series** is about the same **characters** or has the same format each week but each programme is complete in itself.

Films originally made in a different language may have **sub-titles** so you can read a translation of what the characters are saying or be **dubbed**, so you hear what they are saying in your own language.

TV aerial

satellite dish

camcorder

headset/headphones

C Newspapers and publishing

Parts of the newspaper: headlines news reports editorial [an opinion article written by the editor] feature articles, e.g. about fashion or socials trends horoscope cartoons crossword small ads business news sports reports scandal the letters page

A **popular** or **tabloid newspaper** focuses more on sensation than real news whereas a **quality newspaper** professes to be more interested in real news than in sensation. A **tabloid** usually has a smaller format than a **quality paper**, it has larger **headlines** and shorter stories and, in Britain, it prefers stories about film stars, violent crimes and the royal family. A **journal** is the name usually given to an academic **magazine.** A **colour supplement** is a **magazine** which comes out once a week (often on Sundays) as an addition to a newspaper. A comic is a **magazine**, usually for children or teenagers, with lots of picture stories and/or cartoons.

D

Make sure you know the verbs in these sentences.

The BBC World Service **broadcasts** throughout the world.
I can **receive / pick up** broadcasts from Moscow on my radio.
They're **showing** a good film on TV tonight.
This book was **published** by CUP and it was **printed** in Cambridge.
The film was **shot / made on location** in Spain.
They **cut/censored** the film before showing it on TV.
This article/programme has been badly **edited.**

See Unit 99 for the language of newspaper headlines.

Exercises

59.1 **What sort of TV programmes do you think these would be?**

1 Murder at the Match
2 The Amazing Underwater World
3 World Cup Special
4 The $10,000 Question
5 Last Week in Parliament
6 Hamlet from Stratford

59.2 **Give the name of one programme you know in your country of each type mentioned in B.**

59.3 **Match the media job on the left with its definition on the right.**

1 make-up artist	writes a regular article in a newspaper or magazine
2 foreign correspondent	shoots films
3 sub-editor	writes reviews
4 publisher	is responsible for the production and sale of a book
5 continuity person	reports on events in other countries
6 columnist	lays out and adds headlines to newspaper pages
7 camera operator	makes up the faces of people who are to appear on TV
8 critic	ensures scenes in a film connect smoothly

59.4 **Fill in the gaps below with the most appropriate word from the opposite page.**

1 You get better reception if you use a .... rather than an ....
2 You can hear BBC news .... all over the world.
3 A short wave or a VHF radio can .... many interesting stations.
4 Although our .... was expensive, we've taken some priceless film of our children.
5 Children often prefer looking at .... to reading books.

59.5 **Match two words to make a common collocation.**

affairs cassette chat colour control current dish forecast news newspaper opera remote report satellite show soap supplement tabloid video weather

59.6 **Choose any newspaper (it could be in your own language if you can't find an English one) and complete the following sentences.**

1 The main story today is about ....
2 The editorial is about ....
3 There are readers' letters on page .... and they deal with the following topics:
....
4 The most interesting feature is about ....
5 There is some scandal on page ...., a crossword on page ...., a cartoon on page .... and some small ads on page ....
6 The most interesting business story is about .... and the largest sports article is about ....
7 The most striking photograph shows ....
8 There are advertisements for ...., ... and ....
9 An article about .... on page .... made me feel ....

60 Politics and public institutions

A Types of government

republic: a state governed by representatives and, usually a president (e.g. USA, France)
monarchy: a state ruled by a king or queen (e.g. UK, Sweden)
federation: a union of political units (e.g. provinces) under a central government (e.g. USA)
democracy: government of, by and for the people
dictatorship: system of government run by a dictator
independence: freedom from outside control; self-governing

B Presidential and parliamentary government (US and UK)

United States

Presidential government: The powers of the **President** and the **legislature** (**Congress**) are separate. These **branches** of government are elected separately.

The **President** is **elected** for a four-year **term** and can **appoint** or **nominate** high officials in government, including **cabinet** members (who advise) and federal **judges**. The President leads a major party, usually, but not always, the **majority party** in Congress.

Congress consists of two **houses**, the **House of Representatives** and the **Senate**. **Congressmen** or **women** and **Senators** are elected for fixed terms.

The **judiciary** is a separate branch. The **Supreme Court**, the highest court, can overrule the President and Congress.

United Kingdom

Parliamentary government: The government consists of a **legislature** (**Parliament**) and a **Cabinet of Ministers** from the majority party in Parliament.

The **Prime Minister** is the head of the government and the leader of the majority party in the **House of Commons**, holding office while the party holds a majority. The Prime Minister **selects** high officials and **heads** the Cabinet.

Parliament consists of two **chambers**, the **House of Commons** and the **House of Lords**. **MPs** are **members of parliament** elected from each **constituency** [geographical area] to the House of Commons.

The **judiciary** is independent but it cannot **overrule** the Prime Minister or Parliament. The **Highest Court** consists of a group of Lords.

C Parliamentary elections

During a **general election** each **constituency** has to choose which **politician** it wants as its **representative**. Usually there are several **candidates** to choose from. These candidates are all **standing** (or **running**) for Parliament. They present the **policies** that they represent. On **polling day** each citizen goes to the **polling station** and **casts a vote** by marking a cross on their **ballot paper**. The candidate who gets the **majority** of votes wins the **seat**. If the vote is very close, the constituency may be referred to as a **marginal seat**. If an MP dies **in office**, then there has to be a **by(e)-election** to replace him or her. The public can also occasionally vote in a **referendum** – a **direct vote** by the people on an important public issue.

TIP Probably the most useful political words for you will be the ones that relate to your own country. Highlight the words on this page that could be used about your country's political system.

Exercises

60.1 **Choose the correct word from the choices offered.**

1 India gained republic/independence/democracy from the UK in 1948.
2 Our MP's just died and so we'll soon need to have a vote/referendum/by-election.
3 She's running/sitting/walking for Parliament in the next election.
4 His father was voted/stood/elected MP for Cambridge City.
5 What is your country's economic politics/policy/politician?
6 The USA is a legislature/federation/judiciary of fifty states.

60.2 **Look at this text about politics in the UK. Fill in the missing words.**

Parliament in the UK consists of two .... (1): the House of Commons and the House of Lords. In the House of Commons there are 650 .... (2), each representing one .... (3). The ruling party in the Commons is the one which gains a .... (4) of seats. The main figure in that party is called the .... (5). The Commons is elected for a maximum period of 5 years although the Prime Minister may call a general .... (6) at any time within that period.

60.3 **Make some more words based on those you studied opposite.**

abstract noun	*person noun*	*verb*	*adjective*
revolution	revolutionary	revolutionise	revolutionary
representation	....	....	....
election	....	....	....
dictatorship	....	....	....
presidency	....	....	....

60.4 **Try this political quiz.**

1 Name three monarchies.
2 Which is the oldest parliament in the world?
3 Name the President and the Vice-President of the USA.
4 Who is the current Prime Minister of the United Kingdom?
5 What politicians represent you in local and national government?
6 What are the main political parties in the country where you now are?
7 What are the main political issues in that country and what are the policies of the different parties on those issues?
8 What do these political abbreviations stand for – MP, PM, UN, EU, NATO, OPEC?

60.5 **Using the words on the left-hand page, write a paragraph about the political system in your country.**

Follow-up: Find a newspaper article in English relating to a political issue that interests you. Note down any further useful vocabulary in it.

You will find words about types of political belief in Unit 63.

61 Crime

A

Note the difference between the verbs: **steal** and **rob**. The object of the verb '**steal**' is the thing which is taken away, e.g. they stole my bike, whereas the object of the verb '**rob**' is the person or place from which things are stolen, e.g. I was robbed last night. A masked man robbed the bank. '**Steal**' is irregular; steal, stole, stolen.

B

The table below gives the names of some other types of crimes together with their associated verbs and the name of the person who commits the crimes.

crime	*definition*	*criminal*	*verb*
murder	killing someone	murderer	murder
shoplifting	stealing something from a shop	shoplifter	shoplift
burglary	stealing something from someone's home	burglar	burgle
smuggling	taking something illegally into another country	smuggler	smuggle
kidnapping	taking a person hostage in exchange for money or other favours, etc.	kidnapper	kidnap

All the verbs in the table above are regular.

C

Here are some more useful verbs connected with crime and law. Note that many of them have particular prepositions associated with them.

Bill **committed a crime** when he robbed a bank. Someone **witnessed** the crime and told the police. The police **charged** him **with** bank robbery. They also **accused** his twin brother, Ben, **of** being his accomplice.

The case came to court and they **were tried**. The trial did not last very long. Bill and Ben both **pleaded not guilty** in court. Their lawyer did her best to **defend** them but the **prosecuting** lawyer produced a very strong case against them.

After brief deliberations, the jury **passed verdict on** them. They decided that Bill was **guilty** but Ben was **innocent**. The judge **acquitted** Ben **of** any involvement in the robbery but **sentenced** Bill **to** three years in prison. He also had to **pay a** large **fine**. Bill **served** two years in prison [jail] but **was released from** prison a year early. He **got time off** for good behaviour.

D

Here are some useful nouns.

trial: the legal process in court whereby an accused person is investigated, or tried, and then found guilty or not guilty
case: a crime that is being investigated
evidence: information used in a court of law to decide whether the accused is guilty or not
proof: evidence that shows conclusively whether something is a fact or not
judge: the person who leads a trial and decides on the **sentence** i.e. the punishment
jury: group of twelve citizens who decide on the **verdict** i.e. whether the accused is guilty or not

Exercises

61.1 **Put the right form of either *rob* or *steal* in the sentences below.**

1 Last night an armed gang .... the post office. They .... £2,000.
2 My handbag .... at the theatre yesterday.
3 Every year large numbers of banks ....
4 Jane .... of the opportunity to stand for president.

61.2 **Here are some more crimes. Complete a table like the one in B opposite.**

crime	*criminal*	*verb*	*definition*
terrorism	....	....	....
blackmail	....	....	....
drug-trafficking	....	....	....
forgery	....	....	....
pickpocketing	....	....	....
mugging	....	....	....

61.3 **Fill the blanks in the paragraph below with one of the verbs from C opposite.**

One of the two accused men ....(1) at yesterday's trial. Although his lawyer ....(2) him very well, he was still found guilty by the jury. The judge ....(3) him to two years in prison. He'll probably ....(4) after eighteen months. The other accused man was luckier. He ....(5) and left the courtroom smiling broadly.

61.4 **Here are some words connected with law and crime. If necessary, use a dictionary to help you check that you understand what they all mean. Then divide them into three groups, in what seems to you to be the most logical way.**

member of a jury   judge   smuggling   witness   prison   fine   bribery
detective   hi-jacking   community service   probation   traffic warden   death penalty
rape   drunken driving   lawyer

61.5 **Look at all the crimes named in this unit. Look both at the left-hand page and at exercises 61.2 and 61.4. Which do you think are the three most serious and the three least serious?**

61.6 **Write a paragraph to fit this newspaper headline. Give some details about the crime and the court case, using as many words from this unit as is appropriate.**

Local girl's evidence gets mugger two years prison

Follow-up: If possible look at an English language newspaper. List all the words connected with crime and the law which you can find in it.

62 Money – buying, selling and paying

A Personal finance

Sometimes in a shop they ask you: 'How do you want to pay?'
You can answer: **'Cash. / By cheque. / By credit card.'**

In a **bank** you usually have a **current account**, which is one where you **pay in your salary** and then **withdraw** money to **pay your everyday bills.** The bank sends you a regular **bank statement** telling you how much money has gone in and out of your account. You may also have a **savings account** where you **deposit** any extra money that you have and only **take money out** when you want to **spend** it **on** something special. If you spend more than you have in your account you can have an **overdraft.** The bank allows you to spend more and **charges** you **interest.** If your account is **overdrawn** [you have taken more out of your account than you had in it] you are **in the red** (as opposed to **in the black** or **in credit**).

Sometimes the bank may **lend** you money – this is called a **bank loan.** If the bank [or **building society**] lends you money to buy a house, that money is called a **mortgage** /ˈmɔːɡɪdʒ/.

When you **buy** [or **purchase** more formally] something in a shop, you usually **pay** for it **outright** but sometimes you buy **on credit.** Sometimes you may be offered a **discount** or a **reduction** on something you buy. For example, you might **get £10 off** perhaps because you are a student. You are often offered a discount if you buy **in bulk.** It is not usual to **haggle** about prices in a British shop, as it is in, say, a Turkish market. If you want to return something which you have bought to a shop, you may be given a **refund,** i.e. your money will be returned, provided you have a **receipt.**

The money that you pay for services, e.g. to a school or a lawyer, is usually called a **fee** or **fees**; the money paid for a journey is a **fare.** If you buy something that you feel was very **good value,** it's a **bargain.** If you feel that it is definitely **not worth** what you paid for it, then you can call it **a rip-off** [very colloquial].

B Public finance

The government collects money from citizens through **taxes. Income tax** is the tax collected on **wages** and **salaries. Inheritance tax** is collected on what people inherit from others. **Customs** or **excise duties** have to be paid on goods imported from other countries. **VAT** or **value added tax** is a tax paid on most goods and services when they are bought or purchased. Companies pay **corporation tax** on their profits. If you pay too much tax, you should be given some money back, a **tax rebate.**

The government also sometimes pays out money to people in need, e.g. **unemployment benefit** [also known as **the dole,** informal] **disability allowances** and **student loans** [money lent to help pay for studying]. Recipients **draw a pension / unemployment benefit** or are **on the dole** or **on social security.**

Every country has its own special **currency.** Every day the **rates of exchange** are published and you can discover, for example, how many dollars there are currently to the pound sterling.

A company may sell **shares** to members of the public who are then said to have **invested** in that company. They should be paid a regular **dividend** on their **investment,** depending on the **profit** or **loss** made by the company.

Exercises

62.1 **Answer the following money quiz.**

1 What currencies are used in Japan, Australia, India and Russia?
2 What does the expression 'hard currency' mean?
3 Give two examples of imports that most countries impose customs duties on.
4 Give three examples of kinds of income that would be classed as unearned.
5 What is the Dow Jones index and what are its equivalents in London and Japan?
6 Give an example of something that is priceless and something that is valueless.
7 Name the coins and banknotes used in your country and one other country.

62.2 **Match the words on the left with their definitions on the right.**

1 interest	a bank account with a negative sum of money in it
2 mortgage	money paid towards the cost of raising a family
3 an overdrawn account	money paid on what is inherited after someone dies
4 savings account	an account that is used mainly for keeping money
5 current account	money paid to people after a certain age
6 pension	an account for day-to-day use
7 disability allowance	money chargeable on a loan
8 child benefit	money paid to people with a handicap
9 inheritance tax	a loan to purchase property

62.3 **Is the ordinary 'person-in-the-street' pleased to see these newspaper headlines or not?**

Mortgage rate goes up

Wages to be frozen

Pension age raised

Interest rates down

VAT to be reduced

NUMBER ON DOLE RISES

62.4 **Complete the sentences with words from the opposite page.**

1 If you get something more cheaply, perhaps because you buy in bulk, you get a ....
2 If the bank lends you money, you have a bank ....
3 If you have some money in your account you are in the ....
4 I paid too much tax last year so I should get a .... soon.
5 If it's no good, take it back to the shop and ask for a ....

62.5 **Fill in the table below for your own, or any other, country.**

Rate of inflation	Basic level of income tax ....
Exchange rate (against the US dollar)	Rate of VAT ....
Interest rate	Monthly state pension ....

62.6 **Draw two bubble networks (see Units 2 and 3 for examples with CAT and TRAVEL). At the centre of one bubble network put PAYING MONEY and at the centre of the other put GETTING MONEY. Include as many words as possible from this unit.**

Follow-up: To improve your financial vocabulary, read articles on business in any English magazine or newspaper. Write down any new words or expressions that you come across.

63 Belief and opinion

A Verbs connected with beliefs and opinions

You probably already know **think** and **believe**; here are more:

I'm **convinced** we've met before. [very strong feeling that you're right]

I've always **held** that compulsory education is a waste of time. [formal; used for very firm beliefs; **maintain** could be used here]

She **maintains** that we're related, but I'm not convinced. [formal; insist on believing, often against the evidence; **hold** could not be used here]

I **feel** she shouldn't be forced to do the job. [strong personal opinion]

I **reckon** they'll get married soon. [informal; usually an opinion about what is likely to happen / to be true]

I **doubt** /daʊt/ we'll ever see total world peace. [don't believe]

I **suspect** a lot of people never even think about pollution when they're driving their own car. [fairly formal; have a strong feeling about something negative]

B Phrases for expressing opinion

In my view / In my opinion, we haven't made any progress. [fairly formal]
She's made a big mistake, **to my mind.** [fairly informal]
If you ask me, he ought to change his job. [informal]

Note how **point of view** is used in English:

From a teacher's **point of view**, the new examinations are a disaster. [how teachers see things, or are affected]

C Prepositions used with belief and opinion words

Do you **believe in** life after death? What are your **views on** divorce?
What do you **think of** the new boss?
Are you **for** or **against** long prison sentences? [neutral/informal]
I'm **in favour of** (opposite: **opposed to**) long prison sentences. [formal]
I have my doubts about this plan.

D Beliefs, ideologies, philosophies, convictions

If you would rather organise this word tree differently or can add more examples, do so; it will probably help you to remember the words better.

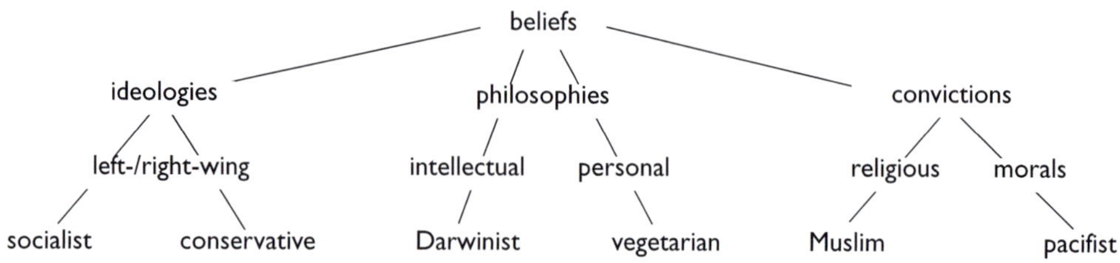

E

Some adjectives for describing people's beliefs and views, in pairs of similar, but not exactly the same, meaning:

fanatical/obsessive   eccentric/odd   conservative/traditional
middle-of-the-road/moderate   dedicated/committed   firm/strong

Exercises

63.1 **Draw lines connecting the left and right, as in the example, adding an appropriate preposition.**

1 I have strong views	my opinion.
2 Most people believe	the proposed changes.
3 I was in favour	marriage.
4 What does she think	my mind.
5 This is absurd,	life after death.
6 He's quite wrong,	the new teacher?
7 Well, that's just silly,	our point of view.

on

63.2 **Use adjectives from E opposite which fit the phrases describing the beliefs and views of these people, as in the example.**

1 A person who insists that the earth is flat. (an ...eccentric... belief)
2 A person who believes absolutely in the power of love to solve world problems. (a .... believer in the power of love)
3 A socialist neither on the left or the right of the party. (a .... socialist)
4 A vegetarian who refuses even to be in the same room as people who love meat. (a(n) .... vegetarian)
5 Someone who is always suspicious of change. (a rather .... view of the world)

63.3 **Rewrite these sentences using the verbs in brackets.**

1 I've always suspected that ghosts don't really exist. (doubt)
2 My view has always been that people should rely on themselves more. (hold)
3 Claudia is convinced that the teacher has been unfair to her. (maintain)
4 I had a very strong feeling that I had been in that room before. (convince)
5 In his view, we should have tried again. (feel)

63.4 **Are you ... ? Consider how many of these words apply to you, and in what situations. Some ideas for situations are given in the box, but you can add your own. Look up any words you don't know in a dictionary. Write sentences about yourself.**

a perfectionist
a moralist
a traditionalist
middle-of-the-road
narrow-minded
dedicated
left-wing
an intellectual
a philosopher
a radical thinker
open-minded
dogmatic

food preferences	politics
learning English	sport
sexual relations	life and existence
religion	work

64 Pleasant and unpleasant feelings

A Happiness and unhappiness

You feel:

ecstatic when you experience an intense and overpowering feeling of delight.
content(ed) when you are satisfied with what you have. Notice that **content** is not used before a noun. You can say 'She is content' or 'She is contented' but only 'a contented person'.
cheerful when life is looking bright and positive.
grateful when someone has done something thoughtful for you.
delighted when something has happened that gives you great pleasure, when you hear news of someone's good fortune, for instance.
miserable when everything seems wrong in your life.
discontented when your life is not giving you satisfaction.
fed-up / sick and tired when you have had enough of something disagreeable. You could **be fed-up** with someone's rudeness, or **sick** (**and tired**) of someone's behaviour.
depressed when you are miserable over a long period of time. Depression is considered an illness in some severe cases.
frustrated when you are unable to do something that you want to do.
confused / mixed up when you cannot make sense of different conflicting feelings or ideas: mixed up is more colloquial.

B Excitement, anger and anxiety

You feel:

excited when you are expecting something special to happen, e.g. before a party.
inspired when you are stimulated to create deeds or words. You might feel **inspired by** a really talented musician to learn how to play a musical instrument.
enthusiastic when you have very positive feelings about something, **enthusiastic about**, e.g. a new project.
thrilled (informal) when something extremely exciting and pleasing happens. She was **thrilled** when the film star kissed her.
cross (informal) when you are angry or bad-tempered. It is often, though not exclusively, used about small children. Stop getting so **cross with** me.
furious/livid/seething with someone **about** something when you are extremely angry; **livid** and **seething** are more informal; **in a rage/fury** also mean furious or violently angry.
anxious when you are afraid and uncertain about the future. I am so **anxious about** the results of my exams that I can't sleep.
nervous when you are afraid or anxious about something that is about to or may be about to happen. I feel **nervous about** going to the dentist. Feeling nervous is a little bit like feeling excited but it is a negative feeling whereas excitement is positive.
apprehensive about, e.g. an important meeting; when you are slightly nervous or anxious about something in the future.
worried about, e.g. an operation; when anxious thoughts constantly go through your head.
upset about, e.g. a quarrel; when something unpleasant has happened to disturb you. It often combines feelings of both sadness and anger.

> **TIP**
> **Really** can be used with all the adjectives on this page. **Absolutely** goes only with the words describing extreme states i.e. *ecstatic, delighted, fed-up, sick and tired, thrilled, furious, livid* and *seething*. With these words **quite** means **absolutely** but with the other less extreme words, **quite** means **rather**.

Exercises

64.1 **Complete the following table.**

adjective	*abstract noun*	*adjective*	*abstract noun*
furious	....	frustrated	....
....	anxiety	....	cheerfulness
grateful	....	enthusiastic	....
....	ecstasy	....	apprehension
inspired	....	excited	....

64.2 **Choose the best word from those given to complete each of the sentences which follow.**

enthusiastic confused cross thrilled depressed fed-up frustrated discontented

1 I didn't know who was telling the truth. I felt totally ....
2 Some unfortunate mothers are .... for months after the birth of a baby.
3 I think she is bad-tempered because she is .... She wanted to be an actress and not a school-teacher.
4 Although he seems to have everything he could want, he is still ....
5 He went skiing for the first time last month, but now he is so .... about it that he can talk of little else.
6 My baby brother gets very .... by the evening if he doesn't have an afternoon sleep.
7 This rainy weather has gone on for so long. I feel really .... with it.
8 She was .... when she learnt that she had won the first prize.

64.3 **Write sentences about when you have experienced the following feelings.**

EXAMPLE anxious *I felt anxious until we heard the results of my mother's medical tests.*

1 apprehensive 3 in a rage 5 inspired
2 grateful 4 miserable 6 enthusiastic

64.4 **The words opposite that end in -ed (apart from (dis)contented, delighted and mixed up) also have -ing forms e.g. depressing and exciting. Add the correct ending -ed or -ing.**

EXAMPLE She was thrill*ed* by her present.

1 I found the film very excit............
2 The poet was inspir............ by the sunset.
3 This weather is terribly depress............
4 It's very frustrat............ when the phones don't work.
5 She was confus............ by his ambiguous remarks.

64.5 **You, of course, know the basic expressions: 'I'm hungry/thirsty/hot/cold/tired/cross'. Colloquially, we often say the same things using a much stronger expression. What do you think people mean when they say:**

1 I'm boiling 3 I'm seething 5 I'm starving
2 I'm dying for a drink 4 I'm freezing 6 I'm worn out

65 Like, dislike and desire

A Words and expressions relating to liking

Dear Anna,
*It was great to hear from you after so many years. Fancy you already being married with a baby! I'm not married but I do have a boyfriend called Tom, I must tell you about him. We've known each other for three years. **I quite liked** Tom when we first met. However. although lots of my friends said they found him attractive, I didn't **fancy** him at all. He invited me out and I admit that I was more **tempted** by his sports car than by him at first. However, I really **enjoyed** spending time with him. He **fascinated** me with his stories of his travels around the world and something mysterious about this past also **attracted** me. Moreover, we were both very **keen on** sailing. Soon I realised I had **fallen in love** with him. His sense of humour really **appealed to** me and I was also **captivated by** his smiling eyes. Now, three years later I absolutely **adore** him and I can't understand why I didn't **fall for** him the moment we first set eyes on each other. He's a very **caring** person, **fond of** animals and small children. He's always **affectionate** and **loving** towards me and **passionate** both **about** me and about the causes he believes in and the people he **cares for**. I hope we'll always **worship** each other as much and be as **devoted to** our life together as we are now. Do write again soon and tell me all about how you are!*
Love Jude

B Words and expressions relating to disliking

Loathe, detest, despise, hate, cannot stand and **cannot bear** are all stronger ways of saying dislike and they are all followed by a noun or an -ing form.

I loathe / detest / despise / hate / cannot stand / cannot bear bad-mannered people.

Repel, revolt, appal and **disgust** are all strong words used to describe the effect which something detested has on the person affected. His paintings **disgust** me. I was **revolted** by the way he spoke. We were **appalled** by the conditions in the refugee camp. His behaviour **repels** everyone.

C Words and expressions relating to desiring

NOTE
After **looking forward**, 'to' is a preposition and not part of the infinitive and is followed by a noun or an -ing form.

Desire is used either as a formal verb to express a sexual wish for someone or else it is quite a formal word for wish. He **desired** her the moment he saw her.
I have a strong **desire** to see the Himalayas before I die.

Look forward to means think about something in the future with pleasant anticipation. The opposite of **look forward to** is **dread.**

I am **looking forward to** going to Fiji but I'm **dreading** the flight.

Long for means to wish for something very much. After this long, cold winter, I'm **longing for** spring.

Yearn for is a more poetic way of saying **long for.** He will never stop **yearning for** his country although he knows he can never return.

D Ways of addressing loved ones

(!)

dearest **sweetheart** **darling** **love** **dear** **pet**

Pet is used mainly to children. Note that the last three words in the list are not confined to use with people who are really loved. It is not uncommon for a London bus conductor, for example, to address any girl or woman as **'love'**. (His Glasgow equivalent calls his female passengers **'hen'**.) It's best for you, however, to keep such words for people you have a close relationship with!

Exercises

65.1 **Complete the following table. Use a dictionary if necessary.**

verb	*noun*	*adjective*	*adverb*
–	passion	....	....
tempt	....	....	....
attract	....	....	....
appeal	....	....	....
disgust	....	....	....
hate	....	....	....
repel	....	....	....
–	affection	....	....
adore	....	....	....

65.2 **Complete the following sentences. Use a dictionary if necessary.**

1 Misogynists hate ....
2 Ornithologists are fascinated by ....
3 People who suffer from arachnophobia find .... repulsive.
4 Kleptomaniacs are constantly tempted to ....
5 Masochists enjoy ....
6 Optimists look forward to ....

65.3 **Reword the sentences without changing the meaning. Use the word in brackets.**

EXAMPLE I very much enjoy his novels. (love) I love his novels.

1 I strongly dislike jazz. (stand)
2 Beer makes me feel sick. (revolt)
3 I don't really care for tea. (keen)
4 His art attracts me. (appeal)
5 She has totally charmed him. (captivate)
6 Do you fancy a pizza tonight? (like)
7 She likes rowing and golf. (keen)
8 I'm dreading the exam. (look)

65.4 **In each pair of sentences which person probably feels more strongly?**

1 a Dear Louise, How are things? b Darling Louise, How are things?
2 a He's devoted to his sister. b He's very fond of his sister.
3 a I dislike his poetry. b I loathe his poetry.
4 a She's yearning to see him. b She's longing to see him.
5 a He worships her. b He loves her very much.

65.5 **Complete the sentences or answer the question in any way that is true for you.**

1 What kind of food do you like? I like .... and I adore .... but I can't stand ....
2 I'm longing for ....
3 I'm fascinated by ....
4 What attracts you most in a person of the opposite sex?
5 What do you enjoy most about your job?
6 If you were on a diet, what food or drink would tempt you most to break the diet?
7 What characteristics in people do you most detest?
8 What do you dread most about getting old?
9 What do you fancy doing this evening?
10 Are there any characteristics in people that you particularly despise?

66 Speaking

A

The verbs in the table below describe how loudly a person is speaking and also, often, indicate mood. These verbs may be followed by clauses beginning with 'that'.

verb	*loudness*	*most likely mood*
whisper	soft	–
murmur	soft	romantic *or* complaining
mumble	soft (and unclear)	nervous *or* insecure
mutter	soft	irritated
shout	loud	angry *or* excited
scream	loud (usually without words)	frightened *or* excited
shriek	loud (and shrill)	frightened *or* amused
stutter, stammer	neutral	nervous *or* excited

Stuttering and stammering may also be the result of a speech impediment.

B

The following verbs indicate how the speaker feels. (*Note*: sb = somebody, st = something)

verb	*patterns*	*feeling*	*verb*	*patterns*	*feeling*
boast	– to sb about st – that	proud of oneself	complain	– to sb about st – that	displeased
insist	– on st – that	determined	maintain	– that	confident
object	– that – to + ing	unhappy with a situation	confess	– that – to + ing	repentant
threaten	– that – to do st	aggressive	urge	– sb to do st	encouraging
argue	– with sb about st – that	not in agreement	beg	– sb to do st – for st	desperate
groan	– that	despair, pain	grumble	– about st	displeased

C

To give an idea of the way someone speaks and their feelings, you can use a speaking verb, plus an adverb. For example, 'He said **proudly**. She spoke **angrily**'. This is most common in written style. Some useful adverbs describing the way someone is feeling while they are speaking.

If someone feels angry: crossly   furiously   bitterly (about something in the past)
If someone feels unhappy: unhappily   gloomily   miserably   uneasily   sadly
If some feels happy: happily   cheerfully   gladly   hopefully   eagerly
If someone feels worried: anxiously   nervously   desperately   hopelessly

Other useful adverbs are boldly, excitedly, gratefully, impatiently, passionately, reluctantly, shyly, sincerely.

Exercises

66.1 **Choose the verb which best fits the meaning of the sentences.**

EXAMPLE 'I love you,' he murmured.

1 'It was me who broke the vase,' he ....
2 'I am the cleverest person in the class,' the little boy ....
3 'Look, there's a mouse over there!' he ....
4 'I'll stop your pocket money if you don't behave,' she ....
5 'I-d-d-d-did it,' he ....
6 'Please, please, help me,' he ....
7 'This hotel is filthy,' she ....
8 'Go on, Jim, try harder,' he ....

66.2 **Change the sentences above into reported speech using the same verbs.**

EXAMPLE He murmured that he loved her.

66.3 **Add the appropriate adjectives and nouns to the table below.**

adverb	*adjective*	*noun*
angrily	....	....
furiously	....	....
bitterly	....	....
miserably	....	....
cheerfully	....	....
gratefully	....	....
anxiously	....	....

66.4 **The answers to the following questions are all words which are from the same root as the verbs on the page opposite. Use a dictionary if necessary.**

EXAMPLE How do you describe a person who boasts a lot? boastful

What do you call:

1 what you make when you threaten?
2 what you make when you complain?
3 what you make when you object?
4 a person who begs for money on the streets?

How do you describe:

5 someone who insists a lot?
6 someone who argues a lot?

66.5 **Look at the verbs in the table in B and answer the following quiz.**

1 Which verbs could replace ask in the sentence 'She asked me to dance with her', without changing the grammar of the sentence?
2 Which prepositions usually follow a) object b) insist c) complain?
3 Which verb could grammatically replace promise in 'He promised to do it'?
4 Which of the verbs can be followed by 'that' and a clause?
5 Find a synonym for each of the six verbs in the fourth column of the table.

66.6 **Write a sentence to match each of the eight adverbs listed at the end of C.**

EXAMPLE Excitedly. 'Let's go at once,' she said excitedly.

67 The six senses

A

The five senses are **sight, hearing, taste, touch** and **smell**. What is sometimes referred to as a 'sixth sense' (or extrasensory perception) is a power to be aware of things independently of the five physical senses, a kind of supernatural sense. The five verbs referring to the senses are modified by an adjective rather than an adverb.

He **looks** dreadful. The trip **sounds** marvellous. The cake **tastes** good.
It **felt** strange. The soup **smelt** delicious.

B Sight

Yesterday I **glanced** out of the window and **noticed** a man **observing** a house opposite through a telescope. I thought I **glimpsed** a woman inside the house. Then I **saw** someone else **peering** into the window of the same house. I **gazed** at them wondering what they were doing. Suddenly the first man stopped **staring** through his telescope. He went and hit the other one on the head with the telescope and I realised that I had **witnessed** a crime.

C Hearing

Scale of loudness **noiseless → silent → quiet → noisy → loud → deafening**

D Taste

sweet (honey) **salty** (crisps) **bitter** (strong coffee) **sour** (vinegar) **spicy** (Indian food)

If you say something tastes **hot** it may mean **spicy** rather than **not cold**. Food can be **tasty**, but **tasteful** refers to furnishings, architecture or a style of dressing or behaviour. The opposite of both is **tasteless**.

E Touch

She nervously **fingered** her collar. He **stroked** the cat and **patted** the dog.
She **tapped** him on the shoulder. He **grasped** my hand and we ran.
She **grabbed** her briefcase and ran to the bus stop.
The thief **snatched** her handbag and disappeared into the crowd.
Press the button. Please **handle** the goods with great care.

F Smell

Here are some adjectives to describe smells:

stinking **evil-smelling** **putrid** **aromatic** **pungent**
musty **fragrant** **sweet-smelling** **perfumed/scented**

G Sixth sense

Different phenomena which a person with sixth sense may experience:

telepathy [experiencing someone else's feelings even though you are apart]
premonition [knowing something is going to happen before it occurs]
intuition [instinctive understanding]
déjà vu [an inexplicable feeling that you have already been somewhere or experienced something]

Exercises

67.1 **Make a sentence about the situations using any of these verbs plus an adjective, *look*, *sound*, *taste*, *touch* and *smell*.**

EXAMPLE You see a film about the Rocky Mountains. They look magnificent.

1 You come downstairs in the morning and smell fresh coffee.
2 A friend has just had her hair cut.
3 You hear the song that is top of the pops.
4 A friend, an excellent cook, tries a new soup recipe.
5 A friend asks how you feel today.
6 A little boy asks you to listen to his first attempts at the piano.
7 You see a friend of yours with a very worried look on her face.
8 Someone you are working with smells strongly of cigarettes.

67.2 **Which of the verbs in the text in B suggests looking in the following ways:**

1 as a crime or accident occurs?
2 closely, finding it hard to make things out?
3 in a scientific kind of way?
4 quickly?
5 fixedly?
6 at something but getting only a brief view?

67.3 **Write sentences using each of the nine verbs in bold in B in ways that illustrate their specific meanings as clearly as possible.**

67.4 **Replace the underlined words with more precise verbs from the opposite page.**

1 I <u>touched</u> the dog <u>a number of times</u>.
2 He <u>knocked lightly</u> on the door.
3 She <u>took</u> my hand <u>firmly</u>.
4 <u>Touch</u> the button to start.
5 The lecturer <u>touched</u> his notes nervously.
6 He <u>touched</u> the cat <u>affectionately</u>.
7 The robber <u>took</u> the money and ran.
8 She <u>picked up, carried and put down</u> the boxes carefully.

67.5 **Are the following best described as *sweet*, *salty*, *bitter*, *sour*, *spicy* or *hot*?**

1 strong, unsweetened coffee
2 chocolate cake
3 chilli powder
4 lime
5 Indian cooking
6 sea water

67.6 **Which of the adjectives in F best describes for you the smell of the following?**

1 herbs in a kitchen
2 old socks
3 rotten eggs
4 roses

5 a room filled with cigar smoke
6 a beauty salon
7 an attic used for storage
8 a skunk

67.7 **Which of the phenomena mentioned in G have you experienced if you:**

1 suddenly think of someone two minutes before they phone you?
2 feel certain someone cannot be trusted although you have no real reason to believe so?
3 walk into a strange room and feel you have been there before?
4 refuse to travel on a plane because you feel something bad is going to happen?

67.8 **Write a sentence about a memorable experience each of your six senses has had.**

68 What your body does

NOTE

All the verbs on this page (except **shake** and **bite**) are regular verbs; almost all the words have an identical noun form: **to yawn / a yawn, to cough / a cough** /kɒf/ etc. (except to **breathe** /bri:ð/ and **to perspire**; their nouns are **breath** /breθ/ and **perspiration**).

A Verbs connected with the mouth and breathing

breathe: A nurse gave the old man artificial respiration and he started **breathing** again.
yawn: If one person **yawns** everyone else seems to start too.
cough: It was so smoky in the room that he couldn't stop **coughing**.
sneeze: Dust often makes me **sneeze**.
sigh: She **sighed** with relief when she heard the plane had landed safely.
hiccough /hɪkʌp/: Holding your breath and swallowing can help you stop **hiccoughing**.
snore: She **snored** all night with her mouth wide open.

B Verbs connected with eating and digestion

burp: He patted the baby's back to make it **burp** after its feed.
chew: My granny used to say you should **chew** every mouthful ten times.
rumble: It's embarrassing if your stomach **rumbles** during an interview.
swallow: Take a drink of water to help you **swallow** the pills.
suck: Sometimes in an aeroplane, you are given a sweet to **suck** – it can stop your ears popping!
lick: The cat **licked** the bowl clean.
bite: Don't **bite** that hard sweet – you'll hurt your teeth.

C Verbs connected with the eyes and face

blink: She **blinked** several times to try and get the dust out of her eye.
wink: He **winked** at me across the room to try to make me laugh.
frown: Why are you **frowning**? What's the problem?
grin: She was so delighted with the present that she **grinned** from ear to ear.
blush: He **blushed** with embarrassment when she smiled at him.

D Verbs connected with the whole body

perspire/sweat /swet/: When it's hot you **sweat/perspire**. [**perspire** is more formal]
tremble: My hands **tremble** when I've been drinking too much coffee.
shiver: Look at him! He's so cold that he's **shivering**!
shake: She laughed so much that her whole body **shook**.

Exercises

68.1 Find the word to match the definitions below.

EXAMPLE draw the eyebrows together to express displeasure or puzzlement frown

1 go pink from embarrassment
2 tremble especially from cold or fear
3 hold something in the mouth and lick it, roll it about, squeeze it, etc. with the tongue and teeth
4 shut and open both eyes quickly
5 deliberately shut and open one eye
6 breathe out deeply, especially to express pleasure, relief or boredom

68.2 Say what could be happening in each of the situations below.

EXAMPLE (*Parent to child*) Take your thumb out of your mouth! The child is sucking it's thumb.

1 Listen to that! I can't sleep in the same room as him.
2 Am I boring you?
3 If you have a drink of water, it might stop!
4 I'd have a honey and lemon drink if I were you!
5 Are you hungry?
6 You shouldn't eat so much so quickly!

68.3 Which of the words on the opposite page do these pictures illustrate?

EXAMPLE 1 blink

68.4 Complete the puzzle.

1 a special kind of gum
2 a more formal word for sweating
3 what you need to do to a stamp
4 try to do this quickly with pills
5 smile broadly
6 James Bond liked to have his drinks .... not stirred.

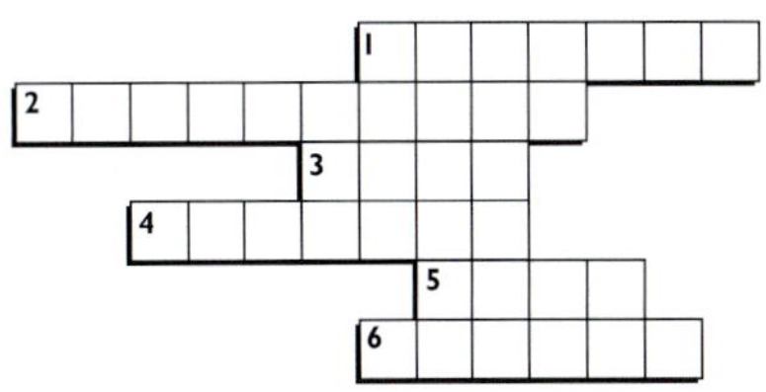

68.5 Organise the words on the opposite page into one or more bubble networks (see Units 2 and 3 for examples of bubble networks). Add any other words that you wish to the networks.

69 Number, quantity, degree and intensity

A Number and quantity

Number is used for countable nouns (e.g. **a large number** of students), **amount** for uncountable nouns (e.g. **a large amount** of money).

Scale of adjectives useful for expressing number and quantity:

tiny	small	average	large/considerable	gigantic /dʒaɪ'gæntɪk/	enormous/ huge/vast

Add just a **tiny amount** of chilli pepper, or else it may get too hot.
A **considerable number** of people failed to get tickets. [formal]
Vast/huge amounts of money have been wasted on this project.
Were there many people at the airport? Oh, about **average**, I'd say. [fairly informal]

NOTE
Much and **many** do occur in affirmatives, but they sound formal and are best kept for formal written contexts.

Much/many, a lot, lots, plenty, a good/great deal

example	*comments*
Is there **much** work to do? No, not **much**.	mostly used in questions and negatives with uncountable nouns
There are **lots of** nice shops in this street.	mostly for affirmatives; has a rather positive feeling; informal
Don't worry, there's **plenty** of time.	mostly for affirmatives; used in positive contexts
You were making **a lot of** noise last night.	used in all structures; neutral, better than **lots** in negative contexts
There's **a great deal of** hard work still to do.	+ uncountables, more formal

Much criticism has been levelled at the government's policy.
Many people are afraid of investing in stocks and shares.

B Informal and colloquial words for number/quantity

I've got **dozens** of nails in my tool box. Why buy more? [especially good for countables]
There's **heaps/bags/loads** of time yet, slow down! [countable or uncountable and informal; usually with singular *there is*, not *there are*]
There was absolutely **tons of** food at the party; far too much. [especially good for things, not so good for abstract nouns; again, note singular *there is*]
There are **tons of** apples on this tree this year; last year there were hardly any. [note how the verb here is plural because of 'apples', but singular in the example before with 'food' – number depends on the *noun* following, not on **tons/lots/loads**]
Just **a drop** of wine for me, please. [tiny amount of any liquid.]

C Degree and intensity

Typical collocations of adverbs: a bit/quite/rather/fairly/very/really/awfully/extremely combine with 'scale' adjectives such as tired, worried, weak, hot.

Totally/absolutely/completely/utterly combine with 'limit' adjectives (not measured on a scale; they are 'all or nothing' words) such as ruined, exhausted, destroyed, wrong.

Exercises

69.1 **Write responses to these statements using words from A opposite.**

EXAMPLE The Government will only give us a grant of £20. But that's a tiny sum of money. How mean!

1 £5 billion was wasted on developing the new rocket.
2 Over 50 people came to Sally's lecture yesterday. We were pleasantly surprised.
3 We have 120 students most years, and we'll probably have about that this year, too. Is that typical?
4 There was only five pounds in my purse when it was stolen.
5 We've wasted over 100 hours in meetings and got nowhere.

69.2 **Here are some more adjectives which can combine with *amount*. Divide them into two groups, *small* and *large* and fill in the bubbles. Use a dictionary if necessary.**

minuscule /mɪnɪskjuːl/ gigantic overwhelming minute /maɪnjuːt/ meagre excessive insignificant sizeable

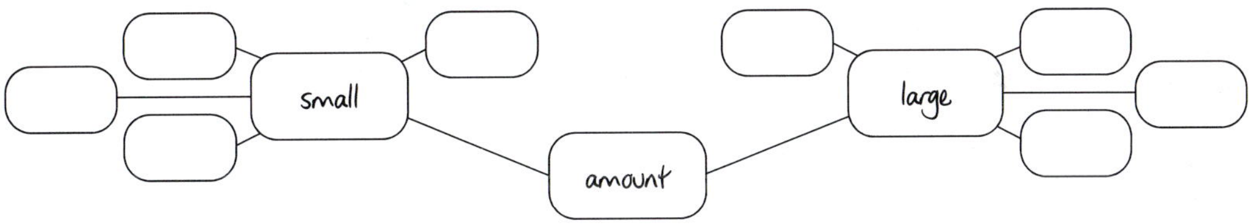

Now try using them to fill in the gaps below. More than one answer may be possible.

1 Even a .... amount of sand can jam a camera.
2 I've had an absolutely .... amount of work lately. I'm exhausted!
3 Oh, you've given me a .... amount of food here! I mustn't eat too much.
4 It takes a .... amount of money to start a business.
5 An .... amount of fat in your diet is dangerous.

69.3 **Fill in the gaps with *much/many*, *a lot/lots of*, *plenty of*, *a good/great deal of*.**

1 There's .... dust on these books. Fetch me a duster.
2 Please eat up; there's .... food.
3 There wasn't .... we could do, so we went home.
4 We've put .... energy into this plan. I hope it works.
5 .... people seem unable to cope with computers.

69.4 **Using intensifiers from C opposite, say how you might feel if the following happened.**

1 You heard that a friend was in trouble with the police.
2 A close friend coming to stay did not turn up, and sent no message to say why.
3 Three people gave you different directions to get to the same place.
4 You passed an exam you expected to fail.
5 Your best friend was going abroad for two years.
6 You had been working non-stop for 18 hours.

69.5 **Make four sentences of your own using the informal words from B opposite. Write about yourself / where you live, etc.**

70 Time

A Periods of time – words and typical contexts

the Ice Age **the Stone Age** **the Middle Ages** **the computer age**
[major historical/geological periods]

After the war, a new **era** of stability began. [long period, perhaps several decades]
The doctor said I needed a **period** of rest and relaxation, so I'm taking three months' unpaid leave. [very general word]
A **spell** of hot weather. He's had a couple of **spells** in hospital in the last two or three years. [indefinite but short]
During the 1980s I lived in Cork for a **time**. [vague, indefinite]
D'you want to borrow this book for a **while**? [indefinite but not too long]

B Useful phrases with time

The doctor says you should stay in bed **for the time being**. [not specific]

He can get a bit bad-tempered **at times**.

By the time we get home this pizza will be cold!

One **at a time**, please! I can't serve you all together.

We got there **just in time** for dinner.

I expected you to be late, the trains are never **on time**.

I've told you **time and time again** not to ring me at the office!

C Verbs associated with time passing

1980 → 1990 Ten years have **passed/elapsed** since I last heard from her.

Elapse is more formal and is normally used in the perfect or past, without adverbs. **Pass** can be used in any tense and with adverbs.

Don't worry. The time will **pass** quickly. Time **passes** very slowly **when** you're lonely.

London → 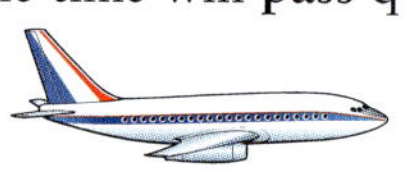 → Singapore It **takes** 12 hours to fly to Singapore.

The batteries in this radio usually **last** about three or four months.

This video tape **lasts/runs** for three hours.

The meeting **went on** for two hours.
[suggests longer than expected or desired]

Note also: **Take your time**, you don't need to hurry.

D Adjectives describing duration (how long something lasts)

He's a **temporary** lecturer; the **permanent** one's on leave.
Could we make a **provisional** booking now and confirm it later?
Venice has a **timeless** beauty. Christians believe in **eternal** life after death.

Exercises

70.1 **Fill the gaps with *age*, *era*, *period*, *spell*, or *time*.**

1 The Minister said that before the new law came into force there would be a .... of six months when people could hand in firearms without being prosecuted.
2 The twentieth century will be seen by historians as the .... of the car.
3 These factories mark the beginning of a new .... of industrial development for the country.
4 For a .... I thought I would never find a job, but then I was lucky.
5 We had a very cold .... in February. All the water pipes froze up.

70.2 **Which phrases from B opposite could you use in the following situations? Write exactly what you might say.**

EXAMPLE To a child who repeatedly leaves the fridge door open despite being told off often.
I've told you time and time again not to leave that fridge door open!

1 To someone you're happy to see who arrives just as you are serving tea/coffee.
2 On a postcard you expect will arrive at someone's house after you do.
3 A large group of people want to talk to you but you'd prefer to see them individually.
4 Ask someone to use an old photocopier while the new one is being repaired.
5 Explain to someone that the weather occasionally gets very cold in your country.
6 Tell someone you'll do your best to arrive punctually at a meeting.

70.3 **Complete the sentences using verbs from C opposite.**

1 The ferry crossing ...
2 Use this cassette to record, it will ...
3 These shoes have been great, they've ...
4 Everyone got bored because the speeches ...
5 The disaster occurred in 1932. Many years ...
6 I'll miss you terribly. I only hope the weeks ...
7 There's no hurry at all, just ...

70.4 **Match the queries with suitable responses.**

1 So, she's been promoted?	Well, provisionally.
2 Is it a lovely, quiet landscape?	Yes, she's permanent now.
3 So she's agreed to do it?	It's a temporary measure.
4 So, after death, life goes on?	Yes, absolutely timeless.
5 Language classes in the gym?	Yes, I believe it's eternal.

Follow-up: Your country/culture may have names for important periods of its history (for example, British people often refer to the years 1840–1900 as the 'Victorian era/period' because the monarch at the time was Queen Victoria). Make sure you can name or describe (in English) such time periods from your culture.

71 Distances and dimensions

You probably know all the common words for distances and dimensions. In this unit we concentrate on derived words and compounds and other connected words/phrases you may not know or may be unsure of how to use accurately.

A Broad and wide and tall and high

Wide is more common than **broad**, e.g. It's a very **wide** road/garden/room.

Make a note of typical collocations for **broad** as you meet them, e.g. Economics is a very broad subject; We came to a broad expanse of grassland. [big area]

Note the word order for dimensions, e.g. The room's **five metres long** and **four wide**.

(!) Don't forget that **tall** is for people but can be used for things such as buildings and trees when they are **high** and **thin** in some way. Otherwise, use **high** for things.

She's very **tall** for a five-year-old. Her office is in that **tall** building in the square.
There are some **high** mountains in the North.

B Deep ≠ shallow

The **deep** and **shallow** ends of a swimming pool.

C Derived words, phrases and compounds

long: Let's measure the **length** /leŋθ/ of this rope.
I swam 20 **lengths** (of the swimming pool).
I've **lengthened** her skirt for her. [**shorten**, see below]
Getting a visa can be a **lengthy** process. [usually refers to time; rather negative]
Can I make a **long-distance** phone call?

short: The new road will **shorten** our journey by ten minutes.
There's a **short cut** to the station. [quick way]

wide: Let's measure the **width** /wɪdθ/ of the room.
They're **widening** the road.

broad: I want to **broaden** my experience. [usually more abstract contexts]
She's very **broad-minded** and tolerant of others.

high: The **height** /haɪt/ of the wall is two metres.
The fog **heightened** the feeling of mystery. [usually used only for feelings and emotions]

low: You can **lower** the microphone if it is too high.

far: He loves travelling to **faraway** places.

deep: The **depth** of the river here is about 3 metres.
His death so soon after hers **deepened** our sadness. [often with feelings]

D Other verbs for dimensions and for changing them

Our garden **stretches** all the way to the river, so we have plenty of room to **extend** the house if we want to.

The cities are **spreading** [getting bigger] and the countryside is **shrinking** [getting smaller].

Exercises

71.1 **Complete B's replies using a suitable form of the dimension/distance words opposite.**

1 A: These trousers I've bought are too long.
B: Well, why don't you get ...

2 A: He's a big boy, isn't he? 1.90 metres!
B: Yes, he's ...

3 A: Why are we going across the field?
B: Just to get there a bit quicker; it's ...

4 A: We'll have to measure how high the room is.
B: That's not necessary; we already know the ...

5 A: The traffic seems to move far quicker on this road since I was last here.
B: Yes, well, they ...

6 A: Why do they have music on TV news programmes? It seems totally unnecessary!
B: Well, I think they want to create a feeling of drama, and the music is supposed to ...

71.2 **Give opposites for:**

1 a length of the pool
2 to shorten
3 a very broad range of goods
4 a local call
5 deep water
6 nearby places
7 narrow-minded

71.3 **Match the left- and right-hand columns.**

1 The city's spread a lot;	for miles along the river.
2 It takes ten weeks;	you should broaden it.
3 We extended the house	it's much bigger now.
4 You can choose;	there's a wide range.
5 Your experience is too narrow;	it's a lengthy business.
6 The forest stretches	to give us more room.

71.4 **Fill in the prepositions. If you are unsure, try looking up the word *distance* in a good dictionary.**

1 The car was parked .... a distance .... about 150 metres from the scene of the robbery.
2 I saw you .... the distance yesterday but didn't call out as you were with someone.
3 She's a great shot. She can hit an empty can .... a distance of about 100 feet.
4 What's the total distance .... here .... Paris?

71.5 **Use these verbs to fill the gaps. Check their usage in a dictionary if necessary.**

expand extend stretch shrink grow contract

1 AIDS .... rapidly during the 1980s.
2 The steel industry .... when the economy was strong, but now it has .... and only employs 8,000 people.
3 This sweater of mine has .... in the wash!
4 Our land .... as far as those trees there.
5 Our problems have .... since that new boss came.

72 Obligation, need, possibility and probability

A Obligation

Must is an instruction or command; that is why we see it on notices, e.g. Dogs **must** be kept on a lead. Cars **must** not be parked here. It is sometimes used to show urgency, e.g. It's an emergency; I **must** see the doctor right now!

Have (got) to says that circumstances oblige you to do something. Often, the meanings of *must* and *have to* overlap and either could be used, but not always.

I **must** get my hair cut! It looks awful! [command to yourself]

I've got to get my hair cut. I've got an interview tomorrow. [circumstances]

There's no bus service, so **I have to** walk to work. [circumstances]

I really **must** get a bicycle. [instruction to yourself]

The company **is obliged** to give a refund if the tour is cancelled.
You will **be liable** /'laɪəbəl/ for any damage when you rent a car. [obliged to pay; formal/legalistic]
The bank robbers **forced** him at gunpoint to open the safe.
We **had no choice/alternative but** to sell our house; we owed the bank £100,000.
The death sentence is **mandatory** /'mændətrɪ/ for drug-smuggling in some countries. [automatic; there is no alternative]
Was sport **compulsory** /kəm'pʌlsrɪ/ **obligatory** /ə'blɪgətrɪ/ at your school? No, it was **optional**. [/'ɒpʃənəl/ you can choose]
I am **exempt** /ɪg'zemt/ from tax as I'm a student. [free from obligation]

The negative of **must** and **have (got) to** are formed with **need** and **have to**, when we mean something is not necessary/not obligatory.

You **don't need to / don't have to / needn't** wash up; we've got a dishwasher.

B Need

The grass **needs** cutting (badly).[or '**wants** cutting', informal]
This plant is **in need of** water. [more formal than 'needs/wants']
The miners died through a **lack of** oxygen. [formal; there was none]
There is a **shortage** of doctors. [there are not enough]
There's a **need for** more discussion on the matter. [formal; we feel a need]

C Scale of probability: 'cannot happen' to 'has to happen'

impossible → unlikely → possible → probable → certain → inevitable

I've been given **an opportunity** to go to Bonn. [a real chance] *but*, Is there any **chance/possibility** you'll be free next week? [**chance** is less formal than **possibility**]

Exercises

72.1 **Continue the sentences using obligation words and phrases from A opposite with the words in brackets.**

1 They were losing £10 million a year, so the company ... (close down)
2 You don't have to buy the travel insurance; it's an ... (extra charge)
3 You can hire a video camera, but you ... (pay a deposit)
4 We'll have to sell the house, I'm afraid we have ... (otherwise, bankrupt)
5 This jacket's got curry stains on it; I really ... (the cleaners)
6 He didn't want to give them the money, but they had guns; they ... (hand it over)
7 No, he couldn't choose to pay a fine; a prison sentence is ... (for dangerous driving)
8 I didn't want to do maths, but I had to. It's ... (in all secondary schools)
9 How kind of you! You really ... (buy us a present)
10 If you're over 50, you're ... (military service)

72.2 **List something in your world which ...**

1 regularly needs cutting. my hair, the lawn
2 there is a lack of.
3 is obligatory once a year.
4 you are in need of.
5 is inevitable.
6 you no longer have to do.
7 was compulsory when you were at school.

72.3 **Use a dictionary to try to fill in the rest of this matrix. One line has already been done for you. If you cannot find out the collocations at all, use the key to this unit.**

✓ = typical ✗ = not a typical collocation

	highly	*quite*	*very*	*absolutely*
possible	✗	✓	✓	✗
impossible				
probable				
(un)likely				
inevitable				
certain				

72.4 **Use the collocations in 72.3 to say how probable/possible these are.**

1 Most people will have a videophone in their homes by 2025.
2 There will be rain in the Amazon forest within the next 8 days.
3 A human being will live to be 250.
4 We will all be dead by the year 2250.
5 A flying saucer will land in Hong Kong.
6 You'll be given an opportunity to meet the US President.
7 There will be a third world war.

Follow-up: Look at an English language newspaper and see how many possibility/probability words you can find in the main news stories.

73 Sound and light

A General words to describe sound

I could hear the **sound** of voices/music coming from the next room. [neutral]
The **noise** of the traffic here is pretty bad. [loud, unpleasant sounds]
The children are making a terrible **racket** upstairs. Could you go and tell them to be quiet? [informal; very loud, unbearable noise, often of human activity]

Noise and **sound** can both be countable or uncountable. When they are of short duration or refer to different sounds/noises, they are countable. When they mean a lot of continual or continuous sounds, they are uncountable.
Their lawnmower makes **a lot of noise**, doesn't it? [uncountable]
The **sound** of the sea is very relaxing. [uncountable]
I heard **some** strange **noises/sounds** in the night. [countable]

B Sound words and things that typically make them

The words can be used as nouns or verbs:
I could hear the rain **pattering** on the roof. We heard the **patter** of a little child's feet.

verb/noun	*example of what makes the sound*
bang	a door closing in the wind, someone bursting a balloon
rustle /ˈrʌsəl/	opening a paper/plastic bag, dry leaves underfoot
thud	a heavy object falling on to a carpeted floor
crash	a big, solid, heavy object falling on to a hard floor
clang	a big bell ringing, a hollow metal object being struck
clatter	a metal pan falling on to a concrete floor
hiss	gas/steam escaping through a small hole
rumble	distant noise of thunder, noise of traffic far away
roar /rɔː/	noise of heavy traffic, noise of a huge waterfall
ring	a small bell ringing, a telephone

C Darkness

Some adjectives for **dark** conditions. (For adjectives describing brightness, see Unit 76).
These brown walls are a bit **gloomy**. We should paint them white.
This torch is getting a bit **dim**. I think it needs new batteries.
It was a **sombre** /ˈsɒmbə/ room, with dark, heavy curtains. [serious, imposing]

D Types of light

Note these collocations.

The sun **shines** and gives out **rays** of light.
A torch gives out a **beam** of light.
A camera gives a **flash** of light.
Stars **twinkle**.
A candle-flame **flickers** in the breeze.
White-hot coal on a fire **glows**.
A diamond ring **sparkles**.
A gold object **glitters**.

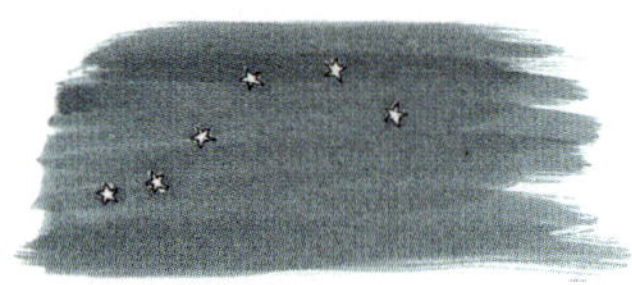

Exercises

73.1 **Choose *sound, noise*(s) or *racket* to fill the gaps. You may use the words more than once.**

1 There was a terrible .... outside the pub last night; it was a fight involving about six people.
2 I could sit and listen to the .... of the river all day.
3 My car's making some strange .... I'll have to have it checked.
4 Gosh! What an awful ....! I think you should take up a different instrument; the violin's just not for you!
5 I can't sleep if there's .... of any kind, so I use ear-plugs.

73.2 **Using the table opposite at B, what sound do you think each of these might make?**

1 A bottle of sparkling mineral water being opened.
2 A typewriter being dropped down an iron staircase.
3 A mouse moving among dead grass and leaves.
4 A rather overweight person falling on to a wooden floor.
5 A starting-gun for a sporting event.
6 A train passing at high speed a few feet away from you.
7 A slow train passing, heard through the walls of a house.

73.3 **As in the table at B opposite, make a note of something that might make the sound.**

verb/noun	*typical source(s) of the sound*
hum	....
rattle	....
bleep	....
screech	....
chime	....

73.4 **Join up the left-hand sentences with the right-hand ones so that they make sense.**

1 I saw a beam of light coming towards me.
2 The jewels sparkled in the sunlight.
3 The candle began to flicker uncertainly.
4 The first rays of the sun shone into the room.

Then it died, leaving us in complete darkness.
It was a police officer holding a flashlamp.
It was clearly time to get up and move out.
I'd never seen such a beautiful bracelet.

73.5 **Which do you think is the correct meaning of the underlined words in these sentences?**

1 She <u>beamed</u> at him.
a) smiled b) shouted c) attacked
2 After a day of skiing, our faces <u>glowed</u>.
a) were frozen b) were dried up c) were full of colour
3 He has a <u>twinkle</u> in his eyes.
a) a piece of grit b) a sign of humour/enjoyment c) a sign of anger

74 Possession, giving and lending

A Possession

All his **possessions** were destroyed in the terrible fire. [everything he owned]
Don't leave any of your **belongings** here; we've had a few thefts recently. [smaller things, e.g. bag, camera, coat; always plural]

Estate in the singular can mean a big area of private land and the buildings on it, or all of someone's wealth upon death.

She owns a huge **estate** in Scotland. [land, etc.]
After his death, his **estate** was calculated at £3 million. [all his wealth]

Property (uncountable) is used in a general sense for houses, land, etc.
He's only fourteen; he's too young to own **property**.

A **property** (countable) is a building (e.g. house, office-block) or land.
She owns some valuable **properties** in the town-centre.

B Words for people connected with ownership

The **proprietor** /prəˈpraɪətə/ of this restaurant is a friend of mine. [formal; used for shops, businesses etc.; **owner** is less formal]
The **landlord/lady** has put the rent up. [owner of rented property]
Do you own this house? No we're just **tenants**. [we rent it]

C Giving

The river **provides** the village **with** water / **provides** water **for** the village. [or supplies]
Would you like to **contribute/donate** something to the children's hospital fund?
Jakes Ltd. **supplies** our school **with** paper and other items. [often for 'selling' contexts]
It gives me pleasure to **present** you **with** this clock from us all.
The school restaurant **caters for** 500 people every day. [looks after the needs of]
That uncle of mine that died **left** £3,000 to a dogs' home.
When she died she **donated** all her books to the library. [for large gifts to institutions]
You've been **allocated** Room 24. Here's your key.

D Lending, etc.

(!) We've decided to **hire/rent** a car. Can you recommend a good **car-hire/car-rental** firm? [**rent** and **hire** are both commonly used]
We'd like to **rent** a flat in Oxford for six months. [not hire]
We've **hired** the lecture-room for a day. [not **rent**; short, temporary arrangements]

Remember: when you **lend**, you give, when you **borrow**, you receive.

(!) That tape-recorder you **lent** me last week, could I **borrow** it again?
I'm trying to get a **loan** from the bank to buy a boat.

Exercises

74.1 **What questions do you think were asked to get these answers?**

1 Oh no, we own it. Most houses here are owner-occupied.
2 Well, sorry, no; I need it to take photos myself.
3 You will be in Room 44B. It's quite a big office.
4 No, you have to buy exercise books and pens yourself. The school doesn't do that.
5 Actually, I've already given something. Sorry.
6 Oh, just a small house with a garden, you know, typical.
7 Yes, the charge is £200 for one that seats 30 people.

74.2 **The verbs in the middle column have been jumbled. Put them in their right sentences.**

1 A millionaire	provided	his entire library to the school.
2 The Director was	presented	the best parking-place.
3 My mother's cousin	donated	me £5,000 in her will.
4 A farmer nearby	catered	us with logs for the fire.
5 When I retired they	left	me with a camcorder.
6 The restaurant	allocated	for vegetarians.

74.3 **Some phrasal verbs connected with 'giving'. Check their meaning in a dictionary and then fill the gaps below.**

hand over   give out   let go of   give away   hand down

1 That bed has been .... in the family. It was my great-grandmother's originally.
2 Would you help us .... some leaflets in the shopping-centre?
3 I don't want to .... that old painting. It might be valuable one day.
4 When Tim's bike got too small for him we .... it ....; it wasn't worth trying to sell it, too much bother.
5 The landlord will .... the keys as soon as you pay the deposit and the first month's rent.

74.4 **Think of something that ...**

1 you would hand over to a mugger if threatened.
2 has been handed down in your family.
3 you have given away at some time in your life.
4 is often given out in classrooms.
5 you value and would not want to let go of.

74.5 **The rise and fall of Mr Fatcatt – a sad story. Fill the gaps with suitable words.**

Horace Fatcatt began his career by buying up old ....(1) in the city when prices were low. He got ....(2) from several banks to finance his deals, and soon he was one of the biggest private ....(3) in the city, with some 10,000 ....(4) renting houses and flats from him. He was also the ....(5) of many shops and businesses. He became very rich and bought himself a huge ....(6) in Scotland, but he ....(7) more and more money from the banks and soon the bubble burst. Recession came and he had to sell all his ....(8) and ....(9) – everything. He was left with just a few personal ....(10) and finally died penniless.

75 Movement and speed

Move is the basic verb for all movement, but do not forget it also means 'to move to a new house/flat', e.g. We've **moved**. Do you want our new address?

A Particular types of movement

Cars, lorries, etc. **travel/drive** along roads.
Trains **travel** along rails.
Boats/ships **sail** on rivers / across the sea.
Rivers/streams **flow/run** through towns/villages.

Things often have particular verbs associated with their types of movement. You should learn these as typical collocations as you meet them, and record them with a phrase or sentence.

White clouds **drifted** across the sky.
The flag **fluttered** in the wind.
The leaves **stirred** /stɜːd/ in the light breeze.
The trees **swayed** back and forth as the hurricane grew stronger.
The car **swerved** /swɜːvd/ to avoid a dog which had run into the road.

B Verbs to describe fast and slow movement

The traffic was **crawling along** because of the roadworks.

Stop **dawdling**! /'dɔːdlɪŋ/ We'll be late!

Suddenly a car came round the bend and **tore along** the road at high speed. Seconds later, a police car **shot past** after it.
Everyone was **hurrying/rushing** to get their shopping done before closing time.
The train was just **creeping/plodding along** at about 20 miles per hour. I knew we'd be late.

C Nouns to describe speed and their typical contexts

speed is a general word: used for vehicles, developments, changes, etc., e.g. We were travelling at high **speed**.
rate is often used in statistical contexts; the rate of increase/decrease, e.g. The birth **rate** is going down.
pace shows how you experience something as happening fast or slow, e.g. The lesson was going at a very slow **pace**.
velocity /və'lɒsɪti/ is used in technical/scientific contexts, e.g. The **velocity** of a bullet.

Exercises

75.1 **Write sentences which could come immediately *before* each of these sentences so that they make sense together.**

1 It was moving so much I thought it would break altogether.
2 It sails at dawn.
3 It flows through the capital city.
4 I had to swerve hard and nearly ended up in the river.
5 It was travelling at 80 miles per hour when it happened.

75.2 **What other things do you think could be described by each verb apart from the contexts given on the left-hand page. Use a dictionary if necessary.**

1 **sway:** a tree, ...
2 **crawl:** traffic, ...
3 **shoot:** a car, ...
4 **flutter:** a flag, ...
5 **drift:** a cloud, ...

75.3 **Fill the gap with *speed*, *rate*, *pace* or *velocity*. Use the guidelines on the left-hand page to help you.**

1 The .... of decline in this species is alarming.
2 I just couldn't stand the .... of life in the city, so I moved to a small village.
3 The police scientist said the bullet had come from a high .... rifle.
4 A: What .... were you doing at the time? B: Oh, about 60, I'd say.

75.4 **Use a dictionary to make notes to help you learn the difference between these near-synonyms. Make notes under the headings *usage* and *grammar*, as in the example.**

	usage	grammar
fast	e.g. fast car / fast train – refers to speed	adjective and adverb – 'she drove fast'
quick	refers to speed	
rapid		
swift		

75.5 **In what situations might you ...**

1 tear out of the house?
2 deliberately dawdle?
3 plod along at a steady pace?
4 not even dare to stir?
5 shoot past somebody's office/room?
6 creep around the house?

75.6 **People and verbs of motion. What sorts of people do you think these are? Use a dictionary if necessary.**

1 a slowcoach 2 a drifter 3 a plodder 4 a toddler

76 Texture, brightness, weight and density

A Texture – how something feels when you touch it

adjective	*typical examples*
smooth /smuːð/	the paper in this book
polished	varnished wood / a shiny metal surface
silky	silk itself / fine, expensive tights or stockings
sleek	highly polished, streamlined, new car bodywork
downy	new-born baby's hair
slippery	a fish just out of the water
furry /ˈfɜːri/	a thick sheepskin rug
rough /rʌf/	new, unwashed denim jeans / bark of a tree
coarse /kɔːs/	sand
jagged /ˈdʒægɪd/	sharp, irregular edges of broken glass or metal
prickly	a thistle, cactus, thorns on a rose
gnarled /naːld/	twisted, dead wood from an old tree

Your hair has a silky **feel**. This cotton is very smooth **to the touch**.
The table had a beautiful polished **surface** /ˈsɜːfɪs/. The ground was rough **underfoot**.

B Brightness

shiny leather shoes

carnival costumes full of **vivid** colours

a **shady** corner of the garden

a **dazzling** light

You wear such **dull** colours: why not get some **brighter** clothes?
The light's too **dim** to read in here. We need another lamp.
I wear sun-glasses when I drive because of the **glare** of the sun.

C Density and weight

A **solid** ≠ **hollow** object. She has **thick** ≠ **thin/fine** hair.
An area with **dense** ≠ **sparse** vegetation.
These boxes are rather **weighty**. [heavier than expected]
Your bag's **as light as a feather**! Have you brought enough?
Your bag's as **heavy as lead**! What's in it, bricks?
This suitcase is very **bulky/cumbersome** /ˈkʌmbəsəm/. [difficult, big and heavy]

Exercises

76.1 **How would you expect the following things to feel?**

1 The cover of a well-produced brochure.
2 The feathers in a pillow or duvet.
3 A wet bar of soap.
4 The branches of a rose-bush.
5 A gravel pathway.
6 The inside of a pair of sheepskin gloves.
7 The edge of a piece of broken, rusty metal.
8 Heavy, stone-ground wholemeal flour.
9 The surface of a mirror.
10 An old, dead log on the forest floor.

76.2 **Look round your own home and find:**

1 something sleek to the touch.
2 something rough underfoot.
3 something with a polished surface.
4 something furry.
5 something smooth.

76.3 **Here are the most common British weights with their metric equivalents. Try and answer the questions that follow.**

weight	*written as*	*approximate metric equivalent*
ounce	oz	28 grams } used for goods in shops, etc.
pound	lb	454 grams } used for goods in shops, etc.
stone	st	6.3 kilos → used for personal weight

1 A friend tells you her new baby weighed seven pounds at birth. Is this a huge, tiny or more or less average baby?
2 Someone tells you their cousin weighs 20 stone. What would you expect the cousin to look like?
3 You ask someone to get a piece of cheese at the market, enough for you personally for a week. They ask if 8 ounces will do. What would you say?
4 Make a note (a private one if you wish!) of your approximate weight in British terms.

76.4 **Quiz. Name the following.**

1 A creature with a sleek coat.
2 A slippery creature.
3 A prickly creature.
4 A creature with a furry coat.
5 A creature with a downy coat.

76.5 **Pair-puzzles. Each word has a letter in it that is part of a *related* word from the left-hand page. Fill in the letters, as in the example.**

				C	D
P		D	S	O	A
O	SHADY	E	H	A	Z
OUNCE	U	N	VI_ _ _	RO_ _ _	Z
N	_	S_ _ _ SE	N	S	GL_ _ _
D	_	E	Y	E	E

Can you make pair-puzzles with *cumbersome/bulky*, *lead/feather*?

77 Success, failure and difficulty

A Succeeding

We **succeeded in** persuad**ing** a lot of people to join our protest. [**in** + **ing**]
I **managed** to contact him just before he left his office.
I don't think I can **manage** the whole walk. I think I'll turn back. [**manage**, but not **succeed**, may have a direct object in this meaning]
We've **achieved** /ə'tʃiːvd/ **accomplished** /ə'kʊmplɪʃt/ a great deal in the last year. [both are used with quantity phrases such as 'a lot' / 'a little'; **accomplish** is rather formal.]
The company has **achieved** all its **goals/aims/targets** for this year. [**achieve** is more common than **accomplish** with nouns expressing **goals** and **ambitions**]
D'you think his plan will **come off**? [succeed; informal]

Matrix for some typical collocations with 'succeeding' verbs

	reach	*attain*	*secure*	*realise*	*fulfil*	*achieve*
an ambition		✓		✓	✓	✓
a dream				✓		✓
an agreement	✓		✓			
an obligation					✓	
a target	✓	✓				✓
a compromise	✓					✓

B Failing and difficulty

Plans and projects sometimes **go wrong** or **backfire**. [don't run out as intended]
Companies, clubs and societies often **fold / go under** through lack of success. [close down; **go under** is informal]
A plan or project may **falter** /'fɒltə/, even if it finally succeeds. [have ups and downs]
All your plans and hard work/efforts may **come to nothing**.
I have great **difficulty** in getting up in the morning. I **find it difficult** to remember the names of everybody in the class. [**hard** can also be used here; it is more informal]
It's hard/difficult to hear what she's saying.
I often **have trouble** starting the car on cold mornings. [more informal]
We've **had a lot of bother with** the neighbours lately. [very informal]
Can you **cope with** three more students? They've just arrived.
I've no money, my girl-friend's left me; I need help; I just **can't cope** any more.

C Word formation

verb	*noun*	*adjective*	*adverb*
succeed	success	successful	successfully
accomplish	accomplishment	accomplished	–
achieve	achievement	achievable	–
attain	attainment	attainable	–
fulfil	fulfilment	fulfilling	–
harden	hardness	hard	hard

Exercises

77.1 **Choose a suitable verb to fill the gap. If the exact word in the sentence is not in the vertical column of the matrix on the opposite page, look for something that is close in meaning. More than one verb is often possible.**

1 The management have .... an agreement with the union which will guarantee no strikes for the next three years.
2 Now that I've .... all my responsibilities to my family, I feel I can retire and go round the world.
3 The school building-fund has failed to .... its target of £250,000.
4 I never thought I would .... my ambition, but now I have.
5 Very few people .... all their hopes and dreams in life, very few indeed, I can tell you.
6 We hope the two sides .... a compromise and avoid war.
7 I'm afraid that little plan of mine didn't .... off.

77.2 **Fill in the missing word forms where they exist.**

verb	*noun*	*adjective*
realise	....	....
–	difficulty	....
....	target	....
fail	....	....
....	trouble	....

77.3 **Correct the mistakes in these sentences. The part which contains a mistake is underlined.**

1 I find ___ very difficult to understand English idioms.
2 She succeeded <u>to rise</u> to the top in her profession.
3 Do you ever have any trouble <u>to use</u> this photocopier? I always seem to.
4 I've <u>accomplished to work</u> quite hard this last month.
5 I'm amazed that you can cope ___ all the work they give you.

77.4 **What might happen if ... *or* What would you do if ...**

1 a plan backfired? *Abandon it. / Look for an alternative.*
2 you were having a lot of bother with your car?
3 a club had only two members left out of fifty?
4 a student faltered in one exam out of six, but did well in all the rest?
5 you started a small business but it came to nothing?
6 you couldn't cope with your English studies?

77.5 **In what sorts of situations would you hear the following remarks? Check any new words/phrases if you are not sure.**

1 We'll have to get an au pair. I just can't cope.
2 £5,000 and I've got nothing to show for it!
3 It collapsed, I'm afraid, and he's bankrupt now.
4 Yes, she pulled it off despite the competition.

78 Idioms and fixed expressions – general

Idioms are fixed expressions with meanings that are usually not clear or obvious. For example, the expression **to feel under the weather**, which means 'to feel unwell' is a typical idiom. The words do not tell us what it means, but the context usually helps.

A Tips for remembering idioms

Think of idioms as units, just like single words; always record the whole phrase in your notebook, along with information on grammar and collocation.

This tin-opener **has seen better days.** [it is rather old and broken down; usually of things, always perfect tense form]

(!) Idioms are usually rather informal and include a personal comment on the situation. They are sometimes humorous or ironic. As with any informal words, be careful how you use them. Never use them just to sound 'fluent' or 'good at English'. In a formal situation with a person you do not know, don't say,

'How do you do, Mrs Watson, Do **take** the **weight off your feet.**' [sit down].
Instead say 'Do sit down' or 'Have a seat'.

Idioms can be grouped in a variety of ways. Use whichever way you find most useful to help you remember them. Here are some possible types of grouping.

By grammar

get the wrong end of the stick [misunderstand] **pull a fast one** [trick/deceive somebody] **poke your nose in**(to) [interfere]	} verb + object
be over the moon [extremely happy/elated] **feel down in the dumps** [depressed/low] **be in the red** [have a negative bank balance]	} verb + prepositional phrase

By meaning e.g. idioms describing people's character/intellect

He's **as daft as a brush.** [very stupid/silly]
He **takes the biscuit.** /'bɪskɪt/ [is the extreme / the worst of all]
You're **a pain in the neck.** [a nuisance / difficult person]

By verb or other key word e.g. idioms with **make**

Why do you have to **make a meal out of** everything? [exaggerate the importance of everything]
I think we should **make a move.** It's gone ten o'clock. [go/leave]
Most politicians are **on the make.** I don't trust any of them. [wanting money/power for oneself]

B Grammar of idioms

(!) It is important when using idioms to know just how flexible their grammar is. Some are more fixed than others. For instance, **barking up the wrong tree** [be mistaken] is always used in continuous, not simple form, e.g. I think you're **barking up the wrong tree.** (*Not* I think you bark up the wrong tree.)

A good dictionary may help, but it is best to observe the grammar in real examples.

Note how Units 82–87 group idioms in different ways.

Exercises

78.1 **Complete the idioms in these sentences with one of the key words below, as in the example. If you are not sure, try looking up the key word in a good dictionary.**

clanger	shot	ocean	plate	block	handle	~~pie~~

1. All the promises these politicans make! It's just ..pie... in the sky. [big promises that will never materialise]
2. The small amount of money donated is just a drop in the .... compared with the vast sum we need. [tiny contribution compared with what is needed]
3. You really dropped a .... when you criticised the Americans last night; that man opposite you was from New York! [said something inappropriate/embarrassing]
4. I can't do that job as well; I've got enough on my .... as it is. [have more than enough work]
5. When I told her she just flew off the .... and shouted at me. [lost her temper]
6. His father was a gambler too. He's a real chip off the old .... [just like one's parents/grandparents]
7. I wasn't really sure; I guessed it; it was just a .... in the dark. [a wild guess]

78.2 **Use a good dictionary or a dictionary of idioms to see if it can help you decide which version of these sentences is correct for the idiom concerned, as in the example. Check the meaning too, if you are not sure.**

EXAMPLE You bark / are barking up the wrong tree if you think I did it. (see B opposite)

1. Holland is springing / springs to mind as the best place to go for a cycling holiday; it's very flat.
2. That remark is flying / flies in the face of everything you've ever said before on the subject.
3. He was innocent after all. It just goes / is just going to show that you shouldn't believe what you read in the papers.
4. You sit / 're sitting pretty! Look at you, an easy job, a fantastic salary, a free car!
5. His attitude is leaving / leaves a lot to be desired. I do wish he would try to improve a little.

78.3 **How would you organise these idioms into different groups? Use some of the ways suggested on the opposite page, plus any other ways you can think of.**

be in a fix child's play rough and ready be up to it hold your tongue
be out of sorts hold your horses a fool's errand odds and ends
stay mum give or take

78.4 **Without using a dictionary, guess the meaning of these idioms.**

1. It's midnight. Time to hit the sack.
2. This is just kid's stuff. I want something more difficult and challenging!
3. He was down and out for two years, but then he got a job and found a home for himself.
4. I can't understand why he's giving me the cold shoulder. He's usually so friendly.
5. I haven't seen Sam for ages. We only get together once in a blue moon.

79 Everyday expressions

Everyday spoken language is full of fixed expressions that are not necessarily difficult to understand but which have a fixed form which does not change. These have to be learnt as whole expressions. These expressions are often hard to find in dictionaries, so it is important to be on the lookout for them.

A Conversation-building expressions

These are some common expressions that help to modify or organise what we are saying. There are many more expressions like these. (See also Units 27 & 28.)

expression		*meaning/function*
As I was saying, I haven't seen her for years.	→	takes the conversation back to an earlier point
As I/you say, we'll have to get there early to get a seat.	→	repeats and confirms something someone has already said
Talking of skiing, whatever happened to Bill Jakes?	→	starting a new topic, but linking it to the present one
If you ask me, she's heading for trouble.	→	if you want my opinion (even if no-one has asked for it)
That reminds me, I haven't rung George yet.	→	something in the conversation reminds you of something important
Come to think of it, did he give me his number after all? I think he may have forgotten.	→	something in the conversation makes you realise there may be a problem/query about something

B Key words

Some everyday expressions can be grouped around key words. **This** and **that**, for example, occur in several expressions:

THIS/THAT

This is it. [this is an important point]

That's it. [that's the last thing, we've finished]

We talked about **this and that,** or **this, that and the other.** [various unimportant matters]

So, **that's that,** then. [that is agreed, settled, finalised]

C Common expressions for modifying statements

If the worst comes to the worst, we'll have to cancel the holiday. [if the situation gets very bad indeed]

If all else fails, we could fax them. [if nothing else succeeds]

What with one thing and another, I haven't had time to reply to her letter. [because of a lot of different circumstances]

When it comes to restaurants, this town's not that good. [in the matter of restaurants]

As far as I'm concerned, we can eat any time. [as far as it affects me / from my point of view]

As luck would have it, she was out when we called. [by chance]

Exercises

79.1 **Complete the fixed expressions in these sentences, without looking at the left-hand page, if possible.**

1 Come ...., I don't remember giving her the key. I'd better ring her and check, just in case.
2 If you ...., the economy's going to get much worse before it gets any better.
3 .... holidays, have you got any plans for next year?
4 A: It's going to be expensive.
B: Yes, it'll be fun, and a great opportunity, but as ...., it will be expensive.
5 That ...., I have a message for you from Sid.
6 As ...., before the telephone interrupted us, we plan to extend the house next spring.

79.2 **Which of the expressions with *this/that* opposite would be most suitable for the second parts of these mini-dialogues?**

1 A: What were you and Lindsay talking about?
B: Oh, ...
2 A: How many more?
B: No more, actually, ...
3 A: Here comes the big announcement we've been waiting for.
B: Yes, ...
4 A: OK, I'll take our decisions to the committee.
B: Right so, ..., then. Thanks.

79.3 **See if you can complete this network of everyday expressions with *now*, as with the *this/that* network opposite. Use a dictionary if necessary.**

....
[occasionally]

NOW

.... [attract attention because you're going to say something]

.... [immediately; also used to emphasise your point]

Use the expressions with *now* to rewrite these sentences.

1 Do you want me to do it straight away, or can it wait?
2 So, everybody, listen carefully. I have news for you.
3 I bump into her in town occasionally, but not that often.

79.4 **Which expressions in this unit contain the following key words?**

1 comes 2 luck 3 fails 4 worst 5 far 6 thing

Follow-up: Make a list of common expressions like the ones in this unit in your language. How do you say them in English?

80 Similes

A As ... as

As ... as similes are easy to understand. If you see the phrase **as dead as a doornail**, you don't need to know what a doornail is, simply that the whole phrase means 'totally dead'. But, remember fixed similes are usually informal/colloquial and often humorous. Those marked * are derogatory. Use all these expressions with care and keep them generally as part of your receptive vocabulary.

Creating a picture in your mind can often help you remember the simile:

as **blind** as a **bat***

as **thin** as a **rake***

as **strong** as an **ox**

as **quiet** as a **mouse**

Some can be remembered as pairs of opposites.

as **heavy** as **lead** /led/ ≠ as **light** as a **feather**   as drunk as a **lord*** ≠ as sober as a **judge**
as black as **night** ≠ as white as **snow** [particularly used in fairy tales]

Some can be remembered by sound patterns.

as **brown** as a **berry**   as **good** as **gold** [this is used about children's behaviour]
as **cool** as a **cucumber**   as **busy** as a **bee**

Some other useful **as ... as** phrases.

The bed was **as hard as iron** and I couldn't sleep.
I'll give this plant some water. The soil's **dry as a bone.**
He's **as mad as a hatter***. He crossed the Atlantic in a bathtub.
She told the teacher, **as bold as brass**, that his lessons were boring.
You'll have to speak slowly and clearly; he's **as deaf as a post***.
Don't worry. Using the computer's **as easy as falling off a log.**
She knew the answer **as quick as a flash.**
When I told him, his face went **as red as a beetroot.**

Sometimes the second part can change the meaning of the first.

The Princess's skin was **as white as snow**. [beautifully white]
When he saw it, his face went **as white as a sheet**. [pale with fear/horror]
The fish was bad and I was **as sick as a dog**. [vomiting]
She ran off with my money; I felt **as sick as a parrot**. [bad feeling of disillusionment/frustration]

> **TIP** You can usually make a simile using **as ... as can be**. For example, I need a drink, I'm **as thirsty as can be**.

B Like

My plan **worked like a dream**, and the problem was soon solved.
Be careful the boss doesn't see you; she **has eyes like a hawk**.
No wonder he's fat. He **eats like a horse** and **drinks like a fish***.
Did you **sleep** well? Yes, thanks, **like a log**.
Sorry, I forgot to ring him again. I've got a **brain/head like a sieve!**
The boss is **like a bear with a sore head** today. [in a very bad temper]
She goes around **like a bull in a china shop***. [behaving in a very clumsy, insensitive way]
Criticising the government in his presence is **like a red rag to a bull**. [certain to make him very angry]

Exercises

80.1 **Complete the as ... as similes.**

1 Rosie is as mad as a ....; you wouldn't believe the crazy things she does.
2 You're not eating enough; you're as thin as a ....
3 He never says a thing; he's as quiet as a ....
4 You'll have to shout; she's as deaf as a ....
5 I'm afraid I can't read this small print; I'm as blind as a .... without my glasses.

80.2 **Different similes contain the same word. Fill the gap with the appropriate words.**

1 I feel great now. I .... like a log.
2 No! It's as easy as .... off a log.
3 After eating that bad cheese I was as sick as a ....
4 I knew she had deceived me. I felt as sick as a ....
5 The old man's hair was as white as ....
6 Her face suddenly went as white as a ....

80.3 **Put the correct number in the right-hand boxes to complete the similes, as in the example. There are two that are not on the left-hand page. Try and guess them.**

	1	quick			daisy
	2	red		5	ox
as	3	flat	as a(n)		flash
	4	fresh			beetroot
	5	strong			pancake

80.4 **Simile word puzzle. Fill in the answers, as in the example.**

Across	Down
1 bold	1 blind
2 mad	2 iron
4 white	3 log
5 fresh	6 cold
7 quiet	8 cool
9 dry	10 light

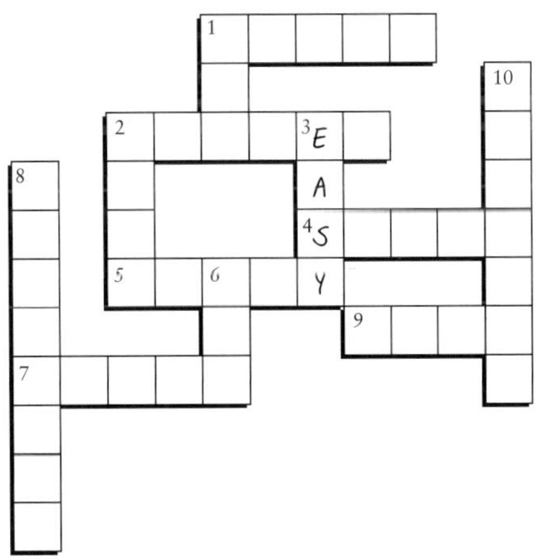

80.5 **What can you say about ...**

1 a person who sees everything and never misses a thing?
2 a plan or course of action that works very well?
3 someone who eats and drinks a great deal?
4 someone with a very bad memory?
5 someone who has been very active and busy all day?

81 Binomials

Binomials are expressions (often idiomatic) where two words are joined by a conjunction (usually 'and'). The order of the words is usually fixed. For example:

odds and ends: small, unimportant things, e.g. Let's get the main things packed; we can do the **odds and ends** later. (We cannot say 'ends and odds'.)

give and take: a spirit of compromise, e.g. Every relationship needs a bit of **give and take** to be successful.

A

You can often tell something is a binomial because of the sound pattern.

Tears are **part and parcel** of growing up. [part of / belong to]
The boss was **ranting and raving** /'reɪvɪŋ/ at us. [shouting / very angry]
The old cottage has gone to **rack and ruin.** [ruined/decayed]
He's so **prim and proper** at work. [rather formal and fussy]
The hotel was a bit **rough and ready.** [poor standard]
She has to **wine and dine** important clients. [entertain]

B

Other times, the clue is that the words are near-synonyms.
You can **pick and choose**; it's up to you. [have a wide choice]
My English is progressing in **leaps and bounds.** [big jumps]
It's nice to have some **peace and quiet.** [peace/calm]
The doctor recommended some **rest and recreation / R and R.** [relaxation]
First and foremost, you must work hard. [first / most importantly]

C

Many grammar words combine to form binomials.

There are cafés **here and there.** [scattered round]
We've had meetings **on and off.** [occasionally]
I've been running **back and forth** all day. [to and from somewhere]
To and fro can be used just like **back and forth.**
He is unemployed and **down and out.** [without a home or money]
She's better now, and **out and about** again. [going out]
She ran **up and down** the street. [in both directions]

D

Your language probably has many binomials. Make sure those which look similar in English have the same word order as your language. These four are very neutral binomials and can be used in formal or informal situations. Try translating them.

A **black and white** film, please. **Ladies and gentlemen**, your attention, please!
She ran **back and forth**. There was **hot and cold** water in every room.

E

Binomials linked by words other than **and.**

You've got your sweater on **back to front.** [the wrong way]
He won't help her; she'll have to **sink or swim.** [survive or fail]
Slowly but surely, I realised the boat was sinking. [gradually]
Sooner or later, you'll learn your lesson. [some time/day]
She didn't want to be just friends; it had to be **all** or **nothing.**
Well I'm sorry, that's all I can offer you; **take it or leave it.**
It's about the same distance as from here to Dublin, **give or take** a few miles. [perhaps a mile or two more, or a mile or two less]

Exercises

81.1 **Here is a list of words that can combine to form binomials (some are from the left-hand page and some are new). Using similarities in sound, join them with *and*. Then check opposite or in a dictionary that you have the right word order and meaning.**

prim dine high ruin rough dry
rack ready proper sound safe wine

Now use them to fill the gaps in these sentences.

1 I was left .... and ...., with no-one to help me.
2 The room's a bit .... and ...., but you're welcome to stay as long as you like.
3 I'm glad you're .... and .... after such a dangerous journey.
4 My hosts .... and .... me at the best restaurants.
5 Our old house in the country has just gone to .... and ....; nobody looks after it now.
6 The secretary is always so terribly .... and ....; the whole atmosphere always seems so very formal.

81.2 **Match words from the left-hand box with words from the right-hand box to form binomials, as in the example *law and order*. There are more words on the right than you'll need. Look for words that are either near-synonyms or antonyms (opposites) of the left-hand word.**

law	now	hit	clean
pick	sick	leaps	

and

money	tidy	drop	tired	soon
snow	pay	bounds	terrible	
clocks	after	whisper	order	
then	dogs	scratch	heart	
choose	flowers	miss	chase	

81.3 **Now rewrite these sentences using the binomials you formed in 81.2. The new sentences will often sound more informal than the original sentences.**

1 There are lots of courses. You can make your own selection.
2 The flat looks all neat and spotless now for our visitors.
3 I have had enough of traffic jams. I'm going to start using the train.
4 Finding the right people was rather difficult; sometimes we succeeded, sometimes we failed.
5 My knowledge of English has progressed rapidly since I've been using this book.
6 The new Prime Minister promised that efficient policing would be the most important policy.
7 I've seen her occasionally, taking her dog for a walk.

81.4 **These binomials do not have *and* in the middle. What do they have? Check the opposite page or in a dictionary if you are not sure.**

1 sooner ...... later
2 all ...... nothing
3 back ...... front
4 sink ...... swim
5 slowly ...... surely
6 make ...... break

82 Idioms describing people

A Positive and negative qualities

positive

She has a heart of gold.
[very kind, generous]

He's as good as gold.
[generous, helpful, well-behaved used generally for children]

negative

She's as hard as nails.
[no sympathy for others]

He's rather a cold fish.
[distant, unfriendly]

Note also:
He's such **an awkward customer**. [difficult person to deal with]
She's **a pain in the neck**. Nobody likes her. [nuisance, difficult]
He **gets on everyone's nerves**. [irritates everybody]

B People's 'fast' and 'slow' qualities

fast

He's very **quick off the mark**; he always gets things before everybody else.

You've asked him to marry you! You're **a fast worker**! You only met him three weeks ago!

slow

I was a bit **slow off the mark**; the job had been filled by the time I got the forms.

Come on! Hurry up! You're such **a slowcoach**!

C How people relate to the social norm

She's a bit of **an odd-ball**; very strange. [peculiar, strange]
He's really **over the top**. [very exaggerated in behaviour]
He's (gone) **round the bend**, if you ask me. [absolutely crazy/mad]
My politics are very **middle-of-the-road**. [very normal; no radical ideas; neither left- nor right-wing]

D Who's who in the class? Idioms for 'people in the classroom'

teacher's pet

Mary's **top of the class**

a real **know-all**

a bit of **a big-head**

a lazy-bones

The last three idioms are used of people outside the **classroom situation**, too.

Exercises

82.1 **Try to complete these idioms from memory if possible.**

1 She does a lot of voluntary work; she has a heart ...
2 Don't expect any sympathy from the boss; she's as hard ...
3 I'm sure Gerry will help you; he's as good ...
4 I was too late to get on that course; I was a bit slow ...
5 You won't find him very friendly; he's rather a cold ...
6 Tell him to hurry up! He's such a ...

82.2 **What do we call ...**

1 an irritating person who knows everything?
2 the person who is the teacher's favourite?
3 someone who thinks they are the best and says so?
4 the one who gets the best marks?
5 a person who is very lazy?

82.3 **You can also learn idioms by associating them with a key word or words. For example, two idioms on the left-hand page have *gold* in them and two have *mark*. Which are they? Here is a word-fork based on *to have + head*. Use the expressions to finish the sentences below.**

to have
- one's head screwed on [be sensible]
- a head for heights [not suffer from vertigo]
- a head like a sieve [bad memory; see Unit 80]
- a good head for figures [be good at maths]
- one's head in the clouds [unaware of reality]

1 I'd better write it in my notebook. I have ...
2 Ask Martha to check those sums. She has ...
3 Don't ask me to go up that tower. I'm afraid I don't ...
4 She's very sensible and knows what she's doing. She ...
5 He's quite out of touch with reality. He really ...

Look for other sets of idioms based on key words.

82.4 **Mini-quiz. Which part of the body might a difficult person (a) *get on* (b) *be a pain in*?**

82.5 **Which idioms do you think these drawings represent?**

1

2
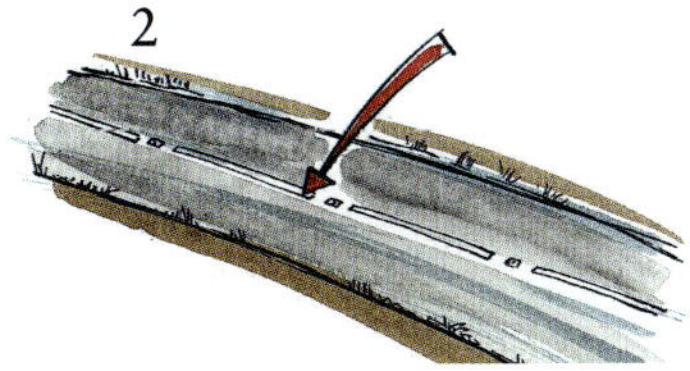
3

82.6 **Try guessing from the context what the underlined idioms mean.**

1 Don't get angry with him. <u>His heart's in the right place</u>.
2 Joe's <u>a bit of a square peg in a round hole</u> here. I think he should get a job which suits his character better.
3 A: Hey! I'm talking to you! B: Sorry, I <u>was miles away</u>.

83 Idioms describing feelings or mood

A Positive feelings, moods and states

Mary seems to be **on cloud nine** these days. [extremely pleased/happy]
Everyone seemed to be **in high spirits.** [lively, enjoying things]
She seems to be **keeping her chin up.** [happy despite bad things]
Jo's **as happy as the day is long.** [extremely content]

B Negative feelings, moods and states

He had **a face as long as a fiddle.** [looked very depressed/sad]
She certainly **looked down in the dumps.** [looked depressed/sad]
Gerry is **in a (black) mood.** [a bad mood/temper]
Martin was **like a bear with a sore head.** [extremely irritable] (See Unit 80.)

C Physical feelings and states

I could eat a horse! [very hungry]
I'm **feeling all in.** [exhausted]
You're looking **a bit under the weather.** [not very well / ill]
She looked, and felt, **on top form.** [in good physical condition]
I suddenly **felt as if my head was going round.** [dizzy]
I was almost **at death's door** last week! [very sick or ill]
Old Nora's **as fit as a fiddle.** [very fit indeed]

D Fear/fright

She was **scared stiff.** [very scared]
She **frightened the life out of him.** [frightened him a lot]
We were all **shaking in our shoes.** [trembling with fear]
The poor lad was **scared out of his wits.** [very scared indeed]
I **jumped out of my skin** when I heard the bang. [gave a big jump]

NOTE
There is an element of **exaggeration** in these idioms in B, C and D. They make comments on the situation and lighten the tone of what you are saying. So use them only informally.

E

Horoscopes are often a good place to find idioms about moods and states, since the horoscope usually tries to tell you how you are going to feel during the coming day/week/month. Look at these horoscopes and note the idioms in italics.

Capricorn (21.12–19.1)
Don't *get carried away*[1] by promises that won't be kept. *Keep a cool head*[2] and take everything as it comes. On the work front, things are looking better.

Taurus (21.4–20.5)
Someone will say something that will *make you swell with pride*[3] and you may *feel on top of the world*[4] for a while, but the evening will not be so easy.

(1) be fooled (2) stay calm (3) feel very proud (4) very happy indeed

Exercises

83.1 **Here are some more idioms that can be grouped as expressing either *positive* or *negative* feelings. Try to group them, using a dictionary if necessary.**

to be over the moon   to feel/be a bit down
to feel/be as pleased as Punch   to feel/be browned off

83.2 **Using the idioms from 83.1 and from A and B opposite, say how you would probably feel if ...**

1 you were told you had just won a vast sum of money. I'd be over the moon!
2 your boss said you had to do again a piece of work you'd already done three times.
3 you were told you'd got a very high mark in an exam.
4 you had a bad toothache and your neighbour was making a lot of noise late at night.
5 nothing seemed to have gone right for you that day.
6 someone you were secretly in love with told you they were in love with you.

83.3 **Complete the idioms in these sentences.**

1 Don't creep up behind me like that! You frightened the ...
2 I don't need a doctor, I just feel a bit under ...
3 As long as he has his car to work on, he's as happy ...
4 Last year, when I won that medal, I really was on ...
5 I wasn't expecting such a loud bang; I nearly jumped ...
6 I've had nothing since lunch; I could ...
7 I feel a bit down this week; last week I felt on top ...

83.4 **Find idioms to do with feelings, moods and states in these horoscopes. Underline them, then check the meaning in a dictionary if necessary.**

Scorpio (23.10–22.11)
You may get itchy feet today, but be patient, this is not a good time to travel. Events at work will keep you on the edge of your seat for most of the day. Altogether an anxious time for Scorpios.

Leo (21.7–21.8)
You'll be up in arms over something someone else close to you says rather thoughtlessly today, but don't let it spoil things. You may be in two minds over an invitation, but think positively.

83.5 **Now use the idioms from 83.4 to rewrite these sentences.**

1 I can't decide about that job in Paris.
2 I've been in suspense all day. What's happened? Tell me!
3 Her son became restless to travel and went off to Uruguay.
4 Everyone protested loudly when they cancelled the trip.

83.6 **Which idioms opposite include the words *head*, *wits*, *swell*, *black* and *carried*? Write a sentence using each one.**

Follow-up: Collect more horoscopes from popular English magazines and make a list of any idioms you find in them.

84 Idioms describing problematic situations

A Problems and difficulties

idiom		*literal phrase*
to be in a **fix**	=	be in difficulty
to be in a **tight corner**	=	be in a situation that is hard to get out of
to be in a **muddle**	=	be confused / mixed up

(these three go together as all having **be + in + a**)

Reacting in situations: more or less opposite idioms

to **take a back seat** [not to do anything; let others act instead]	≠	to **take the bull by the horns** [act positively to face and attack the problem]
to **stir things up** [do/say things that make the situation worse]	≠	to **pour oil on troubled waters** [do/say things that calm the situation down]
to **keep one's cards close to one's chest** [hold back information]	≠	to **lay one's cards on the table** [be very open, state exactly what your position is]

B Idioms with get

This has to be done by next week; we must **get our act together** before it's too late. [organise ourselves to respond; informal]

We need a proper investigation to **get to the bottom of things**. [find the true explanation for the state of affairs]

It's quite difficult to **get** people **to sit up and take notice**. [make them pay attention]

I'm trying to **get a grasp** of what's happening; it's not easy. [find out / understand]

C Changes and stages in situations

The tide has turned for us; better days are ahead.

We can see **light at the end of the tunnel** at last.

I'm afraid we've just **come to a dead end** with our plans.

I think I've **reached a turning-point** in my career.

The government and the unions have **buried the hatchet** for the time being. [made peace / stopped fighting each other]

All that trouble last year was just **swept under the carpet** in the end. [ignored / deliberately forgotten, without solving it]

You should say sorry. **It would go a long way.** [would help a lot]

Exercises

84.1 **When looking up words and idioms in your dictionary, look at what is just before and after the information you are looking for. In this way you can pick up some related words and/or expressions which you can record together. For example, if you look up *take the bull by the horns* in a dictionary, you will probably also find these idioms:**

(to be/act) **like a bull in a china shop** [be very clumsy]
(to talk) **a load of bull** [talk nonsense; informal]

Look up these idioms using the words underlined as your key word and see what other idioms or useful phrases you can find around them in the dictionary.

1 let the cat out of the bag
2 be in a fix
3 to pour oil on troubled waters
4 to stir things up

84.2 **Choose suitable idioms from the opposite page to fill the gaps.**

1 I think I'll just .... and let everyone else get on with sorting matters out.
2 No, please, don't say anything: you'll only ....
3 It's been a long, hard struggle, but I think at last we can see ....
4 The police are trying their best to get to ...., but it's a real mystery at the moment.
5 I'm sorry, I'm in ....; could you explain that again?
6 At last I've managed to get him to sit ....; he's done nothing at all for us so far.
7 I find it difficult to get a .... this global warming business, don't you?
8 I think we should take the bull .... and sort it out. I don't think it should be just swept ....

84.3 **Here are some more idioms connected with situations. Can you paraphrase their meaning, as in the example?**

1 It's not working; we'll have to go back to square one. go back to the beginning again
2 The teachers want one thing, the students want the exact opposite. I'm sure we can find a happy medium.
3 We were on tenterhooks all night waiting for news from the hospital. They finally rang us at 6.30 a.m.
4 Poverty and crime go hand in hand in this part of town.
5 You've been in a lot of trouble lately; you'd better toe the line from now on.

84.4 **What *questions* could be asked to get these answers?**

1 Well, we've buried the hatchet for the moment, but I'm sure it's not for good.
2 Yes, it's been a real turning-point in my career.
3 Yes, I think it would go a long way. You know how sensitive he is, and how he appreciates little gestures.

Follow-up: In an English language magazine, find an article that discusses some kind of problematic situation. Are any idioms used in the discussion of the problem? Write sentences of your own including any new and interesting idioms.

85 Idioms connected with praise and criticism

A Idioms connected with praise

Saying people/things are better than the rest

Mary is **head and shoulders above** the rest of the girls. *or* She's **miles better** than the other girls. [used usually of people]

When it comes to technology, Japan **is streets ahead** of most other countries. [can be used of people or things]

When it comes to exam passes, St John's school usually **knocks spots off** the other schools. [used of people or things]

That meal was just **out of this world**. [outstanding/superb; usually used of things]

Saying people are good at something

She's a **dab-hand at** carpentry, just like her father. [usually for manual skills]

He's a really **first-rate / top-notch** administrator, the very best.

When it comes to grammar, she's **really on the ball**. [knows a lot]

Bill **has a way with** foreign students. The other teachers envy him. [good at establishing good relations / motivating them, etc.]

Marjorie really **has green fingers**; look at those flowers! [good at gardening]

Let him do the talking; he's **got the gift of the gab**. [good at talking]

B Idioms connected with criticism

NOTE
There are far more of these idioms in common use than ones connected with praise!

You can group some according to form; for example, **'s** idioms include several connected with criticising people and things.

She thinks she's **the cat's whiskers** /'wɪskəz/ **the bee's knees**. [thinks she's wonderful]

He was dressed up like a **dog's dinner**. [over-dressed in a showy way]

When it comes to time-keeping, he's **the world's worst**. [no-one is worse]

I'm sorry, this essay of yours is a **dog's breakfast**. [a mess / very badly done]

This group could be learned in association with 'food' words.

When it comes to unreliability, he really **takes the biscuit**. [is the epitome / most striking example of some negative quality] (See Unit 78.)

Mary **wants to have her cake and eat it**! [wants everything without any contribution from her side]

I think he's just trying to **butter me up**. [give false praise in order to get something]

A pay-rise and a company car! **You want jam on it**, you do! [have totally unreasonable expectations/demands]

Note these idiomatic synonyms of the verb **to criticise**:

You shouldn't **run down** your own country when you're abroad.

Why do you always have to **pick holes** in everything I say?

Exercises

85.1 **Using idioms from A opposite, rewrite these sentences without changing the meaning.**

1 The hotel we were staying in was absolutely superb.
2 Joe is a long way above the other kids when it comes to doing hard sums.
3 This restaurant is much, much better than all the other restaurants in town.
4 You're a long way ahead of me in understanding all this new technology; I'm impressed.

85.2 **Which idioms from A and B opposite might these pictures help you to remember?**

1

2

3

4

85.3 **Which of the expressions in 85.2 is most suitable for:**

1 praising someone's knowledge/ability in their profession?
2 saying that something is a real mess?
3 saying someone has a very high opinion of themselves?
4 praising someone's gardening skills?

85.4 **Express the *opposite* meaning to these sentences using idioms from the left-hand page.**

EXAMPLE He's a third-rate athlete. He's a first-rate (or top-notch) athlete.

1 She was dressed beautifully, just right for the occasion.
2 Penny has such an inferiority complex.
3 She's hopeless at DIY; just look at those bookshelves she made.
4 He is no good at talking to people at all.
5 Mick doesn't get on with the secretaries; just look at how they react when he wants something done.
6 He wants a new office, a secretary and a new computer. But compared to what Geoff wants he isn't expecting much!
7 She said I was the best boss they'd ever had. It was obvious she was praising me sincerely. I wonder what she wants?
8 He often says how wonderful his school is.
9 She always praises everything I say.

85.5 **Using a good dictionary or a dictionary of idioms, find more idioms that include the 'food' words below for praising or criticising people/things/actions. Make sentences with the expressions.**

1 ham 2 tea 3 icing 4 nut 5 onion 6 cream

Follow-up: Look at the agony column (the place where people send letters telling their personal problems) in a magazine, and see how many idioms are used to describe people in positive and negative ways.

86 Idioms connected with using language

A Idioms connected with communication problems

They're **talking at cross-purposes.**

He's **got the wrong end of the stick.**

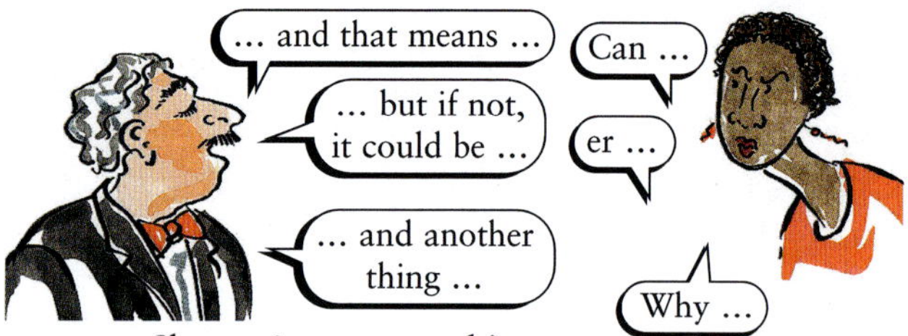

She **can't get a word in edgeways** /ˈedʒweɪz/.

I can't make head or tail of what she's saying.

B Good talk, bad talk

The boss always **talks down** to us. [talks as if we were inferior]

My work-mates are always **talking behind my back.** [saying negative things about me when I'm not there]

It was just **small talk,** nothing more, I promise. [purely social talk, nothing serious]

Let's sit somewhere else; they always **talk shop** over lunch, and it bores me rigid. [talk about work]

Hey! Your new friend's become a real **talking-point** among the staff! Did you know? [subject that everyone wants to talk about]

It's gone too far this time. I shall have to **give him a talking to.** [reproach/scold him]

C Talk in discussions, meetings, etc.

1 start the discussion
2 say it in few words
3 come to the important part of the matter
4 say exactly what I think
5 finish the discussion
6 says intelligent, reasonable things
7 says stupid things
8 says things in a long, indirect way

Exercises

86.1 **Look at these dialogues and comment on them, as in the example.**

EXAMPLE A: £98 for a meal! That's outrageous!
B: Not the meal, you twit! The room!
They seem to be talking at cross-purposes.

1 JOE: So that's what I'm going to do, take it all away.
ANN: What about –
JOE: And if they don't like it they can just go and do what they like.
ANN: If she –
JOE: Not that I have to consult them, anyway, I'm in charge round here.
ANN: I wonder whether it –
JOE: You see, I'm the kind of person who can take a hard decision when it's needed.
It seems that Ann can't get ....

2 MICK: I got very upset when you said I was childish.
GRACE: I didn't, honestly! All I said was that you seemed to get on very well with the children. Honestly.
MICK: Oh, I see. Oh, sorry.
It seems that Mick got the ....

3 DAN: So, area-wise the down-matching sales profile commitment would seem to be high-staked on double-par.
REG: Eh? Could you say that again? You've got me there.
It seems that Reg can't make ....

4 MADGE: I don't expect someone with your intelligence to understand this document.
ERIC: Thank you.
Madge seems to be talking ....

86.2 **What idioms opposite do these drawings represent?**

1 the discussion

3 start

2 talk

4 get to / come to

86.3 **Fill the gaps to complete the idioms.**

1 She is very direct and always .... her mind.
2 I got bored with small ....; let's get down to serious matters. I'm in love with you.
3 The boss gave me a real .... to after that stupid mistake I made. Still I was in the wrong.
4 You're behind the times! Darren's girlfriend was *last* week's .... point.

87 Miscellaneous idioms

A Idioms connected with paying, buying and selling

He **bought a real pig in a poke** when he got that car. [buy something without examining it properly first]

We'll probably have to **pay over the odds** for a hotel room during the week of the festival. [pay more than the usual rate]

He did £600 worth of damage to the car and his parents had to **foot the bill**. [pay up, usually a large amount]

That restaurant was a **real rip-off**. *or* That taxi-driver really **ripped us off**. [made us pay much too much; very informal]

If I were you I'd **drive a hard bargain**. She's desperate to buy a flat and wants yours. [ask a lot and resist lowering the price]

See also **pay through the nose** below.

B Idioms based on parts of the body

He's **made quite a bit of headway** with his maths lately.

I've got that song on the brain! [just can't stop myself singing it]

I hope you didn't mind me telling you. I just had to **get it off my chest**. [tell something that's been bothering you a lot]

We **had to pay through the nose** for those tickets. [pay a huge amount]

You've **got to hand it to** her; she's a great singer. [acknowledge/admit]

Oh, he's **got a finger in every pie**. [is involved in many different things]

C Idioms connected with daily routine

Come on! **Rise and shine!** We've got to leave! [a command to someone to get up, often said to someone who doesn't want to and at a very early hour]. There's no time for breakfast. We can **get a bite to eat** on the motorway [have a snack or meal]. I'll drive and you can **have a nap** in the back seat [a short sleep]. When we get there, there'll be time to **freshen up** before the meeting [wash and tidy oneself]. It's going to be a long day; I'll **be ready to crash out** about 8 o'clock, I should think [be very tired / ready to sleep almost anywhere]. Still, we can stay home tomorrow and **put our feet up** [relax], and just **watch the box** [watch television].

Exercises

87.1 **Look at these mini-dialogues and answer the questions using idioms from the opposite page.**

1 A: I'll give you $85.
B: No, $100 or nothing.
A: Oh, come on. Look, $90, there.
B: No, I said $100 and I mean $100.

What's B doing?

2 A: I'm president of the squash club, I'm on the teacher–parent committee and I run three youth clubs.
B: Really?
A: Yes, oh, and I'm on that working party at the Social Centre, and there's the Union ...

What sort of person could A be described as?

3 A: Lady in red, la-da-da-di-da ...
B: I wish you'd stop singing that blasted song!
A: What? Oh, sorry ... Lady in red, la-la ...

What's A's problem?

4 A: Oh, no! You know that box of wine glasses I bought from that guy in the street? Half of them are cracked!
B: Well, you should have looked at them first. It's your stupid fault.

What has A done?

87.2 **Rewrite these sentences using an idiom instead of the underlined bits.**

1 Can I tell you about a problem I have? I just have to tell somebody. It's been bothering me for a while now.
2 They charged us £100 for a tiny room without a bath. It was just robbery!
3 There'll just be time to have a quick meal before the show.
4 I must admit, Maria coped with the situation brilliantly.
5 I think I'll just go upstairs and have a sleep for a while, if nobody objects.
6 Well, I was very tired and fell asleep on the sofa at about two o'clock, and the party was still in full swing.

87.3 **Can you think of a situation where you might ...**

1 have to get a bite to eat on the way?
2 have to pay over the odds for a hotel room?
3 find it hard to make any headway?
4 be willing to pay through the nose for tickets?

87.4 **Which idioms do these drawings suggest?**

1

2

3

Follow-up: Look up idioms under other parts of the body, for example, *tongue*, *heels*, *toe*, *back*, and make a note of examples.

88 Proverbs

Speakers tend to use proverbs to comment on a situation, often at the end of a true story someone has told, or in response to some event. Like all idiomatic expressions, they are useful and enjoyable to know and understand, but should be used with care.

A Warnings/advice/morals – dos and don'ts

proverb		*paraphrase*
Don't count your chickens before they are hatched.	→	Don't anticipate the future too much.
Don't put all your eggs in one basket.	→	Don't invest all your efforts, or attention in just one thing.
Never judge a book by its cover.	→	Don't judge people/things by their outward appearance.
Never look a gift-horse in the mouth.	→	Never refuse good fortune when it is there in front of you.
Take care of the pence and the pounds will take care of themselves.	→	Take care of small sums of money and they will become large sums.

B Key elements

Proverbs can be grouped by key elements, for example, animals and birds.

When the **cat's** away, the **mice** will play. [people will take advantage of someone else's absence to behave more freely]

You can lead a **horse** to water but you can't make it drink. [you can try to persuade someone, but you can't force them]

One **swallow** doesn't make a summer. [one positive sign does not mean that all will be well. A swallow is a very fast-flying bird that returns to Britain in late spring]

C Visualising

As with learning all vocabulary, visualising some element often helps.

There's no smoke without fire. *or* Where there's smoke, there's fire. [rumours are usually based on some degree of truth]

Too many cooks spoil the broth /brɒθ/. [too many people interfering is a bad way of doing things]

People who live in glass houses shouldn't throw stones. [don't criticise others' faults if you suffer from them yourself]

Many hands make light work. [a lot of people helping makes a job easier]

Exercises

88.1 Find proverbs on the left-hand page that fit these situations.

EXAMPLE Someone says they have just been offered a free two-week holiday, but are hesitating whether to take up the offer. *Never look a gift-horse in the mouth.*

1 Someone thanks you and your friends for helping to load heavy boxes into a van.
2 Someone says they can't be bothered applying to different universities and will just apply to one.
3 Three different people have made different arrangements for the same meeting, and so everyone comes at different times and the result is total confusion.

88.2 Some proverbs are similar in meaning. Which proverbs on the left go with which on the right, and what do they have in common in terms of meaning?

1 A bird in the hand is worth two in the bush.
2 Don't count your chickens before they are hatched.
3 All that glitters is not gold.
4 Absence makes the heart grow fonder.

Never judge a book by its cover.
Familiarity breeds contempt.
Never look a gift-horse in the mouth.
Don't cross your bridges before you come to them.

88.3 People often refer to proverbs by only saying half of them and leaving the rest for the listener to 'fill in'. Complete the proverbs in these dialogues.

1 A: Joel's always criticising people who are selfish, yet he's terribly selfish himself.
B: Yes, well, people who live in glass houses ...
C: Exactly.

2 A: The people in the office have been playing computer games all day since the boss fell ill.
B: Well, you know what they say: when the cat's away ...
A: Right, and they're currently doing that.

3 A: I didn't believe those rumours about Nick and Gill, but apparently they are seeing each other.
B: You shouldn't be so naive, you know what they say, where there's smoke ..., eh?
A: Mm, I suppose you're right.

4 A: Amazing, he's made a fortune from just one little shop!
B: Well, I think it's a case of take care of the pence ...
A: Sure, he's always been very careful with his money.

Follow-up: Try translating some proverbs from your language, word for word into English. Then, if you can, ask a native speaker if they recognise any English proverb as having the same or similar meaning.

89 Expressions with do and make

The next seven units deal with phrasal verbs and other expressions based on common verbs. Phrasal verbs are basic verbs which can combine with different prepositions (or particles) to make verbs with completely new – and often unguessable – meanings. Phrasal verbs are used more in speaking than in writing.

A

Here are some of the most useful phrasal verbs based on **do** and **make**.

phrasal verb	*meaning*	*example*
do without	manage without	We'll have to do without a holiday this year as money is so short.
do away with	abolish	Slavery was not done away with until the nineteenth century.
do out of	prevent from having (by deceit)	He did me out of my rightful inheritance.
make for	move in the direction of	Let's make for the city centre and find a restaurant on the way.
make of	think (opinion)	What do you make of him?
make off	leave hurriedly	He made off as soon as he heard their car turn into the drive.
make up for	compensate for	The superb food at the hotel made up for the uncomfortable rooms.
make up to	be nice to in order to get st	He made up to her until she agreed to help.

B

Some phrasal verbs have a number of different meanings; **do up** can mean not only 'fasten' but also 'renovate' and 'put into a bundle'. Similarly, **make out** can mean 'claim', 'manage to see' and 'understand' as well as 'write' or 'complete'; **make up** can mean 'compose' or 'invent'; it can also mean 'constitute' or 'form', 'put cosmetics on', 'prepare by mixing together various ingredients' and 'make something more numerous or complete'.

C

There are a lot of other common expressions based on **do** and **make**. Note that most expressions referring to work or duty use **do** whereas those which lead to an end product (e.g. tea, a cake, a noise, a toy boat, a profit, a noise) use **make**.

You **do**: the housework / some gardening / the washing up / homework / your best / the shopping / the cooking / business with … , and so on.

You **make**: arrangements / an agreement / a suggestion / a decision / a cup of tea / war / an attempt / a phone call / the best of … / an effort / an excuse / a mistake / a profit / a loss / love / the most of / a noise / a good or bad impression / a success of … / a point of … / allowances for … / a gesture / a face / fun of … / a fuss of … / a go (a success) of … , and so on.

TIP The more collocations with **do** and **make** you learn, the more you will get a 'feel' for the difference between the two verbs.

Exercises

89.1 **Here are some different ways in which *do up*, *make up* and *make out* can be used. What is the meaning of the phrasal verb in each case?**

1 Take this prescription to the chemist and she'll make it up for you.
2 Can you make out the little grey house on the shore?
3 A human being is made up of many, often conflicting, desires.
4 If you do up the newspapers, I'll take them to be recycled.
5 I find it impossible to make Jo out.
6 Let's advertise the talk in the hope of making up the numbers a bit.
7 He made out that he had never loved anyone else.
8 We're planning to do up our bathroom at the weekend.

89.2 **Add the necessary prepositions or particles to complete this story.**

Last weekend we decided to start doing ....(1) our bedroom. We agreed that we could do ....(2) the old fireplace in the corner. As we began to remove it from the wall we found some old pictures done ....(3) in a bundle behind a loose brick. At first we could not make ....(4) what was in the pictures but we wiped them clean and realised they all depicted the same young man. We spent an enjoyable evening making ....(5) stories to explain why the pictures had been hidden.

89.3 **In each sentence below, there is an error either with word order or with choice of preposition. Correct the mistakes.**

1 This weekend we are planning to make the seaside for.
2 Vast amounts of money do not always make of happiness.
3 He makes up for anyone he thinks can help him.
4 Your shoelaces are untied. Do up them or you'll trip.
5 They like to make away that they are very important people.

89.4 **Write word forks (see Unit 2) to help you learn the meanings of *make up*, *make out*, *do with* and *do up*.**

89.5 **Divide the expressions in C opposite into any groups which will help you to learn them.**

89.6 **Complete the following sentences using an appropriate expression from C.**

1 Pacifist posters in the 1960s used to say 'MAKE LOVE NOT ....!'
2 It doesn't matter if you pass the exam or not, as long as you do ....
3 Companies that once made a huge .... are now going bankrupt.
4 I don't like doing .... but someone has to clean, wash, iron and cook!
5 You must make .... the fact that he's only seven years old.
6 Dressing smartly for an interview helps you to make ....

89.7 **Choose ten phrasal verbs and other expressions from the opposite page that you particularly want to learn and write a paragraph using them.**

90 Expressions with bring and take

A

Here are some common phrasal verbs with **bring**. Each is exemplified in a typical spoken sentence and a more formal equivalent is provided in brackets.

My father's parents **brought** him **up** in the country because they thought that country life was better for children. [raised]
Don't give up. I'm sure you'll **bring** it **off** in the end. [succeed]
Cold winds always **bring on** her cough. [cause to start]
The strike **brought about** a change of government. [cause to happen]
I hope they don't **bring back** capital punishment. [re-introduce]
They promised to **bring down** taxes but they have actually raised them. [lower]
Inflation will probably **bring down** the government. [destroy, remove from power]
Ford Motors are **bringing out** an interesting new model in the spring. [introducing]
Keep trying to persuade him and you'll **bring** him **round** to your point of view. [persuade]

B

Here are some common phrasal verbs with **take**.

Doesn't he **take after** his father! They even sound the same. [resemble]
I wish I could **take back** what I said to her. [withdraw]
It's hard to **take in** his lectures – he speaks in such an abstract way. [absorb, understand]
She was completely **taken in** by him and agreed to give him all her money. [deceived]
Sales have really **taken off** now – we should make a good profit this year. [started to improve]
The plane **took off** two hours late. [left the ground]
She's very good at **taking off** her teacher – she sounds just like her. [imitating]
We'll have to **take on** more staff if we're to **take on** more work. [employ; accept]
She **took to** him at once and they soon became close friends. [formed an immediate liking for]
When did you **take up** golf? [start (a hobby)]

C

Here are some other common idioms with **bring** and **take**.

The new regulations will **be brought into force** in May. [become law]
His research **brought** some very interesting facts **to light**. [revealed]
Matters **were brought to a head** when Pat was sacked. [reached a point where changes had to be made]
It's better that everything should be **brought into the open**. [made public]
His new girlfriend has really **brought out of the best in** him. [been good for him]
Don't let him **take advantage of** you. [unfairly use superiority]
After 20 years of marriage he **takes** her **for granted**. [doesn't appreciate her qualities]
I **took it for granted** you'd come – you always do. [assumed]
She immediately **took control** of the situation. [started organising]
His unkind words **took my breath away**. [surprised]
She loves **taking care** of small children. [looking after, caring for]
We **took part in** a demonstration last Saturday. [participated]
The story **takes place** in Mexico. [happens]
He doesn't seem to **take pride in** his work. [draw satisfaction from]
Mother always **takes** everything **in her stride** – she never makes a fuss. [copes calmly]

Exercises

90.1 **Complete these sentences with the appropriate preposition or particle.**

1 The new school reforms which plan to bring .... regular exams for young children are generally unpopular.
2 The bumpy journey brought .... labour and the baby was born on the bus.
3 I think the strikes will bring .... some changes in management.
4 If anyone can bring it ...., he can.
5 He won't agree to it for me but she can always bring him ....
6 She brought .... six children all on her own.

90.2 **The diagram below can be called a bubble network (see Unit 2). Can you complete it?**

90.3 **Write possible answers to these questions using one of the phrasal verbs in A or B opposite.**

1 What is the Conservative Party promising in its manifesto?
2 How did you like her?
3 What causes your rash?
4 Who does your little boy resemble?
5 Have you any special hobbies?
6 How's your new business doing?
7 What is a mimic?
8 Do you think you'll manage to persuade him to let you come?

90.4 **Reword these sentences using expressions from C opposite.**

1 The story of the film happens in Casablanca during the war.
2 Today's newspaper has revealed some fascinating information about the Prime Minister.
3 The situation reached crisis point when the union called for a strike.
4 How does she always manage to be so calm about things?
5 The view from the top of the hill was astonishing.
6 He capitalised on her weakness at the time and she sold it to him.
7 The main function of a nurse is to look after the sick.
8 You shouldn't assume that anyone or anything will always be the same.

90.5 **Make up a bubble network like the one in 90.2, based on phrasal verbs with *bring*.**

90.6 **Which of the expressions in C mean the opposite of:**

1 to keep quiet
2 to look on
3 to disregard
4 to drop an old law
5 to be careless about
6 to be subordinate to

91 Expressions with get

A

Get is used frequently in spoken English. It has the following basic meanings:

- receive, obtain or buy something, e.g. Please get me a newspaper when you're in town; I **got** a letter from John today; She **got** top marks in her exam.
- change position – move or be moved, e.g. How are you **getting** home tonight?
- change state – become or make, e.g. We are all **getting** older if not wiser.

B

Get also has many other more specific meanings.

It's my turn to **get dinner** tonight. [prepare a meal]
I don't **get it**. Why did he speak like that? [understand]
His behaviour really **gets** me at times. [annoy]
Once we **got to know** each other, we became great friends. [become acquainted]

C

This table shows just some of the phrasal verbs based on **get**.

phrasal verb	*meaning*	*example*
get at	reach, find	I hope the enquiry will get at the truth.
get away with	do wrong without being caught	The robbers got away with several thousand pounds.
get behind	fail to do something by a certain time	I've got terribly behind with my work.
get by	manage (financially)	We couldn't get by on my salary alone.
get down	depress	This weather is really getting me down.
get down to	begin to give some serious attention to	It's time you got down to some work.
get on	manage	However will we get on without you?
get on	advance, develop	Jo is getting on very well at school now.
get out of	avoid a responsibility	I'll try to get out of my lesson tomorrow.
get over	recover from	She's getting over a bad attack of flu.
get round	spread	The news soon got round the village.
get through	come to a successful end	I'm glad she got through all her exams!
get through	use up all of	He got through his month's salary in just one weekend.
get up to	to do (especially something bad)	They're very quiet. I wonder what they're getting up to?

D

Here are some other common expressions based on get.

You seem to have **got out of bed on the wrong side** today. [be in a bad mood]
The meeting **got off to a good/bad start** with JR's speech. [started well/badly]
I'm organising a little **get-together**. I hope you can come. [informal meeting/party]
When they broke up he **got rid of** everything of hers. [threw away / destroyed]
I'm going to **get my own back** on her somehow. [take my revenge]

Exercises

91.1 **There are a lot of instances of *get* in this text. Replace them all with another way of conveying the same idea. Notice that by doing this you are changing the text from something very informal to something slightly more formal.**

I don't often get interesting advertising circulars these days. However, quite an unusual one came this morning. It was headed 'Are you worried about getting out of touch?' And it went on, 'If so, get some of our special tablets today. Taking just one in the morning will help you get on well at work and at home. It will stop little problems from getting you down and will ensure that you get rich and successful with the minimum of effort on your behalf. Send just $25 today and you will get your tablets and your key to success within ten days.'

91.2 **Fill in the blanks in the sentences below in the most appropriate way.**

1 Although they had only told their parents about their engagement, the news soon got .... the village.
2 She must have made a good impression last week because she has got .... to the second round of interviews for the post.
3 I love watching TV cookery programmes but when they describe a recipe, it can be hard to get .... all the details in time.
4 We get .... only because we live very economically.
5 What have you been getting .... since we last met?
6 Surely you haven't got .... all the biscuits already?

91.3 **Match the situations in list A with the appropriate expressions in list B.**

A 1 Someone has been very impolite to one of your friends.
2 Someone is about to throw something away.
3 Someone is being negative about everything you suggest.
4 Someone has done something very cruel to you.
5 A good friend is leaving.

B 1 I don't know how we'll get by without you!
2 You wait! I'll get my own back on you one day!
3 Don't get rid of that yet!
4 You got out of bed on the wrong side this morning!
5 Your rudeness really gets me!

91.4 **Complete the following sentences in any appropriate way.**

1 I should hate to get rid of ...
2 The dinner got off to a bad start when ...
3 I find it very hard to get down to ...
4 I wish I could get out of ...
5 I don't think she has got over ...
6 ... is really getting me down.

91.5 **There are a number of other common phrasal verbs and expressions based on *get* which are not listed on the opposite page. Write example sentences using any that you can think of. Use a dictionary to help you if you wish.**

92 Expressions with set and put

A

Look at these examples of phrasal verbs based on **set**.

Since his daughter's birth, Robert had been **setting aside** [reserving] money for her wedding. Now he and his wife were **setting off** [beginning a journey] to meet Carl, her new fiancé. Carl was a mountaineer who had **set out** [begun work with a particular aim in mind] several times to climb Mount Everest but had had to turn back because bad weather had **set off** (caused) avalanches. Now he was trying to **set up** [establish] a sports equipment business. Robert didn't like the sound of Carl but he was doing his best to **set aside** [ignore (not think about)] his negative feelings.

B

NOTE
It would not normally be natural to use all of these expressions together.

Here are some of the many phrasal verbs with **put**.

Sarah **put** her own name **forward** [proposed] for election to the tennis club committee. Ten other people had also **put in** [submitted] proposal forms but Sarah was elected because she is very good at **putting** her ideas **across** [communicating to others]. She also has a talent for **putting** her opponents **down** [making someone look small]. At the first meeting she was largely silent though occasionally she would **put in** a remark [say something]. At the next meeting she was more involved. She supported the proposals that central heating should be **put in** [installed] at the club house and that the local school could use the club to **put on** [present] a play. She insisted that the play would not **put** members **out** [inconvenience] at all provided that the school **put** all their props **away** [tidy] after each performance. She said that she would **put up** [give accommodation to] grandparents coming from other towns to watch the play. She argued that they should **put off** [postpone] making their decision about **putting up** [raising] the club subscription until they had found out how members felt about this. She agreed to **put up** [fix] posters encouraging all members to come to the next meeting. The meeting ended dramatically with a small fire in the club-house but it was quickly **put out** [extinguished]. Sarah told her mother all about the meetings. She was very good at **putting on** [pretending to have] all sorts of accents and she made her mother laugh as she imitated her fellow committee members. 'The chairperson really **put** me **off** [distracted] with his constant sniffing,' she said, 'and I don't know how they **put up with** [tolerate] the secretary's rudeness.'

C

Here are some more common expressions with **set** and **put**.

He has **set his heart/sights on** becoming a ballet dancer. [longs to become]
They sat up till the small hours **setting/putting the world to rights**. [discussing important problems]
Did someone **set fire to** the house deliberately? [put a match to]
The house was **set on fire** by a match thrown on to some old newspapers. [ignited]
Di had never **set foot in** Italy before. [been to]
Jill is very **set in her ways** – she could never change her habits now. [fixed in her habits]
Teachers have to try to **set a good example** for young people. [be a good example]

to put your foot down: to be firm about something
to put all your eggs in one basket: to risk all you have on a single venture
to put your mind to: to direct all your thoughts towards
to put two and two together: to draw an obvious conclusion
o put something in a nutshell: to state something accurately and in a few words only
to put someone's back up: to irritate someone
a put-up job: something arranged to give a false impression

Exercises

92.1 **Put the following sentences into slightly more formal English by replacing the phrasal verbs with their formal equivalents.**

1 They have recently set up a committee on teenage smoking.
2 We try to set aside some money for our holiday every week.
3 Set aside all your negative feelings and listen with an open mind.
4 If we hadn't set off so late, we would have arrived on time.
5 The government's unpopular proposals set off a wave of protests.

92.2 **Write three nouns which could follow each of the verbs. Remember that their meanings might be different depending on the noun which follows.**

EXAMPLE put in money / a comment / a telephone system

1 put out	3 put off	5 put up	7 put away
2 put forward	4 put across	6 put on	8 put up with

92.3 **Write responses to the following statements or questions using any appropriate phrasal verb from A or B opposite.**

EXAMPLE He's always so rude. I wouldn't put up with it if I were you.

1 How should we publicise our play?
2 This room is in a terrible mess.
3 What time do we have to leave for the airport tomorrow?
4 Any chance of a bed on your floor this weekend?
5 Why have you suddenly lost interest in the project?
6 What is Geoff planning to do when he gets his business degree?

92.4 **Using the expressions in C opposite, reword the following sentences without changing their meaning.**

1 He never wants to do anything in a new or different way.
2 He's bound to draw the obvious conclusion if you keep on behaving like that.
3 Her aim is to become Prime Minister.
4 I find her terribly irritating.
5 It's sound business advice not to risk everything at once.
6 Please concentrate on the problem in hand.
7 She is determined to get a seat in Parliament.
8 She threw petrol on the rubbish and put a match to it.
9 She's very good at stating things succinctly.
10 The building started burning because of terrorist action.
11 This is the first time I've ever been to the southern hemisphere.
12 We spent most of our evenings discussing the problems of the world rather than studying.
13 You really should be firm with him or there'll be trouble later.
14 If the teacher doesn't behave properly, the children certainly won't.

92.5 **Choose ten of the phrasal verbs and other expressions with *set* and *put* which you particularly want to learn and write them down in example sentences of your own.**

93 Expressions with come and go

A

Here are some phrasal verbs based on **come**.

Did the meeting you were planning ever **come off**? [take place]
Unfortunately, I don't think his jokes ever quite **come off**. [succeed]
When do the exam results **come out**? [be published, made public]
I must tell you about an important point which **came up** at the meeting. [was raised]
Please **come round** and see me sometime – I'm usually at home in the evenings. [pay an informal visit]
Nothing can **come between** him and football. [separate; be a barrier between]
I **came across** a lovely old vase in that junk shop. [found by chance]
How did you **come by** that bruise / that car? [receive, obtain]

B

Here are some expressions with **come to** (usually with an idea of arriving at) and **come into** (often with an idea of starting or acquiring).

come to: an agreement / a conclusion / a standstill [stop] / an end / a decision / blows [to start fighting] / to terms with [acknowledge and accept psychologically] / one's senses [to become conscious after fainting or to become sensible after behaving foolishly]
come into: bloom / flower / contact / a fortune / money / a legacy / operation [start working] / sight / view / power [of a political party] / existence / fashion / use

C

Here are some phrasal verbs based on **go**. Some have a number of different meanings.

Go on: What is **going on** next door? [happening]; They **went on** working despite the noise. [continued]; As the weeks **went on**, things improved. [passed]; You **go on**, we'll catch you up later. [go in advance]; The oven should **go on** at six. [start operating]; He's always **going on at** me about my untidy hair. [complaining]
Go through: I wouldn't like to **go through** that again. [experience, endure]; Let's **go through** the plans once more. [check]; Unfortunately, the business deal we were hoping for did not **go through** in the end. [was not completed or approved]; He **went through** a fortune in one weekend. [spent, used]
Go for: He really **went for** her when she dared to criticise him. [attack]; He **goes for** older women. [is attracted by]; Which course have you decided to **go for**? [choose]

Those shoes don't **go with** that dress. [suit, match]
He would never **go back on** his word. [break a promise]

D

Here are some expressions based on **go**.

I hope they'll **make a go of** the business but they are taking a big risk. [make a success of]
He's been **on the go** all day and he's exhausted. [very busy, on the move]
It **goes without saying** that we'll support you. [clear without being said]
Your work is good, **as far as it goes**. [but is limited or insufficient]
The story goes that they were once very close friends. [It is said that … / It seems that …]
I'm sure she'll **go far** whatever career she decides to take up. [be very successful]
They **went to great lengths** to keep it a secret. [took a lot of trouble]
The business has **gone bankrupt**. [not got enough money to pay debts]

Exercises

93.1 Which meanings do these underlined verbs have?

1 He went on composing music till his eighties. continued
2 She was so suspicious that she used to go through his pockets every night.
3 The dog went for the postman.
4 The actor's interpretation of Hamlet was interesting but it didn't quite come off.
5 He has a new book coming out in June.
6 I wish you'd stop going on at me!
7 I was sure he'd go for a sports car.
8 I went through three pairs of tights this weekend.

93.2 Choose one of the expressions in B to complete each of the sentences.

1 I found it really hard to make up my mind but in the end I came ....
2 When his grandmother dies, he'll come ....
3 I love it in spring when my cherry tree comes ....
4 Halfway up the steep hill, the bus came ....
5 They say that long skirts are coming .... again.
6 The telephone first came .... over a hundred years ago.
7 They disagreed so strongly that I was afraid they'd come ....
8 As we rounded the corner the house came ....

93.3 Replace the underlined expressions with one of the expressions in D.

1 I don't need to say that we wish you all the best in the future.
2 They took great pains to avoid meeting each other.
3 I've been moving around all day and I'm longing for a shower now.
4 His school-teachers always said that he would be a success in life.
5 It seems that they were together that night.
6 The film is good up to a point but it doesn't tackle the problem deeply enough.

93.4 Which answer on the right fits each question on the left?

1 Why is she looking so miserable?	Any time after eight.
2 Did anything new come up at the meeting?	The firm went bankrupt.
3 When does your alarm clock usually go off?	A bit of a fight, I think.
4 What's the worst pain you've ever gone through?	From a doting aunt.
5 How did he come by so much money?	Seven thirty, normally.
6 When should I come round to your place?	Only Jack's proposal.
7 What's going on over there?	When I pulled a ligament.

93.5 Complete the following sentences in any appropriate way.

1 I'm sure they'll make a go of their new clothes boutique because ...
2 The stain won't come out unless you ...
3 Those shoes don't go with ...
4 I never want to go through ...
5 As the party went on, it ...
6 It is not easy to come to terms with ...
7 The interview committee came to the conclusion that ...
8 I came across not only some old letters in the attic ...

94 Miscellaneous expressions

Here are some of the expressions formed with **look**, **see**, **run**, **turn**, **let** and **break**.

A

If you don't know what the expression means, **look** it **up** in a dictionary.
I'm tired of living abroad and I'm **looking forward to** going home soon.
If you don't **look out**, he'll steal your girlfriend from you.
She **looks down her nose at** anyone she thinks is inferior to her.
It's hard to be optimistic but do try to **look on the bright side**.

B

Try to **see about/to** arrangements for the conference at least a year in advance.
We all went to **see** Jim **off** at the airport.
It's sometimes hard **to see the wood for the trees** but it is important not to get too distracted by small details.
That can't be John. He's in Paris this week. I must be **seeing** things.

C

I **ran into** an old friend yesterday – I had no idea he was in town.
Her patience has **run out** and she has told him to make more effort or she'll stop helping him.
Let's **run over** the plans again to make sure we've thought of everything.
The children have **run me off my feet** today and I'm absolutely exhausted.
She **runs** the business while her husband looks after the children.

D

There was a very large **turnout** at the concert – far more than we'd expected and some people had to stand at the back.
Everyone was very surprised when she **turned down** the promotion and explained that she was leaving the company.
Naoko **turned up** last night. I haven't seen her for years!
I'm going to **turn over a new leaf** this year and answer all my letters the day I get them!
He did me a **good turn** when he offered me a lift into town. If he hadn't, I'd have been waiting at the bus stop for hours.

E

He has been **let down** so many times in the past – I hope he won't be disappointed again.
Don't **let go of** the rope or she'll fall and hurt herself.
Please **let me be** – I just want to read the newspaper in peace.
When she **let it slip** that she had been given a pay rise, the other workers were very angry.

F

The car **broke down** again this morning and I had to cycle to work.
Burglars **broke into** our house while we were on holiday and stole the TV.
I'm dreading **breaking the bad news** to him. He's going to be very upset.
When he left her, he **broke her heart**.
The athlete not only won the gold medal but also **broke the record** for the 1000 metres.

Exercises

94.1 **Use the expressions on the opposite page to help you fill in the gaps in the text below. Use one word only in each gap.**

Let's run ....(1) the plans for tomorrow's disco just once more. First, I must see ....(2) the food arrangements while you make sure that none of the equipment is likely to break ....(3). I don't imagine that many people will turn ....(4) until later but Nick and Jill have promised to come early to help us and I'm sure they won't let us ....(5).

94.2 **Rewrite the following sentences. Use an expression containing the words in brackets.**

1 Do try to be optimistic if you possibly can. (look)
2 I met Jack by chance at the station yesterday. (run)
3 I cooked the dinner yesterday. It's up to you to do it today. (turn)
4 I thought I was hallucinating when I saw a monkey in the garden. (see)
5 I wish you'd stop bothering me. (let)
6 He told us in secret that they were planning to break into the house. (let)
7 An enormous crowd came to hear the Prime Minister speak. (turn)
8 My aunt despises people who don't have a good job. (look)

94.3 **Complete the sentences in an appropriate way.**

1 I'm really looking forward ...
2 A person who cannot see the wood for the trees does not make a good ...
3 Halfway up the mountain he let go ...
4 Although the turnout for the meeting was not large ...
5 He felt terribly let down when ...
6 She didn't turn up ...
7 I'm afraid we've run out ...
8 He asked if I could see my way ...

94.4 **Answer the questions below.**

1 Have you ever turned down an offer or invitation that you later regretted?
2 Have you ever had problems because of something (a vehicle or a piece of equipment, perhaps) breaking down at an inconvenient time? What happened?
3 Who really runs the country, in your opinion?
4 Have you done anyone a good turn today? If so, what did you do?
5 Which record would you most like to break?
6 Do you think it is possible for someone's heart to be broken?
7 Have you ever resolved to turn over a new leaf? In what way(s)?
8 Have you any particular jobs that you must see to today? If so, what?
9 Has your home ever been broken into? What happened?
10 Have you looked anything up in a reference book today? What did you look for?

94.5 **The expressions opposite are only some of many expressions using these six verbs. Can you think of two other phrasal verbs or other idiomatic expressions using each of the verbs? If you can't, look up the base verbs in a dictionary and see what you can find.**

95 Formal and informal words (1)

Formality is all about your relationship with the person you're speaking or writing to. If you use formal language, it may be because you wish to show respect, politeness, or to put yourself at a distance (for example, 'official' language). Informal language can show friendliness, equality or a feeling of closeness and solidarity with someone. You should *never* use informal language just to sound fluent or clever.

A Scales of formality

Some groups of words can be put on a scale from formal to neutral to informal.

formal	*neutral*	*informal*
offspring	children	kids
abode/residence	house/flat	place
goodbye	bye-bye	bye or cheerio
alcoholic beverages	drink	booze
go amiss	go wrong	go pear-shaped

B Short, monosyllabic informal words

Informal versions of words are often short and monosyllabic, as we can see in the right-hand column in the table above. They include slang words. (Unit 96 has more examples.)

It cost me ten **quid**. [pounds] I'll help you peel the **spuds**. [potatoes]
My **bike's** been stolen. [bicycle] Come and meet my **Mum** and **Dad**. [mother and father]
I always go by **tube**. [word used for the London Underground]
Hi! Can't stop; see you, **bye!** [hello; goodbye] I'll get a **cab** from the station. [taxi]

C Clippings

Shortening a word tends to make it less formal, as in **bye** in B.

I'll meet you in the **lab**(oratory). What's on **telly** tonight? [television]
We should put an **ad**(vertisement) / an **advert**(isement) in the (news)**paper**.
Shall I (tele)**phone** them? Her sister's a **vet**(erinary surgeon).
Can I use your **mobile** (phone)?

D Formality in notices, instructions, etc.

You will often see rather formal words in signs, notices and directions. Make sure you know the meaning of the words used so that you could tell someone what the notice says using less formal words.

THIS PUBLIC HOUSE IS CLOSED UNTIL FURTHER NOTICE.

Articles deposited must be paid for in advance.

DO NOT ALIGHT WHILE THE BUS IS IN MOTION.

We regret we cannot accept cheques.

Do not address the driver unless the bus is stationary.

Tickets must be purchased before boarding the train.

TIP If you ask someone to explain a new word, also ask them if it is formal, informal or neutral.

Exercises

95.1 **If you look up an informal word in a monolingual dictionary, you will often find a neutral equivalent as part of the definition or explanation. For example, the *Cambridge International Dictionary of English* entry for *kid* says: '*infml a child or young person.*'**

Use a monolingual dictionary to find neutral or more formal words for these:

1 kip   2 a pal   3 a chap   4 swot   5 ta!   6 brainy

95.2 **Make this conversation more *informal* by changing some of the words. Refer to the left-hand page if necessary.**

JIM: Annie, can you lend me five pounds?
ANNIE: What for?
JIM: Well, I have to go and visit my mother and father, and my bicycle's not working, so I'll have to take a taxi.
ANNIE: Can't you telephone them and say you can't come?
JIM: Well, I could, except I want to go because they always have lots of food, and the refrigerator at our flat is empty, as usual.
ANNIE: Can't you go by Underground?
JIM: Erm ...
ANNIE: Anyway, the answer's no.

95.3 **Say whether you feel the following remarks/sentences are *OK*, *too formal* or *too informal* for each situation described. If the remark/sentence is unsuitable, suggest what the person might say instead.**

1 (*Teenage boy to teenage girl at disco*): D'you fancy an appointment one night next week?
2 (*Parent to another parent at a school parents' meeting*): How many offspring do you have at the school?
3 (*Dinner-guest to host/hostess*): No thanks, I never consume alcoholic beverages when I'm driving.
4 (*Student to university professor*): Will there be lab demonstrations next week?
5 (*Business letter to a newspaper office*): Dear Sir/Madam,
I should like to enquire about the current charges for ads in your newspaper.
My company is considering ..., etc.

95.4 **Mini-quiz: Find words on the left-hand page for the following.**

1 The opposite of **stationary**.
2 The opposite of **to board**.
3 a) to be sorry b) to buy c) to speak to
4 Informal versions of **Greetings!** and **Farewell!**

95.5 **Express these notices in neutral or informal language.**

1

> **CHILDREN ARE REQUESTED NOT TO DEPOSIT LITTER IN THE PLAY AREA.**

2

> **Expenses can only be reimbursed upon production of dated receipts.**

(See also Units 96 and 100 for other informal and formal words and expressions.)

96 Formal and informal words (2)

This unit looks at very informal or slang words. Slang is extremely colloquial language. Slang helps to make speech vivid, colourful and interesting but it can easily be used inappropriately. Although slang is mainly used in speech, it is also often found in the popular press.

A Using slang appropriately

Remember, it can be risky for someone who is not a native speaker to use slang. Firstly because some slang expressions may cause offence to some sections of the population. For example, most policemen are quite happy to be referred to as **coppers** but are offended by the term **pigs**. Similarly, you could probably use the word **sozzled** (meaning drunk) in front of anyone but using the words, **pissed** or **arseholed**, which also mean drunk, could upset some people.

Secondly, slang words date very quickly. Different generations, for instance, have used different slang expressions to say that something was 'wonderful'.

pre-war:	**top-hole**	1970s:	**ace, cosmic**
1940s:	**wizard**	1980s:	**brill, wicked**
1960s:	**fab, groovy**	1990s:	**cool, class**

It can be possible to work out a native speaker's age from the expressions which they use, as people tend to stick with the slang expressions of their youth.

B Some common slang words and expressions

The words and expressions which are most likely to cause offence are underlined.

Expressions for money: **dough** **bread** **dosh** **loot** **brass** **readies**
Expressions for the police: <u>**pigs**</u> **fuzz** **cop(pers)** **bill**
Expressions for drunk: <u>**pissed**</u> **pie-eyed** <u>**paralytic**</u> <u>**legless**</u> <u>**arseholed**</u>
Expressions for a stupid person: **wally** **prat** <u>**wanker**</u> **jerk** <u>**dickhead**</u> **plonker** <u>**pillock**</u> **dork** **clueless** **out-to-lunch** <u>**doesn't know his arse from his elbow**</u>
Expressions for lavatory: **loo** **lav** <u>**bog**</u> **john**
Expressions for drink: **booze** **plonk** (wine) **a bevvy**
Drug-related expressions: **a fix** **dope** **grass** **high** **stoned** **snow** (heroin)
Prison-related expressions: **nick** (prison) **nark** (informer) **screw** (warder)

C

Slang is often used by one particular group and is unintelligible to other people. Here are some examples from American truck-drivers using CB radio to talk to each other.

grandma lane: slow lane **five finger discount:** stolen goods **super cola:** beer
doughnuts: tyres **anklebiters:** children **affirmative:** yes **motion lotion:** fuel
eyeballs: headlights

TIP If you are interested in slang, you can find more examples in films or in the tabloid press but it is probably safest to keep it in your passive rather than your active vocabulary.

Exercises

96.1 **Replace the slang words which are underlined in the sentences below with more formal equivalents. If the meaning is not given opposite, then it should be possible to guess what it is. Notice that some of the words have a slang meaning which is different from their everyday meaning.**

1 The newsreader on TV last night seemed to be pissed as he was reading the news.
2 He's quite a nice geezer really.
3 I've got a terrible belly ache – I think I'd better make an appointment with the quack.
4 Are you and Pat an item?
5 Can you lend me some dosh till tomorrow?
6 I know there'll be plenty of nosh but do we need to take some booze to the party?
7 The footballer said he was gutted by the result.
8 I'm dying for a cuppa. I haven't had one since breakfast.
9 Can I use your loo, please?
10 I was absolutely gobsmacked when she told me she was leaving.

96.2 **Match the statements on the left with the responses to them on the right.**

1 How was the party?	Let's take him home.
2 What does that guy over there do?	Sure. I'll keep my eyes skinned.
3 He's getting legless.	He's in the nick.
4 Keep a lookout for the pigs.	It's in a drawer, over here.
5 Where's the dough?	He's a cop.
6 Where's her hubby?	Let's borrow dad's wheels and go for a spin.
7 What'll we do tomorrow?	Cool!

96.3 **A particular well-known kind of slang is Cockney rhyming slang where an expression is used in place of something that it rhymes with.**

EXAMPLE trouble and strife = wife apples and pears = stairs

How would you translate the Cockney rhyming slang expressions in the sentences below?

1 Let's have a butcher's (short for butcher's hook) at your homework.
2 Just look at those Gawd forbids playing football!
3 It's on the Cain and Abel next to the phone.
4 What a set of Hampstead Heath!
5 She'll get him to the lean and lurch by hook or by crook.
6 Have you seen my titfer? (short for tit for tat)

96.4 **Another common way of making slang words is by using short forms or loosely pronounced forms of ordinary words. Thus *fab* is a slang form of 'fabulous' and *hubby* is a slang form of 'husband'. Can you work out the meanings of the following underlined slang words?**

1 Let's have brekkie.

2 He's a brickie.

3 Let's have a barbie.

97 US English

A

English in the USA differs considerably from British English. Pronunciation is the most striking difference but there are also a number of differences in vocabulary and spelling as well as slight differences in grammar. Yet, on the whole, speakers of British and American English have little difficulty in understanding each other.

B

American spelling is usually simpler. For example, British English words ending in **-our** and **-re**, end in **-or** and **-er** in American English, e.g. colour/color, centre/center. Words ending **-ise** in British English end in **-ize** in US English. There are differences in individual words too, e.g. British 'plough' becomes 'plow'.

C

Here are some common US words with their British equivalents.

Travel and on the street		**In the home**	
American English	*British English*	*American English*	*British English*
gasoline	petrol	antenna	aerial
truck	lorry	elevator	lift
baggage	luggage	eraser	rubber
sidewalk	pavement	apartment	flat
crosswalk	zebra crossing	closet	wardrobe
line	queue	yard	garden
vacation	holiday	drapes	curtains
parking lot	car park	flashlight	torch
trunk (of car)	boot	kerosene	paraffin
hood (of car)	bonnet	Scotch tape	sellotape
freeway/highway	motorway	cookie	biscuit
round trip	return	candy	sweets
one way	single	bathroom, rest room	toilet, WC
railway car	railway carriage	garbage, trash	rubbish
engineer (on train)	engine driver	diaper	nappy
baby carriage	pram	pantihose	tights
subway	underground	french fries	chips

Note: the fall = autumn   semester = term (academic) [semester is becoming more common in Britain.]

D

Here are some words and phrases which can cause confusion when used by Brits and Americans talking together because they mean something different in each 'language'.

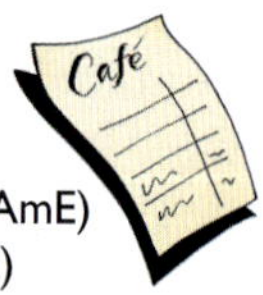

check (AmE)
bill (BrE)

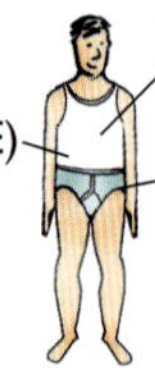

vest (BrE)
undershirt (AmE)
underpants (AmE/BrE)
pants (BrE)

the second floor (BrE)
the second floor (AmE)
the first floor (BrE)
the ground floor (BrE)
the ground floor/the first floor (AmE)

bill (AmE)   (bank) note (BrE)

vest (AmE)
waistcoat (BrE)
pants (AmE)
trousers (BrE)

wash the dishes (AmE/BrE)
wash up (BrE)

wash up (AmE)
wash your hands (BrE)

Exercises

97.1 **If you saw words spelt in the following way would you expect the writer in each case to be British or American? Why?**

1 labor	3 hospitalized	5 favour
2 centre	4 a movie theater	6 thru

97.2 **What are (a) the American and (b) the British words for the following things?**

1
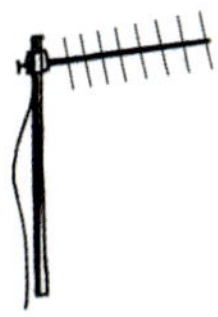
2

3
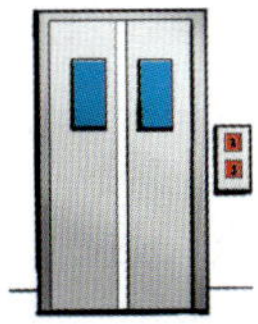
4

5

6
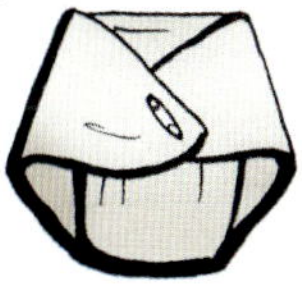
7

8
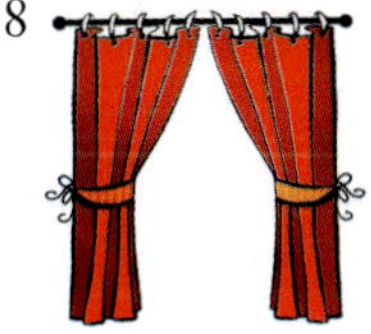
9

10

97.3 **You are going on holiday to the States. Which of the words listed in C and D opposite do you think it would be most important for you to know? Which of the words would a person travelling with a baby might well need to know?**

97.4 **Translate the following into British English.**

1 I had a blow-out.	6 Our bags are in the trunk.
2 Pass me the cookies.	7 One-way or round trip?
3 It's in the closet.	8 Buy a one-way ticket.
4 Open the drapes.	9 We're leaving in the fall.
5 We've run out of gas.	10 I hate waiting in line.

97.5 **Can you avoid some of the most common confusions arising between British and American speakers? Try the following quiz.**

1 Where would you take (a) an American visitor (b) a British visitor who said they wanted to wash up – the kitchen or the bathroom?
2 Which would surprise you more – an American or a British man telling you that he wanted to go and change his pants?
3 You have just come into an unknown office block. If (a) an American (b) a Brit says that the office you need is on the second floor, how many flights of stairs do you need to climb?
4 If (a) an American (b) a Brit asks for a bill, is he or she more likely to be in a bank or a café?
5 Would a man wear a vest under or over his shirt (a) if he is British (b) if he is from the USA?

97.6 **Do you know any other examples of American English? Make a list at an appropriate place in your vocabulary notebook or file.**

See also Unit 98 for English in other parts of the world.

98 Other Englishes

A

US or American English (see Unit 97) is not the only special variety of English. Each area of the English-speaking world has developed its own special characteristics. This is usually mainly a matter of vocabulary and pronunciation. This unit just gives you a small taste of some of the different varieties of English by drawing your attention to vocabulary used in various English-speaking regions. You may come across many of the words covered in this unit in your own reading, listening or viewing.

B

Australian English

Australian English is particularly interesting for its rich store of highly colloquial words and expressions. Australian colloquialisms often involve shortening a word. Sometimes the ending '-ie' or '-o' is then added, e.g. a **truckie** is 'a truck or lorry-driver' and a **milko** delivers the milk; **beaut**, short for 'beautiful' means 'great' and **biggie** is 'a big one'. **Oz** is short for Australia and an **Aussie** is an Australian.

C

Indian English

Indian English, on the other hand, is characterised by sounding more formal than British English. It has retained, in everyday usage, words that are found more in the classics of nineteenth century literature than in contemporary TV programmes, e.g. The **bereaved** are **condoled** and the Prime Minister is **felicitated** on his or her birthday. An Indian might complain of a pain in his **bosom** (rather than his chest) and an Indian bandit is referred to as a **miscreant**.

D

Scottish English

Scottish English uses a number of special dialect words. Some of the more common of these are worth learning.

aye /aɪ/: yes **loch**: lake **dreich**: dull **ben**: mountain **to mind**: to remember
janitor: caretaker **brae**: bank (of river) **bairn**: child **lassie**: girl
dram: drink (usually whisky) **bonny**: beautiful **outwith**: outside
glen: valley **burn**: stream **wee**: small **kirk**: church **stay**: live
ken: know

E

Black English

Black English is the term used to refer to the English which originated in the Caribbean islands and is now also spoken in many parts of the UK, Canada and the USA. Listed below are some words which are characteristic of Black English but are also now used in other varieties of English. Many are particularly associated with the music world.

dreadlocks: Rastafarian hairstyle **beat**: exhausted **chick**: girl
dig: understand **jam**: improvise **pad**: bed **rap**: street-talk **square**: dull

Exercises

98.1 **What do you think these examples of Australian colloquialisms mean? They are all formed by abbreviating an English word which you probably know.**

1 I'm exhausted – let's have a smoko!
2 She wants to be a journo when she leaves uni.
3 We got terribly bitten by mozzies at yesterday's barbie.
4 He's planning to do a bit of farming bizzo while he's in the States.
5 What are you doing this arvo?
6 We decided to have a party as the olds had gone away for the weekend.

98.2 **The words on the left are more common in Indian English than British English. The words on the right are equivalent words more frequently used in British English. Match the Indian word with its British English equivalent.**

1 abscond	catch (e.g. by police)
2 nab	man who annoys girls
3 bag (i.e. a seat in an election)	plimsolls, sneakers
4 Eve-teaser	underwear
5 car-lifter	flee
6 fleetfoots	people awaiting trial
7 undertrials	car-thief
8 wearunders	capture/obtain

98.3 **Below you have some statements made by a Scot. Answer the questions about them.**

1 Mary had a bonny wee lassie last night. What happened to Mary yesterday?
2 They stay next to the kirk. What noise is likely to wake them on Sunday mornings?
3 It's a bit dreich today. Is it good weather for a picnic?
4 He's got a new job as janitor at the school. What kind of duties will he have?
5 Would you like a wee dram? If you say 'yes', what will you get?
6 'Are you coming, Jim?' 'Aye.' Is Jim coming or isn't he?
7 They have a wonderful view of the loch from their window. What can they see from the window?

98.4 **Answer the following questions relating to Black English.**

1 Would you be pleased to be called square?
2 What does hair that is in dreadlocks look like?
3 When might you feel dead beat?
4 If musicians have a jam session, what do they do?

Follow-up: If you have access to the Internet, use a search engine to look up a variety of English that interests you, for example US English, Indian English, Singaporean English. What can you find out about it?

99 Headline English

A

Newspaper headlines try to catch the reader's eye by using as few words as possible. The language headlines use is, consequently, unusual in a number of ways.

- Grammar words like articles or auxiliary verbs are often left out, e.g. EARLY CUT FORECAST IN INTEREST RATES
- A simple form of the verb is used, e.g. MAYOR OPENS HOSPITAL
- The infinitive is used to express the fact that something is going to happen in the future, e.g. PRESIDENT TO VISIT FLOOD AREAS

B

Newspaper headlines use a lot of distinctive vocabulary. They usually prefer words that are shorter and sound more dramatic than ordinary English words. The words marked * can be used either as nouns or verbs.

newspaper word	*meaning*	*newspaper word*	*meaning*
aid*	help	key (adj.)	essential, vital
axe*	cut, remove	link*	connection
back (verb)	support	move*	step towards a desired end
bar*	exclude, forbid	ordeal (noun)	painful experience
bid*	attempt	oust (verb)	push out / remove
blast*	explosion	plea (noun)	request
blaze*	fire	pledge*	promise
boost*	incentive, encourage	ploy (noun)	clever activity
boss*	manager, director	poll*	election / public opinion survey
head*		probe*	investigation
clash*	dispute	quit (verb)	leave, resign
curb*	restraint, limit	riddle (noun)	mystery
cut*	reduction	strife (noun)	conflict
drama	tense situation	talks (noun)	discussions
drive*	campaign, effort	threat	danger
gems (noun)	jewels	vow*	promise
go-ahead	approval	wed (verb)	marry
hit (verb)	affect badly		

Newspaper headlines often use abbreviations, e.g. PM for Prime Minister, MP for Member of Parliament. (See Unit 16 for more abbreviations.)

C

Some newspapers also enjoy making jokes in their headlines. They do this by playing with words or punning, e.g. a wet open air concert in London by the opera singer Luciano Pavarotti was described as:

TORRENTIAL RAIN IN MOST ARIAS ['most areas']

An announcement that a woman working at the Mars chocolate company had got an interesting new job was:

WOMAN FROM MARS TO BE FIRST BRITON IN SPACE

(Note that the word 'Briton' is almost exclusively found in newspapers.)

Exercises

99.1 Match the headlines on the left with the appropriate topic on the right.

1 PM BACKS PEACE PLAN
2 MP SPY DRAMA
3 Space probe fails
4 QUEEN'S GEMS RIDDLE
5 Star weds
6 Key witness death threat

a marriage of famous actress
b royal jewels are stolen
c person who saw crime in danger
d proposal to end war
e satellite is not launched
f politician sells secrets to enemy

99.2 Explain what the following headlines mean in ordinary English.

EXAMPLE SHOP BLAZE 5 DEAD. *Five people died in a fire in a shop.*

1 MOVE TO CREATE MORE JOBS
2 GO-AHEAD FOR WATER CURBS
3 Woman quits after job ordeal
4 POLL PROBES SPENDING HABITS
5 BID TO OUST PM
6 Prince vows to back family

99.3 The words marked * in the table opposite can be either nouns or verbs. Note that the meaning given is sometimes in the form of a noun. In the headlines below you have examples of words from the table used as verbs. Look at the underlined verbs and explain what they mean. You may need to use more than one word.

EXAMPLE PM TO CURB SPENDING *limit*

1 BOOK LINKS M15 WITH KGB
2 CHANCELLOR CUTS INTEREST RATES
3 BOMB BLASTS CENTRAL LONDON
4 PM PLEDGES BACKING FOR EUROPE
5 PRESIDENT HEADS PEACE MOVES

99.4 Would you be interested in the stories under the following headlines? Why (not)?

1 Mortgages cut as bank rates fall again
2 Teenage £4m fraud riddle
3 NEW TENNIS CLASH
4 Royal family quits
5 Price curbs boost exports
6 WOMEN BARRED FROM JOBS

Follow-up: Look through some English language newspapers and find some examples of headlines illustrating the points made on the opposite page. Beside each headline make a note of what the accompanying story is about. Try to find some examples of amusing headlines.

100 The language of signs and notices

Signs and notices in English often use words and expressions that are rarely seen in other contexts. Look at the signs and notices below with their 'translations' into more everyday English.

1 **Do not alight from the bus whilst it is in motion**

Don't get off the bus while it's moving.

2 **TRESPASSERS WILL BE PROSECUTED**

People who walk on this private land will be taken to court.

3 **KINDLY REFRAIN FROM SMOKING IN THE AUDITORIUM**

Please don't smoke in the theatre/hall.

4 **PENALTY FOR DROPPING LITTER – UP TO £100 FINE**

You can be taken to court and made to pay £100 for dropping rubbish.

5 **Lunches now being served**

You can buy lunch here now.

6 **NO ADMISSION TO UNACCOMPANIED MINORS**

Young people under 18 years old can only come in if they are with an adult.

7 **FEEDING THE ANIMALS STRICTLY PROHIBITED**

You are not allowed to feed the animals.

8 **No through road for motor vehicles**

There is no way out at the other end of this road for cars.

9 **NO BILL-STICKING**

You mustn't put up any posters here.

10 ***Please place your purchases here***

Please put the things you are going to buy / have bought here.

11 **This packet carries a government health warning**

What is in this packet is officially considered bad for your health.

12 **Reduce speed now**

Start going more slowly now.

13 **Pay and display**

Buy a ticket and put it in a place where it can easily be seen.

14 **Cyclists dismount here**

Cyclists should get off their bikes here.

15 **FISHING: PERMIT HOLDERS ONLY**

Only people with special cards giving them permission are allowed to fish here.

TIP If you are in or go to visit an English-speaking country, make a collection in your vocabulary book of any notices that you see.

Exercises

100.1 **Where would you expect to see each of the notices on the opposite page?**

EXAMPLE 1 *on a bus.*

100.2 **Match each of the words on the left with their meanings from the list on the right.**

1 to prosecute	a young person under the age of 18
2 a penalty	to get off a bicycle or a horse
3 a purchase	to bring a legal case against
4 a trespasser	not to do something
5 to refrain	to forbid something
6 to alight from	a means of transport
7 to prohibit	a punishment
8 an auditorium	something which has been or is to be bought
9 to dismount	to get off a means of public transport
10 a minor	large place where an audience sits
11 a vehicle	someone who goes on private land without permission

100.3 **Explain the notices below. Where might you see each of these notices?**

1 SHOPLIFTERS WILL BE PROSECUTED

2 *French spoken here*

3 Nothing to declare

4 Clearance sale starts today

5 Admission to ticket holders only

6 *No vacancies*

7 FISHING STRICTLY PROHIBITED

8 Cycles for hire or sale

9 Flat to let

10 Dogs must be carried

11 These seats are appreciated by the old and infirm

100.4 **What notice would a café-owner put up if they wanted to:**

1 indicate that their café was now open for coffee?
2 let people know that the café staff can speak Spanish?
3 stop people from smoking in their café?
4 let people know that they can buy free-range eggs there too?
5 ask people not to fix notices on to their wall?
6 tell people that they could rent rooms there overnight?

Follow-up: Look at the notices in your own language that you see around you every day. How would they be expressed in English? Try to find out, if they are not included in this unit.

Key

Many of your answers will depend on your own particular interests and needs. It is only possible for the key to suggest answers in some cases.

Unit 1

A 1 d 2 b 3 b 4 a

5 the most common twenty words in written English are (in order starting with the most frequent): the, of, to, in, and, a, for, was, is, that, on, at, he, with, by, be, it, an, at, his; and in spoken English: the, and, I, to, of, a, you, that, in, it, is, yes, was, this, but, on, well, he, have, for (Source: David Crystal, *The Cambridge Encyclopedia of Language*, second edition, CUP, 1997, p. 86.)

B 1 *Some possible answers*:

a) a **royal palace, the royal family**
b) to **dissuade** someone from doing something
c) a popular **king** / to crown a **king**
d) **up to my ears** in work
e) **independent** of someone / an **independent** country
f) **get married** to someone

2 a) scissors – only used in plural; if you want to count **scissors**, you have to say, for example, 'two pairs of **scissors**'.
b) weather – uncountable
c) teach, taught, taught; **teach** someone to do something; **teach** someone French.
d) advice – uncountable; a piece of **advice**; verb = to advise (regular).
e) lose, lost, lost (irregular)
f) trousers – only used in plural; if you want to count **trousers** you have to say, for example, 'three pairs of **trousers**'.

3 a) The 'b' in **subtle** is silent, as it is in **comb, tomb** and **lamb** too.
b) The final 'e' in **catastrophe** is pronounced as a syllable as it is in **apostrophe**. **Catastrophe** has 4 syllables. (See Index for pronunciation)
c) The stress is on the first syllable in **photograph**, and on the second syllable in **photographer**; it is on the third syllable in **photographical**. The 'rule' is that the stress in long words in English very frequently falls on the third syllable from the end of the word.
d) The 'w' in **answer** is silent. The final syllable is a schwa sound /ə/ and the 'r' is not usually pronounced in standard British English, unless it is followed by a vowel, e.g. Answer all the questions ...

4 guys is informal, persons is formal (most commonly found in legal documents) and people is neutral

5 *Some useful phrases from the text*:
periods of contact, foreign languages, sets of words, add greatly to, to express (subtle) shades of meaning.
If you have included other phrases from the text that seem useful to you, then that is fine too.

D Research into language learning can help you to prepare a sensible vocabulary learning plan. What you plan to do will, of course, depend very much on your own circumstances.

You cannot realistically aim to learn as many new words a day if you are working a full day at something else as if you are doing a full-time English course. In general, however, 10 to 20 words a week is probably a reasonable aim.

It does not matter where you try to learn vocabulary but it seems to be better to do a little on a regular basis rather than a lot infrequently. Research also suggests that it is a good idea to revise your work on a very regular basis – once a week, perhaps, but do not revise only the words that you've learnt in that week. Look back over your work of the previous month(s).

Unit 2

A 1 The network could be completed and added to like this:

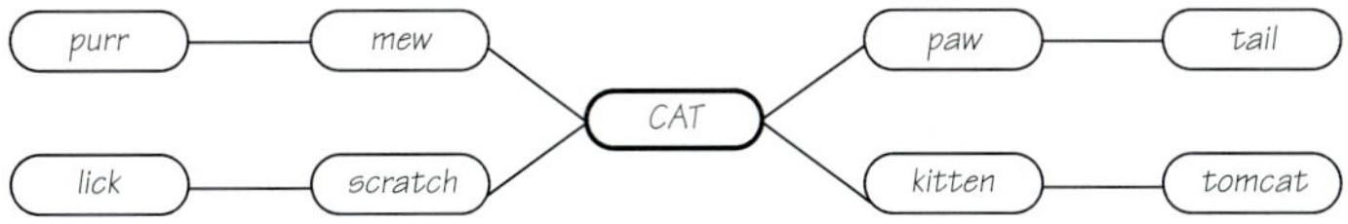

2 a) **Child, tooth** and **mouse** are all words with irregular plurals (**children, teeth, mice**). You could add more examples, e.g. **foot** (**feet**); **goose** (**geese**); **ox** (**oxen**); **phenomenon** (**phenomena**).

b) **Information, furniture** and **luggage** are all uncountable nouns – you could add **milk, money** and **work** to this group.

3 *Possible words and expressions to add*:

a) **pricey, underpriced, price tag** b) **to lend someone a hand**, a **handful**; a **handbag**, **underhand**, etc.

B 2 *Possible word tree for* **school**:

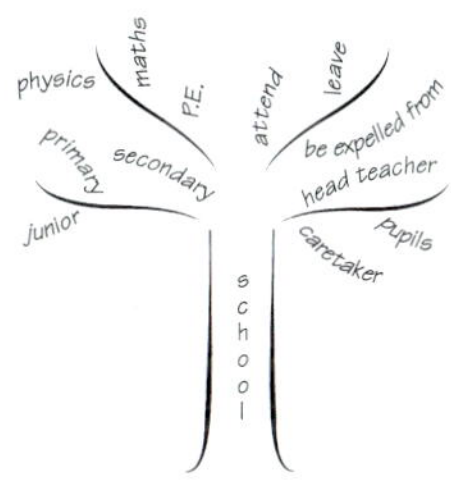

3 *Possible ways to complete the word forks*:

magnificent	views
breath-taking	
superb	
stunning	
splendid	

kick	a ball
hit	
bounce	
catch	
throw	

4 *Possible bubble diagram* for **make**:

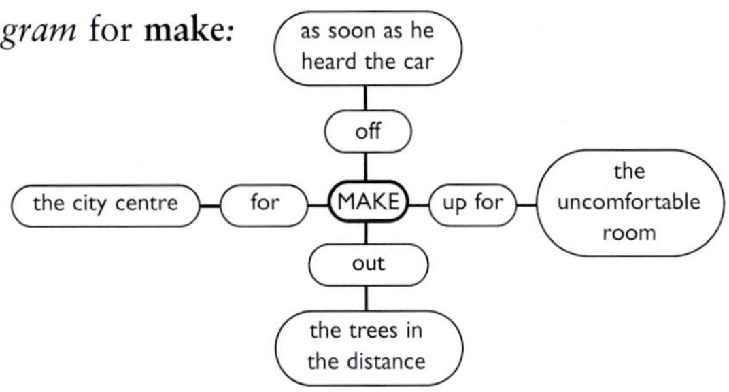

5 a) drive b) fly c) Riding

Unit 3

3.1 The list is probably connected to a lesson or lessons about time or a text about someone's relationship with time. A possible organisation might include bringing the **clock** words together in a word-map or bubble diagram (**clock, wristwatch, hands, minute-hand**); other words could then be added later (**hour-hand, face/dial, digital**, etc.).

Tell the time and **What time do you make it?** could form a separate list of 'time phrases', to which others could be added, e.g. **Have you got the time?, My watch is fast/slow**, etc. **Drowsy** and **wide awake** could be treated as antonyms, and some notes about the usage of **beneath** and **under** would be useful. This list could have information about word-class too.

3.2 **Theatre** seems the obvious word.

3.3 Other testing systems include re-entering any word you have difficulty remembering, so that it appears more than once in the notebook. Another useful discipline is to set yourself a fixed number of words to memorise each week, e.g. 20, and to tick them off in the book as you do them. You could also take out any 10 words from your book and put them on individual slips of paper which you stick in prominent places around your room or house, e.g. on the fridge door, so that you are regularly looking at them.

3.4

noun	*verb*	*adjective*	*person*
production	produce	productive	producer
industry	industrialise	industrial	industrialist
export	export	export	exporter

Note the change in stress from **ex**port (noun or adjective) to **export** (verb) and **exporter** (person), e.g. Our **ex**port figures have increased; we ex**port**ed 20% more goods last year.

Unit 4

4.1 *Suggested answers*:

1 style situation slang
2 be have refer
3 informal colloquial suitable
4 extremely mainly frequently
5 of to for

Obviously your answers here depend on how you answered 4.1. If you chose the same words as we did, then your answers to 4.2 will be as follows: style C situation C slang *U* be *IT, IR* have *T, IR* refer *IT, R*

4.2

verb	*infinitive*	*-ing form*	*past participle*
define	define	defining	defined
mean	mean	meaning	meant
write	write	writing	written

4.3 1 root – *form* prefix – *in* suffix – *al*
2 formal
3 casual e.g. of dress; colloquial e.g. of language; relaxed e.g. of occasion
4 form, formality, formless, deform, reform, reformation, and so on.

4.4 syllable colloquial pejorative collocation comma semi-colon apostrophe (note that there are four syllables in **apostrophe**) hyphen exclamation mark question mark brackets inverted commas capitals

4.5 1 converse 2 lavatory 3 man 4 tolerate 5 violin

4.6 1 terrorist 2 skinny 3 wordy 4 mean 5 cunning 6 extravagant

4.7 uncountable/abstract noun; intransitive/regular verb; colloquial expression/language.

4.8

( ) brackets	? question mark	’ apostrophe	, comma
; semi-colon	- hyphen	– dash	“ ” inverted commas

Unit 5

5.1 Open any page in your dictionary and look at the first word at the top of the page. Do you know it? If not, read the definition or translation and write the word (without the definition or translation) in your notebook. One week later, look at your notebook and see if you can remember what the word meant. If not, look it up again.

To improve your reading of phonetics for pronunciation, take six words from anywhere in the dictionary and copy only the phonetic pronunciation into your notebook or to a separate sheet of paper. After one week, see if you can read what the original words were. If you can’t, consult the list of pronunciation symbols in your dictionary.

5.2
1 All the words are possible. Some people feel that **sofa** and **couch** are a bit ‘lower class’, and that **settee** is the so-called ‘refined, middle-class’ word. **Divan** could also be used, but its normal British English meaning is a kind of bed with a very thick base. It can also, less commonly, mean a kind of sofa with no back or arms.
2 **Luxury** most typically collocates with **yacht**, though **ketch** (a double-masted sailing ship) would also be possible. A **dinghy** is a very small, open boat, hardly suitable for going around the world. **Sailing boat** sounds just too general here, since it covers all types of boats with sails.
3 **Wellingtons** is the most likely word, since they are rubber boots designed to keep the water out. **Boots** are any kind of high-sided footwear. **Bootees** suggests a kind of ankle-length shoe, fairly lightweight, usually with fur inside for cold weather, often referring to what babies wear. (**Wellingtons** is usually abbreviated to **wellies**.)
4 **Dinghy** would be a good word here (see 2 above), though **sailing boat** would also fit, as it’s quite general.

5.3 1 INFORMAL 2 CHANCE 3 NOT INTERESTED 4 TEMPORARY

5.4 1 education 2 passport 3 length 4 liberty 5 revision 6 brother

5.5 exciting, worrying, frightening

Follow-up: Cambridge University Press (CUP) publishes major learners’ dictionaries for International English and American English, as well as dictionaries of idioms and phrasal verbs. CUP also publishes bilingual thesauruses (dictionaries organised around meaning instead of alphabetically), for French-English, Italian-English, Greek-English, Spanish-English, Catalan-English and Portuguese-English.

There is no key for Unit 6.

Unit 7

7.1 The picture is a good clue to help you understand **tortoise**. You may recognise the word **shell** in **shelled** (as in **egg shell**, for example). Similarly, your knowledge of **long** and **life** together with the context should enable you to work out what **longevity** and **lifespan** mean. The whole context of the sentence should help you to work out the meaning of **tended**. Some of the underlined words may be similar to words in your own language which can be another useful way of working out the meaning of a word you have not seen before. The meanings of the underlined words are provided here for you to check your answers.

shelled: with a shell or hard protective cover
reptile: kind of animal that lays eggs and uses the heat of the sun to keep its blood warm (e.g. crocodiles, snakes)
famed: well-known (famous)
longevity: living a long life
lifespan: time from birth to death
tended: cared for
hibernate: go into a sleep-like state throughout the winter (as some animals and insects do)

7.2 *Possible answers*:
(These answers all give correct information in more detail than you would need to have provided in your own answers.)

1 Buzzards must be some kind of big bird, a sort that eats small animals.
2 A vole must be a kind of small animal, something like a mouse perhaps.
3 A chisel is something you use for shaping marble. It's a kind of tool used by sculptors.
4 A tureen must be a kind of very large bowl, a bit like a pot, used for soup.
5 To ladle is a way of serving soup by using something like a very large spoon.
6 To clamber means something like climbing with difficulty.
7 Ratty must be a bit like bad-tempered.

7.3 *Possible answers*:

1 It says on the can that this drink contains no sugar.
2 More and more shops now have their own special credit cards that can only be used in one specific chain of shops and offer you a discount if you use one of them.
3 I find Mo a very kind person.
4 I've been terribly busy with work ever since I got back from holiday.
5 We walked down a street with trees along both sides of it towards the station.
6 The little boys were fascinated by the machine used for mixing cement.

7.4

1 to change the address on an envelope so that it is sent somewhere else
2 anger that can't be controlled
3 drinks before dinner
4 a report that comes out either twice every month or every two months (both meanings of bi-monthly exist)
5 the person who used to be my boss (and no longer is)
6 feelings that are hostile to tourists

7 to break the telephone connection (e.g. by unplugging it from the wall or by doing something at the telephone exchange so that calls can no longer be made, possibly because a bill has not been paid.)
8 letters that have not been delivered to the people they were addressed to

Unit 8

8.1
1 windscreen wiper(s)
2 classical violinist
3 professional photographer /fəˈtɒgrəfə/
4 amateur actor
5 payee
6 dishwasher (normally written as one word)
7 organ donor
8 addressee

8.2
1 stapler
2 grinder
3 can-opener (*or* tin-opener)
4 nail-clipper
5 coat-hanger

8.4
1 a cooker – a thing (the stove on which you cook); the person who cooks is a **cook**.
2 a typewriter – a thing (machine for typing); the person is a **typist**.
3 a ticket-holder – person or thing; a person who has a ticket, e.g. for a concert, or a kind of wallet for holding tickets, e.g. a season ticket for the train/bus.
4 a CD player – a thing (machine for playing CDs).
5 a cleaner – person or thing; person who cleans, e.g. in an office or other place of work; a substance or instrument for cleaning, e.g. 'this cleaner will get the grease off your oven'.
6 a smoker – a person or thing; a person who smokes; a short name for a seat in the smoking area of a plane or a train (or the whole smoking compartment on a train).
7 a drinker – a person (someone who drinks alcohol, usually regularly or in large quantities).
8 a dresser – a person or thing; the person is someone who helps actors with their costumes; the thing is a piece of furniture.

8.5
1 forgivable
2 admission
3 laziness
4 productive
5 readable

8.7
1 neighbourhood: it is a place (an area); all the others refer to human relationships, quantities or identities.
2 handful: it is a noun; all the others are adjectives.
3 compliment: all the others are verb + 'ment', e.g. appoint + ment. There is no verb 'compli'.
4 worship: all the others are kinds of human relationships; **worship** refers to paying tribute to a God, or, figuratively, as a verb, to loving someone very, very much, e.g. 'They worshipped their teacher'.

Unit 9

9.1
1 indiscreet
2 insensitive
3 unconvincing
4 irrelevant
5 disobedient
6 inefficient
7 irresponsible
8 ungrateful
9 disloyal
10 intolerant

9.2
1 Unmarried
2 Inedible
3 Illiterate
4 Unemployed
5 Impartial
6 Irreplaceable

9.3 1 unwrapping 2 disagree 3 disprove 4 unveiled 5 to unload 6 disconnected

9.4 1 microwave 2 antibiotic 3 multi-national 4 on auto-pilot 5 postgraduate 6 subway

9.5 1 mispronouncing 2 are overworked but underpaid 3 post-dated his cheque 4 her ex-husband 5 rewrite it

Follow-up: Some possibilities:

prefix	*examples*	*prefix*	*examples*
anti	anti-government antiseptic	over	overrun overcharge
auto	autocue automobile	post	post-colonial post-industrial
bi	bi-plane bi-focals	pre	predict pre-conference
ex	ex-flatmate ex-partner	pro	pro-Iranian pro-nuclear
ex	express extort	pseudo	pseudo-democracy psuedo-liberal
micro	micro-chip microprocessor	re	rephrase redefine
mis	misspell mislead	semi	semi-literate semi-conscious
mono	monorail monosyllable	sub	sub-editor sub-human
multi	multi-cultural multi-faceted	under	underachieve underweight

Unit 10

10.1 The stress is on the underlined syllable in each of the words in the table.

verb	*person noun*	*adjective*	*abstract noun*
convert	convert	converted	conversion
produce	producer	productive	production, produce, product, productivity
conduct	conductor	conducive	conduct, conduction
impress	–	impressive	impression
support	supporter	supportive	support
impose	–	imposing	imposition

10.2 1 oppressive 2 deported 3 advertisements 4 introduce 5 inspector(s) 6 introductory 7 inspect 8 composed

10.3 1 It isn't easy to find synonyms for these words; the meanings are as follows: 'She spends a lot of time thinking about her own thoughts and feelings and so does he; he's quite shy and not very talkative.'
2 argue against
3 hold back
4 work out
5 made public
6 hold back
7 put into an appropriate form

10.4 support – hold up
reduce – cut down
postpone – put off
deposit – put down
oppose – go against
divert – turn away
inspect – look at

In each case the word based on the Latin root is more formal than its two part verb equivalent.

Follow-up: Some possibilities:
SPECT: circumspect behaviour; a retrospective exhibition; a fresh perspective.
VERT: an extroverted person; inverted commas; to pervert the innocent.
PORT: a railway porter; reported speech; transportation costs.
DUC, DUCT: to reduce taxes, to induce labour; a railway viaduct.
PRESS: blood pressure; compressed air; an original expression.
POSE, PONE: to pose for a photograph; to suppose something to be true; to repose peacefully.

Unit 11

11.1

1 affection	5 amusement	9 attentiveness	13 equality
2 excitement	6 grace	10 happiness	14 hope
3 kindness	7 originality	11 popularity	15 resentment
4 security	8 stupidity	12 weakness	16 wisdom

11.2

1 collect	5 strengthen	9 produce
2 empty	6 bore	10 own
3 satisfy	7 act	11 imagine
4 intensify	8 excite	12 adjust

11.3

1 amazement	5 replacement	9 sight
2 curiosity	6 stardom	10 freedom
3 brotherhood	7 reduction	11 rage
4 chance	8 neighbourhood	12 prosperity

11.4 1 darkness 2 advice 3 injustice 4 Imitation 5 kingdom

11.5 How you answer this question is a matter of your own originality. Here are some 'real' quotations about these abstract nouns, however:

1 Freedom is an indivisible word. If we want to enjoy it, and to fight for it, we must be prepared to extend it to everyone.
2 Love is a universal migraine. (Migraine = bad headache)
3 Life is a foreign language; all men mispronounce it.
4 Four be the things I'd be better without:
Love, curiosity, freckles and doubt.
5 Where there is no imagination, there is no horror.

Follow-up: Some possible answers:
There are many more possibilities for the B suffixes but not many for the C ones.

B -ment	(un)employment entertainment involvement requirement
-ion	diversion attraction direction rejection
-ness	awkwardness foolishness loveliness madness
-ity	brutality familiarity productivity superiority
-ship	citizenship chairmanship sponsorship championship
C -dom	dukedom earldom
-th	growth wealth stealth
-hood	babyhood nationhood

Unit 12

Note that when you are looking compound adjectives up in the dictionary you may sometimes find the word listed under its second element rather than its first. Sometimes, in some dictionaries, the word will not be listed at all if the meaning is absolutely clear from an understanding of the two elements.

Notice that the descriptions of Tom and Melissa on the left-hand page are light-hearted and far-fetched! They are not examples of good style as such long lists of adjectives would be inappropriate in a normal text.

12.1

1 brown, bright-eyed, wide
2 fool, dust-proof, fire
3 broad, narrow-minded, single
4 polo, round-necked, high
5 British, ready-made, home
6 tax, problem-free, hands
7 hot, pig-headed, bald
8 kind, soft-hearted, hard

Other possibilities are high-minded and hard-headed.

12.2 Here is one possible way of categorising the words. There will be many other ways of categorising them. What is most important is not how you categorise them but the process of doing the exercise itself. The process should help you to learn the words.

Words connected with money: cut-price duty-free interest-free
Words connected with comfort, safety, convenience and quality: air-conditioned hand-made remote-controlled sugar-free bullet-proof
Words connected with time: last-minute long-standing off-peak part-time time-consuming
Words often connected with travelling: long-distance second-class
Words often used to describe people: so-called world-famous
Odd man out: top-secret!

12.3 *Some examples*:

self-assured *P* self-satisfied *N* self-confident *P* self-conscious *N*
self-seeking *N* self-possessed *P* self-indulgent *N* self-employed *neutral*
self-evident *neutral* self-sufficient *neutral* self-willed *N* self-effacing *N*

12.4

1 No, she's long-sighted.
2 No, he's hard-up (or badly-off).
3 No, he's badly-behaved.
4 No, they're flat(-heeled)/low-heeled.
5 No, it's hand-made.
6 No, in north-west England.

12.5 *Some possible answers*:

air-conditioned house/car
bullet-proof car/vest
cut-price clothes/sale
duty-free perfume/whisky
hand-made chocolates/toys
interest-free offer/loan
last-minute preparations/arrival
long-distance train/runner
long-standing arrangement/affair
off-peak viewing/phone calls
part-time work/employment
remote-controlled TV/toy boat
second-class fare/citizen
so-called authority/specialist
sugar-free jam/cola
time-consuming work/preparations
top-secret papers/file
world-famous composer/novelist

12.6 1 up 2 on 3 back 4 off 5 of 6 out

Unit 13

13.1 Here are words which would fit appropriately into the bubble diagrams suggested.

money	*health*	*social problems*
luxury goods	blood donor	race relations
book token	heart attack	human rights
credit card	contact lens	arms race
burglar alarm	birth control	brain drain
income tax	blood pressure	death penalty
mail order	hay fever	generation gap
pocket money	food poisoning	greenhouse effect
	junk food	welfare state

13.2 Here are some possible answers for this question. There are some other possibilities also. Check with a dictionary or a teacher if you are not sure whether your answers are correct or not.

1 music token
2 junk mail
3 sound bite
4 blood ties
5 teapot
6 mother country
7 inheritance tax
8 word-processing
9 level-crossing
10 footlights
11 fast food
12 rat-race

13.3
1 pedestrian crossing
2 the greenhouse effect or global warming
3 hay fever
4 the arms race
5 air-traffic control
6 contact lens
7 the death penalty
8 package holiday
9 answering machine

13.4 *Suggested sentences*:
1 I always like getting one of these so that I can choose the music I like myself. (a music token)
2 I get an enormous amount through the post these days. (junk mail)
3 They say these are thicker than water. (blood ties)
4 He couldn't stand it any longer and went to be self-sufficient on a Scottish island. (the rat-race)
5 They had a huge amount to pay after their father died. (inheritance tax)
6 It is so much more efficient than using a typewriter. (word-processing)
7 We were given a large silver one as a wedding present. (teapot)
8 We've got one at the end of our village and you often have to stop to let the trains pass. (level-crossing)

13.5
1 A token which you can exchange for books of your choice in a bookshop.
2 An alarm in a house which goes off if burglars try to get into the house.
3 Being poisoned or being made ill by food that you have eaten.
4 A gap between different generations making it difficult for parents and children to understand each other's tastes and attitudes.
5 An increase in the amount of carbon dioxide and other gases in the atmosphere which is believed to lead to an increase in the world's temperatures i.e. the effect of temperature increase is similar to the increase of temperature in a greenhouse.

6 Scissors that are especially for use in a kitchen preparing food etc.
7 Goods that are luxuries rather than necessities, cosmetics rather than basic foods, for example.
8 Money that you carry in your pocket i.e. small amounts of money that can be spent on what you wish. (It is usually used about money that parents give their children every week to spend on what the children themselves decide.)
9 The part of the state that provides welfare for the members of society who need it – money for those out of work or pensioners or sick, for instance.

Unit 14

14.1

1 queue of traffic	3 attempt to conceal information	5 delay to traffic
2 burglaries	4 obstacle in the way of progress	6 escape

14.2 *Some possible answers*:

1 radioactive fallout	5 final output (*or* outcome)
2 nervous breakdown	6 sales outlet
3 computer printout	7 positive feedback
4 annual turnover	8 drastic cutbacks

14.3

1 takeover	3 walk-out	5 BREAK-OUT	7 outbreak
2 shake-up	4 input	6 check-out	8 pin-ups

14.4

1 write	3 work; press	5 clear	7 turn
2 hand	4 write	6 hold	8 lie

14.5
1 **Outlook** means prospect whereas a **look-out** is a person watching out for an enemy or danger.
2 **Set-up** means organisation whereas **upset** means disturbance.
3 **Outlet** means place where something is released whereas **let-out** means way of escaping from a difficult situation.
4 **Outlay** means amount of money spent on something whereas **layout** means the way something is arranged, e.g. the **layout** of a page or a room.

Unit 15

15.3 *Some words which fit most obviously into the networks suggested*:

food	*politics*	*the arts*	*animals*
yoghurt	embargo	avant-garde	mosquito
cuisine	junta	piano	poodle
gateau	guerrilla	soprano	dachshund
spaghetti	coup	ballerina	rottweiler
frankfurter	ombudsman	easel	mammoth
hamburger			lemming
marmalade			dodo
delicatessen			jackal
bistro			cobra
aubergine			
sauté			
sherbet			

15.4 *Other networks could include*:

clothes: anorak yashmak caftan shawl
things in the house: futon mattress alcove carafe duvet patio
sports and hobbies: origami judo karate caravan kayak ski yacht easel waltz casino snorkel
geographical features: fjord tundra steppe

15.5
1 military coup
2 strawberry yoghurt
3 pop psychology
4 Chinese cuisine
5 ankle tattoo
6 total embargo
7 long-standing vendetta
8 noisy kindergarten
9 double duvet
10 all-night casino

15.6
1 practise karate
2 paddle a kayak
3 sit on / sleep on a futon
4 place an embargo
5 be a guerrilla
6 live in a cul de sac
7 attempt a coup
8 throw confetti
9 have a siesta
10 go on / take a cruise
11 take/have a sauna
12 attend/give/hold a seminar

15.7 macho man/behaviour/clothes; avant-garde art/design/furniture

Unit 16

16.1

1 **Mr** A. Carlton
Flat **no.** 5
28, Hale **Cresc.**
Borebridge

2 **Ms** /məz/ P. Meldrum
c/o T. Fox
6, Marl **Ave.**
Preston

3 N. Lowe & **Co.**
7, Bridge **Rd.**
Freeminster
UK

Note: **Flat** could be abbreviated to **f.** or **fl.**, though this is not so common. **United Kingdom** is abbreviated, but **Great Britain** is not normally abbreviated in addresses. **Ms** is unusual in that English words do not normally like to have a stressed /ə/ vowel. For this reason, many people say /mɪz/.

16.2
1 Bachelor of Science (A)
2 Federal Bureau of Investigation (A)
3 Father (could also be 'French' or 'Franc') (C)
4 extension (telephone) (C)
5 compact disc (A)
6 as soon as possible (A)
7 personal identification number (B)
8 for example (D)
9 United Nations Educational, Scientific and Cultural Organisation (B)

16.3

Memorandum from Mister Richard Hedd (Managing Director)
To: All staff
Date: The third of May, 1991 Reference: 04056/DC
May I remind you that all new laboratory equipment should be registered with Stores and Supplies, Room 354 (extension 2683). Please note: new items must be notified before five o'clock in the afternoon on the last day of the month of purchase, that is, within the current budgeting month. All account numbers must be recorded.

16.4
1 **OAPs** – British English for 'Old age pensioners': retired people or senior citizens; on a museum entrance.
2 **WC** – 'water closet': a lavatory; **Gents** – gentlemen; on a door in a pub or restaurant.
3 **US** – United States of America; **POWs** – prisoners of war; newspaper headline.
4 **CFC** – Chloro-fluoro-carbons; nasty chemicals sometimes found in sprays, which can damage the ozone layer; on an aerosol can.
5 **Dep** – depart; **Arr** – arrive; on an airline timetable.

16.5
Across
3 UFO (pron. U-F-O) (Unidentified flying object of any kind)
6 EAST (N = north; S = south; W = west)
8 RN (Common abbreviation for the Navy in Great Britain)
9 RIP (usually put on gravestones or in newspaper announcements of deaths)
10 BIO (as in 'bio-degradable plastic')
11 CD (compact disc)
12 AND
13 ESP (this can also mean 'English for Special Purposes' or 'extra-sensory perception', a power some people say they have to see ghosts and spirits of the dead, or to see the future)
15 GB (each country has an abbreviation for car-plates when travelling in another country. What is your country's abbreviation?)
17 US (United States)
19 ET (Extra-terrestrial – a lovable creature from another planet in the film, called *ET*)
20 TUBE

Down
1 PER CENT
2 See 13 across
4 FRIDGES
5 ONO (used in advertisements: e.g. 'Bicycle for sale: £25 o.n.o.' This means perhaps £23 or £24 would be accepted if nobody else offers £25.
7 AIDS
10 BN (Please note = NB)
14 PUB (**pub** is a short form of 'public house')
16 BT (seen on phone boxes in Britain. The abbreviated name of British Telecom, a telecommunications company)
18 SE (NW = north-west, SW = south-west, NE = north-east)

Unit 17

17.1
1 someone who is addicted to shopping
2 someone who aspires to be something or someone else
3 ordinary post rather than e-mail
4 an advert distributed via the Internet
5 disagreeably crude male behaviour
6 a teenager highly skilled at using computers
7 to switch TV stations frequently, usually by using a remote control
8 a TV programme in which a hidden camera has filmed ordinary people going about their everyday lives
9 buying things by phone or computer

17.2

1 cybercafé
2 snail mail
3 singleton
4 snowboarding
5 grey vote
6 hot-desking
7 mouse potato
8 down-sizing
9 wannabe
10 audio book

17.3

1 hidden camera used by the police to detect cars that are travelling too fast
2 having access to banking services via the Internet
3 an alternative term for jet-skiing (using a vehicle powered by a petrol engine which travels over water on skis)
4 short for signature, information about the writer, their name and e-mail address and their affiliation perhaps
5 the practice of abandoning an elderly person in an unfamiliar location
6 a kind of mass-hysterical reaction to anything connected with Diana, Princess of Wales
7 cards for use in a particular shop (customers build up credits which can be used for discounts, special offers, etc.)
8 a set of adverse environmental conditions found in buildings with poor ventilation
9 a fear of computers
10 tourists who like to travel to places with unspoilt natural attractions

Unit 18

18.1

1 They sang a <u>p</u>sa<u>l</u>m to <u>h</u>onour the memory of the wo<u>r</u>ld-famous <u>p</u>syc<u>h</u>ologist as she was laid to rest in the family tom<u>b</u>. (Note that although the 'r' in 'world' is not really pronounced, in Standard British English, it affects the way the word is pronounced.)
2 The <u>p</u>syc<u>h</u>iatrist was <u>k</u>nifed in the <u>k</u>nee as he was wa<u>l</u>king home.
3 He shou<u>l</u>d have w<u>h</u>is<u>t</u>led as he fas<u>t</u>ened his s<u>w</u>ord to his belt. (Note that the 'h' in 'have' is not really pronounced when following an auxiliary verb as in this sentence and the next one.)
4 You cou<u>l</u>d have left me ha<u>l</u>f the C<u>h</u>ris<u>t</u>mas cake on We<u>d</u>nesday.

18.2 The odd one out appears first.

1 worry /ʌ/ sorry, lorry /ɒ/
2 word /ɜː/ sword, cord /ɔː/
3 dome /əʊ/ come, some /ʌ/
4 plead /iː/ head, tread /e/
5 could /ʊ/ doubt, shout /aʊ/
6 plough /aʊ/ rough, tough /ʌ/
7 wand /ɒ/ land, sand /æ/
8 root /uː/ soot, foot /ʊ/

18.3 *Possible answers*:

2 stuff 3 now 4 threw 5 off 6 go

18.4 The stressed syllables are underlined below.

1 <u>trans</u>fer; trans<u>ferr</u>ing
2 sus<u>pect</u>ed; <u>sus</u>pect
3 con<u>flict</u>ing; <u>con</u>flict
4 <u>up</u>set; up<u>set</u>
5 in<u>creased</u>; <u>de</u>crease
6 <u>per</u>mit; per<u>mits</u>
7 re<u>cord</u>; <u>re</u>cord
8 <u>con</u>duct; con<u>duct</u>ing

18.5

1 muscle
2 catastrophe
3 handkerchief
4 chemical
5 subtle
6 receipt
7 height
8 recipe

18.6

1 photograph, photography, photographer, photographically
2 telephone, telephonist
3 zoology, zoologist, zoological
4 arithmetic, arithmetical, arithmetician
5 psychology, psychologist, psychological
6 psychiatry, psychiatric, psychiatrist

Follow-up: Keep this question in mind as you continue with your English studies. Whenever you come across a word whose pronunciation seems strange, write it down with its phonetic transcription too.

Unit 19

19.2

1 click
2 whirred
3 sizzling
4 clinked
5 crash
6 groaned
7 splashing
8 drizzling

19.3

1 spit (spat, spat)
2 grumpy
3 spit (a spit is a long, thin metal spike on which meat is put for roasting)

19.4

1 splosh – colloquial form of splash
2 gargle – wash the throat with liquid kept moving by a stream of breath
3 rustle – make a gentle light sound like dry leaves in the wind
4 mumble – speak softly and indistinctly
5 creak – make a sound like that of an unoiled door hinge
6 whack – hit hard

19.5

1 a gash in someone's arm
2 a referee whistling
3 someone bashing something
4 someone spraying their hair
5 someone sprinkling something on a cake
6 water spurting out of the ground

19.6

schoolchildren giggle   a fire crackles   the bell on a cat's collar tinkles
a bad-tempered person or dog growls   a bored child wriggles   a bicycle chain clanks
a steam train whistles   a church-bell clangs   someone with asthma wheezes

Follow-up: Some possible answers:

gr: **grizzle** and **grudge**, both have rather unpleasant meanings – **grizzle** is to cry because of bad temper rather than pain or discomfort and **grudge** is to be unwilling to give or do something.

cl: **clap** or **clatter**, both represent quite sharp sounds – **clap** is to put your hands together quickly and loudly and **clatter** is to make a long, continuous resounding noise like hard metallic things falling on a hard surface.

sp: **spatter** or **spill** both have an association with liquid or powder – **spatter** means to splash or scatter in drops like hot oil from a frying pan; **spill** means to knock over something liquid.

wh: **whirl** and **whisk** both have associations with the movement of air – **whirl** means to move quickly round and **whisk** means move or sweep quickly through the air.

Unit 20

20.1

1 The girl I live (give) with knows a good pub with live (five) music.
2 The main house (mouse) houses (browse) a collection of rare stamps.
3 It's no use (juice). I can't use (snooze) this gadget.
4 You sow (go) the seeds while I feed the sow. (cow)
5 The violinist in the bow (so) tie made a bow. (now)
6 He's the lead (deed) singer in the group 'Lead (head) piping'.
7 What a row (plough) from the last house in the row! (though)
8 Does he still suffer from his war wound? (tuned)
9 I wound (round) the rope around the tree to strengthen it against the gale.
10 It's hard to wind (find) in the sails in this wind. (tinned)

Note: These sentences do not sound natural. They are only used for the exercise.

20.2

1 waste
2 sole
3 pane
4 heir
5 allowed
6 practise
7 through; phase
8 peel

20.3 *Possible answers*:

Note: Most sentences in 'real' English avoid using pairs of homophones as they may be confusing and often don't sound natural.

1 **They're** going to take **their** aunt to have dinner **there** this evening.
2 **It's** the first time the car has left **its** garage this year.
3 Let's **practise** with these grammar exercises first and then do some vocabulary **practice.**
4 It's **great** to see such a lovely fire burning in the **grate.**
5 Don't **whine** so much, just because the **wine**'s finished.
6 **Brake** now or you'll **break** that toy in the road.
7 The archaeological **site** was a marvellous **sight** at sunset.
8 Let us **pray** that we may never be **prey** to evil thoughts.
9 Although she was a little **hoarse** it did not put her off **horse** riding in the snow.
10 The beautiful sight of the moon's **rays** reflected in the lake did a great deal to **raise** her spirits.

20.4

1 A woolly jumper.
This is a play on words on the two meanings of **jumper** – a sweater and a person or animal that jumps.

2 Let's play draughts.
This is a play on words on the two meanings of **draughts.** One is the game played with round counters and a chess board and the other is a current of air as in 'There's a terrible draught coming from under the door'.

3 He wanted to draw the curtains.
This is a play on words on two meanings of **draw.** The first means make a picture and the second means pull.

4 Because it's full of dates.
This is a play on words on the two meanings of **dates.** One refers to years such as 1066, 1892; the other to a sweet fruit coming from a kind of palm tree or to an evening spent together by two people (usually romantic).

5 A drum takes a lot of beating.
This is a play on words on two meanings of **beating.** A drummer beats a drum. There is also an expression, 'takes a lot of beating' which means 'is hard to improve on'.

20.5 1 tea and tee
2 pair and pear
3 waste and waist
4 toe and tow

Unit 21

21.1 2 Till then
3 By the time / When
4 While/When
5 Previously/Earlier/Before that
6 As soon as /After/When
7 When/Once/After
8 The moment/minute

21.2 *Other possible sentences*:

While she was in Paris, she missed home a lot.
She went to the theatre **after** she'd been to the Pompidou Centre.
While driving home from Glasgow, she saw a bad accident on the motorway.
Prior to going on to Glasgow, she was in Manchester.

21.3 *Possible answers*:
2 ... I usually feel guilty and go on a diet for a while.
3 ... switch on the radio.
4 ... lived in the same house.
5 ... reading a story.
6 ... go back home and look for a job.
7 ... double-check that everything is booked.
8 ... upset and want to make it up as soon as possible.

Unit 22

22.1 1 **as long as / providing / provided that** are all OK; **on condition that** is fine too, and sounds a little stronger and more formal.
2 **In case of / In the event of** (often seen in notices and regulations).
3 **Unless**
4 Since this is legal/official language **on condition that** would be very suitable, or **providing / provided that; so long as** is also possible, but **as long as** sounds just a little too informal.
5 **Supposing / What if** (less tentative, more direct and informal) **/ If**

22.2 *Suggested answers*:
1 You cannot enter unless you have an Entry Visa. *or* You can/may enter providing/ provided that you have an Entry Visa.
2 You can/may go on to university as long as you get 70% or more in the exam. *or* Unless you get 70%, you cannot go on to university.
3 You can't come in unless you're over 18. *or* You may enter the club providing you are over 18.
4 Visitors may enter the mosque on condition that they remove their shoes. *or* You can go in as long as you take off your shoes (informal).

22.3 1 No matter where she goes, she always takes that dog of hers.
2 If anyone rings, I don't want to speak to them, whoever it is.
3 Whatever I do, I always seem to do the wrong thing.
4 It'll probably have meat in it, no matter which dish you choose. They don't cater for vegetarians here.
5 However I do it, that recipe never seems to work.

22.4 *Some possible answers*:
1 For the authors of this book, who are teachers, the prerequisites are a degree and a teaching qualification.
2 Many people might move if they were offered a good job in another part of the country, or if a motorway was going to be built at the bottom of their garden!
3 In Britain, the normal entry requirements are A-level exam passes in relevant subjects. (A-levels are exams taken at 18 years old.)
4 For most people it would be a good idea to make the condition that the person should pay for any breakages (i.e. things that get broken), keep the place clean and perhaps pay coal/gas/oil/electricity and phone bills.

Unit 23

23.1 *Suggested answers*:
1 The announcement **provoked/generated** a strong attack from the opposition.
2 The new Act of Parliament has **brought about / led to** great changes in industry.
3 The train crash was **caused by / due to** a signal failure.
4 A violent storm **caused** the wall to collapse. *or* **Owing to** a violent storm, the wall collapsed.
5 The food shortages **sparked** (**off**) serious riots in several cities.
6 The food shortages **stemmed from / arose out of** bad economic policies.

23.2 1 The reason I didn't contact you was (because) I'd lost your phone number. *or* My reason for not contacting you was ... (this is also acceptable, but sounds more formal).
2 I will not sign, on the grounds that this contract is illegal.
3 The aim of the new law the government passed was to control prices. *or* The government passed a new law with the aim of controlling prices.
4 I wonder what her motives were in sending everyone flowers. (Note the preposition *in*)
5 The high salary prompted her to apply for the job.

23.3 *Possible answers*:
1 There were awful blizzards, which caused the road to be blocked.
2 Owing to the fact that the performance was cancelled, everyone got a refund.
3 The service was terribly slow. As a result / Consequently (more formal), all the customers got angry.
4 We missed the last bus. As a result we had to walk home.

23.4 1 for 2 of 3 with; of 4 in 5 out of *or* from 6 with; to 7 to

Unit 24

24.1 *Suggested answers*:

1 I accept (or more formal: I acknowledge) that you weren't solely to blame, but you must take *some* responsibility. (**Accept** and **acknowledge** are most suitable here since the speaker is prepared to agree with one aspect but wants to go on to make another point to support his/her case.)
2 OK, I admit I was wrong, you were right; he *is* a nice guy. (This seems to be a situation where somebody is accusing someone or trying to get them to say they were wrong. **Admit** is ideal in this case.
3 The company acknowledges that you have suffered some delay, but we do not accept liability. (**Acknowledge** is perhaps best here; it is often used in formal, legalistic situations like this because it simply says 'We understand your message, but we do *not* necessarily accept any blame/responsibility'; **admit** might suggest the company *does* accept legal responsibility; **accept** is also possible though less formal.)
4 She accepted/conceded that we had done all we could, but she was still not content. (**Concede** usually suggests an argument or debate where people might 'give' small points to one another while still holding on to their basic position, and would seem to be a likely choice here; **concede** here suggests she did not really want to say it.)

24.2 *Possible answers*:

2 The house itself is rather small.
3 There is no sign that the government has solved the traffic problem.
4 In most of the rest of Europe, the traffic drives on the right. (Ireland also drives on the left.)
5 I'm not at all hungry, thanks.

24.3

Across	Down
1 yawning	2 apart
3 world	4 divide
5 huge	6 gap
7 poles	

24.4 *Possible comments:*

1 There's a great divide between those who believe in nuclear weapons, and those who believe in world disarmament.
2 There's a huge discrepancy between what she says and what she does.
3 Jim and Sandra are poles apart when it comes to believing in God / on the question of believing in God.
4 There's a world of difference between being a student and being a teacher.

24.5 *Suggested answers*:

1 that's all well and good
2 After all
3 for all that / after all
4 It's all very well

24.6

1 on the contrary (it's *not* true that I'm worried)
2 on the other hand (it *is* true that it's expensive, but if you look at it from another point of view, we need it)

Unit 25

25.1 *Suggested answers*:

1 Further to
2 In addition to / As well as / Apart from / Besides
3 etc. / and so on
4 in addition to / as well as / apart from / besides
5 Furthermore / Moreover / Likewise

Comments: In (2) and (4), the choice is quite wide, but, depending on which one she chooses for (2), the writer would probably then choose a different one, to avoid repeating herself, for (4).

In (3), **etc.** is slightly more formal than **and so on**, and the writer may want to avoid sounding too informal.

In (5), if she wanted to use **what's more**, the writer would probably write it in full as **what is more**, so as not to sound too informal. However, **what's more / what is more** can often sound a little abrupt and argumentative (as if you're trying very hard to convince the reader) and might sound just a bit too strong here.

In (5), **furthermore/moreover** add her previous experience on to the rest; **likewise** not only adds the information but suggests it is of equal value to the other experience she has mentioned. **Equally** would not be suitable here, as it is best used when arguing points and presenting opinions (trying to convince someone of the equal value of a point added on to other points).

25.2
1 Physical labour can exhaust the body very quickly. Equally, excessive study can rapidly reduce mental powers.
2 My cousin turned up, along with some schoolmates of his.
3 As well as owning a big chemical factory, he runs a massive oil business in the USA. *or* He owns a big chemical factory as well as running a massive oil business in the USA.
4 She was my teacher and a good friend into the bargain.
5 In addition to being their scientific adviser, I also act as consultant to the Managing Director.

25.3
1 I work part time as well as **being** a student, so I have a busy life.
2 Besides **having** a good job, my ambition is to meet someone nice to share my life with.
3 Alongside **my** many other responsibilities, I now have to be in charge of staff training.
4 In addition **to** a degree, *or* In addition **to having** a degree, she also has a diploma.
5 My father won't agree. **Likewise**, my mother's sure to find something to object to.
6 She is a good footballer and she's a good athlete **to boot**.
7 He said he'd have to first consider the organisation, then the system, then the finance **and so on and so forth**.

25.4 1 to boot 2 into the bargain 3 plus (+) 4 on top of (all) that

Unit 26

26.1 1 fact 2 issue (*or* problem) 3 belief 4 problem 5 evaluation 6 view

26.2
1 issue (best here because it is something everyone is debating and disagreeing on, **question** and **problem** are also OK)
2 problem/matter; **crisis** if it is really serious.
3 question (**mystery** would also be possible)
4 topic
5 approach/response/solution/answer

26.3
1 Situation in Sahel worsening daily
2 New approach to cancer treatment
3 Scientist rejects claims over fast food
4 Solution to age-old mystery in Kenya
5 Prime Minister sets out views on European Union
6 New argument over economic recession

Unit 27

27.1 'Well, where shall I start? It was last summer and we were just sitting in the garden, sort of doing nothing much. Anyway, I looked up and ... see we have this kind of long wall at the end of the garden, and it's ... like ... a motorway for cats, for instance, that big fat black one you saw, well, that one considers it has a right of way over our vegetable patch, so ... where was I? Yes, I was looking at that wall, you know, day-dreaming as usual, and all of a sudden there was this new cat I'd never seen before, or rather, it wasn't an ordinary cat at all ... I mean, you'll never believe what it was ...'

Comments:

Well is often used to shift the conversation to a different type or topic (here from the ordinary conversation to a story).

Where / How shall I start / begin? ('begin' is much more common in written language than in spoken). This is a very common marker at the beginning of a story or monologue while the speaker is composing his/her thoughts.

Anyway is probably the most common marker in spoken story-telling to divide up the story into its different stages (introduction / main plot / resolution, etc.)

See is often used in informal talk instead of **you see**, when someone is clarifying or explaining something.

Like, sort of and **kind of** are often used when the speaker hesitates, or to make something less precise, a little more vague.

Well here is used to focus on an important point.

So is very commonly used to mark the beginning of the next event in a story.

Where was I? is used when we want to come back to the main subject we were talking about after an interruption or diversion into another point or topic.

Yes is often used when we resume what we were talking about; it does not have to be an answer to a question from someone. **No** is also used in exactly the same way and could have been used here instead of **yes**.

You know is used here to mean 'you can guess what I was like'.

Or rather is used when you change to a different word or a better / more accurate way of saying what you want to say.

I mean is used when you want to explain something or expand or illustrate what you are saying.

This extract is typical of the number of markers found in everyday informal talk. The speaker is not a 'lazy' or 'bad' speaker; everyone uses markers, even if they are not conscious of it or do not want to admit it! Informal conversation *without* markers sounds rather odd and strained, and a little too formal.

27.2 *Possible answers:*

1 A: Are you a football fan?
B: **Well**, I like it; I wouldn't say I was a fan.

2 A: I'll take care of these.
B: **Right**, that's everything.
A: **Fine, so** see you next week.
B: **Good**. That was a very useful meeting.

3 A: It was last Monday. I was coming home from work. I saw this ragged old man approaching me. **Anyway**, I stopped him ...
B: Jim Dibble!
A: **Hang on!** Let me tell you what happened first.

4 A: Which number is yours?
B: **Let me see** ... it's that one here, yes, this one.

5 A: He's looking exhausted.
B: Yes, he is.
A: **Mind you**, he has an awful lot of responsibility, so it's hardly surprising.

6 A: What do you mean 'cold'?
B: **Well**, she's not friendly, very distant, **so to speak**. Last week I gave her a jolly smile and she ... **like** ... scowled at me.
A: **Well** what do you expect? **Look**, I've seen the way you smile at people, it **sort of** puts them off.

27.3
1 Yes, there is a lot of work to do. Anyway, I must rush now, I'll call you tomorrow.
2 There's two reasons I think he's wrong. A, people don't act like that, and b, Paul would certainly never act like that.
3 At the end of the day, money is not the most important thing in life. I really do believe that.
4 I never got a chance to tell him. Still, I'm seeing him next week. I'll tell him then.

Follow-up: If it is difficult or impossible for you to get hold of tape-recordings of natural conversation, there are tapes and transcripts of everyday English conversation in R. Carter and M. McCarthy, *Exploring Spoken English* (Cambridge University Press, 1997), where you will find a wide range of spoken discourse markers in actual use, with commentaries.

Unit 28

28.1
1 First of all / Firstly
2 in other words
3 For example / For instance
4 Next
5 as it were
6 Lastly
7 In summary *or* in sum (more formal). (**In conclusion** would not be suitable here, since it just means 'this is the end of the text', whereas this sentence provides a summing up of the arguments in the text.)

28.2
1 this will not be discussed
2 as an aside / secondary issue
3 change the topic
4 to finish off
5 this document is about another one
6 read something earlier in the text

28.3 1 say, meaning 'for example'
2 the following (introducing a list)
3 further (as in *further details/information*)
4 overleaf (meaning turn the page)
5 in summary, to sum up, in sum

28.4 *Sample letter*:

> Dear Editor,
>
> **With reference to** the article in your newspaper about the closure of Mainton Hospital, I would like to express my strong opposition to the proposal, for **the following** reasons. **Firstly**, the nearest other hospital is 50 kilometres away. **Secondly**, 200 people work at the hospital and they will lose their jobs and the whole region will suffer, **that is to say** the hospital makes an important contribution to the local economy. **Finally**, it is the only hospital in the region with a special cancer unit. But **leaving aside** the economic and medical questions, the hospital is obviously being closed for political reasons, and this is quite wrong.
>
> **To sum up**, the closure of our hospital would be a disaster both for the people and for the economy of this region.
>
> Yours sincerely,
>
> Anne Gree (Ms)

Unit 29

29.1 1 no article 2 no article 3 an 4 no article 5 no article
6 no article; if you said **a film** here it would sound as if you mean one film, and then suddenly change your mind and decide to buy five rolls.
7 no article in both cases

29.2 The words on the left are matched with words on the right in terms of similar meaning.

Uncountable	*Countable*
clothing	garment
information	fact
advice	tip
travel	trip
work	job
baggage	case

29.3 *Some uncountable items you might put into your suitcase*:

soap toothpaste make-up underwear clothing writing-paper
film medicine shampoo suntan lotion

29.4 1 We had such terrible weather that we left the camp-site and got accommodation in town instead.
2 In the North of England, most houses are made of stone, but in the South, brick is more common.
3 I love antique furniture, but I would need advice from a specialist before I bought any. My knowledge in that area is very poor.
4 Her research is definitely making great progress these days. She has done a lot of original work recently.

29.5 *Possible answers*:

A soldier needs a lot of courage, determination, stamina, loyalty and a lot of training.
A nurse needs a lot of patience and goodwill. A bit of charm also helps, and a lot of commitment and training is needed.
A teacher needs great patience, a lot of energy, a bit of creativity, intelligence and some training.
An explorer needs a lot of stamina, courage and determination, as well as energy.
An actor needs a lot of creativity, talent, imagination and some training.
An athlete needs great stamina and determination, and a lot of commitment.
A writer needs a lot of creativity, imagination, talent and a bit of intelligence.
A surgeon needs experience, patience and a lot of training.
A receptionist needs charm, goodwill, reliability and energy.

29.8 Could I have **some** vinegar?
Could I have **a** duster?
Could I have **a** needle?
Could I have **some** thread?
Could I have **some** sellotape?
Could I have **a** tea-bag?
Could I have **some** shoe polish?

Unit 30

30.1 Individual answers. In addition to those on the left-hand page, subjects and areas of study that are plural might include:

arts/humanities natural sciences genetics politics ethics

30.2
2 glasses
3 scissors
4 braces
5 tweezers
6 binoculars
7 pincers/pliers (pliers are usually best for electrical jobs, e.g. cutting wires/cables)
8 handcuffs

30.3 knickers/pants trousers tights shorts dungarees

30.4
1 pyjamas
2 proceeds
3 acoustics
4 whereabouts
5 jodhpurs
6 authorities; goods

30.5 1 trousers 2 billiards 3 scissors 4 dungarees

30.6 I decided that if I wanted to be a pop star I'd have to leave home and get **lodgings** in London. I finally got a room, but it was on the **outskirts** of the city. The owner didn't live on the **premises**, so I could make as much noise as I liked. The **acoustics** in the bathroom **were** fantastic, so I practised there. I made so much noise I almost shook the **foundations**! I went to the **headquarters** of the Musicians' Union, but a guy there said I just didn't have good enough **looks** to be famous. Oh well, never mind!

Unit 31

31.1
1 Yes, most people have a **cloth** somewhere in the kitchen to wipe the work surfaces and in case somebody spills something.
2 It is not likely that most people will have a **wood**. A **wood** is a rather big area of land covered with trees (a small forest).
3 Some people have a **fish** (or several **fish**) swimming around in a tank in their living room.

4 Most people have **pepper** (together with salt) in their kitchen or dining room.
5 Most homes have **glass** somewhere, usually in the windows.
6 Most people have **paper** somewhere, for writing letters and notes, or for wrapping parcels.
7 Only people who consume alcohol would have **drink** in their house; they'd probably keep it in a cocktail cabinet or a cupboard.
8 You would have a **tape** if you have a tape recorder or a video recorder, and you'd probably keep it near the machine.
9 A **rubber** is quite common. It is used for rubbing out writing done in pencil, and would normally be kept with pens and pencils.

31.2 *Suggested answers*:

1 Could I borrow an iron?
2 Could I have some pepper?
3 Could I have a chocolate?
4 Could I borrow some paper?
5 Could I borrow a rubber?
6 Could I have a glass?

31.3 *Possible answers*:

1 I drove over some glass. *or* There was glass in/on the road.
2 No, she's living in a home now.
3 Perhaps he should get a trade, become a carpenter or something.
4 Well, it had a lot of land with it.
5 It's a very famous work of art, a painting.
6 Well, look at the policy; that should tell you everything you need to know.

31.4
1 **Some sauce** here typically means bottled sauce, such as tomato ketchup. **A sauce** means a specially prepared sauce to go with a particular dish, e.g. a white sauce, a cheese sauce.
2 **Plant** means very heavy equipment, e.g. heavy machinery for building. **A plant** means a botanical plant for cultivation. **A plant** can also mean a factory or large installation, e.g. a nuclear power plant – a place where electricity is generated.
3 **Light** (uncountable) usually means light in order to see better, e.g. electric light or a torch. Used countably in the request 'Can I have / can you give me a **light**, please?', it usually refers to a match or lighter to light a cigarette or pipe.

Unit 32

32.1 1 swarms 2 shoal 3 gang 4 pack 5 team 6 pair 7 couple

32.2 1 swimmers 2 a book 3 a hospital 4 cats 5 pigs

32.3
2 a range of mountains*
3 a gang of schoolkids
4 a swarm of flies
5 a row of houses
6 a heap of bed-linen
7 a herd of elephants

*We also say 'a mountain range'.

32.4
1 There's a stack of tables in the next room.
2 There's a crowd of people waiting outside.
3 The staff are very well-paid.
4 A flock of sheep had escaped from a field.
5 She gave me a set of six sherry glasses.
6 She gave me a bunch of beautiful roses *or* a beautiful bunch of roses.

32.5 a whole **host** of a **barrage** of a **string** of a **series** of

Unit 33

33.1

1 a stroke of luck
2 a shower of rain
3 an article of clothing
4 a lump of coal
5 a flash of lightning
6 a blade of grass
7 an item of news/clothing
8 a rumble of thunder

33.2

1 My mother gave me a piece of advice that I have always remembered.
2 Suddenly a gust of wind almost blew him off his feet.
3 We had a spell of terribly windy weather last winter.
4 Would you like another slice of toast?
5 He never does a stroke of work in the house.
6 Let's go into the garden – I need a breath of fresh air.
7 I can give you an important bit of information about that.
8 We could see a cloud of smoke hovering over the city from a long way away.
9 There is an interesting new piece of equipment in that catalogue. *or* There are some interesting new pieces of equipment ...
10 I need to get some pieces of furniture for my flat.

33.3 1 health 2 emergency 3 disrepair 4 uncertainty 5 poverty

33.4 *Possible puzzle:*

1 Did you see that .... of lightning?
2 She sells old .... of clothing at the market.
3 Have you ever seen him do even a .... of work?
4 What a loud .... of thunder. It sounded almost overhead.
5 Let's go and get a .... of fresh air. It's so stuffy indoors.

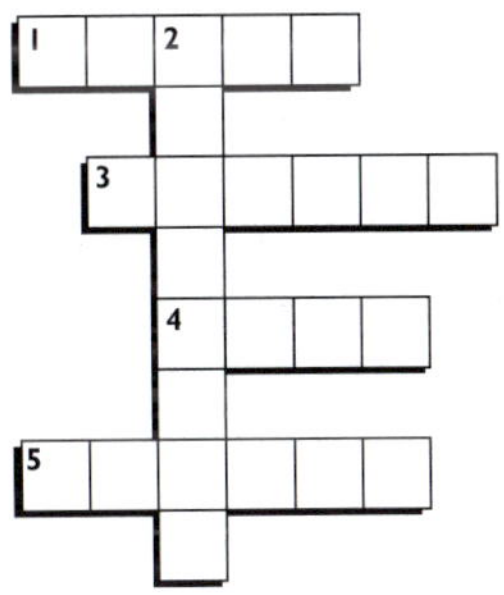

Answers

1 flash
2 articles
3 stroke
4 clap
5 breath

33.5 *Possible sentences*:

1 We moved over a month ago but we are still in a state of chaos.
2 The company has been going through a state of flux for some months now as two chairmen have died in rapid succession.
3 Everything seems to be in an impossible state of confusion at the moment but I'm sure it'll all be sorted out before the wedding.
4 It is not unusual for job candidates to get themselves into a terrible state of tension before a final interview.

Unit 34

34.1

2 bottles/cartons of milk
4 cans of cola
a tin of condensed milk
a packet/box of chocolate biscuits
a packet/carton of cigarettes
a large box of matches
a jar of honey
6 packets of crisps

34.2
1 tub, pot
2 barrel, bottle, sack (of coal/potatoes)
3 can, bottle, barrel, pack, crate, case
4 *any of these*: bottle/carton (of milk), jug (of milk), mug (of tea), packet (of cornflakes), jar (of jam/marmalade/honey), glass (of milk), bowl (of sugar)
5 bag (or perhaps a sack)
6 bag and basket
7 (a) 200 (b) 10 or 20

34.3
1 a jar of peanut butter
2 a packet of washing powder
3 a carton of cream
4 a tube of hand cream
5 a tin of sardines
6 a tin of tomatoes
7 a bag of apples
8 a box of tissues
9 a packet of butter
10 a pack of 12 cans of beer
11 a bottle of washing-up liquid
12 a box of matches

34.4 *Possible answers*:
1 chocolate/tool/match
2 wine/milk/water
3 carrier/shopping/mail
4 milk/cream/water
5 wine/whisky/liqueur /lɪ'kjʊə/
6 flower/tea/coffee

Unit 35

35.1
1 Argentinian Venezuelan Costa Rican Panamanian /pænə'meɪnɪən/ Mexican Peruvian (note the v) Ecuadorian Bolivian Uruguayan Paraguayan etc.
2 Ukrainian Serbian Croatian Slovenian Bulgarian Rumanian Albanian Moldavian etc.
3 Other groupings: -i adjectives seem to describe Middle Eastern or Muslim countries; four of the -ese adjectives are from the Pacific Rim.

35.2 *Possible answers*:
1 Mao-Tse Tung
2 Nelson or Winnie Mandela
3 Pope John Paul II
4 Luciano Pavarotti
5 U2

35.3
1 <u>Pan</u>ama → Pana<u>man</u>ian /pænə'meɪnɪən/
2 <u>Cy</u>prus → <u>Cy</u>priot /'sɪprɪət/
3 <u>Gha</u>na → Gha<u>nai</u>an /gɑː'neɪən/
4 <u>Jor</u>dan → Jor<u>dan</u>ian /dʒɔː'deɪnɪən/
5 <u>E</u>gypt → E<u>gyp</u>tian /ɪ'dʒɪpʃən/
6 <u>Fi</u>ji → Fi<u>ji</u>an /fɪ'dʒiːən/

35.4 1 Princess to marry a **Frenchman**? Royal sensation! (Note how Frenchman is normally written as one word. French woman is usually two words.)
2 **Britons** have highest tax rate in EU
3 **Rwandan** refugees leave Hong Kong camps
4 Police arrest **Dane** (or **Danish man/woman**) on smuggling charge
5 **Iraqi** delegation meets **Pakistani** President

35.5 1 Malays, Chinese (or various ethnic sub-types), and Indians (many are Tamils and Sikhs).
2 If we take Scandinavia as strictly the geographical peninsula, then Sweden and Norway are the only countries completely in Scandinavia. If we consider it more as a language family, then Denmark and Iceland can be added, and if as a cultural family, then Finland can be added too.
3 Approximate populations are China: 975,000,000; India: 638,000,000; USA: 218,000,000; Indonesia: 141,000,000; Brazil: 116,000,000. The former Soviet Union used to be third, with 260,000,000 (source: *The Times Atlas*).
4 A difficult question! However, most linguists seem to agree on around 5,000 mutually incomprehensible tongues. There are, of course, many many more dialects.
5 Kiribati is an independent country in the middle of the Pacific Ocean. It has only about 57,000 people.
6 Inuit is an Eskimo language, and its speakers may be found in Northern Canada.
7 Languages most widely spoken, in the following order, are Chinese, English, Spanish, Hindi, Arabic (source: *The Cambridge Encyclopedia of Language* Cambridge University Press).

Unit 36

36.1 Some of these combinations form one solid word and some remain as two words.

1 thunderstorm
2 torrential rain
3 downpour
4 heatwave
5 hailstones
6 snowdrift
7 gale warning

36.2 1 slush 2 sleet 3 frost 4 blizzards 5 snowdrifts 6 thaws 7 melts

36.3 *Possible answers*:

1 There was a heatwave in July. *or* It was scorching/boiling (hot) last month.
2 It was terrible muggy and humid as we worked.
3 It was absolutely stifling today.
4 There was ice/snow/slush on the roads this morning.
5 We had terrible floods that winter.
6 There was a heavy blizzard that night.
7 Do you remember how mild it was that year?
8 There was a very bad drought that summer.
9 Suddenly there was a very strong gust of wind.
10 After the hurricane/gale, the damage was unbelievable.
11 There was a very dense fog that morning.

36.4 1 *bad*: too dry, a drought, or frost *good*: mild weather just after rain
2 *bad*: cold, windy or wet weather
good: warm, mild, or even cool (if it has been a terribly hot day) and preferably dry
3 *bad*: gales, high winds, hurricanes, storms, wet weather, mist/fog, no wind at all
good: clear, sunny, dry, breezy weather

4 *bad*: cold, wet and windy weather or humid, muggy weather
good: fine, dry, but not too hot
5 *bad*: wet, windy, snowy weather *good*: dry, no wind, warm nights
6 *bad*: fog/mist, rain *good*: clear, dry, sunny weather

Unit 37

37.1 *Suggested answers*:

1 ... the fair, bald guy. *or* straight-/curly-haired man.
2 ... scruffy and untidy-looking/messy-looking.
3 ... that slim, dark-haired woman over there.
4 ... unattractive, in fact. (You could also say he/she was 'rather plain' or 'rather ordinary', if you felt they were neither attractive nor unattractive. 'Ugly' is a very strong word indeed, and could be offensive.)
5 ... a teenager / in her twenties. (Another useful expression is 'she's a youngster', for a person who is a teenager or who is still very young.)

37.2 1 The author who wrote this exercise is tall, with brown hair which is going grey; he's white, in his early fifties and thinks he's good-looking! What about you?

37.3 stocky build overweight middle-aged round-faced
long-haired long-legged /'legɪd/ well-dressed mixed-race
tanned complexion (tanned = brown from the sun) red-haired red-faced

37.4 *Suggested answers*:

Ian Prowse, height 6ft, thin-faced, dark, curly hair, fair skin.
Sandra King, height 5ft 4, dark, wavy hair, stocky build, round-faced.
Louise Fox, age 7, Asian appearance, straight, dark hair.
Jack 'Dagger' Flagstone, 6ft, bald, with beard and moustache; muscular build.

Unit 38

38.1 *Opposites*:

1 clever – half-witted
2 extroverted – introverted
3 rude – courteous
4 cruel – kind-hearted
5 generous – tight-fisted
6 unsociable – gregarious

38.2 1 likes 2 likes 3 likes 4 dislikes 5 dislikes 6 dislikes 7 dislikes 8 likes

38.3 1 Di's very stingy.
2 Molly's usually brusque/blunt.
3 Liz is quite unprincipled.
4 Sam can be assertive.
5 Dick's quite assertive.
6 I find Dave self-assured.
7 Don't you think Jim's inquiring?
8 Jill is peculiar.

38.4 1 sociable 2 pessimistic 3 assertive 4 inquisitive 5 extravagant 6 argumentative 7 sensitive

38.5 *Possible questions*:

1 thrifty – Do you always keep old pieces of string in case they come in handy (might be useful)?
2 blunt – If a friend asks you if you like her awful new dress, would you say 'No'?
3 sensible – If you won a lot of money, would you put it in the bank rather than spend it on a luxury you have always wanted?
4 intelligent – Can you give the next letter in this sequence S, M, T, W, T, F? (If you are not sure of the answer, think of the days of the week.)
5 even-tempered – If someone spills soup on some new clothes of yours, do you just sigh and say 'That's life'?
6 original – Do you never wear blue jeans?
7 obstinate – Do you become even more determined to do something, if people try to persuade you not to?
8 stressed out – Do you find it hard to sleep at night because problems are going round in your head?

38.6 *Possible answers*:

1 self-confident – She's self-confident; speaking in public never bothers her at all.
self-centred – I've never met anyone as self-centred as he is; he thinks the world revolves around him alone.
self-indulgent – Buying a box of chocolates just for yourself is very self-indulgent.
2 bad-tempered – She's always bad-tempered first thing in the morning although she's very good-natured at other times.
good-tempered – The dog is far too good-tempered to be much use as a watchdog.
quick-tempered – She's very quick-tempered; she gets very angry at the slightest provocation.
3 narrow-minded – It's surprising how narrow-minded he is given the fact that he is so well-travelled.
single-minded – He's totally single-minded; he never thinks of anything but work.
open-minded – I'm sure she won't be shocked; she's far too open-minded.

38.7 *Possible answers*:

Anna is even-tempered – she never gets cross with people. She is very bright – she was always top of the class when we were at school. She is totally honest – she would never tell even a white lie. She is generous – even though she doesn't have much money, she gives lovely presents. She is gregarious – she would always prefer to be with other people than on her own. Her one fault is that she can sometimes get a bit wound-up and, when she does, she can do rather daft things.

Unit 39

39.1
1 This is Jack. He's my flatmate. *or* He and I are flatmates.
2 My grandad still writes to his old (*or* former) shipmates.
3 We were classmates in 1988, weren't we? *or* You were a classmate of mine …
4 She's not really a friend, she's just a workmate.

39.2 *Some possible answers*:

John Silver and Lorna Fitt were colleagues in 1994–5.
Josh Yates is Eve Cobb's ex-husband.
Eve Cobb is Josh Yates' ex-wife.
Eve Cobb used to be Bill Nash's flatmate.
Bill Nash and John Silver are colleagues.
Ada Brigg and Nora Costa were Olympic team-mates. (usually written with a hyphen because 'm' is written twice)
Ana Wood is Bill Nash's partner. (or vice versa)
Nora Costa and Ada Brigg were classmates.
Bill Nash and Eve Cobb were flatmates.
Bill Nash is Eve Cobb's ex-flatmate. (or vice versa)
Fred Parks and Ada Brigg were once acquaintances.

39.3
1 A teenage music fan might not see eye to eye with his/her parents, might worship or idolise a pop star, might dislike, but might (secretly) respect a strict teacher, and probably likes or even loves his/her mates.
2 A secretary might like another secretary, might or might not get on well with them, might despise or hate their boss, or perhaps look up to him/her and might fancy a very attractive workmate.
3 A 45-year-old may well dislike teenagers or look down on them, or secretly fancy them if they are attractive; he/she might be repelled by their ex-husband/wife, or might still fancy them.

39.4
1 Jo and Phil don't see eye to eye. *or* ... don't get on with each other.
2 I fell out with my parents ...
3 We had a quarrel but now we've made it up.
4 Do you think Jim and Nora are having an affair?
5 I get on very well with my colleagues at work.
6 She should learn to respect her elders.
7 Jo's attractive, but her mate just leaves me completely cold.

Unit 40

40.1
1 a garden shed *or* a garage
2 a kitchen *or* dining-room drawer
3 a bathroom cabinet (dental floss is a kind of thread for cleaning between your teeth)
4 a wardrobe
5 a cupboard, *or* perhaps an attic / a loft
6 a kitchen or utility room
7 usually in every room
8 in front of one of the entrance doors (front or back)
9 in the kitchen, probably in a drawer or cupboard
10 in the loft *or* in the cellar, *or* in a shed

40.2
1 attic or loft
2 landing
3 the hall
4 utility room
5 pantry or larder

40.3
1 cellar (or perhaps **basement**, though they normally have windows)
2 power point (or you can also say **socket**)
3 coaster
4 bin-liners
5 loft (attic is also possible)
6 shed/garage; terrace/patio (or **balcony** if not on the ground floor; or **verandah**, if it is covered)
7 landing
8 bungalow
9 master; guest/spare
10 drive/driveway

40.5 *Suggested answers*:
1 You could use a grater (or a food processor).
2 A dust-pan and brush (perhaps followed by a vacuum-cleaner).
3 A table-mat.
4 Use the remote-control.
5 Use a chopping-board.

Unit 41

41.1 *Suggested answers*:
1 My car broke down / wouldn't start.
2 Our washing machine broke down / stopped working.
3 Maybe the door-handle has come off, or something that was held on with a screw or screws.
4 Oh dear! I've cut my finger. It's bleeding.
5 I fell and grazed my knee.
6 The batteries have run out / are dead on my radio/walkman. (You can also use **run down**.)
7 I seem to have mislaid my glasses / false teeth, etc.

41.2
1 break down – this means to 'fail mechanically'; **break** and **smash** both mean to break physically.
2 stain – means to 'leave a mark'; **run out** and **stop** can both refer to things failing to work, e.g. the clock has stopped; the batteries have run out.
3 leak – refers to liquids; **come off** and **chip** can both refer to small pieces falling off an object.
4 flood – refers to an excess of water; **cut** and **bruise** are both types of injury.

41.3 *Possible answers*:
1 Contact the bank / credit agency and get them to cancel it at once.
2 Apologise and offer to get them a new one.
3 Sew it back on again.
4 Get it repaired.
5 Put an ice-cube on it. (There are lots of remedies for this, including rubbing good butter on it!)
6 Put it right by moving the hands forward / changing the setting.

41.4 *Things that typically go together:*

	cake-tin	*vase*	*elbow*	*clock*	*moped*	*sink*
banged			✓			
cracked		✓				✓
broken down					✓	
dented	✓					
stopped				✓		
blocked						✓

41.5
1 ... banged/bumped my head.
2 ... locked myself out.
3 ... mislaid her number.
4 ... broken down / not working. (It could also be **jammed** which means mechanically stuck, e.g. by some broken film.)
5 ... fell and twisted my ankle / cut my leg/knee, etc.

Unit 42

42.1
1 Drought; if the plants and trees are **withered,** they are probably dying because they have no water, and since the earth is **cracked** (hard, with a pattern of deep lines over it), it suggests it is very dry.
2 Earthquake; a **tremor** is a trembling movement of the earth. Note how disasters of various kinds can **strike**, e.g. The hurricane **struck** the coastline at noon.
3 A violent storm or wind, a hurricane/typhoon/tornado; if you **board up** your house you cover the windows and doors with wooden boards to protect them.
4 War or a battle of some kind; **shells** and **mortars** are projectiles which cause explosions when they strike.
5 Probably a plane crash; people who witness such crashes often describe the explosion as a **fire-ball**, or **ball of fire**.
6 Probably a flood, since if your house is flooded, the natural thing to do is to go to the upper floor(s) or the roof to escape the water.

42.2

verb	*noun: thing or idea*	*noun: person*
explode	explosion	–
survive	survival	survivor
injure	injury	the injured
starve	starvation	the starving
erupt	eruption	–

42.3
1 getting worse (**spreads** means gets bigger / covers a wider area)
2 a disaster was avoided (the bomb was **defused** – made safe)
3 getting better (the oil is **receding** – going away from where it was heading, for example, towards a beach)
4 getting worse (**to tick away** means to get worse with time)
5 disaster avoided (an **emergency landing** is a landing when the pilot has to land the plane immediately – perhaps he has no proper control over the plane, e.g. if there is an electrical fault)
6 disaster has occurred / is occurring (if you **heed** a warning, you take note, and do something; here the warning was ignored)

42.4 1 victims 2 refugees 3 casualties 4 survivors 5 dead; wounded

42.5 1 malaria 2 leprosy 3 cholera or typhoid 4 rabies 5 yellow fever

Unit 43

43.1

1 primary
2 nursery
3 grammar
4 comprehensive
5 further/higher
6 evening classes
7 grant
8 teacher-training college

43.2

1 I'm **taking/doing/sitting** an examination tomorrow. *or* I've got an examination tomorrow!
2 I hear you **passed / did well in** your examination!
3 You can **study** a lot of different **subjects / take** a lot of different **courses** at this university. (a career is a job or profession you follow for life or for many years)
4 I got some good **marks/grades** in my continuous assessment this term.
5 She's a **teacher** in a primary school. (Professors are only in universities and are very senior teachers.)
6 He gave an interesting 45-minute **lecture** on Goethe. (A **conference** is a big meeting of people with the same interests, usually lasting several days.)
7 She got a **diploma** in personnel management. (Only universities can give degrees.)
8 ... we started having French classes/lessons at school. (**Seminars** are classes held in colleges or universities.)

43.3 *Possible questions*:

1 Do students in your country get a grant?
2 What's the difference between a state university and a private one?
3 What goes on at playschools and nursery schools?
4 Why did you choose a teacher-training college instead of a university?
5 What's the school-leaving age in Britain now?
6 You look terribly tired. What've you been doing?
7 Do you get marks/credits/points/percentages for your exams?
8 Did you skip yesterday's lecture?
9 What are 'A-levels'?

Follow-up: You could look up these things in an encyclopaedia, or else write to your American Embassy and ask them to send you information about education in the USA. Broadly speaking a **high school** is like a British secondary school, **college** means further education, a **sophomore** is a second-year college student and **graduate school** is where you study for further degrees, e.g. MA/MSc, after gaining your first degree.

Unit 44

44.1

1 union representative
2 executive
3 director
4 unskilled worker
5 administrator
6 safety officer (not the security officer – see answer 11)
7 supervisor
8 labourer
9 personnel officer
10 public relations officer
11 security officer
12 receptionist

44.2 *Suggested answers*:

1 This person has been **made redundant.**
2 He/She's **taken early retirement.**
3 This is a person who **works shifts / does shift-work.** (You can also say ... is a **shift-worker.**)
4 She's **been promoted.**
5 **I got the sack** (*or* **I was fired**; *or* **I was dismissed** – more formal).
6 He/She works **nine-to-five.** *or* He/She **has a nine-to-five job.**
7 You're a **workaholic.**

44.3
1 teacher
2 surgeon
3 clerk/secretary/typist/office worker
4 actor/broadcaster/performer of some kind
5 farmer
6 tailor/dressmaker

44.4
1 profession
2 a difficult one; it could be called a trade, but many chefs may prefer to be thought of as 'professionals'
3 trade
4 profession
5 trade
6 trade (though could be called a profession)
7 unskilled job
8 same as 'dressmaker'
9 unskilled job
10 profession

44.5 1 get/have 2 living 3 work 4 offered 5 take ... on

Unit 45

45.1 *Probable answers*:

1 bowling (the bowls have a weight on one side which gives them a bias as they roll)
2 hang-gliding ('at the top' = at the top of the hill from which the hang-glider is launched)
3 motor-racing
4 show-jumping (the winner is the rider who completes the course in the quickest time, knocking off the fewest posts)
5 windsurfing (being able to stay upright on the water)
6 darts (hitting the centre gives the highest score, 50 points). If it was archery, the sentence would have said 'target' rather than 'board'.

45.2 *Equipment*: 1 arrows 2 shuttlecock 3 ball 4 ball 5 dartboard

Clothing:

1 Archers usually wear special gloves, and probably a cap to shade their eyes.
2 Usually sweat-shirt and shorts or a short skirt, with tennis-style shoes, possibly sweat-bands too.
3 Hockey-players usually wear shorts or a short skirt, but also protective gloves, shin-pads and possibly a safety-helmet.
4 Baseball players often wear caps, plus protective clothing (special gloves, shin-pads, etc.).
5 No special clothes, since the game is usually played informally in pubs and clubs.

45.3 1 broken 2 beaten/defeated 3 win 4 take up 5 holds 6 scored

45.4
2 a jockey
3 a racing driver
4 a discus/javelin thrower
5 a gymnast
6 a hockey player
7 a footballer *or* a football player
8 a pole-vaulter

45.5 2 could be golf (golf-course) or horse-racing (racecourse)
3 usually boxing or wrestling
4 used for football, rugby and cricket
5 ice-skating
6 ten-pin bowling or skittles (a traditional British game similar to ten-pin but with only nine pins)
7 skiing

Unit 46

46.1 *Probable answers*:

1 Sculpture (The verb **stand** is often associated with statues; it could also be architecture, if 'Peace' is interpreted as the name of a building or huge monument.)
2 Cinema (Animated films are often associated with Walt Disney, e.g. the Mickey Mouse cartoons, but are also a serious art form.)
3 Dance (**Movement** and **rhythm** are the clues.)
4 Poetry (**Rhyme** (having the same sounds at the ends of consecutive lines) is often thought of as a necessary quality of good poetry.)
5 Painting (Oils and water-colours are the two most popular types of paint used by artists.)
6 Architecture (We talk of the **design** of a building.)
7 Drama texts/plays in written form.
8 Perhaps a novel, but it could be any book divided into chapters, e.g. an academic textbook.
9 A play at the theatre (Plays are divided into **acts** (major divisions) and **scenes** (smaller divisions).)
10 Opera: a tenor is a kind of opera singer, who sings in the middle range of voices (neither very high nor very low).

46.2 1 the (**The arts** relates to all the things in the network on the left-hand page.)
2 no article (the subject in general)
3 the (a particular performance)
4 The (the technique/creative requirements)
5 no article (modern poetry in general – all of it)
6 no article (the speaker is talking about drawing and painting)

46.3 1 What's the name of the **publisher** of that book you recommended? Was it Cambridge University Press? (An **editorial** is an article in a newspaper or magazine giving the opinions of the editor on matters of interest/concern.)
2 'I wandered lonely as a cloud' is my favourite **line** of English poetry. (A **verse** is a collection of lines separated from the next verse by a space.)
3 He's a very famous **sculptor**: he did that statue in the park, you know, the one with the soldiers. (**Sculpture** is the name of the art form; **sculptor** is the person who does it.)
4 Most of the (**short**) **stories** in this collection are only five or six pages long. They're great for reading on short journeys. (**A novel** is a long work (usually more than 100 pages). Here **short story** or just **story** is clearly what the speaker is referring to.)
5 There's an **exhibition** of **ceramics** at the museum next week. (**Exposition** is only used in very formal academic texts to talk about how an argument is presented. **Ceramics** as the name of the art form is always plural.)

6 The **sets** are excellent in that new production of *Macbeth*, so dark and mysterious. (**Scenery** is uncountable and refers to natural beauty in the landscape e.g. 'There's some wonderful scenery on the west coast of Ireland'. The attempt to represent a place on a theatre stage is called the **set**.)

7 **What's on at** the Opera House next week? Anything interesting? (When we want to know what events are taking place, what a cinema is showing, etc., we use the question **what's on**? We also need a preposition for **opera house**; in this case, **at** is the best one.)

46.4 *Suitable questions*:

1 Was the play a success?
2 Would you like a ticket for the Beethoven tonight?
3 What's the architecture like in your home-town?
4 Was it a good production?
5 What are they showing at the Arts Cinema at the moment? *or* What's on at the cinema?

Follow-up:

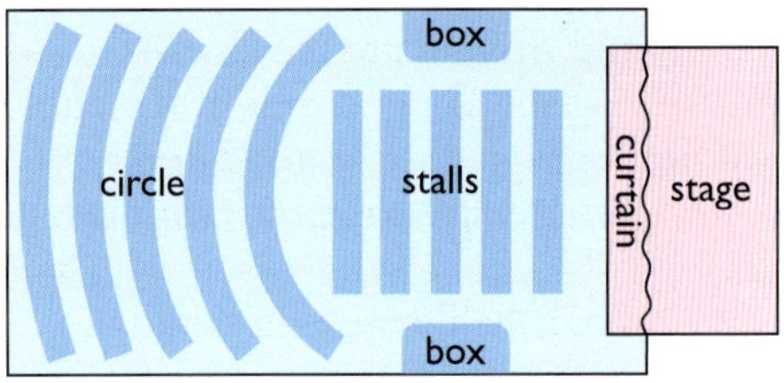

Unit 47

47.1 1 A track is one individual song or piece of music that is part of an album. An album usually contains ten or more tracks.

2 These are both ways for musicians to record their work. A CD is a compact disk (made of shiny metal) and a cassette is made of magnetic tape enclosed in a plastic cover. CDs are said to give a better quality of reproduction and to have a longer life.

3 A lead singer is one main singer featured on a CD or in a concert and a backing group consists of several singers or players who support the lead singer.

4 A hit is a successful single (usually – although albums can be referred to as hits as well if they sell particularly well) and a single is one song issued / released individually.

5 Orchestral music is written for a full orchestra and so can only be played in a large hall and chamber music is classical music written for a small group of people so that it can be played in a small room.

6 Country music is a particular style of US music based on the folk music of the south and west USA and folk music is traditional music from any part of the world.

7 Muzak is the kind of soft background music played in public places and aimed largely at soothing people and disco music is loud and aimed at encouraging people to dance.

8 Soothing music is music that calms and relaxes people and discordant music is music that does not follow the normal rules of harmony and so is rather disturbing for most ears.

47.2 The pictures are intended to suggest the following types of music but if they suggest different types of music to you then that is no problem – there cannot really be said to be right and wrong answers here.

1 classical music
2 country music
3 pop music
4 jazz (or blues) music

47.3 *positive*: tuneful soothing relaxing rousing sweet soft innovative (note that some people will use this word with positive connotations while for others it has negative connotations)
negative: loud deafening discordant tuneless

47.4
1 practise
2 hum
3 chords
4 scales
5 arranged
6 ear
7 whistling
8 making

47.5 *Possible answers*:
1 Yes, it was 'Heartbreak Hotel' by Elvis Presley.
3 I particularly enjoy folk music, guitar music and rock music.
4 I love flamenco music.
5 I'm not that keen on contemporary classical music as I find it rather discordant.
6 I sometimes like to have background music on – something reasonably rousing, some Irish folk songs or some songs from musicals, for example.
7 Music is written on a set of five lines (a stave) with spaces divided into bars. The way the notes are written indicate how long they are i.e. whether they are crotchets, minims, quavers, semi-quavers or semi-breves. Symbols at the beginning of the piece (treble clef or bass clef) indicate the key that the piece should be played in and show which notes are to be played as sharps or flats.

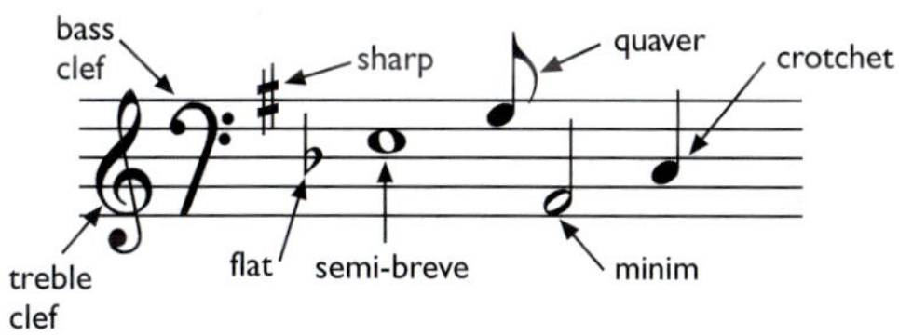

8 I can play the piano a bit but not very well, only for my own pleasure but not for anyone else's.
9 I'd like to be able to play the flute because I love the sound it makes.

Unit 48

48.1 *Possible groupings*:
Found in salads: cucumber green/red pepper lettuce radish celery beetroot cabbage
'Onion family' vegetables: leek shallot garlic onion
Grows underground: potato carrot turnip
Usually long-shaped: aubergine courgette sweetcorn asparagus
There are, of course, other possible groups too.

48.2
1 hot, spicy
2 savoury
3 salty
4 sour
5 sugary, sickly
6 bitter, strong
7 bland, tasteless

48.3 *starters*: pâté and toast prawn cocktail shrimps in garlic
main courses: chicken casserole Irish stew rump steak grilled trout
desserts: coffee gateau fresh fruit salad sorbet chocolate fudge cake

48.4 1 These chips are rather oily/greasy/fatty.
2 This dish is over-cooked.
3 This meat is done to a turn.
4 This is just tasteless / very bland.

48.6 1 *Fish*: sardines mackerel hake plaice trout cod sole whiting
Seafood: prawns squid oysters mussels crab lobster
2 calf – veal, deer – venison, sheep – lamb (young animal), mutton (older animal), pig – pork, ham, bacon.
3 Students' own answers.

Unit 49

49.1

1 waterfall	4 peninsula	7 volcano	10 gorge
2 cliff	5 estuary	8 straits	11 summit or peak of a mountain
3 glacier	6 tributary	9 geyser	12 chain of mountains

49.2 Brazil is **the** fifth largest country in **the** world. In **the** north, **the** densely forested basin of **the** River Amazon covers half **the** country. In **the** east, **the** country is washed by **the** Atlantic. **The** highest mountain chain in South America, **the** Andes, does not lie in Brazil. Brazil's most famous city is Rio de Janeiro, **the** former capital. **The** capital of the Brazil of today is Brasilia.

49.3 1 Mount Kilimanjaro
2 The Volga
3 Venezuela (The Angel Falls)
4 New Zealand
5 A delta is at the mouth of a river where the river divides and flows into the sea in a number of different channels. The River Nile has one.
6 The Straits of Gibraltar are at the western entrance to the Mediterranean and the Cape of Good Hope is at the southern tip of Africa.

49.4 *Possible answers*:

1 Scotland	5 flatter	9 the Western Highlands
2 country	6 agriculture	10 Ben Nevis
3 the north of Britain	7 Scotland	11 Overfishing
4 mountainous	8 the Clyde	12 Scotland

49.5

1 sandy beach/shore	3 shallow brook/bay	5 turbulent river/sea
2 steep gorge/cliff	4 rocky coast/mountain	6 dangerous cliff/current

49.6 *Some possible answers*:
1 Spray cans destroy the ozone layer.
2 Organic farming means that fewer chemicals pollute the land, and our bodies, and unleaded petrol causes less air pollution than leaded petrol.
3 Recycling paper means that fewer trees need to be cut down and using bottle banks means that glass is re-used rather than thrown away. There is, thus, less wastage of resources.

4 Environmentalists are also in favour of using solar or wind power, of using as little plastic as possible (because it is not bio-degradable) and of planting new trees instead of simply increasing the amount of land given over to agriculture.

Unit 50

50.1

1 Cork is in the south of the Republic of Ireland.
2 It lies on an island between two channels of the River Lee.
3 It has a desperately complex one-way traffic system. Moreover, its buses are terribly crowded.
4 St Anne's Church was built on a site where another church stood previously. That church was destroyed during a siege of the city.
5 In the French Gothic style.
6 Probably not as they do not cater specifically for tourists.
7 The Crawford Gallery is worth visiting because it regularly puts on interesting exhibitions of modern art.
8 Well-off people live in fashionable residential areas overlooking the harbour while others live in suburbs on the edge of the city.

50.2 *Some possible answers, based on the city of Cambridge, England:*

Cambridge has the second oldest university in England (after Oxford). The main tourist area of the town lies in the town centre, around the university colleges.

King's College Chapel is in the Perpendicular style.

Most of the main hotels in the town are within walking distance of the centre.

The town centre tends to be terribly crowded on Saturdays.

A number of the colleges are built on the site of former monasteries or convents.

Cambridge has been called the intellectual centre of the world. I am not sure whether or not it still merits this description.

There are plenty of sports facilities catering for both young and old.

Those who enjoy boating must not miss the opportunity to go for a punt on the River Cam.

Most of the more picturesque colleges overlook the River Cam.

An interesting new Science Park has been built on the outskirts of the town.

The Fitzwilliam Museum is well worth visiting.

Kettle's Yard regularly mounts quite varied exhibitions by a range of artists.

Railway enthusiasts do not have to travel far from Cambridge to find a working steam railway open to the public.

Everyone who visits Cambridge is sure to appreciate its character.

50.4

1 natural history
science
folk

2 leisure
shopping
city

3 art
music
community

4 basketball
squash
royal

5 night
tennis
social

6 employment
accommodation
press

50.7 *Some possible answers*:

The most picturesque parts of Cambridge are beside the river.

Cambridge is one of England's most historic towns.

The town could hardly be called spacious as most of its streets are very narrow.

Some of the eighteenth-century buildings are particularly elegant.

The most magnificent building in the town in my opinion, is the Pepys Library.

The town is at its most atmospheric on the day of a student graduation.

Tourists often find Cambridge's narrow lanes very quaint.

Cambridge is very lively at night because so many young people live there.

The city centre is quite hectic at weekends.

When the university is on vacation the town can suddenly seem quite deserted.

The market is particularly bustling on Saturdays.

The shops are always very crowded in the weeks before Christmas.

The shopping centre always seems to be packed with people.

We are lucky in that nowhere in the town is filthy; everywhere is quite clean.

Some of the suburbs have become quite run-down in recent years.

The old buildings in Cambridge are generally not allowed to become shabby but are kept in good repair.

Unit 51

51.1

1. fish
2. oak, willow and chestnut are deciduous; the pine is evergreen
3. pollen
4. hedgehog, tortoise and bear
5. s/he loves me, s/he loves me not
6. rose, daisy and lily; parrot, pigeon and seagull.
7. cheetah
8. a rose; b kiwi (bird)
9. Your answer to this question depends, of course, on where you come from.
10. breathing
11. The dinosaur is extinct; the emu is still in existence and the phoenix was a mythical creature, not a real one.
12. some breeds of tiger or whale, for example

51.2 *Possible answers*:

living things: hedgehog eagle oak willow worm
parts of living things: mane petals bark

51.3

1 roots	4 blossom/flower	7 bud	10 Bats
2 claws; trunk/bark	5 hoof	8 thorns	11 Snails
3 blossom/flower	6 stalks	9 twigs	12 Harvested

51.4 *Possible collocations:*

cuddly creatures complex communities wage war their own kind close relationship

51.5 *Possible sentences:*

Hedgehogs are certainly not cuddly creatures.
Bees live in very complex communities.
Very few animals wage war on others of their own kind.
Some people have managed to build a very close relationship with dolphins.

Unit 52

52.1 1 heel; soles 2 laces 3 dressing-gown 4 slippers 5 belt 6 hem; buttons

52.2 1 pyjamas 2 jeans 3 shorts 4 pairs of pants 5 pair (of tights) 6 tights (*or* new ones)

52.3
1 silk blouse, nightie, dressing-gown
2 cotton shirt, vest, summer dress
3 leather boots, trousers, jacket
4 woollen scarf, sweater, hat
5 suede shoes, skirt, gloves
6 denim jeans, jacket, skirt

52.4 *Possible answers*:

The man is wearing baggy corduroy/striped trousers with a shabby sweater. The collar of a tartan shirt is visible. He has lace-up shoes and one of the laces is undone. He has a pair of mittens on and a flat cap.

The woman is wearing a round-neck close-fitting spotted long-sleeved top with plain cuffs and a knee-length striped skirt. She has high-heeled shoes on and is carrying a handbag and some gloves.

52.5 1 fits 2 matches 3 suits

Unit 53

53.1
1 flu – headache, aching muscles, fever, cough, sneezing
2 pneumonia – dry cough, high fever, chest pain, rapid breathing
3 rheumatism – swollen, painful joints, stiffness, limited movement
4 chickenpox – rash starting on body, slightly raised temperature
5 mumps – swollen glands in front of ear, earache or pain on eating
6 an ulcer – burning pain in abdomen, pain or nausea after eating

53.2
1 For measuring/taking your temperature.
2 For weighing people.
3 For taking blood or giving injections.
4 For doing operations.

53.3 1 c 2 g 3 e 4 a 5 b 6 f 7 h 8 d

53.4

noun	*adjective*	*verb*
breathlessness, breath	breathless	breathe
faint	faint	faint
shiver, shivering	shivery	shiver
dislocation	dislocated	dislocate
ache	aching	ache
treatment	treatable	treat
swelling	swollen	swell

53.5 *Possible answers*:

1 blisters
2 indigestion
3 lung cancer
4 bruises
5 a broken leg
6 sunburn
7 a rash
8 breathlessness
9 sickness and diarrhoea
10 an itch
11 a cold
12 hypochondria

Unit 54

54.1

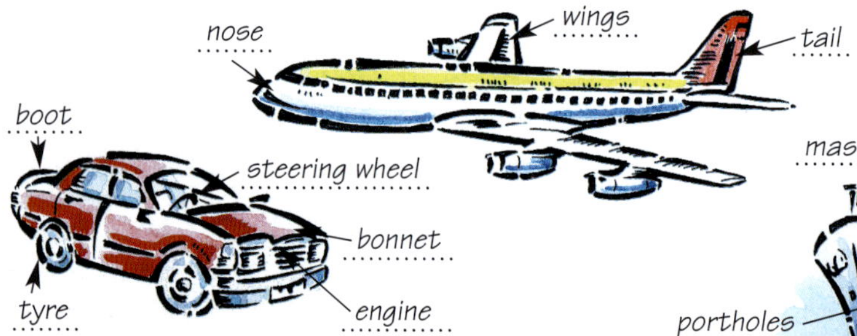

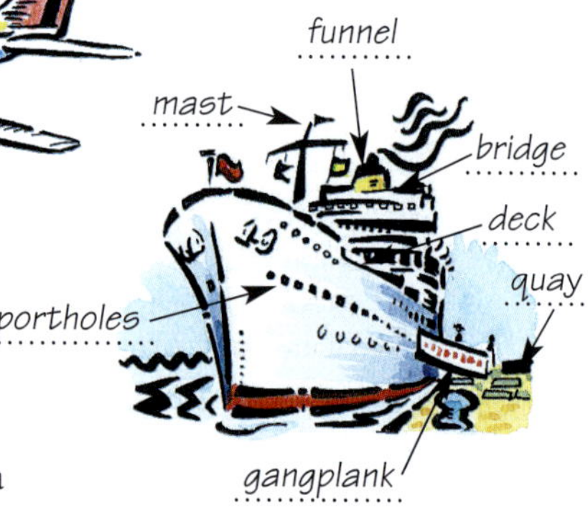

54.2 bonnet – part of vehicle used on the road
balloon, glider – types of transport in the air
deck-chair – facilities used by ship's passenger at sea
guard's van – part of train (rail: parts of vehicle)
mast, anchor, oar, rudder – part of boat (**rudder** can also be part of a plane) (sea: parts of vehicle)
petrol pump, dual carriageway – facilities used by road travellers
bus driver – person working in road transport
left luggage lockers – facilities used by rail or air travellers
check-in desk, control tower – facilities associated with air travel
canoe – type of transport used at sea

54.3

1 travel
2 voyage
3 flight/journey
4 travel
5 trip
6 journey

54.4

1 flight
2 boot
3 bonnet
4 garage
5 mechanic
6 run out
7 check
8 departure lounge
9 delayed
10 train
11 ferry
12 deckchair
13 passengers
14 galleys

54.5 *Possible answers*:

type of transport	*advantages*	*disadvantages*
road	takes you door to door; easy with luggage	tiring for driver; slow for long distances
train	can enjoy scenery; can work on train	poor catering frequent delays
sea	can move around; fresh sea air	slow; can feel seasick
air	quick; convenient	cramped; difficult to get to airports

Unit 55

55.1 *Possible advantages and disadvantages*:

place	*advantages*	*disadvantages*
camp-site	cheap	uncomfortable
self-catering flat	free to eat when you want	hard work
guesthouse	cheaper than hotel	very basic with few services
youth hostel	cheap	no privacy
holiday camp	lots to do	noisy
time-share apartment	can be attractive accommodation	same place every year
package holiday	don't need to take a lot of money with you	you can't eat in lots of different restaurants
cruise	you see a lot of different places	you see them in quite a superficial way

55.2

adjective	*noun*	*verb*
exhilarating	exhilaration	exhilarate
glamorous	glamour	glamorise
intoxicating	intoxication	intoxicate
legendary	legend	–
luxurious	luxury	luxuriate

55.3
1 unspoilt
2 unspoilt/picturesque
3 exhilarating
4 luxurious
5 breath-taking/stunning

55.4
1 pitched
2 bunk
3 chalet/flat
4 quality
5 mighty
6 exclusive
7 slopes/pistes
8 legendary

55.5 The Smiths stayed at a camp-site last summer because all other kinds of holiday accommodation are too expensive for them. Every day Mrs Smith sunbathed, Mr Smith went sightseeing and the children travelled around the island. One day they went on an excursion to a local castle.

55.6 *Possible answer*:

Come and experience the unspoilt charm of this picturesque town nestled on the banks of the mighty River Rhine. Treat yourself to the unsurpassed quality of the accommodation and the sublime cuisine at the exclusive Ritz Hotel. The glamorous restaurant is situated in an exotic roof garden and enjoys breath-taking views of the surrounding mountains. You can spend your days doing exhilarating outdoor activities or visiting the luxurious shops which the town has to offer.

Unit 56

56.1
1 1, 3, 5, 7
2 2, 4, 6, 8
3 1, 2, 3, 5
4 10.6 (ten point six)
5 ³/₈ (three eighths)
6 *e* equals *m c* squared; it is Einstein's relativity equation in which e = energy, m = mass and c = the speed of light
7 two pi r; this is the formula for the circumference of a circle when r = the radius of the circle. π is the mathematical symbol for 3.14159 ...

56.2
1 Two per cent of the British population owned ninety per cent of the country's wealth in nineteen ninety-two.
2 Nought degrees Centigrade (*or* Celsius) equals thirty-two degrees Fahrenheit.
3 Sixty-two point three per cent of adults have false teeth.
4 Two thirds plus one quarter times *or* multiplied by four squared, equals fourteen and two thirds.
5 Two million, seven hundred and sixty-nine thousand, four hundred and twenty-five people live here.

56.3 triangular circular square pentagonal octagonal rectangular oval spherical cubic pyramidal spiral

56.4
1 forty-six point six per cent
2 nine hundred and seventy-nine metres
3 one thousand eight hundred and ninety-two cups
4 one hundred and seventy-three metres or five hundred and sixty-eight feet high
5 twenty-three thousand, two hundred and fifty umbrellas; nineteen eighty-seven to nineteen eighty-eight
6 seven hundred and thirty-three telephones per thousand population
7 nought point four square kilometres
8 thirty-three billion, nine hundred and twenty-three thousand, three hundred and ten million kilometres

56.5

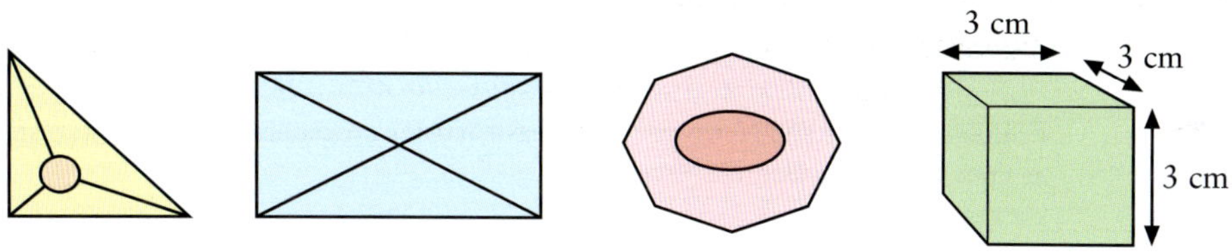

Unit 57

57.1

science	*scientist*
chemistry	chemist
physics	physicist
zoology	zoologist
genetics	geneticist
information technology	information technologist
cybernetics	cyberneticist
civil engineering	civil engineer
astrophysics	astrophysicist

Check in the index for the pronunciation of these words as they are frequently mispronounced. Note: a **physician** is a doctor.

57.2

1 video recorder – a machine which records and plays back sound and pictures
2 photocopier – a machine which makes copies of documents
3 fax machine – a machine which makes copies of documents and sends them down telephone lines to another place
4 tape recorder – a machine which records and plays back sound
5 modem – a piece of equipment allowing you to send information from one computer down telephone lines to another computer
6 camcorder – a camera which records moving pictures and sound
7 word processor – a kind of sophisticated typewriter using a computer
8 food processor – a machine for chopping up, slicing, mashing, blending, etc.

57.3 *Some suggested definitions*:

1 VDU stands for **visual display unit** and it is the part of the computer which includes the screen or monitor, on which you look at your work as you do it.
2 A cordless **iron** is an iron which gets its power from a base unit on which it stands when not in use. It is not connected to the base unit by a flex and so can be used freely and easily.
3 A **coffee percolator** is a useful piece of kitchen equipment which allows you to make fresh coffee.
4 A **stapler** is a useful piece of office equipment which allows you to join two or more pieces of paper together by bending a small bit of wire, called a staple, through the pages which you want to connect.
5 An **alarm clock** is a clock with an alarm which goes off at the time that you want to wake up in the morning.

57.4 1 discovery 2 invention 3 rotation 4 conclusion 5 patent 6 analysis 7 dissection 8 experiment 9 combination

Follow-up: *Time* and *Newsweek* often have articles on general scientific interest as does the newspaper, *The Times*.

Unit 58

58.1 1 mouse 2 desktop computer 3 floppy disk drive 4 spreadsheet 5 printer 6 floppy disk 7 laptop (computer)

58.2 1 scanner 2 virus 3 laptops 4 floppy; hard 5 surfing 6 chat forum / chat room 7 downloaded 8 websites or home pages

Home page is more commonly used for individuals (e.g. The Spice Girls' home page), and website for companies (e.g. Cambridge University Press's website).

58.3 1 scanned 2 clicked 3 crashed 4 attachment 5 down

Unit 59

59.1 1 detective story / film 2 documentary 3 sports programme 4 game show / quiz 5 current affairs programme 6 drama

59.3
1 make-up artist – makes up the faces of people who are to appear on TV
2 foreign correspondent – reports on events in other countries
3 sub-editor – lays out and adds headlines to newspaper pages
4 publisher – is responsible for the production and sale of a book
5 continuity person – ensures scenes in a film connect smoothly
6 columnist – writes a regular article in a newspaper or magazine
7 camera operator – shoots films
8 critic – writes reviews

59.4 1 satellite dish; aerial 2 broadcasts/programmes 3 pick up / receive 4 camcorder 5 comics

59.5
current affairs
video cassette
chat show
colour supplement
remote control
satellite dish
weather forecast
news report
tabloid newspaper
soap opera

Unit 60

60.1 1 independence 2 by-election 3 running 4 elected 5 policy 6 federation

60.2 1 chambers 2 MPs (Members of Parliament) 3 constituency 4 majority 5 Prime Minister 6 election

60.3

abstract noun	*person-noun*	*verb*	*adjective*
representation election dictatorship presidency	representative elector dictator president	represent elect dictate preside	representative elective dictatorial presidential

60.4 1 UK, Sweden, Belgium
2 Iceland
8 Member of Parliament; Prime Minister; United Nations; European Union; North Atlantic Treaty Organisation; Organisation of Petroleum Exporting Countries. (You will find more work on abbreviations in Unit 16.)

Unit 61

61.1 1 robbed; stole 2 was stolen 3 are robbed 4 was robbed

61.2

crime	*criminal*	*verb*	*definition*
terrorism	terrorist	terrorise, commit acts of terrorism (the verb to terrorise is used more generally than in the criminal sense, e.g. The wild dogs terrorised the neighbourhood.)	using violence for political ends
blackmail	blackmailer	blackmail	threatening to make a dark secret public in order to get money
drug-trafficking	drug-trafficker	to traffic in drugs, to peddle drugs, to deal in drugs	buying and selling drugs
forgery	forger	forge	to try to pass off a copy as the real thing
pickpocketing	pickpocket	pickpocket	stealing from someone's pocket or handbag
mugging	mugger	mug	attacking someone, often on the street, generally to get money

61.3 1 was convicted 2 defended 3 sentenced 4 be released 5 was acquitted

61.4 *Possible groupings*:

Crimes: hi-jacking smuggling bribery drunken driving rape
Punishments: prison death penalty probation community service fine
People connected with the law: witness detective traffic warden lawyer judge members of a jury

61.5 The answer to this question is, of course, very much a matter of opinion. Moreover, more details would need to be known about the crime and its circumstances but many people would say that the most serious of all the crimes might be murder, terrorism and rape whereas perhaps the least serious might be bribery, shoplifting and forgery.

61.6 *Possible paragraph*:

Sarah Green (17) was looking out of her bedroom window when she witnessed a crime. She saw a leather-clad young man snatch an old lady's bag and umbrella. She rang the police who managed to apprehend the young man before he could get away. He was charged with mugging and had to appear before a judge and jury a month later. Yesterday, when the case came to trial, Ms Green gave her evidence and John Smith, 19, who pleaded guilty, was convicted of mugging Elsie Jones and sentenced to two years in prison.

Unit 62

62.1
1. Japan – yen; Australia – dollar; India – rupee; Russia – rouble.
2. It is any currency which is reliable and stable.
3. Alcohol and tobacco.
4. Rents from property; winnings from gambling; interest from investments.
5. It is an index used for calculating the value of shares on the Stock Exchange in New York. The FT (or Footsie) Index in London and the Nikkei in Japan.
6. An ancient Greek vase in perfect condition is priceless and an old biro that doesn't work is valueless.
7. Your own answers.

62.2
1. interest – money chargeable on a loan
2. mortgage – a loan to purchase property
3. an overdrawn account – a bank account with minus money in it
4. savings account – an account that is used mainly for keeping money
5. current account – an account for day-to-day use
6. pension – money paid to people after a certain age
7. disability allowance – money paid to people with a handicap
8. child benefit – money paid towards the cost of raising a family
9. inheritance tax – money paid on what is inherited after someone dies

62.3 The only two headlines that most people would be pleased to see are 'Interest rates down' and 'VAT to be reduced'.

62.4 1 discount 2 loan 3 black 4 rebate 5 refund

62.6 Words that could be included in the PAYING MONEY bubble network:

credit card cheque bills mortgage purchase fare fee
income tax inheritance tax customs or excise duties VAT
corporation tax

Words that could be included in the GETTING MONEY bubble network:

salary cheque bank loan interest refund discount fee wages
tax rebate dole unemployment benefit disability allowance
student loan pension social security investment profit dividend

You may be able to justify including other words in these networks as well or even putting some of the ones listed in the other network. For example, if you are the manager of a company you will be paying rather than receiving wages.

Unit 63

63.1
2 Most people believe in life after death.
3 I was in favour of the proposed changes.
4 What does she think of the new teacher?
5 This is absurd, from our point of view / to my mind / in my opinion.
6 He's quite wrong, in my opinion.
7 Well, that's just silly, to my mind / from our point of view.

63.2 *Possible answers*:
2 firm/strong
3 middle-of-the-road/moderate
4 fanatical/obsessive
5 conservative/traditional

63.3
1 I've always doubted that ghosts exist.
2 I have always held that people should rely on themselves more.
3 Claudia maintains that the teacher has been unfair to her.
4 I was convinced (that) I had been in that room before.
5 He feels we should have tried again.

Unit 64

64.1

adjective	*abstract noun*	*adjective*	*abstract noun*
furious	fury	frustrated	frustration
anxious	anxiety	cheerful	cheerfulness
grateful	gratitude	enthusiastic	enthusiasm
ecstatic	ecstasy	apprehensive	apprehension
inspired	inspiration	excited	excitement

64.2
1 confused
2 depressed
3 frustrated
4 discontented
5 enthusiastic
6 cross
7 fed-up
8 thrilled

64.3 *Possible answers*:
1 I felt slightly apprehensive before my first trip to China.
2 I was very grateful to him for lending me his car.
3 I was in a terrible rage when I heard about the unkind things the teacher had said to my best friend.
4 I was miserable for days when I broke up with my boyfriend.
5 I was so inspired by the book, *The Story of San Michele*, that I decided I would become a doctor too.
6 I was initially very enthusiastic about skating but I soon lost interest.

64.4 1 exciting 2 inspired 3 depressing 4 frustrating 5 confused

64.5
1 I'm hot
2 I'm thirsty
3 I'm cross
4 I'm cold
5 I'm hungry
6 I'm tired

Unit 65

65.1

verb	noun	adjective	adverb
–	passion	passionate	passionately
tempt	temptation	tempting	temptingly
attract	attraction	attractive	attractively
appeal	appeal	appealing	appealingly
disgust	disgust	disgusting	disgustingly
hate	hatred	hateful	hatefully
repel	repulsion	repulsive/repellent	repulsively
–	affection	affectionate	affectionately
adore	adoration	adoring	adoringly

65.2 1 women 2 birds 3 spiders 4 steal 5 pain 6 the future

65.3
1 I can't stand jazz.
2 Beer revolts me.
3 I'm not really keen on tea.
4 His art appeals to me.
5 She has totally captivated him.
6 Would you like a pizza tonight? *or* Do you feel like ...
7 She is keen on rowing and golf.
8 I'm not looking forward to the exam.

65.4 1 b 2 a 3 b 4 a 5 a

65.5 *Possible answers*:
1 I like all fruit and I adore curry but I can't stand tripe (animal stomach lining).
2 the holidays
3 language
4 Their eyes, probably.
5 I enjoy meeting people from all over the world.
6 A chocolate ice-cream.
7 Arrogance and a negative attitude to life.
8 Losing my health.
9 I rather fancy going to the theatre.
10 Selfishness and a negative attitude towards life.

Unit 66

66.1 *Possible answers*:

1 confessed 2 boasted 3 shrieked 4 threatened 5 stammered/stuttered 6 begged 7 complained 8 urged

66.2
1 He confessed to breaking the vase (*or* that he had broken ...).
2 The little boy boasted of being the cleverest person in the class (*or* that he was ...).
3 He shrieked that there was a mouse over there.
4 She threatened to stop my pocket money if I did not behave.
5 He stammered/stuttered that he had done it.
6 He begged me to help him.
7 She complained that the hotel was filthy.
8 He urged Jim to try harder.

66.3

adverb	*adjective*	*noun*	*adverb*	*adjective*	*noun*
angrily	angry	anger	cheerfully	cheerful	cheerfulness
furiously	furious	fury	gratefully	grateful	gratitude
bitterly	bitter	bitterness	anxiously	anxious	anxiety
miserably	miserable	misery			

66.4 1 a threat 3 an objection 5 insistent
2 a complaint 4 a beggar 6 argumentative

66.5 1 urged/begged 3 threatened
2 a) to b) on c) about 4 all except **urge** and **beg**
5 complain – grumble; maintain – declare; confess – admit; urge – encourage; beg – plead; grumble – moan.

66.6 *Possible answers*:

1 'We can easily break into the bank,' she said **boldly**.
2 'Thank you so much,' he said **gratefully**.
3 'I wish you'd get a move on,' he said **impatiently**.
4 'I love you so much,' she said **passionately**.
5 'I'll do it if you really want me to,' he said **reluctantly**.
6 'I don't know anyone here,' she said **shyly**.
7 'Of course, I believe you,' he said **sincerely**.

Unit 67

67.1 *Possible answers*:

1 That smells wonderful. 5 I feel great.
2 Your hair looks great. 6 That sounds fantastic.
3 It sounds brilliant. 7 You look upset. What's the matter?
4 This tastes delicious. 8 He smells disgusting.

67.2 1 witness 2 peer 3 observe 4 glance 5 stare 6 glimpse

67.3 *Possible answers*:

Laura hoped her boss wouldn't notice her glancing at her watch every few minutes.
Did you notice anything different about her today? She seemed a little odd to me.
Rebecca is doing some research which involves observing a community of chimpanzees.
As she entered the concert hall, Sandra thought she glimpsed Janet going out through a door on the other side of the auditorium.
If people do not see very well they can often be helped by glasses or contact lenses.
Jack peered through the keyhole trying to see what was happening in the room.
Every evening we sat on the hotel balcony gazing at the lake and the magnificent mountains around it.
Why are you staring at me like that? Is my face dirty?
Simona had to appear in court because she witnessed a traffic accident.

67.4 1 patted 3 grasped 5 fingered 7 grabbed/snatched
2 tapped 4 Press 6 stroked 8 handled

67.5 1 bitter 2 sweet 3 hot 4 sour 5 spicy 6 salty

67.6 *Possible answers*:

1 aromatic
2 smelly
3 evil-smelling, putrid
4 fragrant, sweet-smelling
5 evil-smelling, pungent
6 scented, perfumed
7 musty
8 stinking

67.7 1 telepathy 2 intuition 3 déjà vu 4 premonition

67.8 *Possible answers*:

1 *sight*: I climbed up to the top of a mountain and was above the level of some low clouds. I could not see the ground but could see the tops of half a dozen other mountains rising out of the clouds.
2 *hearing*: I heard my newborn baby crying for the first time.
3 *taste*: I tasted some wonderful soup after a long day's walking in the hills.
4 *smell*: I shall always remember smelling the sea after a long time away from it.
5 *touch*: I touched the fur of a lion cub.
6 *sixth sense*: I have often had the experience of not having written to an old friend for a long time and then our letters to each other cross in the post (we both write to each other at the same time).

Unit 68

68.1 1 blush 2 shiver 3 chew 4 blink 5 wink 6 sigh

68.2
1 Someone is snoring.
2 Someone is yawning.
3 Someone is hiccoughing.
4 Someone is coughing and/or sneezing.
5 Someone's stomach is rumbling.
6 Someone has burped.

68.3
2 blush
3 frown
4 grin
5 sigh
6 sneeze
7 snore
8 wink
9 yawn

68.4 1 chewing 2 perspiring 3 lick 4 swallow 5 grin 6 shaken

68.5 It is possible to draw bubble networks in any way that seems logical to you and that helps you to learn. You could group together words associated with **illness** – **sneeze, cough, shiver** and so on, or you could organise your networks around **parts of the body** – you could put **yawn, lick, bite**, etc. around the word **mouth**. Words that might be added to the networks include **hug, sip** and **stare**.

Unit 69

69.1 *Suggested answers*:

1 That's a vast / huge / an enormous amount of money to be wasted like that!
2 That's a considerable number of people.
3 Yes, that's about average.
4 At least that's only a small amount of money.
5 You've wasted a huge / an enormous amount of time. (*vast* is not quite so suitable here as it does not often collocate with expressions of time)

69.2 *small:* minuscule minute meagre insignificant
large: gigantic overwhelming excessive sizeable

1 minute/minuscule
2 overwhelming/excessive/gigantic
3 a(n) excessive/gigantic
4 sizeable
5 excessive

69.3
1 a lot of (this gives a rather negative feel; **lots of** would be OK, but could sound too positive)
2 plenty of / lots of (a positive quantity)
3 much / a lot
4 a good/great deal of / a lot of / lots of
5 Many / A lot of (**Many** and **much** *are* sometimes used in affirmatives, but they do have a somewhat formal feel about them used in that way; the general rule of thumb is not to use **much** and **many** in simple affirmatives.)

69.4 *Possible answers*:

1 quite shocked / extremely anxious
2 slightly anxious / a bit surprised
3 rather/quite/totally confused
4 quite surprised
5 a bit / rather sad
6 absolutely/utterly/completely exhausted / extremely tired

69.5 *Possible sentences*:

1 There are dozens of empty jam-jars in my kitchen.
2 My neighbours must have heaps of money; he drives an expensive sports car.
3 There's tons of rubbish in the garden; it'll take me months to clear it all.
4 I only ever take a tiny drop of milk in my tea.

Unit 70

70.1 1 period 2 age (era could also be used) 3 era 4 time 5 spell

70.2 *Possible answers*:

1 Hello! Nice to see you! You're just in time for tea/coffee!
2 By the time you get this card, I'll probably already be at your house.
3 I'd rather talk to you one at a time, if you don't mind.
4 Could you use the old photocopier for the time being? The new one's being repaired.
5 It can get extremely cold at times in ...
6 I'll do my best to get there on time.

70.3 *Possible answers*:

1 ... takes about three hours.
2 ... run/last for about half an hour each side.
3 ... lasted me three winters.
4 ... went on for ages.
5 ... have elapsed/passed since then, but people still remember that day.
6 ... pass quickly.
7 ... take your time.

70.4 1 Yes, she's permanent now.
2 Yes, absolutely timeless.
3 Well, provisionally.
4 Yes, I believe it's eternal.
5 It's a temporary measure.

Unit 71

71.1 1 ... them shortened?
2 ... extremely tall.
3 ... a short cut.
4 ... height.
5 ... widened it / ... 've widened it.
6 ... heighten the feeling.

71.2 1 a width of the pool
2 to lengthen
3 a very narrow range of goods
4 a long-distance call
5 shallow water
6 faraway/distant places
7 broad-minded

71.3 1 it's much bigger now.
2 it's a lengthy business.
3 to give us more room.
4 there's a wide range.
5 you should broaden it.
6 for miles along the river.

71.4 1 at; of 2 in 3 from (*or possibly* at) 4 from; to

71.5 1 spread 2 expanded/grew; contracted 3 shrunk 4 stretches 5 grown

Unit 72

72.1 1 ... was obliged/forced to close down / had to close down / had no choice but to close down.
2 ... it's an optional extra charge.
3 ... have to / 'll have to pay a deposit.
4 ... no choice/alternative, otherwise we'll go/be bankrupt.
5 ... must / ought to / should take it to the cleaners.
6 ... forced him to hand it over.
7 ... mandatory (*or perhaps* obligatory) for dangerous driving.
8 ... compulsory/obligatory in all secondary schools.
9 ... needn't have bought us a present / didn't have to buy us a present / shouldn't have bought us a present.
10 ... exempt from military service / not obliged to do military service.

72.2 *Possible answers*:
2 Most people usually suffer from a lack of time or of money.
3 Filling out a tax return is obligatory once a year in many countries.
4 Most people feel they are in need of more time and money, and millions of people in the world are in need of food and a decent home.
5 Death is certainly inevitable for all of us.
6 If you are an adult you probably no longer have to go to school or wear nappies!
7 When I was at school, sport, maths, English and French were compulsory.

72.3 *Suggested answers*:

	highly	*quite*	*very*	*absolutely*
possible	✗	✓	✓	✗
impossible	✗	✓	✗	✓
probable	✓	✓	✓	✗
(un)likely	✓	✓	✓	✗
inevitable	✗	✗	✗	✓
certain	✗	✓	✗	✓

72.4 *Suggested answers*:

1 A videophone in every home is quite possible by 2025.
2 Rain in the Amazon forest within 8 days is highly likely!
3 A human being living to 250 is absolutely impossible.
4 We'll all be dead by 2250: absolutely inevitable.
5 A flying saucer in Hong Kong is highly unlikely.
6 An opportunity to meet the US President is highly unlikely for most people but quite possible for some.
7 A third world war? Very possible if we continue to build nuclear weapons.

Unit 73

73.1
1 **racket** would be an ideal word here
2 **sound**, since it is obviously pleasant
3 **noises/sounds** if you mean different sounds, but **noise/sound** is also possible here if you interpret 'some' to mean not a plural number, but *one* sound of 'a certain, unidentifiable type', e.g. 'Some animal must have come into the garden last night; look at these footprints.' (it's not clear what sort of animal)
4 **racket** (**din** can also be used, often for discordant music)
5 **noise** is probably the best word since it means something negative and can be used uncountably (without *a*)

73.2 *Suggested words*:

1 hiss	3 rustle	5 bang	7 rumble
2 clatter *or* crash	4 thud	6 roar	

73.3

verb/noun	*typical source(s) of the sound*
hum	an electrical appliance when switched on, e.g. computer, freezer, record player
rattle	small stones in a tin being shaken
bleep	the alarm on a battery-driven clock
screech	a car's tyres when the brakes are applied very suddenly or when the car drives off with extremely high acceleration
chime	an old-fashioned pendulum clock or a big public clock on a building when they are sounding the hour or quarter-hour

73.4 1 It was a police officer holding a flashlamp.
2 I'd never seen such a beautiful bracelet.
3 Then it died, leaving us in complete darkness.
4 It was clearly time to get up and move out.

73.5 1 a 2 c 3 b

Unit 74

74.1 *Suggested questions*:

1 Do you rent this house?
2 Could I possibly borrow your camera? / Would you lend me your camera?
3 Which room have I been allocated?
4 Does the school provide exercise books and things?
5 Would you like to contribute to our collection for the disabled?
6 What sort of property do you have / live in / own?
7 Is it possible to hire a room for a meeting?

74.2 1 The millionaire donated his entire library to the school.
2 The Director was allocated the best parking-place.
3 My mother's cousin left me £5,000 in her will.
4 A farmer nearby provided us with logs for the fire.
5 When I retired they presented me with a camcorder.
6 The restaurant catered for vegetarians.

74.3 1 handed down 2 give out 3 let go of 4 gave ... away 5 hand over

74.4 *Possible answers*:

1 your wallet/handbag/money
2 jewellery/furniture
3 a book / a picture of someone
4 hand-outs / tests
5 an antique / a set of books

74.5 1 properties
2 loans
3 landlords
4 tenants
5 owner/proprietor
6 estate
7 borrowed
8 properties
9 possessions
10 belongings/possessions

Unit 75

75.1 *Possible first sentences*:

1 That big tree was swaying back and forth in the wind.
2 The cruise-liner is leaving tomorrow.
3 The most famous river in France is the Seine.
4 A cat ran out in front of the car.
5 A train was derailed near London yesterday.

75.2 1 a person dancing; a person who is drunk trying to walk may sway from side to side; a boat or a bus can also sway from side to side.
2 an insect crawls; a baby does too before it can walk; there is a fast over-arm swimming style called 'crawl'.

3 anything moving extremely fast, e.g. a bird or animal can shoot by, a plane can shoot overhead, a fish can shoot through the water.
4 a bird's or butterfly's wings; a piece of washing on the line in the wind; a person's eyelashes; a curtain in the wind.
5 anything moving slowly on water, e.g. a boat, a piece of wood; a person can drift through life (moving without any sense of purpose or direction); your thoughts can drift to something or someone (it happens unintentionally).

75.3 1 rate 2 pace 3 velocity 4 speed

75.4 *Possible answers*:

	usage	*grammar*
quick	something that takes a short time, e.g. quick snack; quick phone call	adjective only; can be used with 'to', e.g. she was quick to respond
rapid	more formal; used for things like 'rapid increase/decline'	adjective only
swift	more restricted generally; used for things like 'swift-flowing stream'; swift response/ decision/reaction	adjective only; can be used with 'in', e.g. 'He was swift to point out how wrong I was.'

75.5 *Possible situations*:

1 If you are very late for something.
2 If you *want* to be late for something, e.g. something unpleasant.
3 If you aren't in a hurry. You can also say this about your studies, if you are not going either particularly fast or slowly.
4 If you were hiding from someone, e.g. under a bed or behind a door.
5 If you really don't want to meet them or talk to them, or don't want them to see you.
6 If it is late and everyone else is asleep.

75.6 1 A **slowcoach** is a person who does everything too slowly, who takes an unacceptably long time to do things.
2 A **drifter** is someone who may not have a home or job and just moves from town to town, or it could be someone who lacks any sort of direction in their life.
3 A **plodder** is a person who sticks at a task and completes it slowly and usually with great effort and difficulty, no matter how long it takes.
4 A **toddler** is a little child who has only just learnt to walk.

Unit 76

76.1 *Suggested answers*:

1 glossy
2 downy/fluffy
3 slippery
4 prickly
5 rough/coarse
6 furry
7 jagged
8 coarse
9 polished/smooth
10 gnarled

76.2 *Suggested answers*:

1 a pair of silk stockings or a silk blouse or pyjamas; the metal surface of a hi-fi or television.
2 a heavy-duty carpet; a garden path
3 a highly-varnished table-top; a mirror; a brass object

4 a cat / a dog / a pet rabbit; a fur coat
5 bed-linen; the surface of a table

76.3
1 This is about average for a baby.
2 A 20-stone person is a huge, probably very overweight person.
3 8 ounces is half a pound, e.g. 227 grams. It's enough for many people; is it enough for you?
4 The person writing this weighs 11st 7lb.

76.4 *Possible answers:*

1 a big cat such as a panther or leopard
2 a fish; an eel
3 a hedgehog; a porcupine
4 a bear; a panda
5 a baby chick or duckling; the new-born of many animals

76.5

```
S H A D Y             D       S         C             D
      U               E       H         O             A
      L               N     V I V I D   A             Z
      L       S P A R S E     N         R O U G H     Z
                      E       Y         S           G L A R E
                                        E             E
```

Possible pair puzzles:

```
C U M B E R S O M E       L
      U                 F E A T H E R
      L                   A
      K                   D
      Y
```

Unit 77

77.1
1 reached/secured
2 fulfilled
3 reach/attain/achieve
4 attain/realise/fulfil
5 realise/fulfil
6 reach/achieve
7 come

77.2

verb	*noun*	*adjective*
realise	realisation	realisable
–	difficulty	difficult
target	target	targeted
fail	failure	failed, failing
trouble	trouble	troubling/troublesome/troubled

Comments:

targeted is used in sentences such as 'The government has decided to give the extra funds to targeted groups in society'. (specifically chosen)
difficult has no adverb in English; we say 'We did it **with difficulty**.'
troubling: We have seen some very **troubling** developments recently. (worrying)
troublesome: They are a **troublesome** group of students. (cause trouble)
troubled: I've been feeling rather **troubled** lately about my daughter. (worried)

unfailingly: 'failingly' doesn't exist, but 'unfailingly' does, e.g. She is unfailingly honest; you can trust her completely.
failed: They have made three failed attempts to save the company.

77.3
1 I find **it** very difficult to understand English idioms.
2 She succeeded **in rising** to the top in her profession.
3 Do you ever have any trouble **using** this photocopier? I always seem to.
4 I've **managed** to work quite hard this last month. (**accomplish** usually has a direct object, e.g. 'I've accomplished a lot this month'.)
5 I'm amazed that you can cope **with** all the work they give you.

77.4 *Possible answers*:
2 I'd get it seen to / repaired.
3 It would probably fold eventually.
4 The marker(s) might take the overall performance into account and ignore the one bad result.
5 Perhaps try again, or abandon it.
6 Perhaps ask for help and advice from my teacher.

77.5 *Possible answers*:
1 Someone is finding their housework / family responsibilities impossible to manage.
2 Perhaps someone who invested £5,000 and lost it all.
3 It could be about a business someone started, or about a project, or something they were building!
4 Talking about someone's success, e.g. in getting a job / in sport; **pull it off** means to succeed, to win, when it is difficult or people are not expecting you to succeed.

Unit 78

78.1 2 ocean 3 clanger 4 plate 5 handle 6 block 7 shot

78.2
1 springs
2 flies (this is quite formal)
3 just goes
4 're sitting
5 leaves

78.3 *Possible groupings*:
be in a fix (be in trouble / have a serious problem), **be up to it** (be capable of something), **be out of sorts** (be unwell) all have in common the verb **be**, but also the fact that they are followed by prepositional phrases.
child's play (very easy) and **a fool's errand** (a wasted/pointless journey to get something) are both 's idioms. (See Unit 85 for more of these.)
hold your tongue (be silent), **hold your horses** (wait before acting/speaking) both of course contain **hold**, but **hold your tongue** could also go with **stay mum** (be silent) because they are very close in meaning. The difference is that **hold your tongue** is often used in aggressive commands, e.g. Hold your tongue, you! (shut up!).
rough and ready (basic / lacking in comfort), **odds and ends** (small items difficult to group along with others), **give or take** (as in 'It'll cost £700, give or take £50', meaning between £650 and £750 approximately) are all **binomials** (phrases joined by **and, but, or**; see Unit 81).

78.4 1 go to bed
2 a stronger, more informal version of **child's play**, i.e. simple, too easy for me.
3 clearly means more than just 'unemployed', as he didn't have a home; it means totally without money or property, living and sleeping on the streets.
4 not talking; behaving in an unfriendly way
5 infrequently / not often

Unit 79

79.1 1 to think of it 2 ask me 3 Talking of 4 you say 5 reminds me 6 I was saying

79.2 1 this and that *or* this, that and the other 2 that's it 3 this is it 4 that's that

79.3

now and then *or* every now and then
(occasionally)

NOW

now then!
[attract attention because you're going to say something]

here and now / right now
[immediately; also used to emphasise your point]

1 Do you want me to do it here and now, or can it wait?
2 Now then, everybody, listen carefully. I have news for you.
3 I bump into her in town (every) now and then, but not that often.

79.4 1 When it comes to ...
2 As luck would have it ...
3 If all else fails ...
4 If the worst comes to the worst ...
5 As far as I'm concerned ...
6 What with one thing and another ...

Unit 80

80.1 1 hatter 2 rake 3 mouse 4 post 5 bat

80.2 1 slept 2 falling 3 dog 4 parrot 5 snow 6 sheet

80.3 1 as quick as a flash 2 as red as a beetroot 3 as flat as a pancake 4 as fresh as a daisy 5 as strong as an ox

80.4 **Across** 1 brass 2 hatter 4 sheet 5 daisy 7 mouse 9 bone
Down 1 bat 2 hard 3 easy 6 ice 8 cucumber 10 feather

80.5 1 He/She has eyes like a hawk.
2 Our plan worked like a dream.
3 She/He eats like a horse and drinks like a fish.
4 He/She has a brain/head like a sieve.
5 He/She has been as busy as a bee all day.

Unit 81

81.1 1 high and dry 2 rough and ready 3 safe and sound 4 wine and dine / wined and dined 5 rack and ruin 6 prim and proper

81.2 law and order   now and then   hit and miss   clean and tidy   pick and choose   sick and tired   leaps and bounds

81.3 *Suggested sentences*:

1 There are lots of courses. You can pick and choose.
2 The flat looks all clean and tidy now for our visitors.
3 I'm sick and tired of traffic jams. I'm going to start using the train.
4 Finding the right people was rather difficult; it was hit and miss.
5 My knowledge of English has progressed in leaps and bounds since I've been using this book.
6 The new Prime Minister promised that law and order would be the most important priority.
7 I've seen her now and then, taking her dog for a walk.

81.4 1 or   2 or   3 to   4 or   5 but   6 or

Unit 82

82.1 1 ... of gold   2 ... as nails   3 ... as gold   4 ... off the mark   5 ... fish   6 ... slowcoach

82.2 1 a know-all   2 the teacher's pet   3 a big-head   4 top of the class   5 a lazy-bones (or you could say this person is **bone-idle**)

82.3 *Idioms with* gold: to be as good as gold / to have a heart of gold
Idioms with mark: to be quick/slow off the mark

1 ... a head like a sieve.
2 ... a good head for figures.
3 ... have a head for heights.
4 ... has her head screwed on.
5 ... has his head in the clouds.

Another example of a key-word family might be **eye**:

He has eyes in the back of his head. / He has eyes like a hawk. (said of someone who never misses anything, especially when people are doing something wrong) (See Unit 80.)
She has an eye for antiques. (she is good at spotting them)

Look up **eye** in a good dictionary and see how many more idioms there are using the word.

82.4 a) your nerves (always with possessive, **my**, **our**, **John's**, etc.)
b) the neck (always used with **the**)

82.5 1 an odd ball   2 middle-of-the-road   3 over the top

82.6 1 If you say that someone's **heart's in the right place**, you mean they have good intentions and want to do good things, but have actually done something wrong/stupid/irritating without intending to.
2 If a person is **a bit of a square peg in a round hole**, we mean they do not fit in naturally, they are out of place in the situation they find themselves in.
3 If you say **I was miles away**, you mean you were not concentrating on what was happening or what someone was saying, and were thinking about something else.

Unit 83

83.1 *positive*: to be over the moon; to feel/be as pleased as Punch
negative: to feel/be a bit down; to feel/be browned off

83.2 *Possible answers*:

2 Probably quite browned off, or even in a (black) mood.
3 Over the moon, as pleased as Punch, on cloud nine.
4 Probably like a bear with a sore head *and* in a (black) mood!
5 Down in the dumps, a bit down, browned off.
6 On cloud nine, over the moon.

83.3
1 ... life out of me.
2 ... the weather.
3 ... as the day is long.
4 ... cloud nine.
5 ... out of my skin.
6 ... eat a horse.
7 ... form. (You could also say **on top of the world.**)

83.4

Scorpio:
get itchy feet – get a desire to be travelling or moving around.
(to be) on the edge of your seat – to be impatient, excited, in suspense, waiting for something to happen.

Leo:
to be up in arms – to be very angry and protesting loudly.
to be in two minds – unable to decide or make your mind up about something.

83.5
1 I'm in two minds about that job in Paris.
2 I've been on the edge of my seat all day. What's happened? Tell me!
3 Her son got itchy feet and went off to Uruguay.
4 Everyone was up in arms when they cancelled the trip.

83.6
1 felt as if my **head** was going round
2 was scared out of his **wits**
3 **swell** with pride
4 to be in a **black** mood
5 get **carried** away

Example sentences:

1 So many people surrounded me, all wanting to ask me questions. I felt as if my head was going round.
2 That programme about nuclear weapons scared me out of my wits.
3 Seeing her in the graduation procession made her parents swell with pride.
4 Careful! The boss is in a black mood today.
5 I know I shouldn't have listened to his lies, but I got carried away by his charming personality.

Unit 84

84.1 You might find the following idioms and expressions, depending on your dictionary:

1 let the **cat** out of the bag (reveal a secret you should not reveal, often causing problems for other people)
to think you are the **cat's** whiskers (think you're wonderful)
fight like **cat** and dog (fight furiously)
there's not enough room to swing a **cat** (very little room / cramped conditions)

2 to be in a **fix** (be in difficulty)
get a **fix** on your position (find out exactly where you are)
something is **fixed** in your mind/brain (you remember it clearly)
you **fix** somebody up with something (provide them with something)
3 **pour** oil on troubled waters (calm a problematic situation)
pour cold water on an idea / a plan (criticise something so that people don't want to do it any more)
pour your heart out to somebody (tell them all your troubles)
it's **pouring** with rain (raining very heavily)
4 **stir** things up (cause trouble/arguments between people)
cause a **stir** (cause great excitement or anger among everyone)
stir yourself (move yourself, get up, get moving)
stir fry (vegetables, meat, etc. fried very quickly on a fierce heat)

84.2
1 take a back seat
2 stir things up
3 light at the end of the tunnel
4 the bottom of things
5 a muddle
6 up and take notice
7 grasp of
8 by the horns; under the carpet

84.3
2 a compromise
3 in great suspense
4 are found together in the same place and connected to one another
5 behave yourself / follow the rules

84.4 *Possible questions*:
1 Are you still quarrelling all the time with Mabel?
2 Has the new job been a success?
3 Should I ring Maurice? Or send him a little gift, perhaps?

Unit 85

85.1 *Suggested rewrites*:
1 The hotel we were staying in was out of this world.
2 Joe is head and shoulders above the other kids when it comes to doing hard sums.
3 This restaurant knocks spots off all the other restaurants in town.
4 You're streets ahead of me in understanding all this new technology; I'm impressed.

85.2
1 to think you are the cat's whiskers
2 to have green fingers
3 a dog's breakfast or a dog's dinner
4 to be on the ball

85.3 1 – 4 2 – 3 3 – 1 4 – 2

85.4 *Suggested answers*:
1 She was dressed up **like a dog's dinner.**
2 Penny thinks she's **the cat's whiskers / the bee's knees.** (these two are synonyms)
3 She's a **dab-hand** at DIY; just look at those bookshelves she made.
4 He has **the gift of the gab.**
5 Mick **has a way with** the secretaries; just look at how they react when he wants something done.

6 He wants a new office, a secretary and a new computer. But compared to what Geoff wants, he **wants jam on it!**
7 She said I was the best boss they'd ever had. It was obvious she was **buttering me up**. I wonder what she wants?
8 He often **runs down** his school.
9 She always **picks holes** in everything I say.

85.5 1 There is a verb **to ham it up**, which can be used to criticise an actor's performance if it is overdone and grossly exaggerated; we can call such an actor **a ham actor**.
2 If you don't like something or somebody you can say it/he/she **just isn't my cup of tea**, which means you do not feel attracted to it or to the person.
3 If you say something **is the icing on the cake** you are praising it as something extra good on something that is already good. 'Flying first class was wonderful, and being met at the other end by a limousine really was the icing on the cake.'
4 If you call a person **a real nutcase**, you mean they are mad/crazy.
5 If you say someone **knows his/her onions**, you are praising their knowledge of a particular subject.
6 If you say a group of people really **are the cream**, you are saying they are the best possible representatives of a larger group. If they are the absolute best, you can say they are **the cream of the cream**.

Unit 86

86.1 *Suggested answers*:
1 It seems that Ann can't get a word in edgeways.
2 It seems that Mick got the wrong end of the stick.
3 It seems that Reg can't make head or tail of what Dan is saying.
4 Madge seems to be talking down to Eric.

86.2 1 wrap up the discussion
2 talk rubbish
3 start the ball rolling
4 come/get to the point

86.3 1 speaks 2 talk 3 talking 4 talking

Unit 87

87.1 1 B is **driving a hard bargain.**
2 A could be described as someone who **has a finger in every pie.**
3 A seems to **have** the song 'Lady in Red' **on the brain.**
4 A seems to have **bought a real pig in a poke.**

87.2 1 Can I tell you about a problem I have? I just have to **get it off my chest**. It's been bothering me for a while now.
2 They charged us £100 for a tiny room without a bath. It was **a real rip-off!** *or* They **really ripped us off!**
3 There'll just be time to **have a bite to eat** before the show.
4 I've **got to hand it to her**, Maria coped with the situation brilliantly. *or* **I've got to hand it to Maria**, she coped with ... etc.
5 I think I'll just go upstairs and **have a nap**, if nobody objects.
6 Well, I **crashed out** on the sofa at about two o'clock, and the party was still in full swing.

87.3 *Possible answers*:

1 You might have to get a bite to eat on the way if you had to set off on a journey and didn't really have time to eat before leaving, or couldn't get anything before leaving, perhaps because it was too early.
2 Typically, hotels charge over the odds during festival weeks or if there is an important event on in a city. In short, any time when demand is very high.
3 Some people find it hard to make any headway in learning languages, but if you have got this far with this book, you don't have that problem!
4 You might be willing to pay through the nose if it is a performer you like very much and/or a once-in-a-lifetime opportunity to see that person.

87.4 1 foot the bill 2 put your feet up 3 watch the box

Follow-up:

to have a word/name on the tip of your tongue: 'Oh dear, her name's on the tip of my tongue! What is it? Laura? Lona? Laurel? Something like that, anyway.'

to hold one's tongue: 'I'm going to hold my tongue. The last time I said anything it only caused trouble, so this time, I'll say nothing.'

to be head over heels for someone / head over heels in love with someone: 'Jim's absolutely head over heels for that new girl. He talks about her all day long and blushes every time her name's mentioned.'

to toe the line: 'The boss gave him a very hard time yesterday about his lazy attitude and all the absences he's had. He warned him he might lose his job. He's going to have to toe the line from now on.'

to tip-toe / to walk on tip-toes: 'We'll have to tip-toe past the children's bedroom. I don't want to wake them up.'

to get someone's back up: 'Sally won't get any sympathy from her workmates, in fact, quite the opposite, she seems to get everybody's back up with her selfish attitude.'

Unit 88

88.1
1 Many hands make light work.
2 Don't put all your eggs in one basket.
3 Too many cooks spoil the broth.

88.2
1 Never look a gift-horse in the mouth. (Both proverbs advise you to take advantage of good fortune when you have it in front of you.)
2 Don't cross your bridges before you come to them. (Both proverbs warn you not to anticipate future events.)
3 Never judge a book by its cover. (Both proverbs warn against trusting the external or superficial features of something.)
4 Familiarity breeds contempt. (**Absence makes the heart grow fonder** says that if you cannot be with someone or something you will love them/it more. **Familiarity breeds contempt** says that being with someone/something too much makes you despise them.)

88.3
1 People who live in glasshouses shouldn't throw stones.
2 When the cat's away, the mice will play.
3 Where there's smoke, there's fire.
4 Take care of the pence and the pounds will take care of themselves.

Unit 89

89.1 1 prepare by mixing ingredients
2 manage to see
3 constitute / consist of (**make up** with this meaning is usually used in the passive)
4 tie up in bundles
5 understand (with this meaning **make out** is usually combined with 'can' or 'could' and 'not' or 'never')
6 making something more numerous or complete
7 claimed/pretended (**make out** implies that what is being claimed may well not be true)
8 renovate

89.2 1 up 2 without 3 up 4 out 5 up

89.3 1 ... make for the seaside.
2 ... make for happiness.
3 ... makes up to anyone ...
4 Do them up ...
5 ... make out ...

89.4 *Possible word forks:*

make up	
	a story
	her face
	an excuse
	the prescription
	the sum to £50

make out	
	a cheque
	a case for her defence
	some figures in the distance
	the outline of the coast
	a shopping list

do with	
	a cup of tea
	a cold drink
	some help
	some advice
	something to eat

do up	
	the bedroom
	your buttons
	her dress
	the house
	your coat

89.5 *Possible answers:*

Work: do the housework / some gardening / the washing-up / some shopping / the cooking / business with; make a bed / a profit/loss / a cup of tea
Trying, succeeding and failing: do your best; make an attempt / an effort / a mistake / the most of / a success of / a go of / a good/bad impression / a point of / allowances for.
Things you say: make arrangements / an agreement / a phone call / a suggestion / a decision / an excuse / fun of / a fuss of
Physical things: make war / love / a noise / a gesture / a face

89.6 1 WAR 2 your best 3 profit 4 (the) housework 5 allowances for 6 a good impression

89.7 *Possible answer:*

Before we moved into our new house last year, we had an awful lot of work to do. We wanted to do it up before we moved in. We **made an agreement** that I would **do the painting and wall-papering** if Pat would **do** all **the gardening.** We probably **made a mistake** when we decided to **do away with** an old shed in the garden. It would have come in useful for storing our old paint pots once I had done the decorating. Mind you, the extra space we now have in the garden certainly **makes up for** not having the storage space. Pat certainly **made a great success** of the garden. And I **did my best at** the painting and we always find that both the house and the garden seem to **make a** very **positive impression** on our visitors.

Unit 90

90.1 1 about/back 2 on 3 about 4 off 5 round 6 up

90.2 *Here is one way of completing the network*:

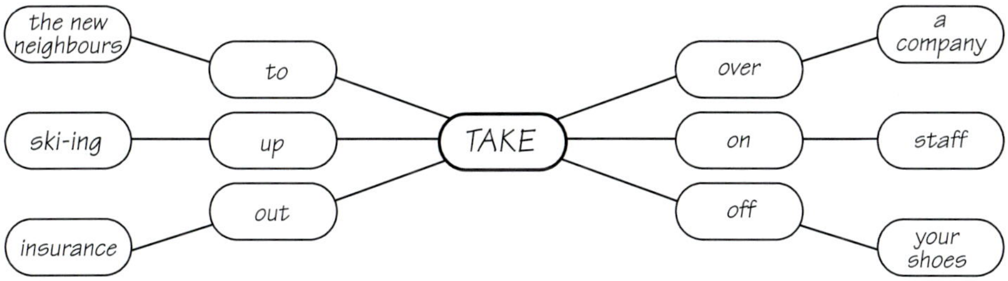

90.3 *Possible answers*:

1 To **bring down** taxes, among other things.
2 I **took to her** at once.
3 It seems to be **brought** on by strong sunlight.
4 He really **takes after** his father.
5 I've **taken up** hang-gliding recently.
6 It really seems **to have taken off** now.
7 A person who **takes off** other people.
8 **I'll bring him round** somehow.

90.4 1 The story of the film **takes place** in Casablanca during the war.
2 Today's newspaper has **brought to light** some fascinating information about the Prime Minister.
3 The situation was **brought to a head** when the union called for a strike.
4 How does she always manage **to take things in her stride?**
5 The view from the top of the hill **took my breath away.**
6 He **took advantage of** her weakness at the time and she sold it to him.
7 The main function of a nurse is **to take care of** the sick.
8 You shouldn't **take anyone or anything for granted.**

90.5 *Possible answer*:

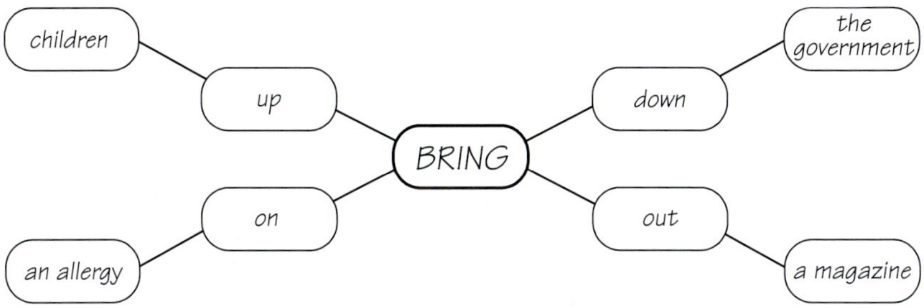

90.6 1 to bring into the open
2 to take part in
3 to take care of
4 to bring a law into force
5 to take pride in
6 to take control of

Unit 91

91.1 I don't often **receive** interesting advertising circulars these days. However, quite an unusual one came this morning. It was headed; 'Are you worried about **losing touch**?' And it went on, 'If so, **purchase/buy** some of our special tablets today. Taking just one in the morning will help you **succeed** at work and at home. It will stop little problems from **depressing you** and will ensure that you **become** rich and successful with the minimum of effort on your behalf. Send just $25 today and you will **receive** your tablets and your key to success within ten days.'

91.2 1 round 2 through 3 down 4 by 5 up to 6 through

91.3 A1 – B5 A2 – B3 A3 – B4 A4 – B2 A5 – B1

91.4 *Possible answers*:

1 ... my old teddy bear.
2 ... Jack spilt tomato soup on Jill's dress.
3 ... study in weather like this.
4 ... going to the meeting
5 ... her father's death yet.
6 Living in such a small place ...

91.5 *Some example sentences*:

She was the first to **get off** the plane. (disembark from)
I don't understand what you are **getting at**. (trying to say)
They are due to **get back** at six. (return)
You **get ahead** in that company only if you are related to the boss. (succeed, are promoted)
Get lost! (colloquial) (Go away, stop bothering me!)

Unit 92

92.1 1 They have recently established a committee on teenage smoking.
2 We try to reserve some money for our holiday every week.
3 Ignore all your negative feelings and listen with an open mind.
4 If we hadn't left home so late, we would have arrived on time.
5 The government's unpopular proposals caused a wave of protests.

92.2 1 put out a bonfire / your host / the rubbish
2 put forward an idea / a proposal / a suggestion
3 put off a football match / an appointment / customers
4 put across your feelings/ideas/opinions
5 put up an umbrella / prices / a picture
6 put on a concert / a limp / clothes
7 put away papers/books/files
8 put up with someone's behaviour / bad manners / temper

92.3 *Some possible answers*:

1 Let's put up some posters.
2 I haven't had time to put things away yet.
3 We'd better set out/off at 7 a.m.

4 Yes, of course, I can put you up.
5 The cost of it all has put me off.
6 He is hoping to set up a travel business of his own.

92.4 *Possible answers*:

1 He is very set in his ways.
2 He's bound to put two and two together if you keep on behaving like that.
3 She has set her sights on becoming Prime Minister.
4 She really puts my back up.
5 It's sound business advice not to put all your eggs in one basket.
6 Please put your mind to the problem in hand.
7 She has set her heart on getting a seat in Parliament.
8 She threw petrol on the rubbish and set fire to it.
9 She's very good at putting things in a nutshell.
10 The building was set on fire by terrorist action.
11 This is the first time I've ever set foot in the southern hemisphere.
12 We spent most of our evenings setting/putting the world to rights rather than studying.
13 You really should put your foot down (with him) or there'll be trouble later.
14 If the teacher doesn't set a good example, the children certainly won't behave properly.

Unit 93

93.1
1 continued
2 check
3 attacked
4 succeed
5 being published
6 complaining
7 choose
8 used

93.2
1 ... to a decision.
2 ... into a fortune / money / a legacy.
3 ... into bloom/flower.
4 ... to a standstill.
5 ... (back) into fashion ...
6 ... into operation/existence ...
7 ... to blows.
8 ... into view/sight.

93.3
1 It goes without saying
2 went to great lengths
3 on the go
4 go far
5 The story goes that
6 as far as it goes

93.4
1 The firm went bankrupt.
2 Only Jack's proposal.
3 Seven thirty, normally.
4 When I pulled a ligament.
5 From a doting aunt.
6 Any time after eight.
7 A bit of a fight, I think.

93.5 *Possible answers*:

1 ... they are determined to succeed.
2 ... put salt on it at once.
3 ... that skirt.
4 ... such a terrible experience again.
5 ... began to get quite noisy.
6 ... having a boss who is younger than you.
7 ... Jack should be offered the job.
8 ... but also a box full of diaries.

Unit 94

94.1 1 over 2 to 3 down 4 up 5 down

94.2
1 Do try to look on the bright side if you possibly can.
2 I ran into Jack at the station yesterday.
3 I cooked the dinner yesterday. It's your turn (to do it) today.
4 I thought I was seeing things when I saw a monkey in the garden.
5 I wish you'd let me be.
6 He let us into the secret that they were planning to break into the house.
7 An enormous crowd turned out/up to hear the Prime Minister speak. *or* there was a large turnout to hear ...
8 My aunt looks down her nose at people who don't have a good job.

94.3 *Possible answers*:
1 ... to visiting Egypt next summer.
2 ... manager.
3 ... of the rope and fell into a crevasse.
4 ... those who came were very enthusiastic.
5 ... she refused to help him.
6 ... until the party was nearly over.
7 ... of sugar.
8 ... to letting him sleep on my floor.

94.4 *Possible answers*:
1 I very much regret turning down an opportunity to work in Greece.
2 A train I was on once broke down making me terribly late for an important interview.
3 Big business runs the country as much as government, in my opinion.
4 I did an old lady a good turn when I helped her to get on the bus.
5 I'd like to break a ski-jumping record.
6 I'm sure it is possible for someone's heart to be broken.
7 Every New Year I resolve to turn over a new leaf – I decide to reply to all my letters promptly and to be generally much more organised.
8 I have to see to some shopping today.
9 My own home has never been broken into but a friend's house was once when I was staying with her. She had some money and jewellery stolen.
10 Yes, I looked up the population of Ireland.

94.5 *Here are two possibilities for each of the verbs in the unit*:

look
He used to look much younger than he really was but now he's beginning to <u>look his age</u>.
I don't <u>like the look of</u> those black clouds – I think we may have to cancel the picnic.

see
His parents have promised to <u>see him through</u> university – then he'll have to start earning his own living.
It's hard to find your way round this building – I'll <u>see you out</u>.

run
I was very sad when our dog was <u>run over</u> by a car.
She <u>ran up</u> an enormous bill at the dressmaker's.

turn
Please <u>turn down</u> your walkman – I can't concentrate.
I'm very tired. I'm going to <u>turn in</u> soon.

let
<u>Let sleeping dogs lie</u> – you might cause trouble if you try to interfere.

This skirt is too tight – I'll have to let it out.

break
I'm broke – can you lend me five pounds for a few days?
Breaking in new shoes can be a painful experience.

Unit 95

95.1

1 **kip** – to sleep / have a sleep
2 **a pal** – a friend; nowadays, **mate** is perhaps the most common informal word for 'friend' in British English
3 **a chap** – a man; **chap** does have associations of being a middle-class word and perhaps not used so much by young people
4 **swot** – study hard, e.g. for an exam; you can call someone a **swot** too
5 **ta** – thank you, or (slightly less formal) thanks
6 **brainy** – clever/intelligent; intelligent is the most formal

95.2 *Suggested changes*:

JIM: Annie, can you lend me five **quid**?
ANNIE: What for?
JIM: Well, **I've got** to go and **see** my mum and dad, and my **bike's** not working, so I'll have to **take/get a cab**.
ANNIE: Can't you **phone/ring/call** them and say you can't come?
JIM: Well, I could, except I want to go because they always have lots of food, and the **fridge** at our flat (or 'our place', which is a common way of talking about your house/flat), is empty, as usual.
ANNIE: Can't you **get the / go by tube**?
JIM: Erm ...
ANNIE: Anyway, the answer's no.

For the sake of practice, we have created a dialogue here that probably has more of a concentration of informal words than would occur in reality. Don't forget the advice given at the beginning of the unit about using too much informal language.

95.3

1 A teenage boy would probably say a **date** (or '**Fancy going out**?'), not an **appointment** in this situation; **appointment** is for business contexts; too formal.
2 **Offspring**, if the parent used it, would be heard as humorous, certainly not the normal word for this situation; **children** or **kids** (informal) would be the normal words. **Offspring** would be suitable for legal contexts, religious language and serious history books / biographies; too formal.
3 As with 2, this would be heard as humorous/mock-serious. Most people would say 'I never drink' or 'I never touch alcohol' in this situation. **Alcoholic beverages** is very formal/legalistic and you might see it on, e.g. a notice prohibiting drinking in a particular place or the sale of drink at particular times; too formal.
4 This is fine, since within institutions and groups of people who work together, an agreed informal vocabulary develops. In universities, terms like 'lab' are used every day.
5 There is a clash here between the very formal style of the letter ('I should like to enquire ...') and the rather informal 'ad'. 'Advertisements' would be more suitable.

95.4
1 in motion
2 to alight
3 a) to regret b) to purchase c) to address
4 Hi! and Bye!

95.5 *Suggested answers*:
1 Children (or **kids**) shouldn't drop (or **throw**, or, more informal, **chuck**) litter in the play-area.
2 You have to show receipts with dates on to get your expenses back / get your expenses paid.

Unit 96

96.1
1 drunk
2 man
3 stomach ache; doctor
4 boyfriend and girlfriend
5 money
6 food; drink
7 very upset
8 cup of tea
9 toilet
10 amazed

(Note the colloquial or slang use of **belly** to mean **stomach** and **quack** to mean **doctor**.)

96.2
1 Cool!
2 He's a cop.
3 Let's take him home.
4 Sure. I'll keep my eyes skinned.
5 It's in a drawer, over here.
6 He's in the nick.
7 Let's borrow dad's wheels and go for a spin.

96.3
1 look
2 kids
3 table
4 teeth
5 church (by hook or by crook means by any method, fair or unfair)
6 hat

(To get someone to the church means to get married to someone.)

96.4
1 breakfast
2 bricklayer
3 barbecue

Unit 97

97.1
1 American; a Brit would write **labour**.
2 Brit; an American would write **center**.
3 American; a Brit would be much less likely to use a word of this type, probably preferring a phrase like 'taken into hospital'. If s/he did, s/he would probably spell it **hospitalised**; however, the ending **ize** instead of **ise** is becoming much more common in British English these days.
4 American; a Brit would spell it **theatre** (and would call it **cinema**).
5 Brit; an American would write **favor**.
6 American, writing in an informal context; a Brit would write **through**.

97.2 *The pictures represent*

for a Brit:	*for an American:*
1 TV aerial	TV antenna
2 wardrobe	closet
3 lift	elevator
4 vest	undershirt
5 sweets	candy
6 nappy	diaper
7 pram	baby carriage
8 curtains	drapes
9 sellotape	Scotch tape
10 lorry	truck

97.3 The words you select here will be a matter of personal choice and so there can be no right or wrong answers.

97.4
1 I had a puncture
2 Pass me the biscuits.
3 It's in the wardrobe.
4 Open the curtains.
5 We've run out of petrol.
6 Our bags are in the boot.
7 Single or return?
8 Buy a single ticket.
9 We're leaving in the autumn.
10 I hate standing in a queue.

97.5
1 You'd take the American to the bathroom and the Brit to the kitchen.
2 The Brit, because people do not usually talk about needing to change their underwear although you might well say that you want to change outer clothes.
3 One flight for the American but two for the Brit.
4 An American would be in a bank and a Brit in a café.
5 The American would wear it over his shirt and the Brit would wear it under his shirt.

97.6 There are many other words you could add. Some might be: AmE eggplant (BrE aubergine); AmE trashcan (BrE rubbish bin); AmE German Shepherd (dog) (BrE Alsatian).

Unit 98

98.1
1 smoking (or tea or coffee) break
2 journalist; university
3 mosquitoes; barbecue
4 business
5 afternoon
6 adults/parents

98.2
1 flee
2 catch (e.g. by police)
3 capture/obtain
4 man who annoys girls
5 car thief
6 plimsolls, sneakers
7 people awaiting trial
8 underwear

98.3
1 She gave birth to a baby girl.
2 Church-bells.
3 No, it isn't, it's too dreary/dull.
4 Looking after the school buildings.
5 A glass of whisky (in theory, a small one).
6 Yes, he is.
7 A lake.

98.4
1 Probably not.
2 It is in lots of small very tight plaits.
3 When you have been working or exercising very hard, for instance.
4 They improvise. In other words, they just play whatever comes into their heads, they don't follow any music score.

Unit 99

99.1
1d proposal to end war
2f politician sells secrets to enemy
3e satellite is not launched
4b royal jewels are stolen
5a marriage of famous actress
6c a person who saw crime in danger

99.2 *Suggested answers*:
1 Steps are being taken with the aim of providing more work for people.
2 Approval has been given to a plan to place restrictions on people's use of water.
3 A woman resigned from her job after undergoing some kind of unpleasant experience there.
4 A public opinion survey has looked into how people spend their money.
5 An attempt has been made to remove the Prime Minister from his/her position.
6 The Prince has promised to give support to his family or to family values, in general.

99.3
1 makes a connection between
2 reduces
3 explodes in
4 promises
5 leads / is a major figure in

Follow-up: Make sure that you note down not only the headline but also a brief indication of what the story was about so that the headline makes sense when you revise your work later.

Unit 100

100.1 *Possible answers*:
1 on a bus
2 in the country
3 in a theatre
4 in the street
5 outside a café
6 outside a cinema
7 at the zoo
8 at the beginning of a road
9 on a wall
10 at a supermarket check-out
11 on a packet of cigarettes
12 on a motorway
13 at the entrance to a car park
14 on a cycle path
15 on a river bank

100.2
1 to bring a legal case against
2 a punishment
3 something which has been or is to be bought
4 someone who goes on private land without permission
5 not to do something
6 to get off a means of public transport (bus, train)
7 to forbid something
8 large place where an audience sits
9 to get off a bicycle or a horse
10 a young person under the age of 18
11 a means of transport

100.3

1 You would see this notice in a shop and it lets people know that people who take things from the shop without paying will be taken to court.
2 You would see this in a shop and it lets people know that the staff there speak French as well as English.
3 You would see this at Customs and it lets people know that this is the way to go if they do not have any goods to pay duty on.
4 You would see this in a shop window and it tells people that things are going to be sold off cheaply because the shop wants to get rid of its stock, perhaps because the shop is about to close down.
5 You would see this outside an exhibition or a dance or concert hall perhaps and it lets people know that they need a ticket to get in.
6 You would see this in the window of a hotel or bed and breakfast and it tells people that there are no free rooms there.
7 You would see this on a river bank and it tells people that fishing is not allowed.
8 You would see this notice outside a bicycle shop and it tells people that they can either hire or buy bicycles there.
9 You would see this outside a block of flats or a house and it tells people that a flat is vacant for renting.
10 You would see this notice at the start of an escalator and it tells people that if they have a dog with them, they must carry it.
11 You would see this notice on public transport, a bus or an underground train, and it asks passengers to leave these seats for people who are elderly or find it difficult to move easily.

100.4

1 Coffee now being served.
2 Spanish spoken here.
3 Kindly/Please refrain from smoking *or* Smoking (strictly) prohibited.
4 Free-range eggs for sale.
5 No bill-sticking.
6 Rooms to let.

Index

The numbers in the index are ***Unit*** *numbers not page numbers.*

Proverbs & Sayings

Abbreviations

Acknowledgements

This book would not have seen a second edition if the first edition had not been so successful, and its success was in no small way due to the support we got as authors from our publisher, Cambridge University Press. Editors, reviewers, designers, marketing staff, sales and publicity staff, all contributed in different parts of the world, and there are just too many to name here. And now many people deserve thanks for helping us prepare the new edition of this book. Since the first edition we have received a huge amount of invaluable feedback from teachers, students, reviewers, Cambridge University Press sales representatives and conference audiences all over the world, and we thank you all for finding glitches, suggesting improvements, praising our successes and pointing out our shortcomings, so that, we hope, this new edition reflects what we have gained and learnt from you.

We would, however, like to thank the following individuals who reviewed drafts of the new edition: Angela Cristina Antelo Dupont, Rio de Janeiro, Brazil; Matylda Arabas, Gydnia, Poland, Tim Bromley, Bath, UK; Melanie Chrisp, Hove, UK; Sue Derry Penz, Cambridge, UK; Susi Dobler, London, UK; Celso Frade, São Paulo, Brazil; Ludmila Gorodetskaya, Moscow, Russia; Ewa Gumul, Sosnowiec, Poland; Marie Homerova, Prague, Czech Republic; Thomas Hull, Rennes, France; Tatyana Kazarritskaya, Moscow, Russia; Gaspar Klara, Budapest, Hungary; Nora Krokovay, Budapest, Hungary; Kim Kyung-Suk, Suwon City, Korea; Zdenka Křížová, Prague, Czech Republic; Magdolna Lutring, Budapest, Hungary; Sally McLaren, Fondi, Italy; Geraldine Mark, Cheltenham, UK; Omnia Ibrahim Mohamed, Cairo, Egypt; Barbara Murphy, Seoul, South Korea; Ewa Modrzejewska, Gdynia, Poland; Nobuhiro Nakamura, Fukushima-ken, Japan; Mona Moustafa Osman, Cairo, Egypt; Hee-suk Park, Mamseoul University, Korea; Tatiana, Shkhvatsabaya, Moscow, Russia; Heshim Song, Seoul, Korea; Andrea Paul, Melbourne, Australia; M Ramzy Radwan, Cairo, Egypt; Davee Schulte, Seoul, South Korea; Elaine Paris, Taipei, Taiwan; Margaret Squibb, Trento, Italy; Susan Tesar, Cambridge, UK; Michael Valpy, Hove, UK; Maria Verbitskaya, Moscow, Russia; Matt Wicks, Wiltshire, UK; Giles Witton Davies, Taipei, Taiwan; Tadeusz Z Wolanski, Gdańsk, Poland; Inas Mohammed Younis, Cairo, Egypt.

Particular thanks must also go to the following people: Ellen Shaw, whose American versions of the books in this series have given us many good ideas for improving the British ones, Nóirín Burke of Cambridge University Press whose expertise and guidance as an editor has been without equal, Jane Cordell, who worked with us in the earlier stages of preparing this edition, and Geraldine Mark, whose meticulous work on the final manuscript transformed the book into what you see now. Finally, we would both like to thank our domestic partners for their patience and unfailing support during the months we were exiled in front of computer screens producing this new edition.

The authors and publishers would like to thank the following for permission to reproduce copyright material in *English Vocabulary in Use upper intermediate*. While every effort has been made, it has not been possible to identify the sources of all the material used and in such cases the publishers would welcome information from the copyright holders.

p.4: extract from *The English Language* by David Crystal (Penguin Books, 1988), © David Crystal, reproduced by permission of Penguin Books Ltd.; p.12: definition of 'malignant' from the *Oxford Advanced Learner's Dictionary of Current English*, edited by A.S. Hornby (fourth edition 1989), reproduced by permission of Oxford University Press; p.12: definition of 'hairy' from *Collins COBUILD English Language Dictionary* (1987), reproduced by permission of HarperCollins Publishers; p.13: definition of 'casual' from *Cambridge International Dictionary of English* (1995), reproduced by permission of Cambridge University Press; p.14: extract from *Language Learning Strategies: What Every Teacher Should Know* by Rebecca L. Oxford (1990), reproduced by permission of Heinle and Heinle; p.102: extract from *Fodor's Ireland*, Fodor's Travel Publication (1989); p.105: extract from *Gorilla* by Ian Redmon, published by Dorling Kindersley Ltd. © 1995 Dorling Kindersley Ltd, London.

Illustrations by Amanda MacPhail, Sophie Joyce

Cover design by John Dunne